WINDOWS
NT
Professional
Library

WINDOWS NT

Windows NT Backup & Recovery

John McMains, MCSE, is a Senior Enterprise Systems Engineer with Network Computing Solutions, Inc., based in Raleigh, North Carolina. He specializes in integrating and migrating Windows NT into existing infrastructures and implementing strategic network plans for medium to large organizations. He has over nine years of industry experience and is a Microsoft Certified System Engineer. He is a qualified trainer in most Microsoft BackOffice products and an international speaker on issues of fault tolerance, disaster recovery, and network stability. He has published articles in several major computer industry magazines. In 1995, John co-founded the Triangle NT User Group and currently serves as president. He is also a board member of the WorldWide Association of NT User Groups. He is a graduate of the Rochester Institute of Technology with a BS in Electrical Engineering.

Bob Chronister is senior consultant at Chronister Consultants based in Mobile, Alabama. He specializes in troubleshooting network and system failures in all types of networks with a preference, of course, for Windows NT networks. He has set up several news organizations with up-to-date networking, software, and hardware. In addition to his monthly column in *Windows NT Magazine,* he has written several chapters in NT books and tech edited many others. Bob has a Ph.D. from the University of Vermont.

WINDOWS
NT
Professional
Library

WINDOWS NT

Windows NT Backup & Recovery

John R. McMains, MCSE
Bob Chronister, Ph.D.

Osborne/**McGraw-Hill**

Berkeley   New York   St. Louis   San Francisco
Auckland   Bogotá   Hamburg   London   Madrid
Mexico City   Milan   Montreal   New Delhi   Panama City
Paris   São Paulo   Singapore   Sydney
Tokyo   Toronto

Osborne/**McGraw-Hill**
2600 Tenth Street
Berkeley, California 94710
U.S.A.

For information on translations or book distributors outside the U.S.A., or to arrange bulk purchase discounts for sales promotions, premiums, or fund-raisers, please contact Osborne/**McGraw-Hill** at the above address.

Windows NT Backup & Recovery

1234567890 AGM AGM 901987654321098

ISBN 0-07-882363-3

Contributing Authors
  Toby Velte, Ph.D.
  Ed Woodrick
  Steven Burnett
  Kenton Gardinier, MCSE

Publisher
  Brandon A. Nordin
Editor-in-Chief
  Scott Rogers
Acquisitions Editor
  Wendy Rinaldi
Project Editor
  Heidi Poulin
Editorial Assistant
  Ann Sellers
Copy Editors
  Kathy Hashimoto
  Claire Splan
  Dennis Weaver
  Peter Weverka

Proofreader
  Karen Mead
Indexer
  Valerie Robbins
Computer Designer
  Peter Hancik
Illustrator
  Brian Wells
Series Design
  Roberta Steele
  Jani Beckwith
  Michelle Galicia

To my lovely wife Christina, whose character and intelligence have been inspirations to me for more than a decade. Thanks for believing in me, for encouraging me to be my best, and for being my greatest friend.
—John McMains

I acknowledge the fact that Martha put up with me. This is by no means an easy thing to do. I am in many ways a purist about things. Her support and love makes all worth while (just do not tell her I said so). I would also like to dedicate this book to my sons Ian and Adam, and my step daughters Aimee, Donna, Karla, and Lauree. Let's face it, a bearded man who loves computers must be a challenge.
—Bob Chronister

WINDOWS NT Professional Library

AT A GLANCE

WINDOWS
NT
Professional
Library

CONTENTS

Acknowledgments

My most sincere thanks go to Wendy Rinaldi for conceiving this project and seeing it through. In addition, I'd like to thank Heidi Poulin, Ann Sellers, and the rest of the staff at Osborne. I would also like to personally thank Bill Catchings from Ziff-Davis for giving me valuable advice, insight, and support both before and during this project. Charles Kelly from WANTUG also deserves mention for his keen ability to knock down doors. Moreover, special thanks goes to Mark Wood at Microsoft, Ned Harvey at IBM Global Services, Scott Blanchard at Cadre Systems, Kenton Gardinier at Network Computing Solutions, Bob Noble at General Electric, David Allsbrook at NCDOT, Jay Mitchell at CMH, Sean Corcoran at Peerless, and all of the other people from all of the different companies who gave me input for this book. Finally, I'd like to thank Bob Chronister for his valuable insight and for helping to bring this book to completion.

—John R. McMains

Many people have helped me understand and appreciate computers and Windows NT. I remember talking to people writing drivers late Saturday and Sunday nights because they knew I was worrying about the same thing at the same ridiculous times. My many friends at Microsoft who simply put up with a scientist's exacting request at bizarre times. Kim, Todd, Darrell, Mark, and many others—I appreciate it all. I must acknowledge the daily conversations I have with my son Ian, who at age 26 has been a VAR, a system administrator, and a network consultant. Our discussions have amazed many, including me. Finally, I would like to thank the many folks at *Windows NT Magazine*. Mark, Warren, Dina, and especially Karen and Tim—thanks for all. Not to be ignored, I truly appreciate the assistance and friendship of John McMains and the numerous people at Osborne/McGraw-Hill. Wendy, Ann, Heidi, the final bottle of wine is on me. Special thanks are also sent to my two Roetweillers, Jake and Brittany, who did not eat me while I worked on this book.

—Bob Chronister

Introduction

▼

This book is the result of years of solid computer industry experience. Between us, we have decades of hands-on, real-world computer knowledge. We were both early pioneers in the Windows NT network environment. In addition, we have experience in almost every major computer operating system of the last 15 years. We have had the luxury of watching the great changes in the computer industry and have gained rare insight into the direction of modern computing.

Many developments in the computer industry are amusing from an historical perspective. When the PC was first introduced, it was considered a breakthrough. No longer was there total reliance on the mainframe design. Shortly thereafter, Windows was introduced and nothing has been the same since. Windows completely dominates the desktop and has placed considerable strain on server abilities to provide the necessary data and GUI environment to workstations. What have been the major attempts to solve this problem? Two major initiatives have begun. One is a return to the network computer (NC) which is almost a revisit to the mainframe (it is an amusing full circle with a dubious future). The other is a move to an OS that is independent of hardware format (i.e., Java). Both of these attempts are currently a performance compromise. Neither provides the power, stability, and utility (perceived or real) of the basic systems most users have at home. It is also interesting to note that some of these solutions elevate the idea of server fault tolerance to a new level; the whole idea of an NC, or even the Java-type solutions, leads right back to the server (the mainframe in the old days) as a major single point of failure. Consequently, if the server goes down, the entire company goes down.

This book is an analysis of NT networks in their entirety. It examines, and indeed exploits, every possible point of failure. We draw from our years of experience to explain which systems actually work and which are just "good ideas." Anyone with industry experience soon learns that what works on paper does not necessarily work in the real world.

This book is about maintaining the integrity of your data and the operability of your computer equipment through any disaster large or small. It is about developing contingency and recovery plans that fit your budget and requirements. It is an examination of the return on investment you can expect for your fault-tolerance and disaster recovery dollars.

The methodologies used by companies to ensure fault tolerance are generally operating system independent and depend upon the availability of specific hardware and software solutions. That is to say, the exact steps or techniques are differ- ent for different OSs but the methodologies are basically the same. Windows NT is not revolutionary in methodology. It is, however, revolutionary in its openness, stability, and ease of administration. In this book, Windows NT is the primary focus and, consequently, most solutions discussed will fall within the capabilities of NT. However other operating systems will be occasionally mentioned to demonstrate other proven solutions.

It is not intended that everyone implements every recommendation in this book. Our recommendations are based on budgetary constraints and specific corporate require- ments. It will be unique to each site and organization. The most important thing is that you identify your points of failure and make your decisions based on solid information and not simply on guesswork. This book is both a guidebook and a call to arms—a plea to administrators to understand that their systems *will* eventually fail. We provide the necessary steps to protect and repair your critical systems.

When writing this book, we tried to stay within the boundaries of the following important ideas:

▼ Every drive will eventually fail and every user will eventually delete a program or file.

■ The difference between a problem and a disaster is small; problems can avalanche into disasters at the blink of an eye.

■ Companies must consider the balance between money, protection, and recovery time.

■ Many companies do not plan for disasters until they have suffered major data losses.

■ Most companies never run recovery tests and dry runs.

■ Fault tolerance is a system cost item. It is a tangible cost of the entire system.

■ Total cost of ownership should be a major factor in purchasing decisions.

■ Companies need to learn how to hunt down and analyze every point of failure (weak point).

■ Good corporate policy is essential to any recovery plan.

▲ Auditing and monitoring are crucial.

This book is about prevention. It is all about building a full-proof disaster recovery plan. It is about understanding the steps you will take in every type of disaster, and being sure you have the necessary tools and backups to completely recover your systems.

▼ **Chapter 1: Introduction to Backup and Recovery Planning**   Provides an overview of the components and procedures for creating a solid disaster recovery plan.

■ **Chapter 2: Windows NT's Built-in Features for Fault Tolerance**   This chapter provides a detailed description of NT as an operating system and analyzes it from a fault-tolerance and disaster recovery point of view. It includes descriptions of NT subsystems and error-handling capabilities, built-in features, and includes a large section on the details of the NT emergency repair process.

■ **Chapter 3: Storage Devices in Perspective**   This is an examination of disk storage systems. It starts with a comparison of EIDE and SCSI and then goes into an in-depth study of these standards. We then discuss the new bus and IO structures such as Fibre Channel Arbitrated Loop, FireWire, and I$_2$O. An in-depth discussion of both hardware and software RAID follows.

■ **Chapter 4: Backing Up Data**   This chapter starts with backup terminology and strategies and explores built-in and third-party backup solutions. Here we also examine some of the most recent tape advances and discuss exotic backup techniques like CD burners and magneto-optical.

■ **Chapter 5: Mirroring, Clustering, and Parallelism**   This chapter analyzes current NT cluster technologies. We first examine mirroring products from Vinca and Octopus. We then look at Microsoft's current cluster offerings. Finally, some of the more robust systems from Veritas and Tandem are also examined.

■ **Chapter 6: Protecting Your NT System from Viruses**   This chapter looks at causes of viruses and, of course, the steps required to prevent and eradicate them from your network. We examine DOS viruses, 32- and 16-bit Windows Viruses, macro viruses, e-mail viruses, hoaxes, and Internet threats.

■ **Chapter 7: Windows NT Security**   This chapter looks at NT security from a disaster prevention point of view. Domains, workgroups, and file system security are all discussed. It includes several checklists you can use to be sure your systems are protected.

■ **Chapter 8: Network Considerations**   This chapter looks at the techniques for building and maintaining a robust NT network. It includes descriptions of network hardware for both WAN and LAN connectivity. DNS, WINS, and other NT network software services are also examined.

■ **Chapter 9: Power Considerations**   This chapter looks at the problems associated with power in a detail never before seen. It looks at types of power anomalies and the equipment you can use to protect your systems. It examines large-scale data center type systems and individual power protection.

■ **Chapter 10: Recovering Data**   This chapter examines what you can do if a disaster has already occurred. It looks at recovery techniques and procedures to bring your system back online as soon as possible.

■ **Chapter 11: Real-World Examples**   This chapter is a conglomeration of examples of networks and systems we have seen in our years of industry experience. It includes examples of good and bad systems. It looks at both small and large systems from around the world.

■ **Appendix A: NT Resource Kit**   This appendix examines the utilities in the NT Resource Kit that are pertinent to NT disaster recovery and fault tolerance.

■ **Appendix B: Sources of NT Information**   This appendix explains where to find additional information on NT, including technical support numbers, newsgroups, and Web sites.

▲ **Appendix C: NT Scheduling with AT**   The final appendix looks at scheduling jobs within NT using the AT scheduler.

One of the more exciting aspects of this book is that the information contained in it has such a long life span. Many of the techniques were as viable ten years ago as they are today. Backup and recovery is still an absolutely critical issue when running a company network and this book is the one-stop location for putting an effective recovery plan in place. This book has come out of years of experience in dealing with real disasters and real situations in real networks.

CHAPTER 1

Introduction to Backup and Recovery Planning

Here is a computer industry statistic that defines the basic importance of fault tolerance and disaster recovery: If a company loses access to a major database and the loss is permanent, there is an 80 percent chance that the company will declare bankruptcy within a year. According to a study by IBM, "Of the 350 businesses that were operating in the World Trade Center at the time of the 1993 bombing, 150 were out of business the next year." That was simply a result of not being able to get to their corporate data for a week or so. Do these statistics seem impossible? Consider how long a business would last if it had no customers, issued no invoices, and had no bills to collect or bills to pay. Clearly, an IS manager must take fault tolerance and disaster recovery into consideration when a company's information, databases, accounting packages, and so on are placed on a computer network.

After an IS manager understands the risks of major data loss to a company, the next issue an IS manger must tackle is what exactly are the potential failures. What level of failure or downtime can the company accept? How much money is the company willing to spend to prevent data and operational loss? Considering such failures is at the very heart of this book. What to do about and how to prepare for failures is formally known as the *disaster recovery plan* (DRP).

In many companies, the disaster recovery plan is nothing more than a few assumptions mixed with a handful of facts. Unfortunately, companies that have carefully formulated a disaster recovery plan are the ones who have already suffered a major data loss. This chapter explores the areas that should be considered when formulating a disaster recovery plan. The key to disaster recovery is preparation and prevention. Formulating the plan requires a true understanding of what exactly puts a system at risk. It is much easier to recover data or an NT system when the proper steps have been taken beforehand. Proper planning can be the difference between a minor problem and a major disaster.

DEFINING THE TERMS OF A DISASTER RECOVERY PLAN

Before you start formulating a disaster recovery plan, understanding the basic definitions of terminology can be very helpful. The following pages describe exactly what a disaster is, what fault tolerance is, and what is meant in this book by the term "disaster recovery." You also learn about redundancy, high availability, scalability, and how to formulate contingency plans.

What Is a Disaster?

For the purposes of this book, a *disaster* is any adverse event that causes data to be lost or computer operations to fail. When most people are asked for an example of a disaster, they immediately respond with "a hurricane" or "an earthquake." These events are indeed disasters of the highest order. However, other examples of disasters include human errors such as accidentally erasing files and records, major system failures, power-related disasters such as lightning strikes and electrical anomalies, floods, security breaches, temperature extremes, thunderstorms, sabotage, theft, fire, damage from magnetic fields, and viruses.

The ways in which one of these disasters can affect computer operations and data are collectively known as *points of failure* or *points of weakness*. As a system manager or designer, it is ultimately up to you to decide which points of failure to consider in your disaster recovery plan.

Different Types of Fault Tolerance

Fault tolerance is an interesting concept because it means different things to different organizations and because, to a large extent, fault tolerance is independent of the operating system. In general, the term refers to the ability to recover from an adverse system event in a predetermined amount of time. How long the system takes to recover can range from seconds to hours to days. A fault-tolerant system ensures data integrity and continued operation after a failure occurs. The "system" might be at the component level (power supply or hard drive) or at the machine level. In other words, if a server goes down, a fault-tolerant system switches to another server or system, or fixes the server that went down without losing data or program functioning.

The most important aspects of fault tolerance are redundancy of hardware and software and, of course, recovery time. There are different levels of time acceptability in fault tolerance:

▼   **Real-time fault tolerance**   This is the most common definition of fault tolerance. The system is operational almost immediately after a failure; downtime is measured in seconds. In this scenario, the company cannot afford for the system to be unavailable for any length of time. For example, a major stock market or a company that sells merchandise seven days a week, 24 hours a day simply cannot afford any downtime. Likewise, a factory that manufactures a product 24 hours a day loses thousands of dollars per minute during downtime. Systems in place in these types of companies allow for "overkill" in the area of redundancy. Up to and including the entire server, no component is ever left as a single point of failure.

■   **Short-time fault tolerance**   A short-time solution is arbitrarily defined as one in which the system can be down for one to two hours. In this scenario, a disaster can be handled for a short period of time by administrative clerks or by some other means. Or systems can be fixed or manually moved to another server or workstation, where work can continue. Many small companies can afford this type of fault tolerance. The basic goal of fault tolerance remains the same: When the systems are up again, all data are intact.

▲   **Long-time fault tolerance**   In this scenario, all that matters is that the data and programs are up and available in the shortest possible time, be it a few hours or a few days. Completely rebuilding the systems that were affected is the typical solution here. In this case, fault tolerance is simply the eventual restoration of service, hopefully in a predefined amount of time. Long-term fault tolerance and disaster recovery are, generally speaking, synonymous.

Disaster Recovery

Disaster recovery is best defined as the ability to recover from a system catastrophe in a predetermined amount of time. Disaster recovery is all about turning a major disaster into a minor inconvenience through proper planning. How is disaster recovery different from real-time fault tolerance? To understand how, consider what happens when a user deletes a crucial file from a real-time fault tolerant server. The fancy fault-tolerant cluster server system simply deletes the file and a disaster occurs. However, with proper planning, the file will have been backed up to a tape device. From there, recovering the file (disaster recovery) is a simple task. However, the recovery is not real-time. It can take several minutes to recover the file from tape and that version of the file may be several hours old or more.

Even in the above scenario, time is an important consideration. To be specific, two times are important: the time it takes the system to recover and the time that has elapsed since the last backup. Some companies actually back up the data on critical servers to a slower media several times each day. Deciding on the frequency of backups is an important policy planning issue.

Redundancy

Webster's Dictionary defines redundancy as "unnecessary repetition." This definition fits well, as a redundant part of a computer system typically does not add any benefit to the system until a primary part of the system fails. Usually, the only purpose of redundancy is to improve the overall reliability of the system. Of course, redundancy can be internal to the system (RAID), at the system level (clusters), or even external to the data center (backup power generator).

High Availability

High availability, a relatively new industry buzzword, denotes redundancy and real-time fault tolerance at the server level (typically clustering). High availability refers to the ability to make servers available at all times (even during and after a major failure) with nearly instant recovery from the failure. Maintaining high availability requires preparing beforehand for the worst types of disasters. In fact, the only disaster recovery technique that is higher on the preparedness scale than high availability is offsite data mirroring.

Scalability

Scalability is the ability to maintain and/or improve your system performance as software is upgraded and load requirements increase. Hopefully, scalability can be maintained within the capabilities of the current operating system. For example, suppose a database was originally designed to be a maximum size of 1GB, but after six months it grows to 5GB. It might perform sluggishly on the original system, but if the operating system supports the necessary hardware upgrades to successfully handle the new database size, all will be well.

You can try one of the traditional scalability methods of adding a faster drive subsystem or additional processors. If that does not work, you may have to turn to a cluster system that supports scalability. Unfortunately, Microsoft Cluster Server Phase I, falls well short of this goal (this was a design decision by Microsoft). In fact, it offers almost no scalability to the system. Its strength is in its availability features. However, Phase I was created in such a way as to add scalability later on (Phase II). Some third-party products such as Oracle Parallel Server (**http://www.oracle.com**) do offer limited static scalability.

It should be mentioned that scalability is defined in this section not because it adds a layer of fault tolerance to a system. Rather, it is often a collateral benefit of highly available cluster systems. It is the parallel nature of clusters that make scalability so attractive. In non-NT cluster systems, scalability has been an important feature for many years. In the future it will be an integral part of the Microsoft Cluster Server.

NOTE: According to Microsoft marketing analysis, only one in five of the implemented Clusters systems on all computer platforms were being used for scalability.

Contingency Plan

For our purposes a *contingency plan* is a comprehensive, company-wide plan of action for confronting almost any adverse event. A contingency plan is different from a disaster recovery plan in that it does not stop at the computer systems and networks. These pieces are simply one component of a contingency plan. Among many other things, a contingency plan might call for phantom leasing of out-of-town office space for the entire company or site. It might call for warehousing of duplicate corporate documentation.

The goal of a contingency plan is the complete continuity of business operations in a defined time span. To formulate a contingency plan the IS staff as well as representatives of all company departments must cooperate. Plans often exist for all functions and levels, and each department, function, and level must take into account others' plans in order to formulate its own plan. Failing to take into account others' plans may result in incompatible strategies and multiple claims on the same resource.

Comprehensive contingency planning requires a huge commitment from senior management. Cost analysis, risk analysis, and impact analyses, as well as return on investment information, are all important factors in the plan. Like a disaster recovery plan, a contingency plan must be tested and modeled as much as possible to be truly effective.

HARDWARE/SOFTWARE FEATURES OF AN NT DISASTER RECOVERY PLAN

As an operating system, Windows NT provides several built-in features that offer some degree of fault tolerance. Its native file system, NTFS, has transaction logging capabilities to help prevent data errors on disks. NT utilizes protected subsystems that prevent programs from crashing an entire machine. By using features like the Emergency Repair Disk and Last Known Good configuration, you can quickly recover a downed server in many instances. In addition, NT offers native versions of software RAID, tape backup, and UPS support.

Several solid third-party options can help you make your NT system more stable. Safe to say, there is a third-party product for just about every point of weakness you can find on an NT server. Nearly every trade magazine offers all kinds of solutions to the fault-tolerance problem. Writers discuss specific software solutions and even Network Computers (NCs) and how they can cure everything from downtime to performance problems. Unfortunately, NCs are not necessarily the cure-all that people might consider them to be. Like bottlenecks, points of failure are hard to find and eliminate. Some are obvious; most are not.

The following sections outline the basic hardware and software issues of fault tolerance for an NT disaster recovery plan. Most of the particular issues and considerations are explored elsewhere in this book.

NOTE: Not everyone should implement every recommendation in this chapter or in this book. Which recommendations you follow are determined by your budget and other requirements. Solutions to problems are specific to each site. The most important thing is to understand where your points of failures are and make decisions based on solid information, not on guesswork.

Redundant Internal Components

To begin with, looking at the internal redundancy of any server is prudent. One of the most common causes of system failure is the power supply. Two or even three hot-swapable power supplies are mandatory in critical servers. Also bear in mind that considerable heat is generated by these systems. Adequate cooling must be established with redundant fans.

You must also examine the output of the power supply. In fact, power supply output is one of the most common points of failure in a computer system. Be sure the power supply is the correct size for the system. A power supply failure can lead to a variety of seemingly unrelated problems. Common complaints include the necessity for multiple boots and components simply disappearing offline, problems that are hard to handle and diagnose. Be sure to examine the power supply if your computer is behaving strangely. Your server may be seriously underpowered due to faulty power or an inadequate supply of power.

Redundant External Power

Here is a surprising statistic: External power failures and surges account for 40 to 45 percent of all system failures that result in data loss. When you consider how little attention is paid to power failures and electrical surges, 40 to 45 percent is an amazing figure. Chapter 9 of this book is dedicated to this issue.

A fascinating topic for concern is what actually needs to be protected. Computers, network cards, modems, and serial ports are all susceptible to power surges. Virtually all companies have experienced some kind of power-related failure. Be sure to protect all sensitive equipment with quality power protection devices.

The obvious answer to the problem of power failures is to purchase an uninterruptible power supply (UPS). Most modern UPSs protect a system from power surges as well as power failure. Be sure to periodically check your UPS to see if the battery is discharged or faulty. Whatever you do, take the power supply and surge protection very seriously. Protect everything on critical servers. Remember that any part that is exposed to power is bound to fail at the least opportune time.

Finally, if your network is required to be up 365 days a year, 24 hours a day, you must have emergency power generation equipment on hand. Large network UPSs can supply power for hours, but a hurricane, for example, can take power away for days or weeks. After Hurricane Fran, parts of North Carolina were without power for a week. Can your system afford to be down that long?

Redundant Storage

Perhaps the most important aspect of servers that you need to consider is how to configure the storage devices. The optimal setup might consist of mirrored boot drives, an emergency installation of NT on a different drive, and all data maintained on a hardware RAID 5 system. Depending on the nature of the data involved, you might consider RAID 5+0 for increased speed. An example of such a need would be for a high-speed database or a workstation that supports photo editing real-time video captures.

Given the rapidly changing nature of storage, several other factors become significant. You should design the storage in a somewhat hierarchical design. Immediate data retrieval should be maintained on the fastest hard drives. You can supply simple storage systems that allow access to data but do not compromise the high-speed hard drive systems.

It seems appropriate to point out that you should never allow a single point of failure in a hard drive. On all critical servers, RAID (preferably hardware RAID) should be the standard solution to the hard drive susceptibility problem. Hardware RAID solutions can offer incredible protection from disk failure. The are some hardware solutions, like those found in Network Appliance systems (**http://www.netapp.com**), that are especially robust. They, of course, support hot swappable drives and hot spares. In addition, a Network Appliance machine can be set up to automatically order a new drive in the event of a failure. Following are some do's and don'ts where RAID is concerned:

- ▼ Never put the page file in a conventional RAID 5 set. Writing the parity bit slows down the system unnecessarily.

- ■ Where possible, place the operating system on a mirrored set and the data on a RAID 5 set.

- ■ Have a system that can be remotely configured.

■ Use monitoring software that runs in NT and lets you know what is going on (including e-mail posting and alerting).

▲ Use hardware RAID wherever possible. This is the number 1 rule of RAID in an NT system.

In an ideal world, you would want to provide complete redundancy, but doing so is not normally economically feasible. You can move to another type of redundancy, such as copying files to a remote storage tower (i.e., a magneto-optical jukebox). These storage towers can provide very large amounts of data storage but are slow to access. Obviously, setting up such a system requires serious attention to detail. Hierarchical storage management (HSM) software can help you with this setup. Data storage is discussed in Chapter 3 of this book.

Clustering

Clustering is a relatively new technology for personal computers. However, in the world of mainframes and microcomputers, mature clustering technology has been around for about fifteen years or longer (see Chapter 5). Companies like Digital Equipment Corporation, Amdahl, IBM, and, of course, Tandem have defined stable and fault-tolerant cluster schemes for their respective systems. Once code-named Wolfpack, NT's current clustering incarnation is somewhat basic compared to these other systems, but this will be greatly improved in the near future. Although it only offers availability features, Microsoft can brag that the Cluster Server system is an extremely open cluster solution compared to traditional industry style clusters. Cluster Server is already approved for operation on more types of hardware systems than any other cluster solution in history. Look for subsequent phases of the Microsoft Cluster Server to offer both fault tolerance and scalability. The scalability of these future systems will complete NT's evolution to a true enterprise network operating system.

The current phase of clustering natively available in the NT Enterprise Server is a standard two-way fall-over application. In this configuration, two buses share a RAID 5 array. If one system fails, the second machine takes over in about 30 seconds, which allows a system to continue working after most minor problems. In addition, the scenario is quite effective for planned downtimes such as those used to maintain the system or perform hardware and software upgrades. If your enterprise requires unattended and automatic system fall-over, the Microsoft Cluster Server might be a cost-effective choice for you.

As previously mentioned, other clustering systems vendors offer products for NT. Tandem has ported its Himalaya cluster technology to Windows NT. This cluster design is almost infinitely expandable. In fact, Tandem and Microsoft have shown a 16-way, 64 processor cluster that ran 2TB (terabytes) of data. In a lot of ways, the Tandem system represents the ultimate in cluster design and performance, with modular systems that are almost completely redundant. This is why Tandem products are found in the majority of stock markets around the world. Deciding to jump to these high-end systems depends upon the amount of data, the required availability, and, of course, finances.

Another important consideration is the choice of software. Software vendors need to build cluster-aware applications that can handle the latency time of a fail-over. Clustering can be very awkward if the users' workstations lock up each time fail-over occurs. Microsoft has gone to great lengths to make cluster DLLs and APIs available to industry programmers. These resources ease the development of cluster exploitive applications and should cement Microsoft NT's position as a serious enterprise solution.

Sometimes having a backup server (a hot spare) can offer a simple, elegant solution. Take the example of a Web site. If the primary goes down, the IP address and name of the hot spare are simply changed to that of the first server. The hot spare doesn't need to have all the power of the primary; it only requires enough to keep things going until the first server is repaired. The fail-over in many cases does not even need to be automatic. An administrator can act as the "fail-over agent" in a cheap, but effective, hot-spare scenario.

Which brings us to the next issue: data mirroring. The basic problem with clustering is that the hard drive subsystem is usually a single point of failure. This need not be the case. Some top-of-the-line RAID systems support two RAID 5 sets connected as mirror sets. Because all clustered machines must have their own boot drive, both systems could boot and continue running even if two drives on one RAID set go offline. The likelihood of this event is perhaps remote, but it has happened. Once more, whether you need such redundancy depends on your type of business and specific availability requirements.

Another point of failure in the standard cluster systems is the building that houses the data center. Events can occur that defeat even an ideal cluster/mirror situation. Assuming that many system failures are caused by environment, these "short distance" solutions may not help. If an earthquake, flood, or fire destroys the building, no amount of internal clustering or mirroring can save the systems.

However, some applications allow remote mirroring of data. In other words, any file being opened or closed is mirrored to a remote site. The remote site can be next door, in the next building, or two thousand miles away. The significance of remote mirroring is simple—it is untouched by local catastrophes. One excellent product for remote mirroring is Octopus. The package works as claimed and can save you from serious system catastrophes that occur on the local level. Many companies will include remote mirroring in their disaster recovery plans. For more details on how these types of applications work and how clustering in general works, see Chapter 5.

Data Backup

A common misconception is that backup is part of real-time fault tolerance. Backup is more related to disaster recovery than to fault tolerance. For example, consider the "disaster" mentioned earlier in this chapter in which a user deletes a file from the server. A fault-tolerant system cannot help in this scenario, as it simply deletes the file as well. However, the tape backup can recover the file (or at least that is the plan). Regardless of what it is considered, a solid backup system is a key component of any network, server, and even workstation.

Surprisingly, backup is one of the least performed and monitored tasks on networks. Most administrators only appreciate how important backup is after a file has been deleted or corrupted. When a recent backup is required, it sometimes turns out to be unavailable. Clearly, this is a situation administrators should avoid.

Your backup plan needs serious forethought and serious testing. Always assume that essential files are on servers and, therefore, provide the most serious attention to detail when it comes to these servers. In general, plan on doing a daily backup of the data and possibly a twice daily or more frequent backup of important servers. If restoring data from tape is crucial to the company, consider implementing tape RAID. You can use tape mirroring to place the backup on a second tape and have that tape moved to a remote site. You could also use RAID 5 tape schemes so that you are protected from the failure of one tape without greatly impacting backup speed.

In addition, remember to consider how much time you have to completely finish the backup scheme. If you have little time, you may have to purchase faster hardware or place a tape drive on each server. For small time windows, you may have to change backup software technologies. For instance, switching to live image backup products such as SnapBack Live from Columbia Data Products, Inc. (**http://www.cdp.com**) can significantly shorten the time to complete a backup job. If these suggestions don't do the job, try using database servers with one tape drive for data files and one tape drive for other files. A properly configured parallel backup scheme such as this can greatly reduce backup times.

The actual restoration is usually quite simple. Most administrators can restore a system from a recent tape backup. However, you need to remember that backups are almost always out-of-date. You cannot do a backup after every change is made to data. Only a mirroring application can provide the latest changes. In Chapter 11, the real-world example chapter of this book, it will be shown that many consultants and IS managers have come up with unique and interesting ways to handle these problems.

Make certain that your backup hardware is adequate for the job. Remember to keep your tapes as fresh as possible and to store them properly. Tapes are relatively fragile. You might consider copying data to MO jukeboxes. The MO diskettes are more stable than the tapes.

Be sure to provide the proper backup capacity. Usually, only a small window of opportunity in which to complete the entire backup is available. Backing up the entire network to a single server usually doesn't suffice. Typically, the amount of data a company stores almost doubles each year, so at least consider setting up multiple backup servers.

Finally, be aware of open files. Where necessary, purchase backup agents or modules to back up databases, mail servers, and applications in which open files are continually maintained. Examples of such agents are those that can be purchased for Exchange Server, SQL Server, and Oracle. Trying to back up these applications without the appropriate modules is not advisable, but if you can afford to bring down the application for a short time, you can back up the files with the application's services turned off. In addition, consider purchasing a product specifically for open files such as Open File

Manager from St. Bernard (**http://www.stbernard.com**). With these agents and products, there is no reason not to back up important open files.

Here are a few other considerations for tape backup plans:

▼ Test tapes periodically by doing a restore from each tape.

■ Make workstation users responsible for backing up their own hard drives if they choose not to store their files on the server. (Simple batch files can always put the user in his or her server directory when booting onto the system.)

■ Always have multiple copies of tapes on hand and be certain that they are okay.

■ Do not overuse tapes. You should expect to have to throw tapes out. If a tape fails once, clean the drive and retry. If it fails twice, remove the tape from the rotation.

■ Be certain that tape devices remain clean and are in a clean environment. Dirt is a serious problem with backup tapes.

▲ Assign personnel to check event logs to be certain that the backups went as planned. Most third-party software products allow e-mail or broadcast notifications.

This brings us to the question of whose software package should be used for the backups. Backup software can be very expensive and require numerous module licenses, which makes the decision even harder to make. Why not just use the built-in NTBackup? NTBackup is fine in a very small environment, but its lack of strong network capabilities and slow recovery speed make it unsuitable for most organizations. In fact, NTBackup only provides a backup of network shares and cannot handle remote registries. Several third-party options are available for NT enterprise level backups.

Following are pointers for developing a tape backup plan:

▼ Back up critical servers once a week and perform incremental backups daily.

■ On any critical server, take alternate day tapes off-site for remote storage or store them in a locked safe that is secure from fire damage.

■ At the end of a day, run batch files on appropriate workstations and transfer data files to a remote server, which then should be backed up with all the other servers at night.

■ Give the network a complete backup each month, a separate backup each week, and incremental backups during the weekdays. This is generally referred to as the "grandfather/father/son" approach.

▲ Have a central authority provide servers with daily backups.

Data backup is discussed thoroughly in Chapter 4 of this book.

Physical Network Issues

The next major issue is the physical network itself—the hubs, routers, cables, switches, and so on. Remember that much of today's network equipment actually consists of computers whose functions are limited. These computers should be treated the same way as a server. If a surge destroys a large router, nothing short of a new router can bring the network back online. You must effectively plan the physical network and make provisions for fault tolerance and service recovery.

Here are some suggestions for designing the network:

▼ If you have to lay cable, do so efficiently and lay the best quality cable that you can afford (use enhanced Category 5 cable, if possible). Use fiber optic cable for long distances and in environmentally unsound areas (factories, electrical plants, and so on).

■ Design the network logically. Try to keep the overall design simple and only share essential data and applications.

■ On the software side, do not overdo domains. Complicated trusts and multiple PDCs can get very confusing and are hard to document. Keep it as simple as possible.

■ Document the network. It is almost impossible to provide too much information here.

■ Think through your needs as far as fault tolerance goes. You undoubtedly have to compromise between what you want and what you can afford.

■ Adopt consistent and reasonable policies.

▲ Determine how much technical support you need from your vendors. Do you need on-site spares? Do you need 12-hour turnarounds on nonfunctional equipment?

Network issues are discussed thoroughly in Chapter 8.

System Protection in General

Numerous problems can cause data loss on a computer network. According to a recent study, the chief causes of data loss are

▼ Power failure: 45 percent

■ Storm damage: 10 percent

■ Fire/explosion: 8 percent

■ Hardware/software error: 8 percent

■ Flood and water damage: 6 percent

▲ Other causes: 15 percent

Other system-protection issues include virus infections and security breaches over the Internet. Terms such as firewalls, proxy servers, firewall containing routers, and, of course, name address translation (NAT) are now being used to describe ways of protecting data from intrusions made over the Internet. Clearly, catastrophes caused by physical problems or software are waiting to occur. For example, many companies have suffered plant fires, flooding, and serious virus attacks. If you run a company of almost any size, you are bound to be hit by a computer-based catastrophe of some kind.

Virus issues are insidious but can be dealt with easily. Preventing viruses is the type of problem that greatly benefits from strong corporate policy. Beware of floppies and programs that come from outside of the office, and, of course, e-mail attachments. Implement virus scanning on your servers, your workstations, and your Internet-connected firewall. Firewall products shunt incoming e-mail—in other words, attachments—to a virus scanner before the mail is delivered internally. Don't forget to also include the issue of Internet downloads in your protection plan. Virus issues are dealt with in Chapter 6 of this book.

Security is another important problem. Be sure that IS personnel understand the security issues involved on a network. NT security, application security, password security, and, of course, Internet security should all be examined. Firewalls are easy to implement so that security breaches over the Internet can be minimized with proper design. Corporate policy should place a strong emphasis on security techniques. It has been said, "Security is one-tenth technology and nine-tenths policy." Security is covered in Chapter 7.

Hidden Weak Links and Other Problems

Unfortunately, hidden problems that everyone failed to consider can cause a network or a server to go down. As mentioned above, large UPSs are often placed on servers but are often ignored on switches, hubs, and routers.

Many problems seem obvious after you have encountered them once; other problems are obscure. For instance, suppose you have set up your network so that it complies reasonably well with fault-tolerance and disaster-recovery techniques. Data is backed up every day and all systems use redundant setups. Then a file is suddenly deleted and must be restored from a tape backup. The tape is inserted, but then you find that the tape is defective. This scenario is actually very common. Be prepared and routinely test tapes. The point here is that you must at least consider all points of failure on your network, on your systems, and on your disaster recovery plans.

OTHER ISSUES OF AN NT DISASTER RECOVERY PLAN

Now that the hardware and software aspects of a disaster recovery plan have been analyzed, what are the other issues? Corporate policy issues become extremely important at this point. Items such as security levels, virus prevention techniques, and acceptable levels of service fall into this category. Also included are documentation issues, IS training issues, and user education.

The next obvious issue is how much money you can spend on the solutions and what return on investment you will accept. Once you have decided what points of failure you are willing to pay to resolve, you then must decide on vendors and compatibility issues. You must decide whether you are going to purchase from the big, tier-one server manufacturers or go low-budget and purchase clone systems.

Purchasing Issues

What distinguishes most of the solutions in this chapter from one another is simply the amount of money that the company is willing to spend and the recovery time that the company is willing to accept. The balance between cost and level of protection defines the financial side of the recovery plan. In fact, striking a balance between the two is a recurring theme in the fault tolerance discussion (and hence in this book). The real-time company can afford no downtime and is usually (but not always) willing to pay for massive redundancy. On the other hand, the company that is willing to be down for several days can perform the redundancy at a surprisingly low cost. Attempting to evaluate what an hour of downtime costs on each of your critical servers and on your network as a whole is important. This information can give you an idea of the return you can expect on your investment in a disaster recovery plan.

Hardware Compatibility List (HCL) and What it Means

One of the more critical purchasing decisions that you need to make is the source of the hardware that you use. By definition, choosing a hardware source sounds like a hardware issue, but it is more an issue of policy. Hardware source choices range from the type of machine to purchase to types of maintenance and support contracts to set up. As pointed out earlier, many of these issues are matters of finance, but they should be carefully examined. They can have a huge impact on the overall system.

Every operating system has a list of components, many of them add-ons by third-party vendors. Finding the right product can be difficult. Microsoft has helped greatly by publishing a key component list of hardware that does, in fact, work with Windows NT. The Hardware Compatibility List (HCL) is your starting point in choosing redundancy methodologies.

The HCL is a very important source of information. It basically tells you what Microsoft has tested and what the company is willing to support. Microsoft's definition of hardware compatibility is stringent: "A specific hardware model is compatible with Windows NT if a Windows NT device driver exists that was designed to interact with that hardware model, and Windows NT and the device driver interoperate with the hardware in a stable manner." After the system is tested, Microsoft can retest it to determine whether specific components fail.

So the HCL is a very important list. If Microsoft has not certified a system (the company does not certify components), it reserves the right to tell you that it cannot help you fix it. Microsoft can't fix the system even if you pay the $195 per incident support fee. Many an administrator has called Microsoft to get help when a system failed only to be told that the company does not support a component of the system because the equipment was not on the HCL. Of course, buying from the HCL is a good idea if official support is what you want. The list, which is available from the Microsoft Windows Hardware Quality Labs, is accessible at **http://www.microsoft.com/hwtest**.

A portion of the compatible systems listed in the NT 4.0-released HCL are shown in Table 1-1. The partial list in Table 1-1 is from the actual list of tested Hewlett-Packard systems published by Microsoft.

Microsoft has gone to great lengths to test NT-compatible hardware systems. The company is very specific about what it will and won't support. Purchasing systems from the list whenever possible is advisable. You don't want to be in a situation where you become the "tester."

Clones vs. Specific-System Purchases

If you want to enter a politically challenging argument, try discussing clones versus non-clones with administrators and other users. One would think that most IS decision-makers are computer savvy, but certain statistics make one suspect otherwise. For example, it is estimated that 80 percent of today's Intel-based servers are clones. This is a ridiculous statistic for many reasons, including support problems, NT compatibility, component consistency, and, of course, cost-of-ownership.

Hewlett-Packard NetServer 5/100 LC	Hewlett-Packard NetServer LH Plus 5/133 SMP (1p)
Hewlett-Packard NetServer 5/100 LH	Hewlett-Packard OmniBook™ 4000CT 4/100 3
Hewlett-Packard NetServer 5/100 LM	Hewlett-Packard OmniBook 5000CT Pentium 90 4,5
Hewlett-Packard NetServer 5/133 LC	Hewlett-Packard OmniBook 5000CTS Pentium 90 4,5
Hewlett-Packard NetServer 5/133 LH	Hewlett-Packard OmniBook 5500CT 5/120
Hewlett-Packard NetServer 5/133 LS	Hewlett-Packard Vectra VA 6/180 PC
Hewlett-Packard NetServer 5/166 LC	Hewlett-Packard Vectra VE 5/133 Series 2 PC

Table 1-1.   A Portion of the NT Hardware Compatibility List

Take the compatibility issue. Very few clones are on the NT HCL in a meaningful manner. As mentioned before, not being on the HCL is a huge issue. It literally gives Microsoft a way out of solving your problem! In truth, most clones run NT very well, but does that make them the materials on which to build fault tolerance and a disaster recovery plan? The answer is, quite simply, no.

The clone is not the issue, but the way the clone components are continually in flux. The constant change in components provides a support nightmare. Furthermore, only a handful of clone manufacturers actually have the staff to truly support NT. Why not take advantage of companies that employ literally thousands of NT-certified engineers? Having a clear escalation path for NT-related problems is important. What good is saving $5000 on your server if it costs you $10,000 in lost productivity in the first year?

Interestingly, some of the people who should use clones the least are the ones who use them the most. A small business that has no on-site support staff to speak of is a classic example of a company that uses clones but shouldn't use them. These companies usually rely on outside contractors and consultants for IS support. The consultants can make between $75 and $150 an hour based on expertise (perceived or not). If a consultant has to waste twenty hours tracking down a clone-related bug, the cost savings of using clones are quickly diminished. With tier-one vendor products, a quick trip to a Web site or a relatively quick phone call can often reveal the problem.

It should be understood that clones have a place in a networked environment. The crux of the problem has to do with supporting clone systems in a controlled fault-tolerant environment. If you feel that using clone products or even making your own clones is in your best interest, keep in mind the following rules:

▼ Stick to a single vendor for as many of your purchases as possible. This gives you a single contact point if things go wrong or a component fails.

■ Figure out which components work in your environment and stick to them. For instance, you might find that a particular Intel motherboard works best in your environment.

▲ Do not skimp on network cards or SCSI controllers. Staying with Adaptec SCSI controllers and 3COM or Intel network cards is usually recommended. They are well supported throughout the industry.

What are the so-called tier-one companies from which to buy NT server systems? Purchasing standard systems from well-established vendors such as Compaq, Dell, Digital, Hewlett-Packard, and IBM is highly recommended. As stated earlier, this recommendation is in no way meant to be critical of other vendors, but support is the key issue here. Hours of downtime can easily translate to thousands of lost dollars.

Once again, try to standardize as much as possible on a single vendor and a single hardware profile. Be sure to standardize on known parts and make certain that all are on the Microsoft HCL. Standardizing impacts cost-of-ownership and the overall user perception of an IS department in a great way. In addition, certain manufacturers optimize drivers for their particular systems (Compaq is one such company). Service packs and updated drivers come directly from these companies and not Microsoft. As such, these companies' drivers often alleviate a variety of problems on the systems for which they were designed.

One last point to mention about this issue: Be sure to compare like systems when making the clone/tier-one comparison. Sometimes people boast that their $1000 server does just as well as a $25,000 "megasever." If you are looking for a basic box with no fault tolerance, tier-one systems can be as low as $2000. Conversely, a multiprocessor clone with a RAID controller, multiple disks drives, redundant power supplies, and similar features may cost upwards of $10,000.

Is Cheapest Best?

"Cheapest is best" is an idea that runs rampant in the computer industry. The idea is to purchase based upon price and not on quality. Capital-expenditure-conscious IS people sometimes look upon network servers as straight commodity purchases. However, the commodity concept makes no sense when combined with cost-of-ownership and system performance. It is a recipe for failure. Do not fall into the trap of thinking that all computers with a similar processor are the same.

Here are some other things to remember when purchasing mission critical server and network hardware:

▼   A server that crashes is not a good server in spite of its speed.

■   A network that is unavailable is a travesty in planning.

■   Certain CPUs are designed for servers and others are designed for workstations. For example, a Pentium II and the Pentium II slot 1 are workstation CPUs, whereas the Pentium Pro and Pentium II slot II are server-based. Make certain you understand your choices and options.

■   Protect all essential components on the network backbone with a UPS.

■   On critical systems and or data centers, have a generator available for emergency supply and make certain that the generator is adjusted to run with the UPS units installed.

▲   Be consistent in your purchases in regard to components, systems, and vendors.

Policy Planning

Some consider policy planning the most important part of a disaster recovery plan. It is interesting to note that policy planning has relatively little to do with actual software or hardware. Effective policy planning can go a long way to prevent data loss, operational loss, and corporate misunderstandings.

Policy must be devised by agreement between the executive, IS, and other branches of a corporation. Allowing one group to have too big an influence on policy usually makes for lopsided decisions. Executive and accounting departments are more likely to push for low-cost systems. Other groups may provide absolutely ridiculous guidelines for implementation, while IS departments are likely to go for all of the latest available gadgetry. Letting IS departments have their way can lead to costly, frivolous solutions, which are obvious overkill for most enterprises. The first step is formulating a consistent and realistic company policy. Failure to do so wastes money and potentially causes data to be lost.

The Costs

One of the first policy issues to discuss is how much money you need to put into a disaster recovery plan. Weighing recovery time against the solution cost is mentioned throughout this book. The cost of a disaster recovery plan can be found in the answers to these questions:

▼ How much money will a minute or hour of downtime cost the company?

■ How much data can the company afford to lose?

■ What points of failure should the company protect against?

■ What level of failure or downtime can the company actually accept?

▲ How long is the company required to keep backups?

The cost of downtime can actually be different for different components on a network. Perhaps a domain controller can be down for days with little or no impact. On the other hand, perhaps the company's SAP database can be down only for a few minutes. Time variations can be the difference between an expensive, highly available cluster solution and a relatively low-cost, manual fail-over system. Either way, figuring the costs of downtime is important. Liebert Corporation (a UPS manufacturer) has an interesting downtime cost calculator on their Web site (**http://www.liebert.com/ technics/calc.htm**). Leibert's Web site is a good starting point for getting a grasp on downtime figures.

After you have figured out the costs of downtime and the required recovery times, you must analyze how much data you can afford to lose. In other words, if a server fails, is it okay to go to a twelve-hour-old tape backup for data recovery? Some companies actually do online backups to a slower media several times during the day on critical servers. Others cannot afford to lose even 30 seconds of existing data. The cost difference between these solutions can be astounding. The frequency of disaster recovery systems is an important policy issue.

Finally, you have to decide how long to store backups of your system data. Some companies simply keep monthly or yearly tapes. Others move their periodic backups to a more permanent media like CD-ROM or MO.

IS Training

Be sure to keep your personnel well trained. Training is good for personnel as well as for the entire system. Nothing is worse than someone who thinks they know what to do but doesn't know how to do it. Many networks are built on trial and error and then duplicated. Someone goes through and sets parameters without really knowing what he or she is doing, until finally the network works, at which time its design is duplicated in all future devices. The result is a poor design that gets repeated and a confused network layout that ultimately leads to higher costs for the corporation.

Another common example of poor training is technical people who do not really know what an NT Emergency Repair Disk is for. At the slightest sign of trouble they run the repair process and essentially destroy the server configuration. This particular issue occurs with amazing regularity. The point is that a money spent on IS training is money well spent.

Contractor/Consultant vs. Internal Staff

Deciding early on who is to be the support component of your network is important. Do you want to outsource to consultants? Will you restrict yourself to Microsoft Solution providers? How do you determine the optimal balance between internal and external support? These questions are hard to answer and must be tailored to each environment. In general, the answer lies in the size of the network and the amount of money that is available for support. Ask Microsoft to provide you with the name of local consultants (always be certain to obtain references).

Using internal support staff as well as competent contractors for specific projects is generally a good idea. For instance, you may decide to bring in a contractor to aid IS personnel with an SMS installation. This frees internal personnel as they are going through the product learning curve.

User Issues

You must also consider user-related issues in the area of corporate policy. Such issues range from training to the choice of the desktop operating systems to a policy of reporting problems. Most companies already have some sort of computer use policy in place, but users may not know the documentation exists.

The first issue to discuss is training and documentation. Be sure users are trained in virus prevention, password protection, and the use of locked screen savers. Unfortunately, locked screen savers are typically the bane of desktop support people.

The documentation issue is actually quite straightforward in today's era of massive corporate intranets. Place documentation on all computer user policies and information on user-related issues in a central repository. Make sure the location is readily accessible to all corporate users. If you do not have an intranet, use your e-mail system. Most major e-mail-based groupware products (Exchange and Notes, for example) support public folders and forms, which make for effective policy containers. Another interesting idea is a network-based corporate help file. In this scenario, you create a Windows-based help file and place an icon that points to the file on all user desktops. There are several other ways to alert users to where they can find documentation. The important thing is to pick a method and stick to it.

Another major user issue is the question of what operating system to place on client workstations. On some networks, the equipment can barely support early versions of Windows, but in other situations the equipment can support a variety of operating systems.

If your choice is going to be some type of Windows product, which should you choose? Windows 95 and Windows 98 are often touted as the ideal network clients, but this is not necessarily true. Windows NT Workstations configured with 32MB of RAM actually run faster than these other operating systems. This book is all about fault-tolerant, secure, and robust designs. Running NT Workstation as your network client is highly recommended, unless you can't run it for a specific reason (i.e. a legacy DOS program that does not run under NT).

The last, obvious point to make about desktop operating systems is to choose as few different operating systems as possible. This can have an amazing impact on the total cost of ownership of your enterprise.

Another desktop issue to consider is the problem of workstation backups. It is bad enough that all critical server data on a network needs to be backed up. Why complicate the issue by adding workstations into the mix? If corporate policy dictates that users must store all data on file servers, workstation backups are not even an issue. In general, you should avoid workstation backups at all costs. Laptop users should be required to periodically dump data to file servers for backup. If you are worried about having to restore the user desktop, a good automatic reinstallation routine is far superior to a workstation backup. Several excellent products can help with automatic reinstallation, from Microsoft SMS to Seagate WinInstall (**http://www.seagatesoftware.com**). If, despite recommendations to the contrary, workstation backups are deemed necessary, run nightly batch files that move critical data to a network server for backup or else purchase a third-party software product that supports remote agents.

One such application, Networker by Legato (**http://www.legato.com**) allows you to back up the workstation automatically to the server. The process is initiated by the workstation, which means that workstation users can back up their machines to a backup server based on their own needs. Networker can truly help solve the workstation backup issue.

The final user policy is the problem of user software purchases. All software should be purchased with network licenses and installed where appropriate. Users should not be allowed to install their own software and expect IS to support it. Publish a list of supported software in your user documentation and carefully explain the procurement process for unsupported items.

Policy for the Network

Be sure to plan the growth of the network. Do not allow the network to be put together in a haphazard manner. A confused network can be an expensive network, especially if you need to bring in outside consultants to solve problems. Keep the network as simple as possible. Sophisticated environments are quite often too complex for people to manage. You might be able to design it, but can the support team support it? Document the network as much as possible. Be sure the documentation is readily available to everyone that needs it.

Server Issues

Server issues are an item for IS people to hash out. Such issues include the common NT discussions about drives (EIDE vs. SCSI), file systems (FAT vs. NTFS), and system purchases (clone vs. tier-one servers). The normal issues of hardware and software as mentioned above (RAID, clusters, and so on) can also be considered server issues.

Another server-related issue is system documentation. Be sure to carefully document the server, including installed software schemes, recovery techniques, and known problems. Log all server work and make sure that the logs are readily available to IS personnel. Documentation should be written carefully, as though the entire IS staff will leave tomorrow. In this way, the loss of a person or two has as little impact as possible.

The last server issue to mention is security. For absolutely no reason should everyone have access to all possible shares on the network. Design the network so that shares on servers can be seen but not necessarily accessed. Working with different departments, decide which shares each group of users should have the right to examine. Be sure to turn on auditing. By auditing the NT server properly, you can help reinforce the security policy.

The Issue of Testing

Another important policy consideration is testing. Some argue that testing does constitute a policy, but proper testing can cost enormous amounts of money and tax the resources of the corporation. Before you roll out new software, always test it on test servers first, then on a controlled group. Poorly tested installation can be a major headache for users and can result in a great deal of bad PR for the IS group.

Another import item to test is the disaster recovery plan itself. Be sure to completely test its design and implementation. Never assume something works until you have demonstrated that it truly does work. Everyone who has been in a fire drill knows how important such drills are. For a business, it seems germane to conduct fall-over and recovery drills periodically.

Problem Escalation Paths

The last policy issue to consider is the issue of problem escalation. Again, this is an area that can be extremely expensive. Many of the tier-one server companies offer paid support contracts for hardware and software. As mentioned above, thousands of NT engineers in their support centers can help you get your equipment back online as soon as possible. It is important to have these escalation paths clearly defined and contracts set up well ahead of time. You don't want to have to worry about getting purchasing approval for support when every minute of downtime is costing you.

In addition, you should work out replacement and service contracts for critical servers ahead of time. For instance, you might decide that a four-hour equipment replacement agreement should be in place for all servers. That is to say, if your administrator calls a server company and you decide that the problem has to do with hardware, the new equipment must arrive within four hours. Other support contracts call for a complete inventory of parts on-site, but these contracts can effectively double your hardware costs! However, if you can spare almost no downtime, you might have to pay the high price.

SUMMARY

A solid disaster recovery plan can make the difference between a company that survives and one that does not. Unfortunately, many companies do not plan for disasters until they suffer major data losses. Planning ahead can save thousands of dollars by protecting information, protecting computer operations, and preventing lost productivity.

CHAPTER 2

Windows NT's Built-In Features for Fault Tolerance

Fault tolerance can be loosely defined as the ability of a computer system to continue functioning with negligible interruption when part of the system hardware or software fails. As one example, an uninterruptible power supply provides an alternate source of power when the wall socket power fails, even if only for a few minutes. The user of that workstation may notice if the power flickers, but should not lose data when it happens. Similarly, a hard disk may fail, but if a second disk mirrors that drive, users may never even notice.

Usually, implementing fault tolerance in computer systems requires some degree of redundancy, which can vary from spare discrete components through the inclusion of redundant subsystems to entirely redundant systems. One example of the latter is Microsoft's clustering strategy, where NT Servers are redundant in a manner similar to the well-known VAX clustering schemes. Fault tolerance may be understood by looking at cars: almost every car has a temporary spare tire that is good for a limited time of use. Many cars have a full-size spare tire that is equal to the other tires on the car. Some people carry spare radiator hoses, belts, and other items that can be replaced easily and quickly. Others own and maintain a spare car so that if their primary car breaks down, they are up and running as soon as they can return to their garaged spare.

> **NOTE:** This isn't equivalent to Microsoft clustering: the automotive equivalent of that would be having a partner drive your spare car following you everywhere you went so that, if your car did break down, you could immediately continue on your way.

On NT systems, some of these fault tolerance areas are:

▼ **UPS (Uninterruptible Power Supply) Service**   Both Windows NT Workstation and Server include a Control Panel applet that allows integration of a UPS with the workstation or server. Administrators and users can be notified of a power failure prior to that failure, causing shutdown of the local workstation or server.

■ **Sector Sparing**   SCSI hard disks formatted as NTFS volumes can identify and skip bad sectors as they fail.

■ **Disk Mirroring**   A real-time backup of a partition, disk mirroring requires multiple disks. Fortunately, storage media has become consistently cheaper in recent years.

■ **Disk Striping with Parity**   Like disk mirroring, disk striping with parity allows for a hard disk in a volume set to fail without a loss of service from applications, or loss of access to data, on that set of disks.

▲ **Backup Domain Controllers (BDCs)**   If the PDC (Primary Domain Controller) fails, a BDC can continue handling domain logon validations. If the account database needs to be modified, a BDC may be promoted to a PDC.

Fault tolerance and backups are like insurance: some people or businesses feel they can do without them. Because not everyone will spend extra money for something they feel they might never need, Microsoft offers several levels of software-based fault tolerance as built-in features of the Windows NT operating system. While third-party vendors who feel they can provide significant improvement in functionality over the included software have improved on many of these areas, the third-party solutions cost additional money.

This chapter will present some of Windows NT's built-in features designed to improve accessibility and reliability. Starting with the architecture of the Windows NT operating system itself that isolates applications from the memory space the operating system uses, this chapter will then discuss the boot process for Windows NT, with discussions of recovery and the preparation for that recovery that should be done before it becomes necessary. The chapter will continue with a discussion of the file systems and disk management capabilities of Windows NT, with a preliminary examination of the Disk Administrator tool, followed by a discussion of the various Registry parameters relevant to the topic.

The chapter will then discuss the Emergency Repair Disk and other recovery options. The chapter will close with a discussion of some of the tools included with Windows NT, such as the Performance Monitor, Event Viewer, UPS tool, and tape backup utilities.

BEFORE YOU BEGIN

The time when people most often think about creating a backup (or an Emergency Repair Disk) is when they are looking at the Blue Screen of Death. Buying insurance after the building burns down doesn't help nearly as much as doing so the day before. Various studies have demonstrated that at least a third of the time needed to recover from a data loss is in assembling the required tools. With this in mind, there are a few things to consider having available before you need them:

▼ **Installation Media**   The Windows NT CD-ROM and the set of three floppy disks.

■ **Emergency Repair Disk**   It is recommended that an Emergency Repair Disk be created during installation, and that it should be updated whenever system configuration changes are made. These changes include installing new software or changing software configuration, altering network configuration, hardware changes, and operating system updates. Maintaining a current ERD is as important as having a current system backup.

■ **Current System Backup**   Reloading a snapshot of a given server with Windows NT with all the Service Packs and applications suites and customizations saved in the Registry from a tape or network backup is often much faster than recreating the server's setup from a basic install.

■ **DOS Boot Floppy**   Even if you are running NTFS, a DOS boot floppy can be helpful in starting and repairing NT.

■ **A DiskSave Image of Server**   This image can be crucial in resolving disk-related problems. It is discussed in detail in Chapter 10.

▲ **Complete Server Documentation**   This should include installation parameters for the server and its applications. Many programs can be recovered with the help of this information.

INSIDE THE WINDOWS NT OPERATING SYSTEM

This section provides an overview of the main components of the Windows NT operating system, and how the components interrelate. Windows NT was created as an object-oriented operating system. Each object may be independently addressed, updated, programmed, or controlled. The use of objects allows abstraction from the actual hardware. For two quick examples, the Virtual Memory Manager allows an application to act as though it is the only process (besides the operating system) running in 4GB of memory. The Hardware Abstraction Layer (HAL), by presenting an idealized abstracted version of the hardware, aids portability of software written for Windows NT by not requiring the application's developers to develop for different motherboards with different device registers, or even different processors (Intel x86 and DEC Alpha).

Windows NT is a preemptive multitasking, multithreaded, symmetrical multiprocessor operating system. What exactly do those terms mean?

▼ **Preemptive Multitasking**   Preemptive multitasking is defined as the operating system allocating processor cycles, as opposed to the applications allocating cycles. In cooperative multitasking, where each application chooses when to release the processor once it has control, a hanging of that application can prevent other applications from using the processor. With preemptive multitasking, a hung application does not prevent the operating system and other active applications from continuing to function. The Windows NT kernel schedules all of the processor time usage, preempting the actively running application to hand the processor over to a waiting application.

■ **Multithreaded**   An application written for Windows NT can be written to be multithreaded. A multithreaded application is written as a set of separate, discrete portions of executable code. Each portion can be individually scheduled to run on a processor. Each individual portion that can be separately scheduled by the kernel is called a *thread*.

■ **Soft Affinity**   Windows NT uses a soft affinity model for multithreaded applications on multiprocessor systems. With soft affinity, the operating system tries to send a thread back to the same processor it started at, but sends the thread to another processor if that processor is busy. Windows NT can be set to behave with hard affinity, where an application thread is set to always run on the processor where it started.

- ■ **Symmetrical Multiprocessor** Windows NT may use multiple processors, but is not quite as flexible as it possibly could be. For multiprocessor use, all the processors must be of the same type, level, and speed.

- ▲ **Virtual Memory** Often the amount of actual memory (RAM) on a system is less than the amount required by all of the applications currently running, in addition to the memory needs of the operating system. One requirement of an operating system is to coordinate the requests for memory from the multiple competing applications. Windows NT uses 32-bit addressing to access RAM in a flat, or non-segmented, memory model. Performance is improved (over DOS, for example) by not having to check for the segment of memory to access, and by moving data in 32-bit words instead of the older 16-bit standard. Like previous versions of Windows, Windows NT uses virtual memory when the physical memory is exhausted. Virtual memory is hard disk space treated as though it is slow RAM. The slowness of accessing a hard disk versus accessing RAM causes two events: page faults and demand paging. A *page fault* occurs when an application attempts to use memory that has been paged out to the swap file on the hard drive. *Demand paging* occurs when data is moved back from the hard disk to the memory. Demand paging is also referred to as *paging in*. During NT installation a swap file called PAGEFILE.SYS is created in the boot partition at the root level. The standard size of PAGEFILE.SYS is approximately 12MB more than the physical RAM. The Virtual Memory Manager object masks actual memory addresses in use by presenting only the virtual memory addresses to applications and processes. With a 32-bit addressing scheme, Windows NT supports a 4GB Virtual Address Space (VAS) of memory. A VAS is associated with a given application, so each application acts as though it is operating in a system with 4GB of RAM. By default, Windows NT reserves 50 percent of the memory space for the operating system, leaving the other 50 percent (2GB) for the application. Windows NT 5.0 is expected to support a 64-bit addressing scheme, which will extend the memory address space to 2^{64} bytes.

Subsystem Architecture

Windows NT is designed as a collection of interrelated objects that interact to provide the services of an operating system. By using an object-oriented design, the operating system provides for reliability, modularity for upgrades and feature improvements, and security. Many of the functions of Windows NT, which in other operating systems are part of the core operating system, have been moved out to subsystems. The Windows NT kernel (sometimes called the microkernel) is actually rather small in terms of the lines of code compared to the rest of the operating system. By isolating the portions of the operating system that do not need to be hardware-dependent, the designers reduced the amount of operating system code that needs to be ported to different platforms and architectures. This section will present the major components of Windows NT and how they interact, including how the design allows for reliability, fault tolerance, and disaster recovery. Windows NT's user mode will be covered first, followed by the components of the kernel mode.

User Mode

An operating system's architecture should be designed in such a way as to reduce the chance of a given application interfering with the operating system's services. In Windows NT, applications are assigned their own processes and their own address space. Applications are prohibited from reading or writing outside of their own address space. While often used to describe code functionality, the terms "user mode" and "kernel mode" actually apply to privilege levels associated with the processor. While hardware privileges can be designed with many levels, Windows NT uses a simple hardware privilege level structure that contains only two levels. These two levels are referred to as *user mode* and *kernel mode*. In simple terms, a process running at the user mode privilege level is not allowed to read or write directly to operating system memory, overwrite virtual memory, or perform other activities that would interfere with the operating system. The Virtual Memory Manager (running at the kernel mode level) provides isolation of one application's activities from other applications. To cross the boundary between user mode and kernel mode, a user-mode process must make what is called a *kernel mode transition*. As part of the transition, the NT Executive checks to see if the process request is legitimate, if the user who initiated the process has access to any files the process is aimed at reading or altering, and so on.

In user mode, Microsoft defines a protected subsystem as a user-mode service that is started at boot time. There are two types of protected subsystems:

▼ **Environmental**   A service that supports applications either written for, or native to, another operating system such as DOS.

▲ **Integral**   A service that performs an operating system-related function such as security.

These protected subsystems run in user mode. Each of the protected subsystems is provided with its own process and private memory space, protected from other user mode subsystems by the kernel mode level Virtual Memory Manager. Where the Virtual Memory Manager provides each application with the illusion it is running in a 4GB memory space, a user-mode application (including the environmental subsystem itself) can only access half of the memory space—as mentioned, the other half of the memory space is reserved for the operating system. This section will present the environmental and integral subsystems of Windows NT.

ENVIRONMENTAL SUBSYSTEMS   As stated previously, an environmental subsystem provides an environment for a non-Windows NT application to run within. An environmental subsystem may be considered as an Application Programming Interface

(API) that acts like a non-Windows NT operating system to a non-native application, and converts the non-native requests to service calls made to the Windows NT kernel-mode services. A user-mode code crash is unlikely to affect applications other than itself: the environmental subsystems form a restricted "sandbox" for applications to run in, similar to the sandbox concept of the Java Virtual Machine (JVM) included with many World Wide Web browsers. The five primary environmental subsystems are shown in Figure 2-1.

▼   **win32**   The win32 subsystem enjoys a special place in the user-mode environmental subsystems as the native execution environment for Windows NT applications. The richest-featured and best-developed subsystem, the win32 subsystem includes the access to user input and output devices such as the keyboard, mouse, and monitor, as well as being the only defined GUI windowing manager. The other environmental subsystems must call the win32 subsystem in order to access these user I/O devices.

■   **OS/2**   The OS/2 subsystem provides the supporting environment required to run OS/2 16-bit applications that were compiled for the Intel x86 platform. The OS/2 subsystem includes support for NetBIOS (both version 2.*x* and version 3.0 functionality), named pipes, and mail slots, as well as supporting reading OS/2 format HPFS drives. The major exception for application support is that

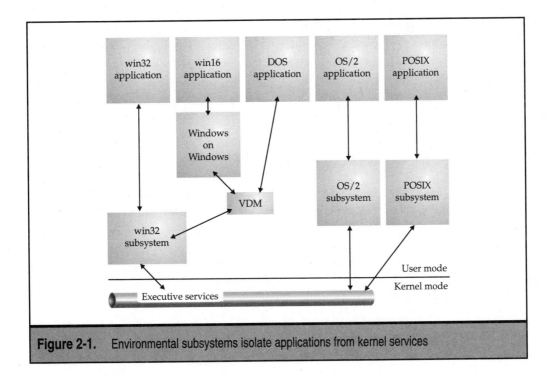

Figure 2-1.   Environmental subsystems isolate applications from kernel services

this subsystem does not provide support for console services (Presentation Manager). The subsystem allows access to NTFS volumes as though they were HPFS volumes, so long filenames are supported. If the ability to run OS/2 applications is perceived as a detriment, the loading of the OS/2 subsystem can be disabled through the removal of the following Registry key:

HKEY_LOCAL_MACHINE\SYSTEM\CURRENTCONTROLSET\
CONTROL\SESSIONMANAGER\SUBSYSTEMS\OS2

■ **POSIX** A common statement is that the POSIX subsystem is only present in Windows NT in order to allow the system to be purchased by clients that have POSIX compliance as a purchase requirement. While the POSIX subsystem does support character-based applications that conform to the POSIX 1003.1 standard, the support is limited. As only a single example of the many limitations of the POSIX subsystem, there is no support for networking. Like the OS/2 subsystem POSIX can be disabled by removing the following Registry key:

HKEY_LOCAL_MACHINE\SYSTEM\CURRENTCONTROLSET\
CONTROL\SESSIONMANAGER\SUBSYSTEMS\POSIX

NOTE: For a fully compliant POSIX environment, the NTFS file system is required. NTFS includes such POSIX-required features as case-sensitive file naming, hard links, creation and last accessed time stamps, and others.

■ **DOS (VDM)** The Virtual DOS Machine (VDM) allows many DOS applications to run within Windows NT. However, there are certain limitations. A DOS application that is designed to access the hardware directly, such as the video card or sound card, will have such a request passed to the Windows NT Executive, which passes such a request to the Hardware Abstraction Layer. The request is then caught in the kernel as a disallowed action, and being denied, is thrown out as an exception. This explains why Windows NT is not a good machine to install DOS-based games on (like Doom). Note that on non-Intel versions of NT the VDM is emulating only an Intel 80486 processor.

▲ **WOW (win16)** The Windows on Windows subsystem is included to support 16-bit Windows 3.*x* applications. However, the same limitation described for the VDM above applies here as well: any direct access of the hardware is strictly prohibited.

NOTE: By default all win16 applications running on the same server share a common VDM (i.e., if the WOW fails, it will take down all 16-bit Windows applications with it).

CORE SUBSYSTEMS The Windows NT core subsystems also run in user mode, but do not provide hosting to non-native Windows NT applications. Windows NT core subsystems perform tasks related to the operating system, instead of related to applications. The four core subsystems presented in this section are

▼   **Winlogon**   The Winlogon application presents the logon dialog to the user, and passes the user's input to the Local Security Authority for authentication. Winlogon also handles remote Performance Monitor data requests. The Winlogon service is highly customizable. The Registry value entries that control the Winlogon service are found under the Registry key:

HKEY_LOCAL_MACHINE\SOFTWARE\MICROSOFT\WINDOWSNT\ CURRENTVERSION\WINLOGON

■   **Local Security Authority (LSA)**   The Local Security Authority subsystem is a user-mode portion of the Security subsystem. The LSA interfaces with the SAM (Security Account Manager) database to verify the user's credentials passed to it by the Winlogon process. When logging into a Windows NT system, the user selects the local computer or domain, which contains his user account information. The Local Security Authority requires the user to specify the account database where the user's account can be authenticated. The From dialog entry only lists the account databases the local security system recognizes as acceptable account databases: the user cannot manually specify the name of a previously unknown domain to connect to.

■   **Security Account Manager (SAM)**   The Security Account Manager is another protected user-mode subsystem, and is used to maintain user and group account information. The Registry value entries that control the Security Account Manager service are found under the Registry key:

HKEY_LOCAL_MACHINE\SAM

Microsoft's recommended limit for the maximum size of the SAM database is approximately 40MB—roughly equivalent to 26,000 users and systems. If a single domain contains more than 26,000 entries, it might be good to consider dividing the domain into smaller portions. Since the SAM is loaded in RAM, and is used for every logon as well as many other transactions, its size affects the amount of memory needed on the server, the length of time a server takes to boot, and the time it take to process a logon request from a user.

▲   **Service Control Manager (SCM)**   The Service Control Manager is the subsystem responsible for loading, unloading, and managing kernel-mode drivers and system services. The SCM, while obviously an integral part of the operating system, runs in user mode.

Kernel Mode

As described earlier, user-mode processes are isolated from the areas of memory the operating system uses. The idea behind kernel mode and its alternative, user mode, is to separate applications from the operating system. Applications run in user mode;

operating systems run in kernel mode. In kernel mode, the code has direct access to all memory, including the address spaces of all user-mode processes and applications, and to hardware. In the Intel x86 processor architecture, Windows NT's kernel mode is equivalent to Ring 0: the process has virtually unrestricted access to the entire memory space, including that of protected applications and the environmental subsystems. Windows NT's user mode is equivalent to Ring 3, and is restricted in its allowed actions. However, "with great power comes great responsibility"—a kernel-mode code failure can crash the operating system.

Three major portions of the Windows NT operating system run in kernel mode:

▼   The Windows NT Kernel

■   The Windows NT Executive

▲   The Hardware Abstraction Layer

This section will present the functions of these three portions of the operating system.

The Windows NT Kernel

The Windows NT Kernel operates at the greatest privilege level on the processor. Every portion of the processor architecture and the assigned memory space may be accessed and written to by the Kernel. Preemption of the Kernel process is not permitted. As the Kernel is non-pageable, all of the code and data for the Kernel resides in physical memory at all times. Paging the Kernel out to disk would cause a massive slowdown of those portions of the kernel code, and also place part of the Kernel (the most privileged and powerful portion of the operating system) under the authority of the Virtual Memory Manager. One design goal of the Kernel was symmetric multiprocessing: the Kernel may be run simultaneously on all processors present in the system.

The Windows NT Kernel provides the basic operating system functions used by the rest of the operating system. The kernel provides process and thread scheduling support, support for multiprocessor synchronization, interrupt handling and dispatching, and other functionality. Since the Kernel is the highest authority in Windows NT, it is designed to reduce its reliance on the other subordinate services, even those other services also in kernel mode. One of the ways in which the Kernel is self-reliant is in the use of objects. The Kernel does not use the Object Manager to define its objects, but instead provides a minimal set of objects and object manipulation functions. These Kernel-defined objects and functions are used by the Windows NT Executive, which takes the Kernel-defined objects and uses them to create more complex objects, which are accessible to user-mode subsystems and their applications.

The Windows NT Executive

The Windows NT Executive is the single largest component of Windows NT. Structured to use the services of the Hardware Access Layer (HAL) and the Windows NT Kernel (both of which are strongly tied to the platform) the Executive is, by comparison, disassociated from the "ground level" operations of hardware access. This comparative isolation from the hardware makes the Executive more portable between the different platforms.

The Windows NT Executive is composed of the following major components:

▼   Object Manager

■   Process Manager

■   Local Procedure Call Facility

■   Security Reference Monitor

■   Video Device Driver

■   Virtual Memory Manager

■   Cache Manager

▲   I/O Manager

This section will present descriptions of these components of the Windows NT Executive.

OBJECT MANAGER   The Windows NT Object Manager manages almost all of the objects within the Windows NT operating system. An object is a data structure defined and originated by a kernel-mode component. An object is opaque to other objects, which do not read, write, or act on the data within the object directly, but send a message to the object with the desired action. The object receiving the message may perform the action requested in the message in one of several ways. For example, consider a light bulb and its operator, a person we'll call Ruth. If you want to turn on the light, you do not turn on the light yourself—you ask Ruth to turn on the light (send a message to the Light Bulb Manager). Ruth, the Light Bulb Manager, may turn on the light in any of several ways: she may simply flip the switch, she may plug the lamp in, she may take the light bulb out of a desk drawer and place it in the fixture, or flip the circuit breaker on for the entire floor of the building. You don't care how she does it, you just ask her to turn on the light. Objects in Windows NT act the same way: an object will have a list of services it can provide, but does not describe how it performs those tasks. In this way, the executive components (you, in the light bulb example) are isolated from the specific hardware issues: you don't have to know the light bulb is kept in a desk drawer and is only inserted when light is requested—all you have to know is that if you want light, ask Ruth.

The rest of the Windows NT Executive subsystems use the Object Manager's services to define, create, and manage objects. Working with the Security Reference Monitor, the Object Manager maintains handle tables for processes. The Windows NT Object Manager provides the following services:

▼   Dynamically adds new object types to the system

■   Allows other subsystems to define security restrictions and protection for instances of that object type

■ Allows other subsystems to define methods (*how* to turn on the light) for instances of that object type

■ Creates and deletes object instances

▲ Maintains a global name space for the operating system

PROCESS MANAGER   The Process Manager allows creation of process and thread objects, ensuring the processes are tagged with access tokens. For an example of why access tokens are useful, consider a user who wants to open a file. Perhaps that file is the evaluation of that user, done by the user's supervisor in the company. The user issues a File | Open request, which is passed to the Windows NT Executive for processing. The system thread for File | Open, while a kernel-mode piece of code, is actually working on behalf of that particular user, so the kernel-mode system thread is tagged with the access tokens for that user. When the File | Open thread attempts to open the file, it compares the requesting user's permissions with the access restrictions placed on the file by the file's creator, and refuses the File | Open request.

LOCAL PROCEDURE CALL FACILITY   The Local Procedure Call (LPC) Facility uses a variation of Remote Procedure Calls (RPC) to pass messages between two processes on the same node using a client/server model. Where RPCs were designed to provide client/server capability between processes on different machines connected by a local or wide area network, the LPC facility is optimized for communication within a node where all processes have access to the same physical memory.

SECURITY REFERENCE MONITOR   Responsible for enforcing security policy on the local node, the Security Reference Monitor subsystem also provides object-auditing facilities. Working with the Object Manager, the Winlogon process, and the Security subsystem, the Security Reference Monitor subsystem ensures access validation and auditing.

VIDEO DEVICE DRIVER   With Windows NT 4.0, the Window Manager, Graphics Device Interface (GDI), and related graphics device drivers were moved from the win32 environmental subsystem (running in user mode) to the Windows NT Executive (running in kernel mode). Both Window Manager and GDI exist in Windows NT 4.0 and forward as Windows NT Executive system services.

By moving the Window Manager and GDI functionality into the kernel-mode Executive service, applications can access the GUI implementation subsystems just as they currently access such non-GUI parts of the win32 API, such as file I/O and memory management. Once applications have called into Window Manager and GDI, those kernel-mode subsystems can now access other Windows NT Executive systems directly without the cost of user/kernel-mode transitions.

VIRTUAL MEMORY MANAGER   Typically, modern workstations and servers have less physical memory (RAM) than the amount desired by the operating system and the active applications. As a basic rule of scarce resources, processes will contend for memory when there isn't enough to satisfy every request. Virtual memory is a way of satisfying the needs of the processes without installing enough physical memory—by pretending that hard disk space is a large and variably sized but significantly slower kind of RAM.

The Windows NT Virtual Memory Manager (VMM) manages the physical memory on the local system, and is also responsible for providing virtual memory management for the rest of the operating system and to all applications that execute on the local system. The Virtual Memory Manager provides services to almost every kernel-mode and user-mode subsystem. One of the few exceptions is the Window NT Kernel, which cannot be paged out. The Kernel must remain entirely in physical memory at all times.

CACHE MANAGER   The Windows NT Executive includes a subsystem responsible for virtual block caching functionality (in system memory) for file data stored on secondary storage media. Closely associated with the Windows NT Virtual Memory Manager, the Cache Manager performs read-ahead on file data by predicting what the user will ask for next, based on the user's previous accesses. For example, if a user opens a file and the first 20KB is loaded into memory, the Cache Manager will read ahead and pre-load the next 64KB of the file data into memory from the hard disk or other slower secondary storage. If the user does not request the next 64KB, the cached read-in data is dumped and the disk is accessed to fulfill the user's actual request.

Similarly, the Cache Manager provides a delayed-write feature for actually writing modified cached data back out to the hard disk or other secondary storage media. Primary responsiveness is given to the user's interaction with the application, and the writing of cached data is delayed to when it does not inconvenience the user. While this delay increases the chance of an application crash or system problem losing the data in the volatile memory, the chance of data loss is reduced on NTFS file systems. NTFS file systems track even cached data changes as transactions, and track whether the transaction is completed. In this way, even an unanticipated power loss will not leave the file system in an unknown state. However, some of the most recent data may be lost in such a case. In almost all instances you will want to use NTFS on your server drives.

I/O MANAGER   The Windows NT I/O Manager provides a framework for all kernel-mode drivers to operate inside. Subordinate portions of the I/O subsystem include file system drivers; network redirectors and file servers; and device, intermediate, and filter drivers.

The NT I/O subsystem consists of the following seven types of components:

▼   **The I/O Manager**   This component manages the framework for the subsystem.

■   **File System Drivers**   These are the local disk-based file systems.

■   **Network Redirectors**   Similar to RPCs as separate from LPCs, a network redirector looks like a local file system driver. A network redirector accepts an I/O request for a non-local file system and sends it to network servers.

■   **Network File Servers**   The servers receive non-local I/O requests and reissue them to local file system drivers.

■   **Device Drivers**   The lowest level, device drivers deal directly with hardware devices such as network interface cards (NICs) and disk drives.

■ **Intermediate Drivers**   One level of abstraction above device drivers, intermediate drivers provide a generalized level of functionality common to all members of a class of device. One example of an intermediate driver would be a generic SCSI-2 driver.

▲ **Filter Drivers**   These are similar to intermediate drivers. However, while intermediate drivers tend to provide a common set of functionality, a filter driver tends to add additional capability the original driver lacked.

The Hardware Abstraction Layer

A major selling point for Windows NT when it was initially released was its multiple architecture portability. Originally designed to be portable across the architectures of Intel x86 platforms, DEC Alpha platforms, MIPS and PowerPC platforms, support for the latter two platforms has since been discontinued by Microsoft. The Hardware Access Layer (HAL) was created with the intention to isolate hardware-specific code from the rest of the operating system. By providing abstract views of the hardware to the other Windows NT kernel-mode subsystems, the other Windows NT subsystems do not need rewriting for new architectures.

The HAL supports several kinds of bus types usable with Windows NT (ISA, EISA, VL-Bus, and PCI among others), managing the differences internally. This concealment allows, for example, a new bus to be supported by Windows NT by extending the HAL, without needing to modify the rest of the operating system. In addition to bus types, the HAL manages and exports hardware-based functionality such as system timers, I/O buses, DMA and interrupt controllers, device registers, and others as messages to the other objects in the operating system.

In most other operating systems, any active program may directly access any device (such as printer ports, communications ports, keyboard controllers, mouse controllers, video controllers, and disk controllers). Any security implemented at the operating system level could be bypassed by simply ignoring the operating system's restrictions and directly accessing the desired devices. While in some cases this was done to improve speed for a given application, direct access is likely to cause difficulty if more than one program wants access to a given device at the same time.

Windows NT prohibits applications from directly accessing any hardware device. When a program wants to access a device, it calls the Windows NT Executive. After the Executive checks the user's security permissions and verifies that the device isn't in use by another program, the application's request is passed as a message to the HAL, which performs the request.

THE NT BOOT PROCESS

The NT boot process follows a predefined set of events that occur each time an NT machine is started. For recovery purposes, understanding the NT boot process and exactly what can go wrong with it is imperative. This process is fully detailed in Chapter 10.

NT FILE SYSTEMS

One of the requirements of an operating system is data management: what types of disks can be used with it, how the operating system chops the disk up into subportions, what format data and files are kept in, and other topics. This section will provide an overview of Windows NT's support for disk types, partitioning of disks, supported file system types, and disk sets. Many of the concepts will be familiar already: Windows NT's Disk Administrator GUI application has many of the capabilities of DOS's command-line application FDISK, in that partitions are controlled through both. Disk Administrator has several other useful capabilities as well, which will also be presented.

Windows NT fully supports two disk file systems:

▼   FAT (File Allocation Table)

▲   NTFS (NT File System)

This section will discuss the advantages and disadvantages of using either file system. As part of this discussion, the partition types used by Windows NT will also be covered. The presentation of partitions, mirrors and stripe sets will lead into a short overview of some of the features of Windows NT's Disk Administrator.

FAT

NT's File Allocation Table (FAT) file system is the same as the FAT file system introduced in Windows 95. A FAT partition or logical drive is accessible by a system running DOS, Windows, or OS/2. The FAT file system used by Windows NT supports both the DOS file-naming convention of up to eight characters followed by a three-character extension and the long file and folder names supported by Windows 95 and Windows NT.

In the FAT file system, files are organized by the File Allocation Table. Every file and directory that exists at the root level in a FAT partition points to a FAT entry identifying the starting cluster number for that file or directory. If the file is larger than a single cluster of sectors (a size dependent on the size of the partition) the cluster points to the next cluster. FAT makes no effort towards file optimization: the next cluster of a file is the next available cluster on the disk, regardless of the location of the previous cluster. The last cluster a file occupies contains an End of File marker.

The FAT root directory is limited to 512 entries (an entry may either be a file or a subdirectory). A *subdirectory* is a file listing the files and subdirectories contained inside, with a marker indicating it is a subdirectory. Subdirectories may contain any number of subdirectories and files.

The FAT file system is limited to a fixed number of table entries: while MS-DOS originally supported a maximum of 4,096 table entries, the Windows 95 and NT version of FAT allows 65,536 entries in the FAT. Since a FAT is limited to a fixed maximum number of clusters, a cluster will not be the same size on two differently sized volumes. At 65,536 clusters and assuming a sector size of 512 bytes, a partition of 32MB or below will have a single sector per cluster, equaling a cluster size of 512 bytes. Above 32GB, each cluster will contain 128 sectors and occupy 64KB on the partition. Only one file may be assigned to a cluster, and any excess space in the last cluster assigned to a file is simply wasted.

NTFS

NTFS (NT File System) is the native file system for Windows NT. Unlike FAT, NTFS is not limited to a fixed number of sectors per cluster. In the NTFS file system, the cluster is the base unit. The cluster factor is defined as a number of bytes, and formatting a volume as NTFS guarantees that the cluster factor is a multiple of the sector size on the drive. As NTFS addresses everything by a cluster number, the file system is isolated from consideration of the sector size of the underlying drive. Due to this isolation from the physical characteristics of the disk, the number of sectors per cluster is a default suggested value rather than a hard and fixed value. NTFS allows modification of the default number of sectors per cluster to better suit the actual usage of the volume. NTFS also seeks contiguous disk space before writing or copying a file to the disk. Because of this, simply copying an NTFS volume off to another disk and back actually helps defragment the disk. This anti-fragmentation feature of NTFS drives work best when they are at less than 60 percent capacity. Over that amount, NTFS is forced to fragment its files.

NTFS' Partition Boot Sector

The partition boot sector is located at the beginning of the NTFS volume, with a duplicate located elsewhere on the volume. Starting at sector 0, the boot sector may be as large as 16 sectors. The contents of the boot sector are

- ▼ The BIOS Parameter Block (BPB)
- ■ The number of sectors in the volume
- ▲ The starting Logical Cluster Numbers (LCNS) of the Master File Table (MFT) and the Master File Table Mirror (MFT2)

A duplicate of the boot sector is located at the end of the volume on Windows NT 4.0 and up, and at the logical center of the volume for Windows NT 3.51 and earlier versions.

The NTFS system or metadata files are created on the volume during the format of the volume by the FORMAT command. The NTFS system files are all defined with fixed file numbers in the MFT. These metadata files, such as the Bad Cluster File, which tracks the location of all identified bad clusters in the partition, follow immediately after the MFT in the root directory of the partition. After the last metadata file are the data files. The MFT2 is not a complete mirror of the MFT, but mirrors the first three records of the MFT (the MFT, MFT2, and the log file) to prevent a bad cluster developing at the beginning of the MFT from corrupting the partition.

NTFS, DOS, and Long Filenames

Windows NT and Windows 95 use the same format for long filenames of up to 255 characters. In order to provide long filenames for FAT volumes, Windows NT used a workaround that allowed for backwards compatibility with applications that require the DOS 8.3 naming convention. When a file is created with a long filename, Windows NT first generates an 8.3 format name for that file. Additional file entries created in the file's directory are used to store the rest of the long filename. DOS applications running under Windows NT can access files stored on NTFS transparently, since they are unaware of the file system actually in use. This "long filename for FAT" workaround is enabled by default. While long filename support for FAT volumes may be turned on or off by editing the Registry, it may only be done at the complete server level, affecting all FAT volumes on that server. Turning off long filename support will result in any file created with a long name after the disabling being invisible to a system viewing that volume with MS-DOS or OS/2.

NOTE: Remember, a FAT root directory is limited to 512 file entries. These additional file entries count against the 512 limit. For this reason, it may be prudent to consider limiting the use of long filenames at the root level of a FAT volume or simply not using FAT.

NTFS includes compression as a basic characteristic for directories and files. While actual compression varies depending on the nature of the data being compressed, the average gain is approximately 2:1. Applications accessing compressed files on NTFS are unaware the file is being decompressed as it's requested. Depending on the performance of the platform, the user may notice some performance degradation. The file is compressed when it is closed or saved. Only the NTFS file system can read the compressed form of the data. When an application or a command such as Copy requests access to the file, the NTFS file system uncompresses the file before the copy occurs. Copying a compressed file to a compressed folder actually involves uncompressing, copying, and recompressing the file. Compression may be enabled for individual files, directories, or entire volumes but is not really recommended in a server environment. Compressed files and folders have an attribute of C when viewed in the File Manager or Windows Explorer.

NTFS improves its efficiency by treating small files in a different manner than large files. A sufficiently small file can actually have all of its attributes, including its data, stored as a resident attribute in the Master File Table. Therefore, the hard disk is accessed only once to find the file and its data. On a FAT file, first the location must be found in the FAT, then the data (however small) must be retrieved from its location, requiring at least two disk accesses. If the file in question is located in a subdirectory, even more disk accesses must happen before reaching the data.

Converting FAT to NTFS

NTFS does offer several benefits over FAT. Microsoft provided a utility to convert a FAT volume to NTFS without losing the data. Often this is done for the purpose of extending the volume size without destroying the contents, or for implementing file-level security. While it is possible to convert a FAT volume to an NTFS volume in the obvious way (by backing up the volume to another drive or to tape, reformatting the drive as NTFS, then copying the files onto the NTFS volume), the convert utility allows direct conversion without such a process. However, it is always prudent to have a current backup on hand in case of disaster.

To convert a FAT volume to NTFS, open a command prompt by clicking on the Start button, then selecting Programs, then selecting Command Prompt. Enter the following command:

```
CONVERT fat_partition_letter /FS:NTFS
```

For example, to convert the F: FAT partition, enter the command

```
CONVERT F /FS:NTFS
```

However, if CONVERT.EXE cannot acquire complete access to the target drive, it will respond with an error message, then prompt with an option to schedule the drive for conversion when the system reboots. If the drive is scheduled for conversion on system boot, the line

```
autocheck autoconv \DosDevices\F: /FS:NTFS
```

(still using drive F as the example) is added to the

```
\HKEY_LOCAL_MACHINE\SYSTEM\CurrentControlSet\Control\SessionManager:Boot
Execute
```

key in the Registry.

In addition to CONVERT.EXE, CUFAT.DLL (for FAT partitions), and CUHPFS.DLL (for HPFS partitions) are necessary to convert a drive to NTFS. By default, these two DLLs are installed in the %SYSTEMROOT%\SYSTEM32 subdirectory.

NTFS and Other File Systems

In addition to the FAT and NTFS file systems, Windows NT also provides limited support for HPFS (High Performance File System, used by OS/2) and Macintosh volumes. While versions of Windows NT previous to 4.0 could both read and write to HPFS, NT 4.0 can only read (but not write to) HPFS partitions. The read-only support allows access to data for purposes of migration to either a FAT or NTFS partition. HPFS security permissions can be converted to NTFS security permissions with the OS/2 utility BACKACC.EXE and the Windows NT utility ACLCONV.EXE. If write capability to an HPFS partition is desired but migration is not desirable for some reason, one workaround would be to copy the appropriate settings and driver from a Windows NT 3.51 or earlier installation.

Windows NT Server can define a portion of an NTFS volume as a Macintosh-accessible volume. Security of files is provided in limited functionality compared to the base NTFS volume: security in a MacFile volume is applied at the directory level, not to individual files.

NOTE: Maintenance of MacFile volumes within an NTFS volume must be done through the File Manager or the Server Manager—this has not yet been included in Explorer's capabilities.

Recoverability: The NTFS Log File

The NTFS file system was designed with recoverability as a design goal, and several characteristics of NTFS were created to support data loss avoidance. As was mentioned earlier, the Master File Table (MFT) has its first three records duplicated as the MFT2. The first record of the MFT is the MFT's location. The second record is the location of the MFT2. The third record of the MFT is the log file, which the operating system uses to restore consistency to the NTFS file system in the event of a system crash.

NTFS uses a recoverable file system strategy, which uses a variation of a "lazy write" method to cache data and write data to the disk in the background. A transaction log of each disk access is maintained to allow a record of all disk write activity to survive a system crash, and therefore to minimize loss of data.

Each modifying I/O request is considered a transaction. The following transactions are logged by NTFS:

▼ Creation and deletion of files

■ Creation and deletion of directories

■ Creation and deletion of attributes

■ Hot fix records

▲ Periodic checkpoint records

Transactions are tracked by the Log File Service and recorded in the log file. The Log File Service is a component of the Windows NT Executive. The *log file* is a circularly reused file that, when full, "loops" back to continue recording of transactions in order to avoid growing indefinitely. Each transaction contains the information required to undo and redo itself. If an error occurs in the transaction, it can be retried using the redo information. If the transaction is marked as incomplete, the transaction is undone (undo). In order to reduce the amount of time needed to perform a recovery, NTFS checks the cache every eight seconds to determine the transaction status, and marks that status as a checkpoint in the log file.

FAT and NTFS: Which Is Better?

FAT and NTFS both have their place. Because of the lower overhead, FAT is more efficient for smaller drives. At the lowest extreme, a floppy disk cannot be formatted as an NTFS volume. However, these are about the only compelling reasons for using FAT. Partitions above approximately 500MB will be more efficiently used if they are formatted as NTFS. Also, NTFS provides several features FAT does not, such as security, inherent defragmentation, compression, and Macintosh sharing. FAT tends to be faster for smaller volumes, but NTFS tends toward better performance for file access on the deep file structure common on most file servers. NTFS tends to use disk space more efficiently than FAT, especially on larger (1GB and upwards) volumes. Security is considerably more granular on NTFS than on FAT volumes; on FAT volumes access control is only at the directory level and affects all users, NTFS access can be controlled down to the individual file level and the individual user. FAT security does not allow you to grant read privileges on a single file to Christina and Andrew, but not Grant.

If the computer needs to start another operating system other than Windows NT, use the FAT file system for your system partition. However, this is definitely not a recommended action on NT file servers.

The last argument in the FAT vs. NTFS debate is the "recoverability" feature of FAT. Some people feel that it is a benefit to be able to boot to a DOS disk and repair damaged NT files. However, you can still use NTFS and have this feature. Simply install a minimal version of NT onto a second disk in the system. Then create an NT boot floppy (to use if the first drive has boot sector problems). This process is spelled out in more detail in Chapter 10.

NOTE: For a RISC-based computer, the system partition must be formatted with the FAT file system. The NTFS file system may be used on the boot partition, which needs to be large enough for all Windows NT system components. Microsoft recommends the system partition on a RISC should be approximately 5 to 10MB, and the boot partition should be about 100MB or more.

Partitions, Volume Sets, and Stripe Sets

The Disk Administrator tool allows manipulation of the drives into a variety of configurations. They range from partitions to sets to mirrors.

Partitions

A *partition* is a defined logical portion of a physical drive's storage space. Partitioning serves several purposes: localizing data, using different file systems such as FAT and NTFS on the same physical disk, or simply providing a different drive letter required by a given application. The two types of partitions are "primary" and "extended." A *primary* partition is a partition not divisible into logical (virtual) drives, and an *extended* partition is a partition that can be divided into logical drives.

On a single physical disk, Windows NT will allow up to four partitions. All partitions may be primary partitions, or one may be extended. Only one extended partition may exist on a single physical disk. The part of a physical disk that is neither partitioned nor formatted is called free space.

> **NOTE:**   DOS, of course, is limited to seeing two partitions. If the OS partition is not the first or second partition, booting from a DOS floppy will not assist in, for example, replacing a bad device driver. In addition, DOS can only read FAT partitions: NTFS partitions will be visible but unreadable.

Volume Sets and Stripe Sets

A *volume set* is a group of 2 to 32 free spaces on drives that is associated together as a single partition. The volume set may then be defined as a FAT or NTFS partition. In a volume set, data is written to the partitions of the set in order. As each partition is filled, data is then written to the next partition. Volume sets are a convenient method of creating a larger area for data, and can be created either by combining multiple areas of free space, or by extending an existing NTFS volume. FAT volumes cannot be extended without losing the data. To extend a FAT volume, the data must be copied elsewhere, a new FAT volume of the desired larger size is then created, then the saved data is restored to the new larger FAT volume set. An NTFS volume set may have free spaces added to the volume set to extend it without requiring the backup/delete/ create/restore process FAT volume sets require. Neither FAT nor NTFS volume sets may be reduced in size without losing the data.

Stripe sets also combine areas of free space on different physical disks to form one large volume (either NTFS or FAT) identified by a single drive letter. However, rather than filling one partition before moving to another, data is written evenly (striped) across the volumes to theoretically gain a performance enhancement. Speed improvements are not actually realized unless the multiple disks are on multiple disk controllers, or controllers that support concurrent disk I/O. A stripe set as described above is equivalent to a RAID (Redundant Array of Inexpensive Disks) level 0, which means that there are no provisions for disaster. A disk crash that contained the second volume of a four-volume stripe set has the same effect as deleting that volume from the disk, which renders the rest of the data in that stripe set inaccessible. To phrase the last point another way, if one partition in a stripe set fills, all data in the stripe set is lost.

Disk Mirroring and Disk Duplexing

Disk mirroring creates an identical copy of a disk partition on another disk. Like a stripe set, the two partitions must be on different disks. All data is written to both disks. The same drive letter is used for both partitions of a mirror set. Any existing partition (including the system and boot partitions) can be mirrored onto another partition of equal or greater size on another disk using either the same or a different disk controller. While expensive in terms of disk space (only 50 percent of the drive space of a mirror is usable—the other half is used for the mirroring) disk mirroring is cost-effective for small setups.

Disk duplexing is a type of disk mirroring that uses a different disk controller for the second drive. In disk mirroring, the single disk controller can fail and cause the data to be lost. By using two disk controllers as well as two disks, another potential point of failure is eliminated. For a more solid RAID configuration, consider purchasing a hardware RAID controller. These devices are discussed more thoroughly in Chapter 3.

Fault Tolerant Stripe Sets

Disk striping with parity is a popular strategy for many installations. In the RAID classification, NT's software disk striping with parity is identified as level 5. The data is striped across all the disks in the array. The parity information for data recovery is also striped across the disks. Data and parity information are always stored on separate disks within the array for a particular stripe.

When you use Windows NT's Disk Administrator to create a stripe set, Disk Administrator divides the total size by the number of disks to create equal-sized unformatted partitions in each of the selected disks and assigns a single drive letter to the collection of partitions that make up the stripe set. If you choose a number that cannot be divided equally, Disk Administrator rounds to the closest higher or lower value.

Stripe sets are created similarly to volume sets, but with the restriction that each member partition of the stripe set must be on a different disk (up to a limit of 32 partitions). In addition, Disk Administrator will make all the partitions approximately the same size, so larger-than-the-average partitions will have their extra space wasted and unusable. If a stripe set is created from a 400MB partition and two 500MB partitions, the effective data space is not 1400MB, but 1200MB. The extra 100MB on the two larger partitions is ignored. If this is a stripe set with parity, the effective space is 800MB.

While the type of disk is effectively irrelevant when creating stripe sets—a mix of IDE, EIDE, and SCSI drives can be used—this practice is not recommended. Using identical disks is preferable for several reasons:

▼ **Disk Performance Matches**   Faster disks do not have to wait for slower disks, so the expense of the faster disks is not wasted.

■ **Space Conservation**   If the disk is configured as part of a mirror set or stripe set with parity, there is no wasted space.

▲ **Driver Compatibility**   Similar disks will use the same drivers and have fewer potential problems.

As with the mirror sets, it is recommended that you purchase hardware RAID 5 controllers for any critical servers. This subject is covered in more detail in Chapter 3.

The Disk Administrator

The Disk Administrator is a tool within Windows NT, and is used to manage disk configuration. While the Disk Administrator is presented in detail in Chapter 3, a short overview here is relevant. To start the Disk Administrator, select the Start button, then select Administrative Tools (Common) | Disk Administrator. The Disk Administrator window is shown in Figure 2-2.

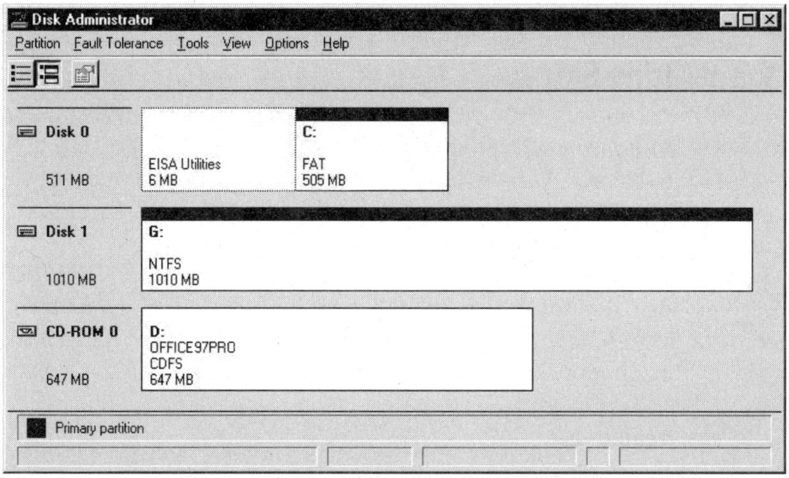

Figure 2-2.   The Disk Administrator allows disk configuration and management

The Disk Administrator provides the following disk configuration and management capabilities:

▼   Creates primary partition

■   Creates extended partition

■   Marks a partition as active

■   Deletes a partition

■   Labels a partition with a volume label

■   Reassigns a drive letter from one partition to another

■   Formats a partition as either NTFS or FAT

■   Creates a stripe set

■   Creates a volume set

■   Manages Fault Tolerance (for NT Server)—the Fault Tolerance menu is located between the Partition and the Tools menu, and controls disk mirroring and creating or regenerating stripe sets with parity

▲   Saves the current disk configuration (the subset of the Registry concerned with the local disk)

Reassignment of drive letters may be necessary occasionally because Windows NT assigns available drive letters sequentially, starting with the primary partition and continuing with the active partitions. If a new hard disk is added to the system, Windows NT will assign the next drive letter—even if that letter is already assigned as a network connection. The local designation takes precedence, thereby disabling the network connection. Therefore a drive letter may be arbitrarily reassigned. As disk configuration settings are stored in the Registry, the change (and therefore the fix) will be present after a restart.

NOTE: In Windows NT 3.51, the Disk Administrator did not show CD-ROM volumes. The ability to show CD-ROM volumes was added to Disk Administrator in Windows NT 4.0.

You cannot use NTFS compression if the cluster size is set to greater than 4K during the formatting process. The Disk Administrator utility allows setting of the cluster size to 4K, but the command-line utility FORMAT.COM allows setting the cluster size to any size. Also, for security on RISC-based computers, Disk Administrator can be used to secure the system partition from modification by users without administrative privileges, even if it is FAT.

Saving the SYSTEM Key

In the Windows NT Registry, the HKEY_LOCAL_MACHINE\SYSTEM key contains configuration for the local disks and volume configuration. This key is saved to the Emergency Repair Disk when RDISK.EXE is run, but the Disk Administrator may be used to save the SYSTEM information to another floppy disk as well.

NOTE: The Windows NT Registry Editor (REGEDT32.EXE) can save the SYSTEM information to any accessible disk, but the Disk Administrator is limited to saving the key to a floppy disk.

To save the SYSTEM key with the Disk Administrator:

1. On the Partition menu, select Configuration | Save. A message is displayed stating that information on assigned drive letters, mirrors, and stripe sets (with and without parity) will be saved to a floppy disk.

2. Insert any floppy disk with enough unused space to hold the configuration information (at least 512K).

3. Click the OK button.

INSIDE THE REGISTRY

All operating systems need some method for keeping track of hardware and software parameters and initialization files. Some operating systems maintain this information in a series of initialization files. For instance Windows 3.1 machines use the SYSTEM.INI, WIN.INI, and other files to keep track of the information. In Windows NT this information is stored in the Registry.

Define

The *NT Registry* (also known as the Registry database or the Registration database) is a hierarchical database of NT configuration settings. It keeps information about your hardware setup, application settings, desktop settings, and user information among other things. Its function is very similar to the INI files in previous versions of Windows. One of the nice things about the NT Registry is that it can be completely examined and modified with a single tool, the Registry Editor (Regedt32).

The Registry is structured in a way similar to a file system. If you open up the Redgedt32 utility you will see an interface very similar to the File Manager of NT 3.*x*. The main Registry screen is shown in Figure 2-3. The first thing you will notice is the series of five windows (There will be six windows if the performance key HKEY_DYN_DATA is included). In File Manager these five windows would be indicative of the root directories of five separate drives. In Registry terminology, the five windows are actually referred to as *root keys* (i.e., HKEY_LOCAL_MACHINE is a root key).

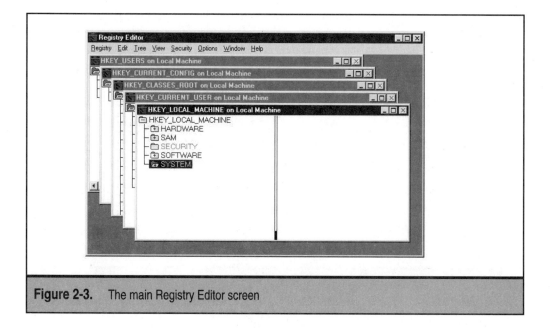

Figure 2-3.   The main Registry Editor screen

If you look at any of the Root Key windows, you will notice a series of "folders" listed. These folders are known as *subkeys*. Actually the terms "key" and "subkey" are often used interchangeably. In Figure 2-3 above, you see five subkeys: HARDWARE, SAM, SECURITY, SOFTWARE, and SYSTEM. If you click on the SYSTEM subkey, an expanded list of subkeys under the SYSTEM subkey will appear. To see some actual values, click on CurrentControlSet | Services | Messenger. When you drill down to the Messenger subkey you'll notice a list that appears in the right-hand pane of the HKEY_LOCAL_MACHINE window. This is the list of values (any key may contain subkeys or values). As shown in Figure 2-4 the values for the Messenger Key include ErrorControl, ImagePath, ObjectName, and so on. The values store the actual Registry data.

This Registry data may come in a variety of types. In fact, there are actually 11 different types which all start with the characters REG_. Generally speaking, you do not need to know what the actual types stand for. If you are asked to make a Registry Value setting, the data type will almost always be included. The most common data types in the NT Registry are

▼ **REG_DWORD**   Numbers (including on/off values) up to four bytes long. It can be Binary, Hexadecimal, or Decimal.

■ **REG_BINARY**   Numbers larger than 32 bits, or raw data such as encrypted passwords; most hardware data is stored this way.

▲ **REG_SZ**   Text strings that can represent names, filenames, paths, types, and variables.

So what are the root keys? The following is a list of the root keys and their purpose:

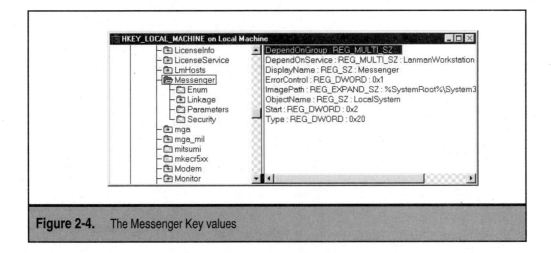

Figure 2-4.   The Messenger Key values

▼   **HKEY_CURRENT_USER**   Contains user profile data associated with the currently logged on user.

■   **HKEY_USERS**   Contains profile information for the default account and the user. The long S-1-5-21... number is actually the user's accounts security ID (SID).

■   **HKEY_CLASSES_ROOT**   Contains file associations and Object Linking and Embedding (OLE) registration information. This tells the machine what file extensions are associated with which programs.

■   **HKEY_CURRENT_CONFIG**   Contains configuration information for the current hardware the machine was booted into.

■   **HKEY_DYN_DATA**   Contains Performance data.

▲   **HKEY_LOCAL_MACHINE**   Contains system-related information about the hardware, programs, and systems running on the machine. This is the most commonly changed root key. Most configuration changes will be performed on this key.

As mentioned above, most of the configuration changes you make on your NT machine will be to the HKEY_LOCAL_MACHINE root key. This key contains an amazing amount of information in its five subkeys: HARDWARE, SAM, SECURITY, SOFTWARE, and SYSTEM. These subkeys are also known as *hives*.

NT Registry hives are actually a series of database files that can be found in the %SYSTEMROOT%\SYSTEM32\CONFIG directory. The only exception is the NTUSER.DAT hive. It exists in the profile directory under the logged on user's profile name. Each hive consists of two files, a data file and a log file. (Note that the term "hive" is often used interchangeably with the "hive data file.") The data file is the actual hive information and the log file is used as a transactive log for fault tolerance (more on this later). Table 2-1 is a list of the hive files and the Registry keys they represent.

Key\Subkey	Data File\Log File\Backup File
HKEY_LOCAL_MACHINE\SAM	SAM\SAM.LOG
HKEY_LOCAL_MACHINE\SOFTWARE	SOFTWARE\SOFTWARE.LOG
HKEY_LOCAL_MACHINE\SECURITY	SECURITY\SECURITY.LOG
HKEY_LOCAL_MACHINE\SYSTEM	SYSTEM\SYSTEM.LOG\SYSTEM.ALT
HKEY_USERS\DEFAULT	DEFAULT\DEFAULT.LOG
HKEY_CURRENT_USER	NTUSER.DAT\NTUSER.DAT.LOG

Table 2-1.   The Hive Files

Modifying the Registry

The NT Registry can be modified in many different ways. The most common way to hand edit the values is with the NT Registry Editor. The easiest way to open the Registry editor is from the Start | Run menu item (Run REGEDT32.EXE). Once the editor is open, you will see five or six Root Key windows. Most customizing changes are made to the HKEY_LOCAL_MACHINE root key.

As a simple example, suppose you want to set a logon message for NT to show when CTRL-ALT-DEL is pressed at logon. The steps are to edit the HKEY_LOCAL_MACHINE\ SOFTWARE\MICROSOFT\WINDOWS NT\CURRENTVERSION\WINLOGON subkey and add two values for the messages. Here are the steps spelled out:

1. From the Registry Editor main screen select the HKEY_LOCAL_MACHINE window.

2. Select the SOFTWARE subkey on the right-hand side of the Editor window.

3. Continue to drill down to the Winlogon subkey through the following path: MICROSOFT\WINDOWS NT\CURRENTVERSION\WINLOGON.

4. With the Winlogon key selected in the left-hand side(see Figure 2-5), select Edit | Add Value.

5. For the Value Name enter LegalNoticeCaption.

6. Leave the Data type at the default REG_SZ and select OK.

7. The String Editor will now appear. Enter your message: Unauthorized Access is Prohibited!

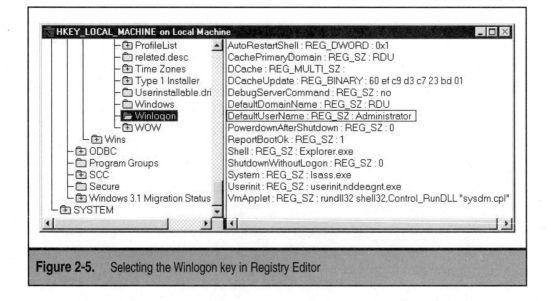

Figure 2-5.   Selecting the Winlogon key in Registry Editor

8. Click OK.

9. Again, select Edit | Add Value.

10. For the Value Name enter LegalNoticeText.

11. Leave the Data type at the default REG_SZ and select OK.

12. The String Editor will again appear. Enter your message: This is My Computer.

13. Click OK.

Figure 2-6 shows the result of this process. Notice the order of the entries: Value - Data Type - Data. Now if you log out and press CTRL-ALT-DEL, the new message will appear.

The Registry Editor also has search capabilities. To use it, select the key or root key that you wish to search. Click View | Find Key and enter the search parameters. The problem is that you can only search for strings within the key names—not values and strings. Luckily, there is another version of a Registry Editor within NT that can handle this job. It is called REGEDIT.EXE. Regedit allows you to easily search the entire Registry for a specific word or words. To use this feature start Regedit. Click on My Computer in the right-hand pane then select Edit | Find. This wonderful feature allows you to search for text in keys, values, and actual data. Both versions of the Registry Editor also support the editing of remote NT systems. If the user has sufficient rights and remote Registry editing has not been disabled, the user can view the remote Registry by selecting Registry | Select Computer in the Regedt32 product.

Another way to modify the NT Registry is through the REGINI.EXE utility in the NT Resource Kit. This is a command line utility that can be used in batch files to modify the Registry. You essentially have to create a Registry script to run the utility against. Regini

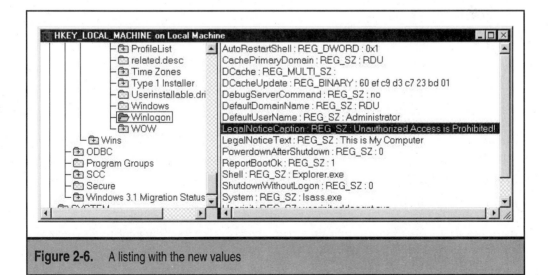

Figure 2-6.   A listing with the new values

does have one important advantage over the GUI Registry Editor products. It supports all 11 possible instances of the values data type.

> *CAUTION:* Adding custom Registry entries should not be performed unless you thoroughly understand the ramifications of each change. Wherever possible, use the NT Administrative tools and Control Panel to make configuration changes in the Registry. These tools are specifically designed to properly add and amend Registry values. If you make an error while changing values with the Registry Editor, you will not be warned. If the error is serious enough the NT install can be damaged.

Registry Fault Tolerance

The NT Registry has fault tolerance built into it. If an NT system loses power while the Registry is being modified, the log files are maintained that allow NT to recover the Registry. In Table 2-1, each Registry hive is shown to have an associated log file. When you run a configuration program that causes a Registry change to occur, the change is first written to the log file. This log is similar to a database transaction log. It is a journal of the changes that are made (or to be made) to the hive's data file.

When the journal entries for a particular change are complete the log file on the disk is updated. It is interesting to note that this write occurs immediately. It is not allowed to wait in the normal cache area that NT would use for a standard write. This is accomplished by forcing the file buffers to "flush" all information waiting in the cache. This ensures that the log file has truly been updated and saved to disk *before* any change is actually made to the data file. If the power were to fail at any time during this process the Registry would still be intact. The information in the log file can be used to undo any partial changes.

The SYSTEM hive is a little different. It is extremely important in NT because it contains some of the most important NT configuration information. Probably the most important areas in the SYSTEM hive are the ControlSet keys. These keys contain information on every device driver and service that is running on the machine. For this reason the SYSTEM hive is completely backed up to the SYSTEM.ALT file. In addition, NT also keeps a log file for this hive.

The last item to notice is that the only subtree of HKEY_LOCAL_MACHINE that does not have an associated hive file is HARDWARE. This is because the HARDWARE subkey is recreated by the NTDETECT.COM process at boot up. This allows the file to be regenerated whenever a user boots up to compensate for a new hardware configuration.

The Last Known Good Configuration

If you inadvertently install an improper driver or make a damaging change to the NT Registry, the Last Known Good start up menu option can save you considerable time. The Last Known Good configuration is literally a copy of all of the Registry entries that were present the last time NT successfully started up.

Using the Last Known Good Configuration

To use the Last Known Good configuration, simply press the SPACEBAR during the boot up sequence when prompted with "Press SPACEBAR now to invoke the Hardware Profile/Last Known Good Menu." This will give you a menu showing your startup options.

Registry Values Related to the Last Known Good Configuration

So where is this information stored? The answer is in the Registry in the HKEY_LOCAL_MACHINE\SYSTEM hive. A control set contains the system configuration information, such as which drivers and services to load and start. There are several control sets.

The HKEY_LOCAL_MACHINE\SYSTEM\SELECT key identifies how the different control sets will be used, and determines which control set to use at startup. The sets are entered as REG_SZ strings where 0×1 equals CurrentControlSet 1. The following is the list of possible values for the Select key:

▼ **Current**   Denotes the actual CurrentControlSet. When you use a GUI Administrative tool or Control Panel to change the configuration, you are actually changing information in the CurrentControlSet.

■ **Default**   Denotes which control set will be used the next time NT is started (unless you select Last Known Good configuration). Note that the default and current values usually contain the same value.

■ **Failed**   Denotes the control set that was used the last time the Last Known Good configuration was used.

▲ **LastKnownGood**   This is the value of the control set that NT considered to be the last configuration that actually worked. A successful start would include booting without problems and having any user actually logon to the console. If this occurs, the Clone control set is copied over the LastKnownGood control set.

The last thing to mention is the Clone control set. The Clone is a copy of Current-ControlSet. It is created each time the system is restarted by the kernel initialization process. As mentioned previously, if the computer starts successfully, the Clone control set is copied over the old LastKnownGood entry.

Backing up the Registry

There are several different ways to back up the NT Registry. The absolute best way is to use a tape backup program. If the backup is run every night you will always have a Registry to fall back on.

There also some manual ways to back up the Registry. You can use the Registry Editors (mentioned previously) through the Save menu. As is discussed in the next section, you can create an Emergency Repair Disk (RDISK /S). In Chapter 10, the method of using the REGBACK Resource Kit utility is shown.

The last way is to boot to DOS (on a FAT partition) or boot to a parallel instance of NT and back up the %SYSTEMROOT%\SYSTEM32\CONFIG and %SYSTEMROOT%\ PROFILES directories. The point is that you need to back up the Registry in some way. It is a key component of any NT disaster recovery plan.

THE WINDOWS NT EMERGENCY REPAIR DISK

The Windows NT Emergency Repair Disk (ERD) can be one of the most important tools in a disaster recovery kit. It is intended to provide enough recovery information to restore a system to a state in which it can start back up. You can use the Emergency Repair Disk to replace damaged system files, rebuild the startup environment, and restore damaged or incorrect Registry information. Unfortunately, the NT Repair Disk can also render an NT server inoperable. It is important to understand the proper use of the ERD. Too many times people turn to the ERD as a cure-all only to find out that it has placed the system in an unrecoverable state. In addition, do not fall into the trap of thinking that a Repair Disk is a substitute for a good backup plan. All critical servers should be backed up to tape at least daily.

Maintaining a current ERD is just as important as having a current system backup. You should always update your ERD before you plan to make a major change to your system (for example, installing new software, changing software, changing network configurations, adding hardware). After the change is complete, test the system to be sure it is fully operational. At that point create a second ERD to cover the new configuration. Of course the "before" disk you create is to protect you from problems with your hardware or software changes.

Several companies have created products that help you update and maintain current Repair Disks. For instance, with ERDisk from Midwestern Commerce, Inc. (**http://www.ntsecurity.com**) administrators can create Emergency Repair Disks for one or a group of servers over a network connection.

Be sure to always save your ERDs in a secure and fireproof area, either offsite or in a fireproof vault. Remember that the disks can sometime contain a full copy of your security database (if the database is small enough to fit on the disk). If a hacker was to gain access to the disks and you use poor password policies, he could theoretically break the passwords with a dictionary attack. (This is discussed in more detail in Chapter 7)

So what is on the basic Emergency Repair Disk? Enough Registry and setup file information to bring the system back to a bootable state. A Repair Disk is essentially an NT-formatted floppy that contains a copy of the files found in the %SYSTEM ROOT%\REPAIR folder. These files are a combination of compressed Registry keys and configuration files. By default, the repair directory only contains the above information from the original installation of NT. To bring it up to date you must periodically run the RDISK command and use the update function. This is examined in more detail later. Table 2-2 lists the files found on the ERD and their basic purpose.

Most of the filenames are fairly obvious (Registry keys). Notice that, by default, the Repair Disk Utility does not save the Windows NT Registry SAM and SECURITY hives.

Filename	Function
AUTOEXEC.NT	The system AUTOEXEC.NT file—used for MS-DOS environment
CONFIG.NT	The system CONFIG.NT file—used for MS-DOS environment
DEFAULT._	HKEY_USERS\DEFAULT Registry key
NTUSER.DA_	%SYSTEMROOT%\PROFILES\DEFAULT USER\NTUSER.DAT (default user profile)
SAM._	HKEY_LOCAL_MACHINE\SAM
SECURITY._	HKEY_LOCAL_MACHINE\SECURITY
SETUP.LOG	NT Setup log file—contains the file cyclic redundancy check (CRC) information for use during the repair process
SOFTWARE._	HKEY_LOCAL_MACHINE\SOFTWARE
SYSTEM._	HKEY_LOCAL_MACHINE\SYSTEM

Table 2-2.   The Files on an Emergency Repair Disk

The files that do appear in the directory are put there during the original installation. The ramification of this is that if you run the repair process at a later date, the SAM and SECURITY hives will be rolled back to their original setup level configurations. The SAM and SECURITY keys can be backed up by using tape backup, the REGBACK Resource Kit Utility, or the RDISK /S switch. This switch is explained in detail later in this chapter.

Another interesting feature of the files in the repair directory is that they are actually Registry hives that have been compressed using the normal file compression routines. This means that any one of them may be uncompressed using the regular Microsoft expand command. For instance typing:

```
Expand SYSTEM._ SYSTEM
```

will yield the actual system hive of the Registry.

The SETUP.LOG file is also particularly interesting. It is a log of the NT system and application files that are installed on the system. The Emergency Repair process searches this file for the system files to replace. After you choose to replace the files during the repair process, the repair driver (actually SETUPDD.SYS) compares the files on the system to the files on the original NT CD-ROM through the CRC information contained in the SETUP.LOG file. If the files are different you are then prompted to replace the files. Figure 2-7 shows the beginning line of a typical SETUP.LOG file. The TargetDirectory is the location of the NT install that this disk was made for, while the TargetDevice is the

```
            [Paths]
            TargetDirectory = "\WINNT"
            TargetDevice = "\DEVICE\HARDDISK0\PARTITION1"
            SystemPartitionDirectory = "\"
            SystemPartition = "\DEVICE\HARDDISK0\PARTITION1"
            [Signature]
            Version = "WinNt4.0"
            [FILES.SYSTEMPARTITION]
            ntldr = "ntldr","2a36b"
            NTDETECT.COM = "NTDETECT.COM","b69e"
            [FILES.WINNT]
            \WINNT40\HELP\31USERS.HLP = "31USERS.HLP","12bfc"
            \WINNT40\HELP\ACC_DIS.CNT = "ACC_DIS.CNT","cc99"
            \WINNT40\HELP\ACC_DIS.HLP = "ACC_DIS.HLP","b82c"
            \WINNT40\INF\ACCESSOR.INF = "ACCESSOR.INF","13070"
```

Figure 2-7.   The SETUP.LOG File

disk and partition that the actual NT install resides on. The SystemPartition lines indicate the system partition that the machine actually boots to.

Notice the FILES.SYSTEMPARTITION section. It indicates the name of the NT loader file (NTLDR) and the name of the NT detection file (NTDETECT.COM). The four or five-digit hexadecimal numbers at the end of the lines indicate the CRC value for these files when originally installed. The [FILES.WINNT] section then continues on for hundreds of lines and shows the NT file names, correct paths and their own CRC values. As mentioned, the Emergency Repair process will use these values and directories to verify each file in the install.

Creating an Emergency Repair Disk

As mentioned above, you should create a new Repair Disk every time you make a major change to your system. The NT installation program will prompt you to create the first one during setup. After that you need to create the files using the RDISK utility from a command prompt. If the system is down and you need to create a Repair Disk, one can be created manually through a parallel NT installation (or through DOS if the drive is FAT).

RDISK

The first method for ERD creation is to use the RDISK utility. NT includes this utility as a quick and easy way to update your repair information. The first thing to understand about RDISK is that it has two distinct functions: 1) to update the %SYSTEMROOT%\

REPAIR directory, and 2) to copy the repair information to a newly formatted floppy. The following steps outline the process:

1. Open a command prompt and type **RDISK**. This will bring up the Repair Disk Utility screen as shown in Figure 2-8.

2. Notice the two buttons on the bottom left: Update Repair Info and Create Repair Disk. The Update Repair Info option will actually take a new "snapshot" of the system, update the files in the %SYSTEMROOT%\REPAIR directory and create a new ERD. The Create Repair Disk button will *only* create the disk from the existing repair information. It will not take a new snapshot of the system. In almost all cases you will want to use the Update button. Select Update Repair Info to start the process.

NOTE: This process will not update the SAM and SECURITY hives in the repair directory (for SAM and SECURITY backups see the "RDISK /S" section below).

---

3. The utility will then issue the following warning: "The repair information that was saved when you installed the system or when you last ran this utility will be deleted. Do you want to continue?" It is telling you that it is going to delete the files that exist in the repair directory and re-create them with the new configuration information. Select Yes to continue.

4. The system will begin to save the new information to the repair directory. You will then be prompted to create the Emergency Repair Disk as shown in Figure 2-9. Select Yes to begin the ERD creation process.

5. When prompted, insert a floppy in the drive. Be sure the write protect tab is off. The floppy does not need to be formatted because the utility automatically formats the disk as part of its routine. Select OK to continue. The utility will now format the disk and then copy the new information from the repair directory to the floppy.

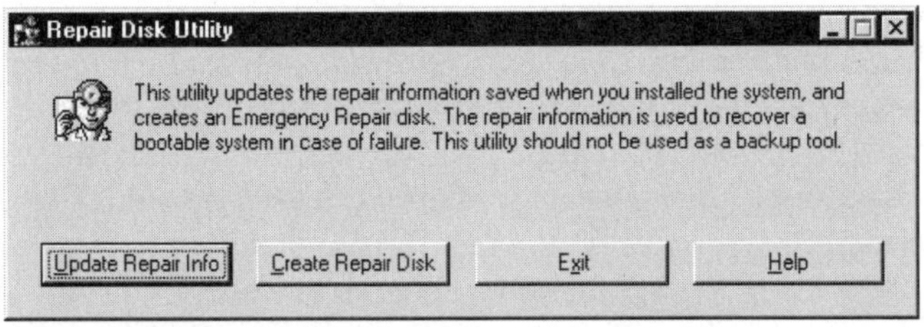

Figure 2-8. The Repair Disk Utility screen

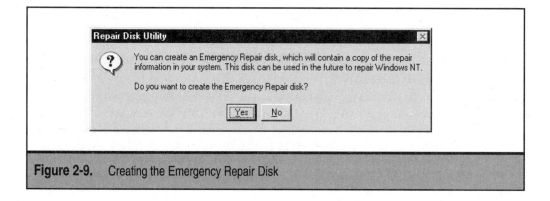

Figure 2-9. Creating the Emergency Repair Disk

RDISK /S By default the RDISK utility will not update the SECURITY and SAM hives of an NT machine. This is because these hives can grow to several megabytes on certain NT machines (usually domain controllers). To copy these hives to the repair directory, RDISK has two switches associated with it: /S and /S-. It should be noted that these hives could also be backed up using tape backup or using the REGBACK Resource Kit utility. REGBACK is explained in detail in Chapter 10.

The RDISK /S option tells the program to skip the initial Repair Disk Utility screen and go directly into saving the configuration. It will then prompt you to create the actual Emergency Repair Disk. The RDISK /S- option tells the program to simply update all of the repair directory information, including the SAM and SECURITY hives, then quit. This switch does not create a Repair Disk.

As mentioned, both of these options overwrite the compressed versions of the SAM and SECURITY Registry hives that were created during the original NT installation on the machine. These original files only contain the default administrator account and password that was used during the NT installation. If you choose either of these switches, RDISK copies the current SAM and SECURITY Registry hive files along with the other files into the \%SYSTEMROOT%\REPAIR directory. The SAM and SECURITY files can become very large and may prohibit the creation of the Emergency Repair Disk. This is due to the fact that the Emergency Repair Disk is simply a copy of the files found in the repair directory.

For this reason, it is not recommended that either of the switches be used on a domain controller or other NT server with a large number of users and/or groups defined. If you are not sure how big the files will be, you can estimate using the techniques shown in the section called "The Problem with Domain Controllers," later in this chapter. A rule of thumb is that a domain of 1,000 users can fit on the disk if the SETUP.LOG is reasonably small. You can also figure it out by brute force. Create a backup to the repair directory and copy the SAM._ and SECURITY._ files to it. Then run RDISK with the /S or /S- switch. After running RDISK with one of these options, check the \%SYSTEMROOT%\REPAIR directory to see if it will still fit on a single floppy. If it turns out the files will not fit on a single floppy, simply copy the SAM and SECURITY keys from your repair backup back to the repair directory. For more information see the section called "What If My Repair Information Does Not Fit on a Single Floppy?" below.

Manually Creating the Disk

You can also manually create an Emergency Repair Disk. This step is usually only necessary when you have a problem during the repair process. If you do not have a Repair Disk, you can normally set the repair process to go to the disk and find the install. It looks at the BOOT.INI file of the machine for an NT install directory. It then runs the repair based on the information in the repair directory of that installation. The problem is that this does not always work, so you are left with the task of creating an Emergency Repair Disk and restarting the repair.

The process is reasonably simple. You take a floppy that has been formatted on any NT system and copy the information from repair directories to the floppy manually. Be sure to include any hidden files. The main problem here is that the fact that you are forced to use this procedure almost by definition indicates that you cannot boot into NT.

So how do you get the files? If the file system is FAT, boot to a DOS floppy and copy the files from the \%SYSTEMROOT%\REPAIR directory to the root of an NT formatted floppy disk. Again be sure to grab any hidden files (usually SETUP.LOG is hidden).

If the file system is NTFS, you will have to boot to a parallel installation of NT to get to the files. This should not be a problem if you have listened to the advice in this book and preinstalled a basic parallel image of NT on the machine. If you have not, you have a couple of options. You can go ahead and install NT into a parallel directory or you can remove the drive to another machine temporarily. You can then copy the files over and reinstall the drive.

▼ **NOTE:**   You can also restore the %SYSTEMROOT%\REPAIR directory from a tape backup and then copy the restored files to the formatted floppy.

What Will an ERD Fix and When To Use It

This section discusses what an Emergency Repair Disk can be used for and when you should use it. As mentioned above, you can use the Emergency Repair Disk to replace damaged system files, rebuild the startup environment, and restore damaged or incorrect Registry information. The ERD is intended as a way to recover the system to an operational state. The Repair Disk should not be your only line of defense. You should also always have a tape backup of critical servers. Chapter 10 discusses a complete list of items that should be in your recovery tool kit. The ERD is just one of the items.

If you have a recent copy of the Emergency Repair Disk and the hard drives are not corrupted and are working properly, you can run the repair process at almost any time without adverse consequences.

> **CAUTION:** Do not run the repair process against the SAM or SECURITY Registry hives unless the Repair Disk was made with the /S switch. This is very important on domain controllers. You can lose your accounts database if this advice is not followed. Unfortunately, domain controllers often have SAMs that are far beyond the capacity of a floppy. Therefore the RDISK /S switch should never be run on them. (You should use other methods to back up the SAM and SECURITY hives on these machines as indicated below.)

If the Repair Disk is old and not indicative of the latest system configurations, you should take care in running the process. In particular, you will not want to run the Inspect Registry Files options. An old Repair Disk will remove any Registry changes that have been made since the Repair Disk's last update. You can use an old ERD or a Repair Disk from a similar system to recover a missing BOOT.INI or similar file, replace other missing NT files, or inspect the boot sector.

During the repair process you are prompted for your choices of what to repair. Each of these choices is described in the sections below.

Inspect Registry Files Option

The Inspect Registry Files option allows the replacement of Registry hives from the Emergency Repair Disk. As always, care must be taken when restoring the SAM and SECURITY files. If you have not run the RDISK with the /S switch, these files will be from the original NT install! This means any existing security or account information on the machine will be rolled back to the original Administrator account and password.

If you have selected the Inspect Registry Files option the repair process will present you with an additional set of menus:

    [ ] SYSTEM (System Key)
    [ ] SOFTWARE (Software Key)
    [ ] DEFAULT (Default User Profiles)
    [ ] NTUSER.DAT (New User Profiles)
    [ ] SECURITY (Security Key)
    [ ] SAM (SAM Database)

Select the Registry files that you suspect to be causing the problem. Do not run repair on any Registry files unless the ERD is up-to-date or unless you have a secondary way to recover the Registry (i.e., tape backup). If you think you have a good tape backup, be sure to verify it before running the repair process. Verify the tape by cataloging it, restoring the directory to a separate location, and confirming that you have up-to-date files in the %SYSTEMROOT%\SYSTEM32\CONFIG directory.

Inspect Startup Environment Option

This option verifies and/or replaces NT startup files on the system partition. It also checks the BOOT.INI and creates a new one if necessary. If files that are needed to start Windows NT are missing or damaged, the repair process replaces them from the NT installation CD-ROM. This choice is generally OK to use if you have an old Repair Disk or a disk from a similar machine.

Verify Windows NT System Files Option

This option tests the NT installation by running a CRC test on all NT files. It checks the CRC information of each file against the values found in the SETUP.LOG on the Emergency Repair Disk. This process also verifies that the system files such as NTLDR and NTOSKRNL.EXE are valid. If a file on the disk does not match the file that is listed in the SETUP.LOG, the option to replace it will appear on the screen. This choice is generally OK if you have an old Repair Disk or a disk from a similar machine. You can always verify the files it will check by examining the SETUP.LOG file.

Inspect Boot Sector Option

This option checks the partition boot sector on the system partition and ensures that it points to the NTLDR file. It replaces the boot sector if necessary. This choice is generally OK if you have an old Repair Disk or a disk from a similar machine (the boot sector can also be replaced by using a DOS boot disk as explained in Chapter 10).

The Repair Process

It is important to understand the actual NT Emergency Repair process. In this section an inoperable machine will be recovered using a recent copy of an NT Emergency Repair Disk. The example will detail the recovery of an NT server that has suffered from corruption or deletion of its Registry files (%SYSTEMROOT%\SYSTEM32\CONFIG). To create the test scenario the entire \WINNT\CONFIG directory was deleted from a parallel installation. If major Registry corruption or deletion such as this has occurred, the machine will give an error upon system startup after the BOOT.INI menu is displayed. A typical error might be

Windows NT could not start because the following file is missing or corrupt: \\WINNT\SYSTEM32\CONFIG\FILENAME. You can attempt to repair this file by starting NT Setup using the original Setup Floppies or CD-ROM.

> **NOTE:** This particular error actually denotes a Registry failure. This can be determined because the file that NT believes is missing is from the NT Registry directory (\\WINNT\SYSTEM32\CONFIG\). If it were a drive failure, you either would get no BOOT.INI menu at all or the missing file would be NTOSKRNL.EXE.

The NT Emergency Repair Disk is not bootable. The basic repair process is started by running the NT installation program. This can be accessed from an NT Server CD-ROM, a directory on the disk, a network share, or from the three NT setup floppies. For this example the machine will not boot so the options are limited. You can boot to a parallel installation of NT or, if one does not exist, use the setup floppies. Let's assume that the floppies must be used and in fact they cannot be located. The following steps take you through the process of creating the disks and preparing disk 2 (a special case for NT 4.0):

1. From any working NT machine, insert the NT CD-ROM and run

   ```
   <CD-drive letter:>\i386\winnt32 /ox
   ```

   (WINNT /OX on a Windows 95 or other DOS-based machine).

2. This will prompt you to create the three NT boot floppies. Insert the disks when prompted and hit ENTER.

3. The next step is to get an updated copy of the SETUPDD.SYS driver (this step is only necessary in NT 4.0 when you require the ERD process to replace system files). The read-only SETUPDD.SYS file on the second NT setup disk must be upgraded to a version from at least NT 4.0 Service Pack 2. It can be found on an NT 4.0 Service Pack CD-ROM in the i386 directory. The file can also be obtained from within the NT Service Pack self-extracting executable (NT4SPX_I.EXE) available from Microsoft. To extract the file run:

   ```
   nt4spX_i.exe /x
   ```

   The updated SETUPDD.SYS driver is required because the original file does not always replace the NT files during a reboot. When the Emergency Repair is run, the process (actually SETUPDD.SYS) searches the SETUP.LOG file for the files to be replaced. If you select the option to replace the files (on the actions screen of the repair process) SETUPDD.SYS compares each file on the system via CRC to the files on the original CD-ROM. If the files are different you are then prompted to replace the files. With the old version of SETUPDD.SYS, if you opt to replace individual files, the files are read from the NT CD-ROM. SETUPDD.SYS compares the version resource date of the files on the install CD to the version resource date of the files on the system. If the version resource date of the file on the computer is newer (i.e., from a Service Pack), then the file is not replaced. The Emergency Repair process does *not* indicate that the file is not going to be replaced. This actually became more of a problem for most administrators than a fix. It is almost always recommended to replace the SETUPDD.SYS file.

So now you have the installation disks. If you also have a recent Emergency Repair Disk you can now recover the system using the following steps:

1. Insert the NT Setup Disk. If you do not have the setup disks see the steps for creating them above.

2. When prompted insert NT Install disk 2.

3. At the Welcome to Setup Screen, press R (as instructed) to begin the repair process.

4. You are then prompted to select the optional repair tasks. These include:

- [X] Inspect Registry Files (allows the replacement of Registry hives from ERD).

- [X] Inspect Startup Environment (verifies and/or replaces NT startup files on system partition, creates/checks BOOT.INI file).

- [X] Verify Windows NT System Files (runs a CRC test on all NT files from SETUP.LOG on ERD).

- [X] Inspect Boot Sector (checks boot sector on system partition. Replaces if necessary).

- Continue.

CAUTION: Be careful when selecting SAM (Accounts Databases) and SECURITY(These are under the Inspect Registry Files option). You should only check these boxes if you feel the problem resides there. If you have not run the RDISK /S switch these files will be from the original NT install! This means the repair process will attempt to roll the SECURITY and SAM information back to the original install values with the original administrator account and password.

By default, all tasks are selected. To deselect an item, highlight it and press ENTER. When you are finished selecting or deselecting options, highlight the Continue item and press ENTER.

5. Next, the Mass Storage Detection screen appears. Press ENTER to continue.

6. When prompted insert disk 3.

7. Setup should detect your controller. If it does not, press S when prompted to select from the default list or add a driver from a third-party disk. Press ENTER to continue.

8. The next screen will ask whether or not you have a valid NT Repair Disk for the installation you are attempting to repair. If you have it, press ENTER to continue. If not, press ESC and setup will attempt to locate your NT installation automatically and use the repair information in the %SYSTEMROOT%\REPAIR directory. In this case, an ERD exists so press ENTER.

9. Insert the Emergency Repair Disk when prompted.

10. The next screen will show you the Registry files NT recommends that you recover. You can deselect any Registry file by removing the X beside its entry. Again, be certain that you understand the ramifications of this step. When finished, highlight the Continue item and press ENTER.

11. NT will now begin to compare the system files in the installation with those from the last install via a CRC comparison process. If any files are found to be different, it replaces them from the NT CD-ROM. You can accept every file change by pressing A or press ESC to skip the file replacement. To replace the files one at a time, press ENTER. You will be prompted to insert an NT Setup

CD-ROM. (If the machine does not have a CD drive attached, see the "Running Repair Without a CD-ROM Drive" section below.) If you have installed any Service Packs on the system, it is very normal to be prompted to replace several files during the repair process. Be sure to rerun the Service Pack after the repair process has completed.

12. This should finish the repair process. When prompted remove the floppies or any CDs from the drives and press ENTER to restart the system. The system should now be back to its original state.

It is important to note the impact of Service Packs on the repair process. As mentioned above, any Service Packs should be reinstalled after completing the repair. There have been instances where repairing certain files (namely TCPIP.SYS) to their original versions has caused NT to Blue Screen upon startup. If this occurs, note the name of the driver that is causing the problem from the Blue Screen of Death. Then boot into a parallel installation of NT and hand-copy the versions from the Service Pack files into the %SYSTEMROOT%\SYSTEM32\ directory.

Problems with Repairs

With any process, there are always times when things don't work out quite as planned. The repair process is much the same. The following section is a list of common problems that occur with the Emergency Repair Process. They include issues such as running repair without an ERD, running it without an attached CD-ROM, and what to do when a repair fails.

Small Business Server

If you have had a problem on a Microsoft Small Business Server 4.0 (SBS) machine you may have noticed that there is no obvious way to run the repair process. This is because the initial SBS install is meant to be as simple as possible. It actually skips over several of the normal install screens and runs in an unattended mode.

To run the repair process on these systems you must make changes to the second SBS 4.0 disk. Open up the disk in My Computer. Select the WINNT.SIF file and rename it (e.g., WINNT.OLD). Then save the changes. Now insert the SBS Setup Disk 1 into the drive and reboot the machine. The install will now stop at the Welcome screen and allow you to begin the repair process by pressing R.

You can also create a new set of three install floppies from the SBS CD-ROM. Insert the CD into the drive. Change to the i386 directory on the CD and type **WINNT32 /OX**.

Running Repair Without a CD-ROM Drive

Windows NT Server allows itself to be installed in many different ways other than from the Install CD-ROM. It can be installed from a zip drive, a network share, or even from a removable hard drive. It is simply a matter of gaining access to the setup files. NT Server setup cannot be completely run from floppy drives (the server product cannot even be purchased in floppy format).

The problem with a machine that lacks a CD-ROM is that the Emergency Repair process requires that the install files be available on a system CD-ROM drive. If the repair process detects that a system file is missing or corrupted, it will prompt you as to whether the file should be repaired. If you select Yes and your system contains no CD drive, the repair process will prompt you for a Windows NT Setup floppy disk that contains the file that needs repair. Of course that floppy does not exist either.

So what do you do if you have no CD-ROM drive on your server? You could temporarily add a CD player to the system and run the repair. You could also figure out which files need to be replaced and copy them to a floppy, or you could trick the repair process into thinking the system has a CD-ROM drive, as follows.

RUNNING THE INSTALL FROM A DRIVE   In order to trick the system into believing it has a CD drive, the system must have at least one operational drive with at least 100MB of free space. This can be a hard drive, a zip drive, or some other temporary device. You will basically move the files from the CD to the drive and modify the repair parameters to tell it to use that drive. The following outlines the steps:

1. Create a directory on an operational hard disk called "install" (i.e., C:\INSTALL).

2. Copy the CDROM_S.40 file from the root of the NT install CD-ROM to the root of the install directory. The file can be obtained from a network share or from any other location that contains the NT installation files. Note that on a machine with no CD-ROM a good practice is to always create this directory proactively.

3. Create a subtree under the install directory called i386.

4. Copy the i386 directories and all subtrees from the NT install CD-ROM into the i386 directory that you created in step 3.

5. If you do not have the setup boot floppies, insert the NT CD-ROM and run

   ```
   <CD-drive:>\i386\winnt32 /ox
   ```

   (WINNT /OX on a Windows 95 or other DOS-based machine).

6. This will prompt you to create the three NT boot floppies. Insert the disks when prompted and hit ENTER.

7. The next step is to get an updated copy of the SETUPDD.SYS driver as mentioned earlier. The SETUPDD.SYS file should be from NT 4.0 Service Pack 2 or above. If the system is an NT 5.0 machine, skip this step.

8. Insert the first NT installation disk (setup) and remove the read-only attribute on the TXTSETUP.SIF file.

9. Using WordPad or your favorite text editor, open the TXTSETUP.SIF file.

10. Search for the [SetupData] area. It will be similar to Figure 2-10.

11. Remove the semicolon from the beginning of the SetupSourceDevice Line.

12. Change the SetupSourceDevice Line to point to the partition that contains the install directory created in step 1.

13. Change the SetupSourcePath Line to point to the install directory created in step 1 (\INSTALL).

14. The File should now look similar to Figure 2-11. Save the file.

You can now run the normal repair process using the disks created in these instructions. When you indicate to the repair process that you wish to replace the files, it will automatically look to the install directory on the partition designated.

```
[SetupData]
;
; SetupSourceDevice is optional and specifies the nt device path
; of the device to be used as the setup source. This overrides
; the CD-ROM or winnt local source.
;
;SetupSourceDevice = \device\harddisk0\partition1
;
; SetupSourcePath specifies the path relative to the source device
; where the setup source tree is to be found.
; All media descriptors are relative to this.
;
SetupSourcePath = \
MajorVersion = 4
MinorVersion = 0
DefaultPath=\WINNT
OsLoadOptions = "/nodebug"
ProductType = 1
LoadIdentifier = %srv_id%
BaseVideoLoadId = %srv_id_vga%
```

Figure 2-10. A normal TXTSETUP.SIF file

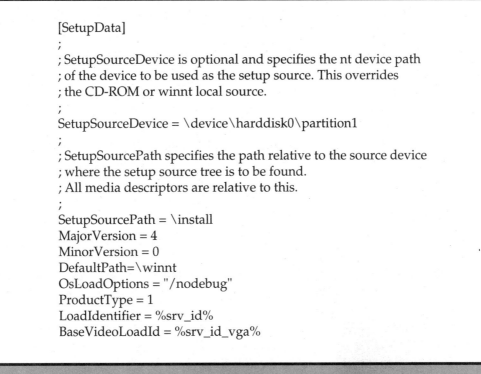

```
[SetupData]
;
; SetupSourceDevice is optional and specifies the nt device path
; of the device to be used as the setup source. This overrides
; the CD-ROM or winnt local source.
;
SetupSourceDevice = \device\harddisk0\partition1
;
; SetupSourcePath specifies the path relative to the source device
; where the setup source tree is to be found.
; All media descriptors are relative to this.
;
SetupSourcePath = \install
MajorVersion = 4
MinorVersion = 0
DefaultPath=\winnt
OsLoadOptions = "/nodebug"
ProductType = 1
LoadIdentifier = %srv_id%
BaseVideoLoadId = %srv_id_vga%
```

Figure 2-11.   The modified TXTSETUP.SIF file

RUNNING REPAIR FROM NEWLY CREATED TAGGED FLOPPIES   In this situation you will need to run the repair process twice. The first time is just to find out the names of the files that need to be replaced. Then you put the files on tagged floppies that you will create and rerun the repair process.

Here are the actual steps:

1. Start the repair process and run it as you normally would (see earlier repair process instructions).

2. Do not replace any files. When you are asked to replace a file, write down the filename and press ESC to skip it.

3. After you have a list of all the files that need to be replaced you will have to modify the SETUP.LOG file on the Emergency Repair Disk.

NOTE: As always, be sure the SETUPDD.SYS file on the second NT install disk is from at least Service Pack 2 if the system is NT 4.0 (see above).

4. Make a copy of the ERD using normal disk copy methods. You will use the copy for the procedure and save the original for a backup.

5. Insert the copy of the ERD into the drive. Remove the hidden and read-only attributes on the SETUP.LOG file.

6. Using a text editor, modify the entries for each file that needs to be repaired by adding a *"path," "medianame," "tagfilename"* entry at the end of each line. *Path* is the path of the files (typically \), *medianame* is floppy, and the *tagfilename* is a disk designation filename. The *tagfilename* is arbitrary; it simply identifies the disk (e.g., DISK1.TXT). It is the name of any file placed in the root directory of the floppy. For instance, suppose you need to modify the entries found in Figure 2-12. You simply add the information to the end of the line: "\,""floppy," "DISK1.TXT." This is shown in Figure 2-13.

7. Save the file and remove the Emergency Repair Disk.

8. Now insert a blank formatted floppy in a machine that has a CD-ROM or a copy of the NT Install Files.

9. Create a file called DISK1.TXT and place it in the root of the floppy.

10. Copy the necessary files from the CD-ROM to the floppy (in this case, NETH.DLL and NETLOGON.DLL).

11. If the floppy fills up, you need to create a second floppy and designate the SETUP.LOG tagfile information accordingly (in this case, create a file named DISK2.TXT in the root of the second floppy).

12. Copy the necessary files to the second floppy (in this case, NETMSG.DLL).

13. Now run the repair process as you normally would.

14. During the repair process insert the disks as required to reinstall the files.

```
\WINNT40\SYSTEM32\NETH.DLL = "NETH.DLL","253f0"
\WINNT40\SYSTEM32\NETLOGON.DLL = "NETLOGON.DLL","2590e"
\WINNT40\SYSTEM32\NETMSG.DLL = "NETMSG.DLL","1cac6"
```

Figure 2-12.   The original SETUP.LOG file

```
\WINNT40\SYSTEM32\NETH.DLL = "NETH.DLL","253f0","\","floppy","DISK1.TXT"
\WINNT40\SYSTEM32\NETLOGON.DLL = "NETLOGON. DLL", 2590e","\","floppy","DISK1.TXT"
\WINNT40\SYSTEM32\NETMSG.DLL = "NETMSG.DLL", "1cac6","\","floppy","DISK2.TXT"
```

Figure 2-13.   The modified SETUP.LOG file

Why Does the Repair Process Fail?

There are several instances when the Emergency Repair process may fail. The most common cause is a problem with the hard drive. This problem could be caused by actual physical damage, or even from the machine running CHKDSK on startup. If the drive has a severe problem a CHKDSK may actually rename the directories (e.g., to FOUND.000 or a similar name). If CHKDSK renames the NT directory the repair process will fail, as it does not know where to place the recovered Registry files.

   If this occurs and you think the drive is OK, boot into a parallel installation of NT and rename the %SYSTEMROOT% directory back to its original name. If the file system is FAT you can boot to DOS and do the same thing.

   If this does not work, you can also reinstall NT and specify that the %SYSTEMROOT% directory should be the same as the original install. Then you can run the repair process to recover the previously saved Registry settings.

   If the repair process fails repeatedly, the problem is probably hardware related. Be sure the system drive is operational.

What If You Do Not Have a Repair Disk?

If you do not have a Repair Disk, you can still recover the system. When you are prompted for the Repair Disk during the installation, you simply specify that you do not have one. The repair process will then look at the BOOT.INI file for an installation path. Setup will try to find the repair directory under the %SYSTEMROOT%\ path specified in the BOOT.INI. It will then use the Registry and configuration information from that repair directory to recover the system.

   If the BOOT.INI file happens to be missing and you have no Repair Disk, you must re-create the file before proceeding. The file can be created by hand or copied from a similar machine. If you follow the advice in this book and always create an NT boot floppy (see Chapter 10), you can also copy the file from that disk. Simply boot to a parallel installation of NT (or to DOS if the partition is FAT) and replace the BOOT.INI file. Then rerun the repair process. To create the file by hand, see the BOOT.INI section of Chapter 10 of this book.

The last option you have if no Repair Disk exists is to make one on a similar machine. This procedure is questionable, as even an identical machine will have Registry differences. However, it will allow the machine to at least start up, so that it can be recovered by some other means (i.e., restored from tape).

What If My Repair Information Does Not Fit on a Single Floppy?

If you look at the total size of the file in the %SYSTEMROOT%\REPAIR directory and this total exceeds the capacity of the floppy, the Emergency Repair Disk Creation utility will fail.

If you have never run RDISK /S the most likely problem is that the SETUP.LOG file is too big. You can edit this file and delete file listings that are not necessary for NT. Simply change the hidden and read-only attributes of the file and delete any entries in the [FILES.WINNT] section that do not begin with %SYSTEMROOT%\ (%SYSTEMROOT%\ is the same as WINNT\ if the default install directory was used). If that does not clear up enough space you can also delete any file listings that do not begin with %SYSTEMROOT%\SYSTEM32\.

> **NOTE:** Take care to not delete anything in the [Files.InRepairDirectory] section, which is located below the [FILES.WINNT] section.

If RDISK /S has been run on the machine, the most likely cause is that the SAM and SECURITY Registry hives are too large to fit on one disk. Remember that on some machines (especially domain controllers) the SAM itself can be several megabytes in size. You can estimate the compressed SAM size using the techniques in the next section.

If it turns out that the SAM or SECURITY hives are too big, you can replace them with a smaller version from an older ERD. You can also get older copies off of an older tape backup. The files from the original NT install, in particular, are very small. After the files are replaced, simply rerun RDISK without the /S switch.

The Problem with Domain Controllers

It has already been mentioned that ERDs for the domain controller of many large domains should not be created using the RDISK /S switch. The SAM hives are much too big for a single floppy.

This can create some problems. The SAM file in the repair directory will consider an NT server to have the status it had at its original installation. That is to say, if you have a machine that was installed as a Primary Domain Controller (PDC), the ERD information will reflect that status.

If the machine has demoted to a Backup Domain Controller (BDC) since the original installation, the information will never be updated on the Repair Disk. When you run the repair process on that machine and update the SAM, the machine will be turned back into a PDC. This will cause a contention on the domain. Therefore, you should remove the machine from the network before running the repair process. After the repair process is complete, restore the Registry from the tape backup to again make the machine a BDC. You can also use the Server Manager Administrative tool to demote the wayward PDC back to a BDC. After the machine becomes a BDC, you can reconnect it to the network and it should resynchronize with the actual primary domain controller.

You can approximate the size of the SAM. In a SAM, a User account uses 1KB, an NT Machine account uses .5KB, and a custom Group account takes 4KB. Built-in groups take up a total of approximately 50K. If you assume a 4:1 compression ratio you can use the following formula:

Required ERD Free Space = (Users(1)+NT Machines(.5)+Custom Groups(4)+built-in Groups)/(Compression Ratio)

For a 1,000-person domain with 50 groups, 500 NT Machines and 600 Windows 95 or 98 Machines (95/98 Machines do not get accounts), the result would be:

Required ERD Free Space = (1000(1)+500(.5)+50(4)+50)/4 = 1500/4=375K

That is to say that repair disks can handle a SAM for 1,000 users in this scenario if it has at least 375KB of free space. If you estimate 200KB for the compressed SECURITY hive, you need a total of 575KB. A typical Repair Disk has between 500 and 700KB of free space before the updated SAM and SECURITY hives are added, so you might just make it. The only other factor is the size of the SETUP.LOG file. Keep in mind these values can be very different in your specific NT installations.

NT RECOVERY OPTIONS

NT has several recovery options that can be set ahead of time to help diagnose and recover from a system failure. These options are set using the Control Panel System applet. To set the options, open up the Control Panel System applet and select the Startup/Shutdown tab as shown in Figure 2-14. There are several options listed under the recovery section:

▼ **Write an event to the system log** This option enters an alert to the machine's system log.

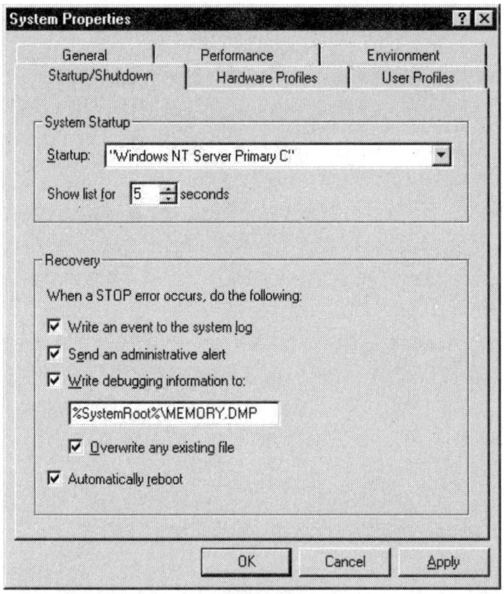

Figure 2-14.   The System Properties Startup/Shutdown tab

■ **Send an administrative alert**   This option issues an administrative alert to the
users specified in the Alerts portion of the Server Manager Administrative Tool.
To set up the alert entries, open the Server Manager and double-click on the
server in question. In the Alerts entry box, enter the user names you would like
to be notified in case of a problem and click Add. This is shown in Figure 2-15.

■ **Write debugging information to**   This option enables the memory dump file.
Check the Write debugging information to box and specify the name of a file
in which to save the dump information. The default is %SYSTEMROOT%\
MEMORY.DMP. Dump file analysis is covered in Chapter 10.

NOTE: Be sure to rename the memory dump file sometime after the machine reboots if you want to
preserve log files. Otherwise, any additional dump files will overwrite the previous one.

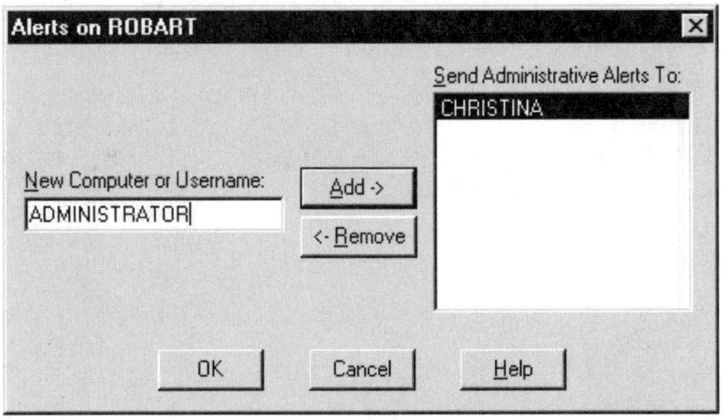

Figure 2-15.   The Alerts section of the Server Manager

▼ **Automatically reboot**   This option causes the system to reboot immediately
   after a crash without the need for manual intervention. This option can be
   important if the crash occurs at a time when the server is not being monitored.

In almost all cases you should enable all of the recovery options. If your system is
directly connected to the Internet it is recommended to not enable the dump file. There is
an arguable security risk if external people are accidentally allowed access to the contents
of the dump file.

WINDOWS NT DIAGNOSTICS

Windows NT also includes a Diagnostics tool (actually the NT version of WinMSD) for
examining the configuration contents of the Registry. Unfortunately, this is a view-only
tool. To make changes, you have to use the specific control panel applets or edit the
Registry directly. Even so, it can be very useful. WinMSD organizes the configuration

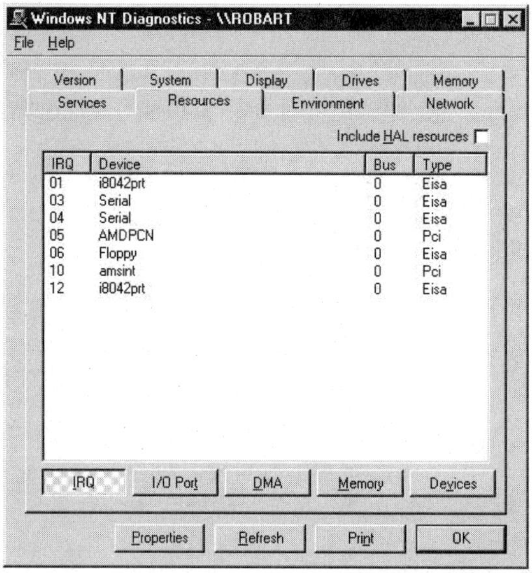

Figure 2-16.   The NT Diagnostics screen

information in an easy-to-understand notebook format. Another important feature of this tool is that it allows you to remotely view other NT machines. In addition, it allows you to quickly save or print the configuration parameters for a specific machine. Figure 2-16 shows the NT Diagnostics screen.

Diagnostics Tabs

The Diagnostics tool is broken down into a number of logical tabs. These include:

▼   **Version**   This tab shows the type of NT machine along with the build number. It also indicates the serial number and the installer registration information.

■   **System**   This tab shows the installed HAL, the system BIOS, and the processors. It's a quick and easy place to find out the processor speed on an NT system. This tab is shown in Figure 2-17.

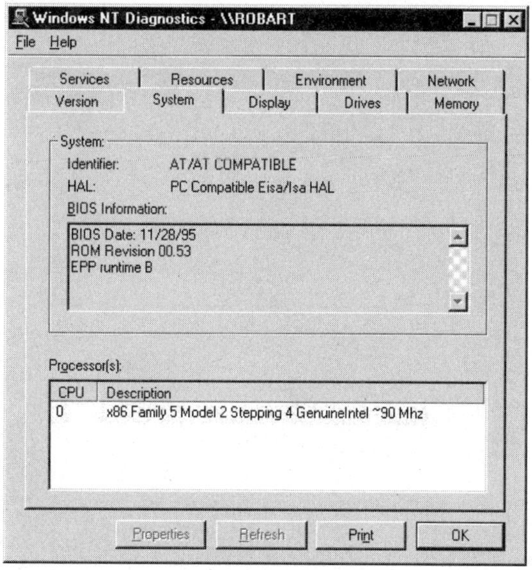

Figure 2-17.   The System tab

- **Display**   This tab gives you a great deal of information about the installed video card and driver. This information includes video BIOS levels, video memory, and chip types.

- **Drives**   The Drives tab has information about all drives in the system. This includes floppies, CD-ROMs, hard drives, and network mapped drives. The information includes free space, total space, and cluster details. The File System subtab includes file system type and other information. This screen is shown in Figure 2-18.

- **Memory**   The Memory tab includes information on both the physical and virtual memory on the NT machine. The Commit Charge section is of particular interest. The Total Value is the amount of virtual memory plus the amount of physical memory that the machine is currently using. The limit is the maximum amount available before requiring the machine to dynamically

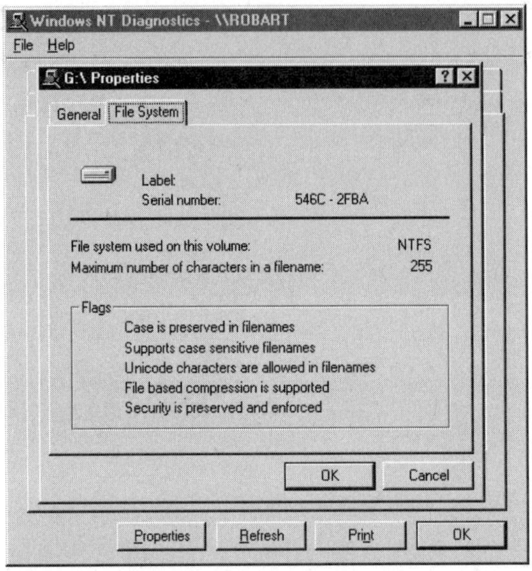

Figure 2-18.   The File System option of the Drives tab

increase the paging file. The peak is the highest attained value. If the peak begins to approach the limit, consider increasing the minimum page file settings. This minimum page file value is modified in the Control Panel System applet under the Performance tab.

■ **Services**   The Services tab includes buttons that show information on both services and devices on the system. Double-clicking on any service or device will bring up another screen that has tabs for both general information and device or service dependencies. Figure 2-19 shows the Dependencies tab for the Microsoft DNS service.

■ **Resources**   If you want to add a new piece of hardware to your system and need to know the available interrupts (IRQs) and I/O ports, then the Resources tab is the place to go. This tab has buttons that group the information by IRQs,

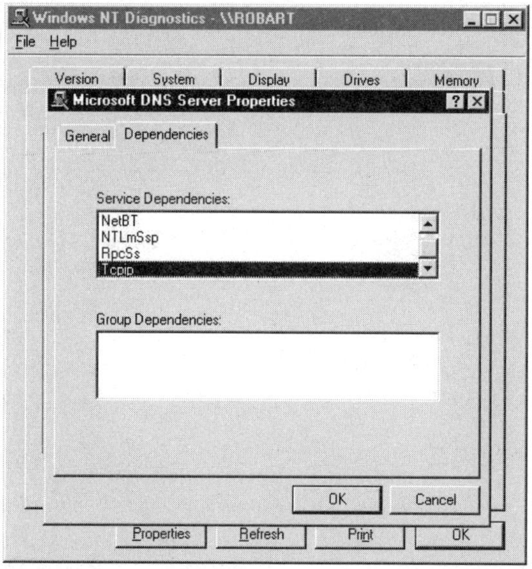

Figure 2-19.   The DNS Service's Dependencies tab

I/O Ports, DMA, Memory, and actual devices. Remember, this screen is for information only. You cannot change any of the values here. Figure 2-20 shows the IRQ information for the server \\ROBART.

- **Environment**   This tab shows the environment variables and their values for the system. To change any of the variables you must go to the Control Panel System applet (Environment tab).

- **Network**   This tabs shows network-related information in four categories: General, Transports, Settings, and Statistics. The General button gives a summary of logged-on users and domain information. Transports gives you bound NIC information similar to running the NET CONFIG SERVER command. The Settings option shows you the configurable parameter for an NT server. Statistics quantifies dozens of counter and network-related statistics including Bytes Received, Bytes Transmitted, and Network Errors.

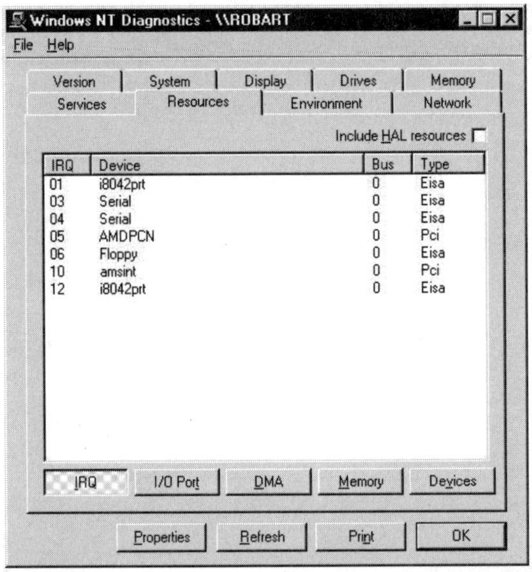

Figure 2-20.   The IRQ information

There are a few other features of the Windows NT Diagnostic tool that are worth mentioning. To start with, the utility allows the printing of reports of the WinMSD information. You can print a single tab or all of the tabs. Figure 2-21 shows the Create Report screen of the utility. It allows you to print to a printer, file, or the Windows Clipboard in either a summary or complete view. This screen is accessed through the File | Print Report menu item.

Another option in the File menu is the Run submenu. The Run item allows you to quickly start many of the utilities you will most likely need to use to change or view the configuration values. The following is the list of programs you can run with this menu:

▼ Event Viewer
■ Registry Editor (REGEDT32.EXE)
■ Disk Administrator
■ Task Manager

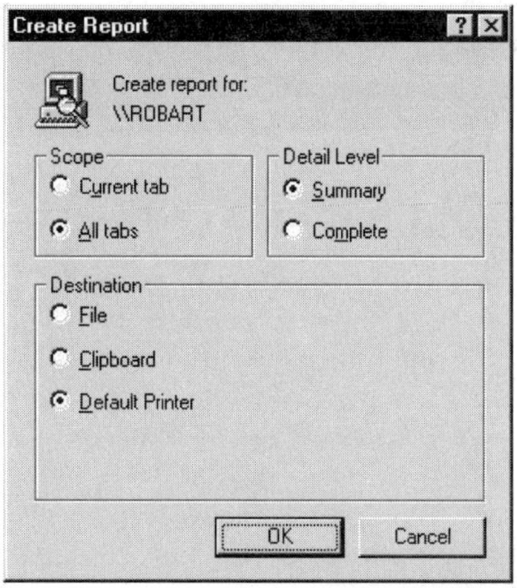

Figure 2-21. The Print options in NT Diagnostics

- Performance Monitor
- Control Panel
- Notepad
- View AUTOEXEC.NT
- View CONFIG.NT
- Start Explorer
- ▲ System Configuration Editor (SYSEDIT.EXE)

Diagnosing Remote Machines

As mentioned, the NT Diagnostic Tool is great for checking out other NT machines. To access another machine, select File | Select Computer and enter the name of the computer you would like to examine. It allows the same capabilities as if WinMSD was being run from the console. Of course, you have to have administrative access on the machine in question.

NOTE: NT has many built-in utilities to monitor remote machines. These include Event Viewer (for viewing logs), User Manager for Domains (for changing and viewing user rights), Registry Editor (for viewing and changing remote registries), and many of the other NT Administrative tools.

NT DOMAIN CONTROLLERS

Windows NT uses the concept of domain controllers to enforce the security model it employs. One nice feature about these controllers is that they have some built-in fault tolerance. The main thing to remember is that every domain, no matter its size, should have at least one Primary Domain Controller and one Backup Domain Controller. Domain controllers are thoroughly discussed in Chapter 7.

DIRECTORY REPLICATION

Windows NT has a built-in replication service that can automatically replicate a single directory tree to other servers and workstations. It has important fault tolerance implications as it allows logon scripts and other information to be passed to Backup Domain Controllers in a domain. In fact, that is one of its most important functions. However, the Directory Replicator Service can also be used to transfer any relatively static information across an enterprise. The information can include file changes, additions, and deletions within the single directory tree. One interesting use of replication is to move files out to a Web server farm. Generally speaking, Web pages hardly ever change. This makes it a perfect candidate for replication.

NOTE: If you are simply trying to move relatively static directories around your network, it may be easier to use an intelligent copy program and some scheduled scripts to replicate the information. One such product is the Robocopy utility contained in the NT Resource Kit. It is intelligent in that it can be configured to only copy files (and even delete files) in the directory trees that have changed. Be sure to only use Robocopy to replicate directories that are coming from and going to NTFS partitions.

Setup

To set up replication, you must first configure a replication service account using user managers for domains. Here are the steps:

1. Open up User Manager for Domains and select User I New User.

2. Give the account a name indicative of its function (e.g., replic). About the only name you cannot give the account is "replicator" as there is already a default group of that name.

3. Assign the replic account to the Backup Operators group.

4. Select Password never expires and be sure that the account has 24-hour logon privileges.

5. Select Add and close User Manager for Domains.

Setting Up the Directory Replicator Service

The next step is to configure the Replicator Service.

1. Open the Control Panel Services applet.

2. Scroll through the list of services to the Directory Replicator Service.

3. Select Startup and set the Startup Type to automatic.

4. In the Logon As: section click This Account and enter the name and password of the replication account created above.

5. Click OK to close the Startup boxes.

6. You can now start the Directory Replicator Service manually by clicking the Start button.

7. Close the Control Panel Services applet.

The above steps must be completed on every machine that will either import or export directories. Be sure to use the same domain-wide service account on all machines involved in this replication set (a set includes importers and exporters). For example, if the replicator account is called "replic" and the domain is RDU, enter the account name as RDU\REPLIC. You can replicate across domains as well. Simply be sure that the same account is used.

Import vs. Export

It is important to understand that the NT Directory Replicator Service has two functions. One is to import and the other to export. For ease of use, only configure one export server. This will be the machine whose directory will be passed out to other machines. The other machines are importers.

NOTE: If you want the export machine to also get the replicated information you must set it up to be an import machine as well. This does not conflict as the import directory is always named differently than the export directory. Figure 2-22 shows the typical configuration. The import servers may be local or even at remote (WAN-connected) sites. By default, the replication directories are set up to be %SYSTEMROOT%\SYSTEM32\REPL\EXPORT (for exporting) and %SYSTEMROOT%\SYSTEM32\REPL\IMPORT (for importing).

It is also important to remember that only directories are exported at the top export directory level. That is to say, you must create a *directory* under the export folder in order to have replication occur. After that point in the tree, all files and directories are completely replicated.

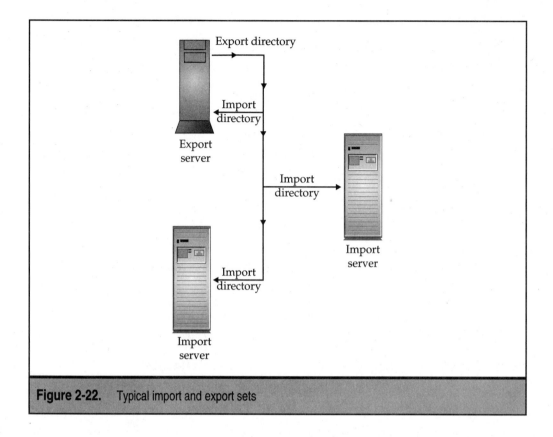

Figure 2-22.   Typical import and export sets

CONFIGURING EXPORT   Now you need to set up replication in the Server Manager Administrative tool. The first step is to configure your export directories and servers.

1. Open the Server Manager and double-click on the server that will be the export machine.

2. Click the Replication button.

3. Now select the Export Directories radio button. Figure 2-23 shows the results. Notice the default export directory is filled in for the path. (You do not have to use the default directory.)

4. Click on the Add button under the To List: window. This is the list of machines or domains the export server will attempt to send the replication information to. If you have import servers that are across a WAN link, you must enter in each individual server name specifically. If you are connected in a LAN environment to *all* of the import servers, you can simply enter the domain to replicate to. The latter option will automatically identify and replicate to all import hosts in the domain. In the case of this example, the domain name will be used, as all import hosts are local.

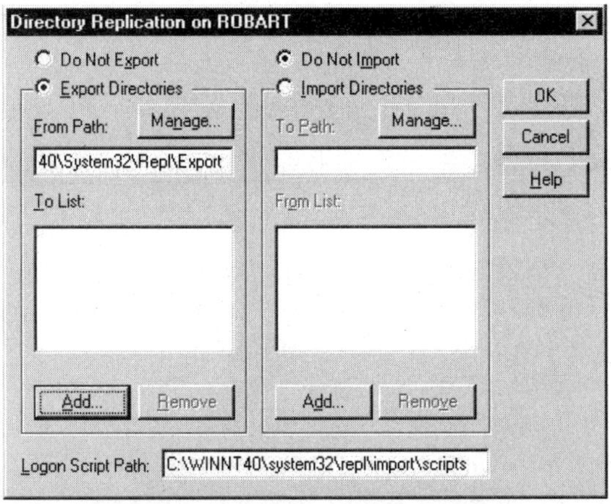

Figure 2-23.   The Replication screen

5. Click OK to add the export information.

Repeat these steps on all exporting machines. For ease of administration it is usually best to limit the number of export machines. Ideally, you should have only one exporter.

NOTE: Only NT Server machines can be exporters. However, NT workstations are valid import computers.

CONFIGURING IMPORT   Now that the export side is configured you must configure the import servers. The steps are quite similar to the export configuration.

1. Open the Server Manager and double-click on the server that will be the import machine. If you wish to have the exported information sent to the import directory of the exporting machine, you must configure import on that machine as well.

2. Click the Replication button.

3. Now select the Import Directories radio button. Again, notice the default directory is filled in for the path.

4. Click on the Add button under the To List: window. This is the list of machines or domains that the importing server will allow replication information from. Again, if the export server is across a WAN link you must enter in each individual server name specifically. If you are connected in a LAN

environment to the export server, you can simply enter the domain to replicate from. In the case of this example, the domain name will be used, as all export hosts are local.

5. Click OK to add the import information.

If the Directory Replicator Service is not started it will do so automatically at this point. Repeat these steps on all servers in the replication set.

TESTING REPLICATION   The easiest method to test replication is to open up NT explorer and add a few files to the EXPORT\SCRIPTS directory that was specified above. If everything is working properly, the files should be created in the IMPORT\SCRIPTS directory within five minutes. Another easy way to determine if replication is occurring is to check out the Replication tab in the Server Manager. On the Import Directories side click on Manage. If replication is occurring it will show the last date and time of replication as in Figure 2-24. If it is not configured properly it will show "No Master." If things do not seem to be working, check out the following:

▼ Are there any Replicator events in the NT Application Logs on the import or export machines? Common errors are coded 5 and 2116. These indicate a missing Registry entry. Check the following key:

   HKEY_LOCAL_MACHINE\SYSTEM\CURRENTCONTROLSET\CONTROL\ SECUREPIPESERVERS\WINREG\ALLOWEDPATHS

   When you double-click this AllowedPaths key, the value should be a listing of several Registry paths. Be sure there is an entry for SYSTEM\ CURRENTCONTROLSET\ SERVICES\REPLICATOR

▼ Does the Directory Replicator account have backup operator equivalence?

■ Is the Directory Replicator account started on both import and export servers?

■ Is a file open in the import or export directories?

   Are the clocks of the import and export machines synchronized? Be sure to periodically synchronize all server clocks. For replication to occur, the system clocks must be within ten minutes of each other. The easiest way to do this is to periodically issue the following command in a batch file or scheduled job:

   NET TIME \\SERVERNAME /SET /Y

▲ Double-check the Server Manager Replication settings.

NOTE: Replication occurs only after a file is closed. If it is open it will not be replicated.

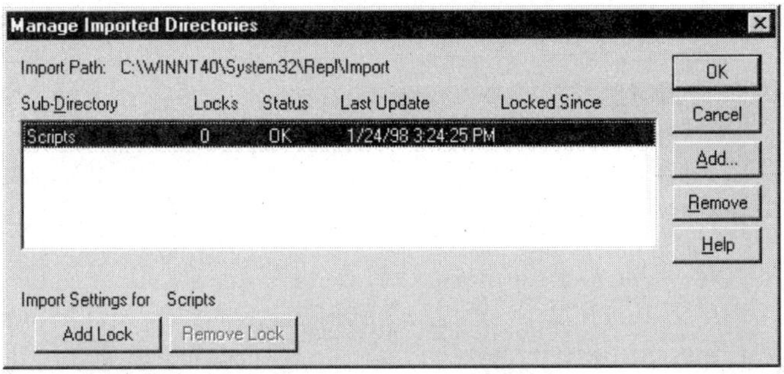

Figure 2-24.   The Manage Imported Directories screen

CONTROLLING REPLICATION

So how does replication actually occur and how can you affect this process? Every five minutes, the export computer actually sends a NetBIOS broadcast out towards its import machines that includes a list of its first-level export directories. The import machine then makes a connection to the exporter's REPL$ share (this is the default Replicator share name). After this, the importer creates a named pipe session to check the exporter's Registry parameters for the replication process. This determines the actions that will be taken and is indicative of the Manage Replication settings in Server Manager | Replication. If an update of files is required, the connection to the REPL$ share is then used to copy the necessary files from the export machine.

You can control many facets of the replication process. To start with, you can modify replication through the Server Manager | Replication | Manage selection shown in Figure 2-25. The Add button to the right of the screen is used to add other subdirectories for replication. The default scripts directory should already be listed. To add an additional directory select Add and enter the directory name exactly as it appears. It must exist *under* the export directory. In Figure 2-25 three test directories have been added. The other settings in the Manage Exported Directories dialog box apply to only one directory at a time. The options are listed below:

▼   **Add Lock**   Use this option to manually prevent an export server from replicating a directory during heavy network usage times. Simply select the directory in question and click on Add Lock. The exporter will not replicate the directory until the lock is removed.

■   **Remove Lock**   Use this option to reenable replication for the directory in question.

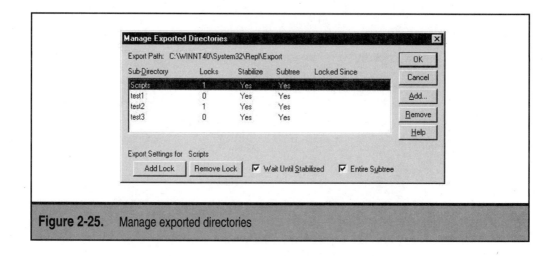

Figure 2-25. Manage exported directories

- ■ **Wait Until Stabilized** If this box is checked, a file must be stable for at least two minutes before replication can occur. This helps prevent partial replication.

- ▲ **Entire Subtree** If this box is checked, all files and directories under the directory in question will be replicated. If not, only the top-level directory that is listed in the box will be replicated.

There are also several Registry parameters that affect replication. They are found in the HKEY_LOCAL_MACHINE\SYSTEM\CURRENTCONTROLSET\SERVICES\ REPLICATOR\PARAMETERS key. They following is a list of the options:

- ▼ **Interval** This value determines how often the exporter checks for changes to its particular directory structure and then sends pulses to its importers. The default value for Interval is five minutes. This can be increased to reduce the frequency of replication. If the data is particularly static, consider changing the number to 120 minutes. This option is ignored on importers.

- ■ **Pulse** This value is the counter that controls how often an exporter contacts the importer. Even if no changes have occurred the exporter will resend old changes after the repeat time (Repeat Time=Pulse × Interval and is expressed in minutes). This allows importers that may have missed the initial announcements to be brought up to date. The default value of Pulse is three minutes. If you use the default values of Pulse and Interval, the exporter will repeat every 15 minutes.

- ■ **Guardtime** This value affects the amount of time that must pass before a change is considered stable. The default is two minutes and is usually sufficient. During debugging you can set this value to zero.

■ **Random**   This value is used to prevent the exporter from being overloaded with requests from the import machines. An importer uses the exporter Random value to generate a random number of seconds from zero seconds to the value of Random (i.e., Random is the maximum wait time). The importer then waits the generated number of seconds before requesting the replication data from the exporter. The default value of Random is 60 seconds.

■ **Replicate**   This value indicates the replicator's type. It is normally set by enabling or disabling a replication type in the Server Manager tool. The possible types are

1. Exporter

2. Importer

3. Both—the machine imports and exports

■ **Export List**   The value is the list of machines or domains to replicate to. Use the Server Manager to set this value. This value is ignored if Replicate is set to 2.

■ **Export Path**   The value is the path that will be replicated out. Use the Server Manager to set this value. This value is ignored if Replicate is set to 2.

■ **Import List**   The value is the list of machines or domains to allow replication from. Use the Server Manager to set this value. This value is ignored if Replicate is set to 1.

▲ **Import Path**   The value is the path that will be replicated to. Use the Server Manager to set this value. This value is ignored if Replicate is set to 1.

PERFORMANCE MONITOR

Performance Monitor is the Windows NT GUI-based Administrative tool that is used to measure individual components and/or the overall performance of NT systems. Bundled with the operating system, Performance Monitor can be configured to gather data on local and remote systems, and alert you when processes go beyond specified boundaries. It allows the system performance data to be analyzed in real time or historically through graphs, reports, and logs. By taking periodic measurements of your NT systems with Performance Monitor, you can even use it to predict impending failures.

What does Performance Monitor have to do with fault tolerance and the prevention of data loss? It can be used to predict failures and determine poorly performing systems. By quantifying measurements of a system under normal load, abnormally high or low values can be discovered preemptively. If you can find changes in a system's behavior through monitoring, you may be able to predict an impending failure. For example, if the queue length on your disk drive has suddenly quadrupled, you will know that something has changed; perhaps the network demand has increased or the disk is simply going bad.

Counters and Objects

Every Windows NT system has characteristics that can be monitored by the Performance Monitor. Since Windows NT is object oriented in design, a process will call on a resource by name, instead of by a physical address or a port. Each object is a representation of a given resource, such as the processor, the cache, the disks, and so on. Each object in Windows NT that consumes system resources has several counters that measure specific characteristics of that object's usage. As such, there are literally thousands of possible counters on an NT server. Counters typically provide information relating to utilization, throughput, or specific queue lengths. For example, all counters pertaining to the computer's processor are organized into the Processor object. Moreover, if a system has more than one processor, the Processor object will have multiple instances. Each instance will represent an individual processor. Figure 2-26 shows the default main screen for Performance Monitor Chart View.

The number of available objects and their respective counters is not limited by what NT provides (the so-called standard objects and counters). Applications, such as those in the Microsoft BackOffice suite, have built-in objects and counters that can be measured with Performance Monitor. In addition, third-party vendors also have the ability to create objects and counters within their products through a Microsoft-provided programming interface (API).

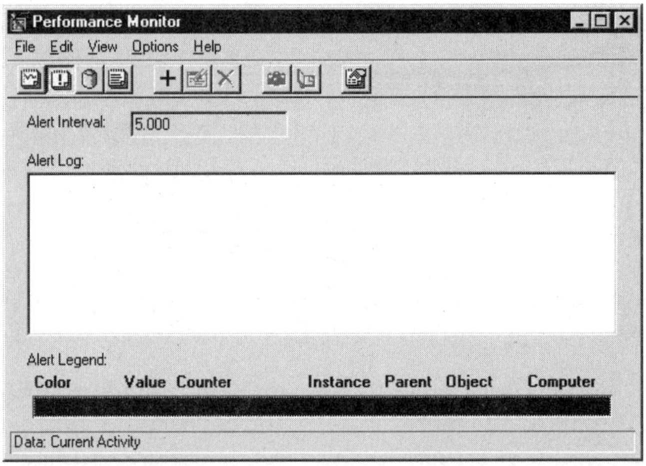

Figure 2-26.   Performance Monitor main screen

Real-time Monitoring

Counter statistics can be monitored either in real time or logged for future scrutiny. To see the Chart View of counters in real time:

1. From the View menu, select Chart View.

2. From the Edit menu, select Add to Chart.

3. To monitor a remote machine, either enter the UNC name in the Computer box or click the ellipsis (...) button to browse for the machine.

4. Choose the desired counters for each object by selecting the counter and clicking the Add button. A common counter to observe is %Processor Time, used to track the percentage of processor time in use at the moment.

NOTE: If you do not know whether or not to add a specific counter, you can always click on the Explain button to get more information.

5. When you are through selecting the counters, click the Done button.

The chart should begin populating as in Figure 2-27.

Logging Data Collection

Performance Monitor can collect data and store the information into a log file for later viewing and analyzing. Logging provides a means in which to store historical system activity data as well as a convenient format that can be analyzed with other applications. To configure Performance Monitor to log activity:

1. From the View menu, select Log View.

2. From the Edit menu, select Add to Log.

3. Choose the desired objects from the pick list and click the Add button.

4. Click the Done button when finished.

5. From the Options menu, select Log, and then provide a path and filename with the .LOG extension for the log file in the Log Options dialog box.

6. Configure the update interval (the interval at which Performance Monitor collects data from the counters).

7. Select Start Log to initiate monitoring of the selected objects.

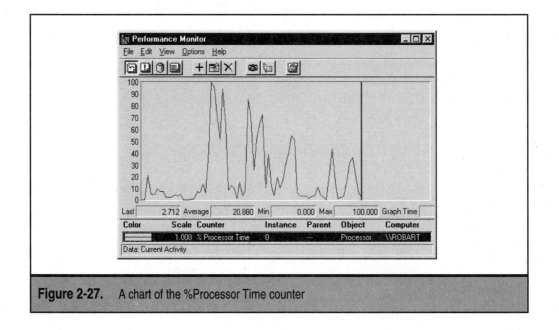

Figure 2-27.   A chart of the %Processor Time counter

When preparing for logging, the interval at which Performance Monitor takes a snapshot of system activity is critical for controlling the growth of log files. Clearly, the shorter the time interval between snapshots, the more rapidly the logs will grow. Make sure you have plenty of disk space to compensate for the potentially rapid growth of the log files. Alternatively, you can limit the number of objects and raise the time interval to conserve on space.

After finishing logging data, you can open and analyze these files with Performance Monitor or other applications such as Microsoft Excel or Access. If you wish to use Excel or Access to analyze the historical data that has been collected, use Performance Monitor's export feature to convert the log file into a file format that the other applications can more easily read. To export a log file for use with another application, do the following:

1. Make sure the data collection has stopped. If it has not stopped, click Stop Log from within the Log Options dialog box.

2. Select Export Log from the File menu.

3. Choose the file location and specify the filename in the Performance Monitor | Export As dialog box.

4. Select a file type: TSV (tab-delimited file) or CSV (comma-delimited file). Most spreadsheet and database applications can accept either format.

5. Choose a path and filename and then click Save.

Configuring Alerts

Alerts can be set to monitor any available counter on an NT system. When a counter exceeds or falls below specified values, Performance Monitor triggers an alert, which then logs the event and can notify an administrator. To configure alerts:

1. On the View menu, click Alert.

2. Add counter(s) by selecting Edit | Add to Alert. For each specified counter, set the desired value to monitor and specify whether this value is the ceiling or floor value (over or under, respectively).

3. To monitor a remote machine, enter the UNC name of the computer in the Computer box or browse for the computer by pressing the ellipsis (…) button.

4. You can also run an application, such as an application that will page you, by providing the location of the executable within the Run Program on Alert box. You can run this program every time the alert occurs or just the first time the value is reached.

5. Click Done when finished selecting counters.

6. Now select Options | Alert to configure the other Alert parameters. This screen is shown in Figure 2-28.

7. Again, note the Interval entry box. Set the interval to a value commensurate with the behavior of the counter being monitored.

8. Click OK when finished. Note that the alert will only function when Performance Monitor is active. It is possible to run Performance Monitor as a service. This is explained in the "Configuring Performance Monitor as a Service" section later in this chapter.

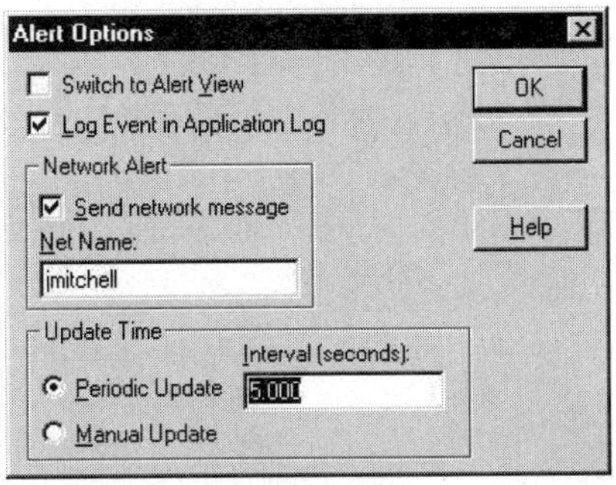

Figure 2-28. The Alert Options dialog box

Reports

Performance Monitor's reporting mechanism is similar to the other views in that you select counters to monitor and it then takes a snapshot of what you have selected. The major difference, however, is that it displays the snapshots in a tabular format. This format can be a particularly useful troubleshooting view when problems arise. You choose individual counters that you want to report on from the objects that were monitored.

To configure reports:

1. From the View menu, select Report.
2. Select Edit | Add to Report.
3. To clear a report or create a new report, choose File | New Report Settings.
4. Be sure to set the report interval on the Options | Report screen.

To export reports:

1. From the File menu, select Export Report.
2. Choose the location and specify the filename in the Performance Monitor | Export As dialog box.
3. Select file type as either TSV (tab-delimited file) or CSV (comma-delimited file) in the Save Type As drop-down list, then click the Save button.

Monitoring a Remote Machine

By default, Performance Monitor measures the performance of the local machine. However, a remote NT machine can also be viewed. The remote machine can be viewed separately or as another machine in the existing scheme.

To monitor a remote NT machine or add one to the existing monitoring scheme:

1. From the Edit menu, select Add To. In the Add To dialog box, type the UNC name (i.e., \\REMOTE_SYSTEM) of the computer in the Computer field and click the Add button. You may also click the ellipsis (...) button beside the Computer field to see a list of available computers to monitor.
2. Select the desired computer and click the Add button.
3. In the Add To dialog box add the objects or counters that you wish to monitor.
4. Click Done when finished.

Critical Resources to Monitor

As mentioned previously, Performance Monitor can monitor many objects native to NT as well as those provided by third-party companies. Selecting too many objects for monitoring can result in information overload, making the useful information difficult or impossible to see. Be particularly frugal in selecting the counters to be monitored. For many, the most critical resources to be monitored are

▼ Memory

■ Processor

■ Disk subsystem

▲ Network subsystem

The role of an NT server determines the additional counters that are necessary to examine. For instance, a server may be used for file and print sharing, applications, domain controller functions, or any combination of the above. While you may want to consider monitoring the effects of replication and/or synchronization between domain controllers, this would not necessarily be an issue on an application server or a file server. It is important to monitor the most common contributors to system bottlenecks such as those listed above, as well as those that pertain to the particular configuration of the server.

Monitoring Memory

The most common cause of serious performance problems in systems is lack of memory. Memory contention arises when the memory requirements of the active processes exceed the available memory resources on the system. When the system is out of physical memory, NT relies more heavily on paging. *Paging* is the process where portions of active processes are swapped out to the disk into a file or files called PAGEFILE.SYS for temporary storage. The more that the system has to rely on paging, the more performance is degraded because hard disk access is much slower than RAM access (actually by several orders of magnitude). To optimize overall performance, steps must be taken to ensure that main memory is used efficiently and the need for paging is minimized.

Windows NT has several important memory-related counters that should be considered. The biggest issue one thinks about in terms of memory is, "How much is enough?" Two counters that indicate whether or not the system is configured with the proper amount of physical RAM are Page Faults/sec and Pages/sec. The counters are shown in Figure 2-29. A page fault occurs when a process requires code or data that is not in its working set. The code can actually be located either in file system cache, in transition to disk, in the working set of another process, or in the paging file. The page fault counter includes both hard faults (those that require disk access) and soft faults

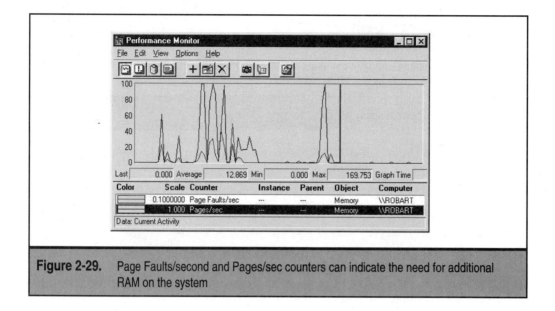

Figure 2-29.   Page Faults/second and Pages/sec counters can indicate the need for additional RAM on the system

(where the faulted page is found elsewhere in physical memory). Most systems can handle large numbers of soft faults without consequence. However, hard faults can cause significant delays because of the relatively slow hard disk access times.

Pages/sec is the number of pages read from or written to disk to resolve hard page faults. As mentioned above, hard page faults occur when a process requires code or data that is not in its working set or elsewhere in physical memory, and must be retrieved from disk. This counter was designed as a primary indicator of excessive paging (thrashing). You can tell whether or not your system is thrashing by checking the Pages/sec counter. If it is consistently above 100, your system is excessively paging and performance is affected. In general, this counter should never consistently exceed 20 pages per second.

The counter Memory | Available Bytes displays the amount of free memory. It is generally accepted that performance is considered degraded if this counter stays consistently below 4MB on Windows NT Servers tuned as "Application" Servers (1MB on servers tuned as File/Print Servers).

> **NOTE:**   Before you make the assumption that your system is not configured with the proper amount of RAM, check the PhysicalDisk | %Disk Time and Avg Disk Queue Length. Acceptable values for these counters are 55 percent and less than 2, respectively. If the system is showing higher than these recommended values, the disk subsystem may be the cause of performance degradation.

Monitoring the Processor

The %Processor Time counter in the Processor object includes instances of all processors on the system. In other words, each processor in an NT system has its own instance. The %Processor Time counter represents the percentage of overall processor utilization. A realistic value for considering an upgrade is when the counter sustains 60 percent or greater processor utilization for long periods of time. When average processor time consistently exceeds 60–75 percent utilization, users will notice a marked degradation in performance that may not be tolerable. Possible solutions to improve performance may be to off-load some services to another less-utilized server, adding another processor, upgrading the existing processor, or distributing the load to an entirely new machine. These values can also be good ammunition when presenting proposals for new equipment.

Monitoring the Disk Subsystem

To view statistics of your disk subsystem you must first activate the disk performance counters with the command:

DISKPERF -Y
DISKPERF -Y \\myserver (for remote machines)
DISKPERF -YE (for systems with a software RAID array)

Disk performance counters are disabled by default because they cause slight performance degradation. This was more of an issue with the older Intel 486 processor systems. Today, these counters can be enabled with virtually no system degradation. The most important disk performance counters to monitor are %Disk Time and Disk Queue Length. %Disk Time represents the elapsed time that the selected physical or logical drive is busy servicing read and write requests. This counter should not exceed 55 percent. Disk Queue Length is the number of outstanding requests on the physical or logical drive. This is only an instantaneous measurement rather than an average over a specified interval. The request delays can be calculated by subtracting the number of spindles from the Disk Queue Length measurement. If the calculated delay is frequently greater than two then the disks are degrading the system's performance.

Disk Queue Length is a parameter that can alert you to an impending drive failure. Be sure to take a baseline measurement of Disk Queue Length and periodically sample for changes. It is much better to identify problem disks before they fail. As added protection, it is recommended to configure Performance Monitor to alert you when this counter exceeds two.

Monitoring Network Performance

The system's configuration will have a great impact upon your choices of network performance counters to monitor. The most important information you can gain from monitoring the network subsystem is network activity and throughput. For example, suppose you have a Windows NT server that is using the NetBEUI protocol. NetBEUI has both connectionless and connection delivery properties. A significant counter is Datagrams/sec. This is an indicator of network activity because *datagrams* are associated with unreliable, connectionless delivery methods and are packets that may or may not reach the intended recipient. This data transfer method is analogous to yelling for a person in a crowded theater. Everyone has to hear the request. In a similar manner, every node is typically broadcast to and there are no generated acknowledgments that the packet was successfully delivered. A key indicator of network throughput for the NetBEUI protocol is Bytes Total/sec counter. It incorporates both frame-based and datagram activity but only counts the bytes in the frames that are carrying data.

Another useful network performance counter is the Server | Total Bytes/sec counter. If this counter is consistently exceeding 0.83Mbps (or approximately 6Mbps) on 10Mbps Ethernet, then the network's capacity is at its maximum. Other counters in the Server object are equally important in determining network bottlenecks. This includes the counters measuring number of requests rejected, pool paged/non-paged failures, and the number of sessions in error.

Configuring Performance Monitor as a Service

One of the major problems with the Performance Monitor tool is that it only will alert, monitor, chart, or log if it is actually running at the console. This implies that someone must be logged in. This can be difficult if you are monitoring a serious problem as the machine reboots; the Performance Monitor would not restart.

The Windows NT Resource Kit includes two other utilities that can be used to fix this problem by creating a performance monitoring service. These two utilities, Monitor and Datalog, can be used to automatically start or stop performance monitoring from the command line as well as automatically initiate performance monitoring at startup. This service starts regardless of who logs into the console. The Monitor Resource Kit utility is the configuration piece and is used to install and control the Data Logging Service. The two utilities combine to perform the same functions as the NT performance Monitor Alert and Logging Facilities. It is a two-step process. First you create the Performance Monitor Workspace, and then you create and start the monitor service.

Creating the Performance Monitor Workspace

First, you must decide which events you wish to set alerts for or monitor with the service. This will depend on the uses of the particular machine and the applications it is running.

For this example assume that a machine is running a new piece of software that you are concerned may be causing memory leakage. That is to say, the software is requesting more and more memory from the system but is never releasing it. The server will automatically issue an alert if the initial memory resource settings are used up. However, it would be more beneficial to find out when approximately 3/4 of the memory is used. Then you can take corrective actions before the server performance is brought to its knees. In the example, a network alert will be sent to administrative personnel if more than 80 percent of the memory resources are used up.

There are actually several counters that can be used to check for this event. In this example, the %Commited Bytes In Use counter on the Memory object will be monitored. This value is the ratio of the Committed Bytes to the Commit Limit. The Commit Limit is the total of the system RAM plus the *minimum* pagefile value. The Commit Limit is actually a soft limit (it can change) as it can increase on demand up to the total of the system RAM plus the *maximum* pagefile size. In an NT system you should never allow the situation to occur where the pagefile has to be dynamically increased by the OS. This results in poor performance of the system as the pagefile will become fragmented over the disk. As mentioned, a Committed Bytes value of 80 percent of the limit signifies a memory problem on a properly configured NT server. Here are the steps to configure the Performance Monitor Workspace for the counter.

1. Start Performance Monitor and go to the Alert Window.

2. Set up an alert on Memory: %Committed Bytes In Use. This is a measure of how much memory NT has reserved for processes and programs as explained above.

3. In the Alert If: Over section set the value to your alert threshold (80).

4. In the Run Program on Alert box, add the name of your alert program. This is typically a script that sends a network broadcast to an administrator. It will include a line such as:

```
net send username Servername Memory Usage Alert... Please Check
Resources!
```

Of course the message (in this case, "Servername Memory Usage Alert... Please Check Resources!") can be any message you desire. In Figure 2-30 the batch file that contains this script is called SEND2ADMIN.CMD.

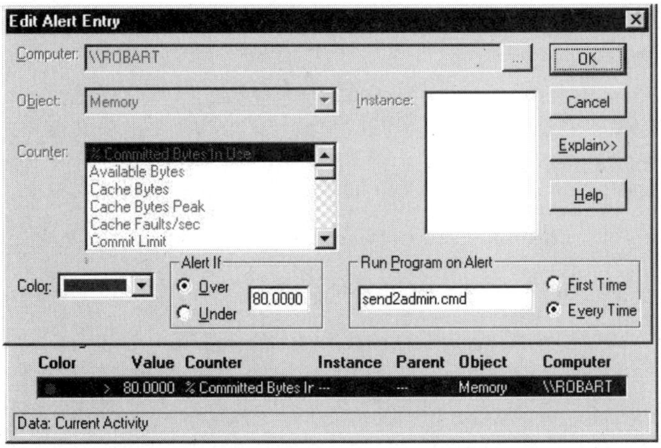

Figure 2-30.   The Performance Monitor Edit Alert Entry screen

NOTE: If you only wish to send alerts to a single user, group, or computer there is a Send Network Alert option on the Options I Alert screen.

5. Don't forget to go to the Options I Alert menu and set an appropriate update interval. In the example above, checking the condition every 300 seconds (5 minutes) should suffice.

6. Continue to add any other alerts as required.

If you wish to add logging capabilities, simply open the Log window and enter the objects you wish to log (you can even log the same events you created alerts for). Again, do not forget to go to the Options I Log menu to set the update time and log file location.

This next step is very important. You need to save the Performance Monitor Workspace as a .PMW file in the %SYSTEMROOT%/SYSTEM32 directory. Simply select File I Save Workspace and enter the appropriate parameters (e.g., WINNT\SYSTEM32\ PERF.PMW).

Creating the Data Logging Service and Starting the Monitor
The next step is to create the Data Logging Service.

1. Copy the DATALOG.EXE file from your Resource Kit directory to the %SYSTEMROOT%/SYSTEM32 folder:

```
copy c:\ntreskit\datalog.exe c:\winnt\system32
```

2. Next, use monitor to install the service. From a command prompt, type: **monitor setup**.

3. You now use monitor to assign the Performance Monitor Workspace created above to the service. It will only look in the %SYSTEMROOT%/SYSTEM32 folder, so it is not necessary to add the full path to the .PMW file: **monitor PERF.PMW**.

4. To actually start the monitor type **monitor start** at a command prompt.

5. To stop the monitor simply type **monitor stop**.

The service has now been added to the NT service list as *Monitor Service.* The startup and service account parameters can be configured like any other NT service through the Control Panel Services Applet. In addition, it can be started and stopped remotely or even added as an NT scheduled job.

THE NT EVENT VIEWER

The Event Viewer is a built-in administration utility used to examine three Windows NT log files (System, Security, and Application). This simple yet resourceful utility is a key component to understanding and monitoring NT local or remote machine events. Moreover, when the Event Viewer is used in conjunction with auditing, it can provide insight into security issues such as who is logging into the machine and what resources users are accessing. By default, the Event Viewer is automatically started each time you run Windows NT.

▼   **System Log**   The System Log records events driven by Windows NT system activity. For example, a driver that fails to load or a protocol that fails to bind to an adapter during startup causes the system to write an event to the System Log. Other events, such as the Event Log service starting or system conflicts, trigger the system to log the event.

■   **Security Log**   By default, the logging of security events is disabled. However, when auditing is enabled, the selected audited events are recorded. Auditing can be established through the File Manager, Windows Explorer, the Print Manager, and User Manager for Domains. You manage what events will be logged to the Security Log. Only the Administrator or user with administrative rights can view the Security Log.

▲   **Application Log**   The Application Log records events triggered by an application. Microsoft's BackOffice, Dr. Watson, and some third-party applications are common applications that write events to the log file to provide informative messages that can be viewed by the Event Viewer.

Configuring Logging

The Event Viewer allows you to control the growth of each log file so that the files do not take up an overwhelming amount of disk space. The default setting, Overwrite Events As Needed, is the easiest to maintain and ensures that all events will be written even if the maximum log file size has been reached. It will automatically overwrite the oldest event once the log file has reached maximum capacity.

If you have administrative rights, you may change event log settings by selecting Log Settings from the Log menu. Other event-logging options are as follows:

▼   **Maximum Log Size**   The maximum size of the specified log file (default is 512KB).

■   **Overwrite Events Older Than [ ] Days**   This option limits the size of the specified log file by overwriting only the events that are older than the selected number of days. The default number of days is seven. This is the recommended option if you plan to archive log files on a periodic basis.

▲ **Do Not Overwrite Events**   The Event Viewer will not overwrite events even when the log file has reached its maximum limitation. You must manually clear the events in the log file to resume logging. Use this option cautiously since event logging will stop once the maximum log size is reached. It is recommended that you increase the maximum log size if you wish to use this setting.

Viewing Events

Each recorded event has seven separate fields that provide specific information concerning the event. These fields are shown in Figure 2-31. In addition to the Date and Time fields, the following information is provided for each entry:

▼ **Source**   An application or system component that logged the event.

■ **Category**   This field represents how the source classifies the event.

■ **Event**   Identifies a specific event, which is unique to the type of event. This Event ID can be used to help troubleshoot and document occurrences on Windows NT. You can use this number to search Microsoft's Knowledge Base for information regarding the event.

■ **User**   The user name of the account that was logged in during the event or responsible for the event.

▲ **Computer**   The machine name where the event occurred.

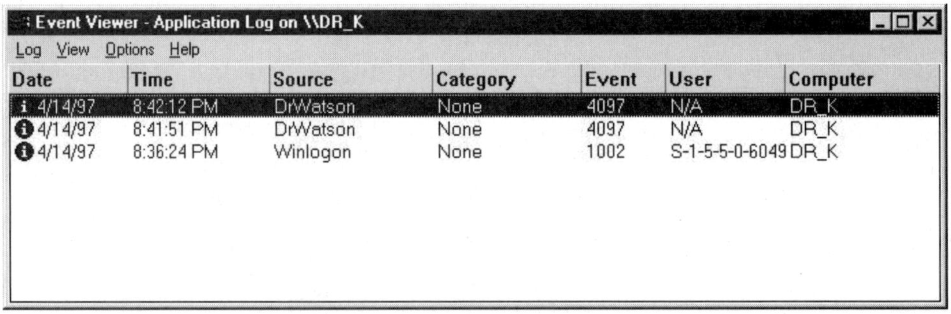

Date	Time	Source	Category	Event	User	Computer
i 4/14/97	8:42:12 PM	DrWatson	None	4097	N/A	DR_K
❶ 4/14/97	8:41:51 PM	DrWatson	None	4097	N/A	DR_K
❶ 4/14/97	8:36:24 PM	Winlogon	None	1002	S-1-5-5-0-6049	DR_K

Event Viewer - Application Log on \\DR_K
Log View Options Help

Figure 2-31.   The Application Log in the Event Viewer

Each event is graphically represented with an icon so that the log is easy to scan visually. Each icon represents the severity of the event, which is extremely helpful in pointing out high priority events.

▼ **Information**   This type of event represents significant occurrences that do not require immediate attention or require no attention at all.

■ **Warning**   A warning event signifies non-critical errors or occurrences that do not pose any immediate problem for the system.

■ **Critical Error**   A critical error event requires immediate attention. This type of event may also present a warning message to the user logged on to the system. For example, a service fails to load or a protocol that is unable to bind causes a critical error.

■ **Success Audit**   A success audit event is associated with the successful execution of an audit function such as completed logons.

▲ **Failure Audit**   Failure audits describe unsuccessful or failed attempts to gain access to system resources.

Paying Attention to Details

To obtain more details on a specific event you may either select Details from the View menu or double-click the specific event you want to view. This view will provide a description of the event and any data from memory that can be used to troubleshoot the problem. Figure 2-32 shows a detailed view of a critical error. As you can see, the information provided in the Event Detail window could be extremely useful in determining the nature of the problem and providing an exceptional solution.

So suppose you find an error code listed in an event log. Now what do you do? The most common method to figure out what error codes mean is to enter them into a Microsoft TechNet query. If you do not have TechNet you can go to the Microsoft Knowledge Base database at the Microsoft Support Web site (**http://www.micro-soft.com/support**). The NT Resource Kit also contains a Microsoft Access database (NTEVNTLG.MDB) that contains most standard NT errors codes. It lists causes and some typical remedies. In addition, some error codes can be found in NT's online help (Start | Help) and at the command prompt:

```
NET HELPMSG ERROR#
```

Viewing Remote Machine Log Files

The Event Viewer extends its capabilities of viewing log files on the local machine to a remote machine running Windows NT. You must have administrative rights in order to view the Security Log on the remote machine. To view a remote machine's log files, select Log | Select Computer and enter the name of the machine you wish to view.

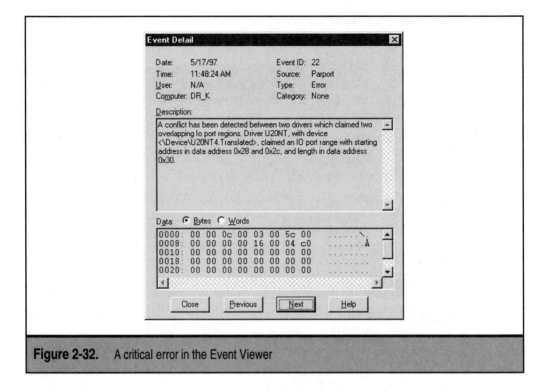

Figure 2-32. A critical error in the Event Viewer

Viewing Another Log File

Only one log file can be viewed at a time. However, you can easily toggle among the log files by selecting the System, Security, or Application Log from the Log menu.

Sorting and Filtering Events

You may chronologically sort events by selecting either Oldest First or Newest First from the View menu. The Event Viewer allows you to filter/search events by date and time, type, source, category, user, computer, or event ID. The Event Filter screen is shown in Figure 2-33. The abundance of options available for filtering events can be extremely useful when you are searching for particular system occurrences or types of events. For example, you can filter all failure audits in the Security Log that occurred within a specified time period. To filter events, select Filter Events from the View menu.

Event Viewer Utilities

There are several utilities in the NT Resource Kit that are useful for creating and keeping track of NT events. These include LOGEVENT, Crystal Reports, and Dump Event Log.

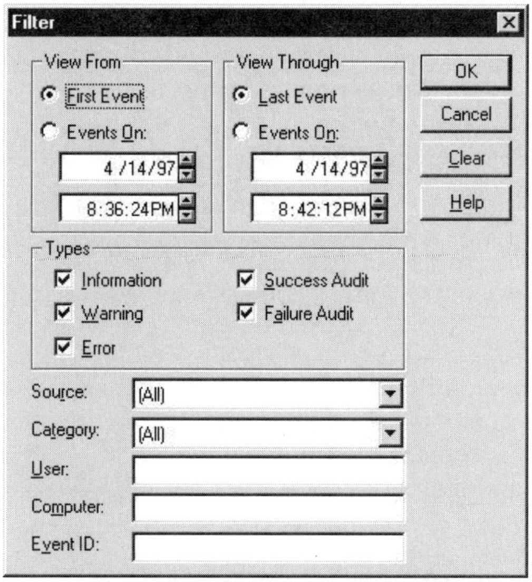

Figure 2-33. The Event Filter screen

Event Logging Utility (LOGEVENT.EXE)

The LOGEVENT utility is an application that writes events to the Windows NT Event Log on local or remote machines. It can be called from the command prompt or any batch file. For example, you can call LOGEVENT from within batch files executing from an AT command or from a logon script. Moreover, you can associate an Event ID and comment each time you call LOGEVENT to signify unique events. LOGEVENT is available in the Windows NT Resource Kits.

Crystal Reports Event Log Viewer

Crystal Reports Event Log Viewer is an excellent enhancement to the Event Viewer. It is useful for reporting NT events as well as viewing multiple log files from many different machines simultaneously. In addition to its reporting and viewing facilities, it provides a means by which to analyze, filter, and export data from event logs. Crystal Reports Event Log Viewer can be found on the Windows NT Resource Kit.

Dump Event Log (DUMPEL.EXE)

Dump Event Log is a command-line utility that dumps an event log for a local or remote system into a tab-separated text file. This utility can also be used to filter for or filter out certain event types.

UPS SUPPORT

An uninterruptible power supply is a wonderful and comparatively cheap hardware addition that provides short-term insurance against the local power grid fluctuations. In addition to keeping the workstation or server up and running in the event of a short power outage, most UPSs filter the wall socket power for spikes and minor fluctuations.

To start the UPS utility:

1. Double-click the My Computer icon on the Windows NT desktop.

2. Double-click the Control Panels Folder, then on the UPS icon.

Figure 2-34 shows the UPS applet configuration window.

If UPSs are used, make sure that all relevant portions of the system are on the UPS's current flow. If you're in a home or small office and Internet connectivity is important, make sure the modem is protected with the workstation. Or, if every workstation in a LAN has its own UPS and the file server is unprotected, what happens when the power

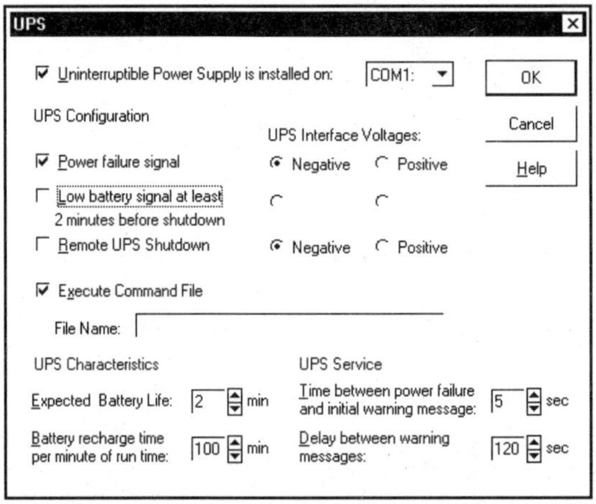

Figure 2-34.   The UPS window allows configuration of Windows NT for a variety of uninterruptible power supplies

flickers? If the servers and workstations are protected, what about the network hub or routers? "A chain is only as strong as its weakest link" is a cliché, but is a good rule to observe. It is also a good idea to test the UPS system at some point, preferably not during a time when access to the file server is urgently needed by the rest of the company. Power devices including UPSs are thoroughly covered in the Chapter 9.

TAPE BACKUP SUPPORT

Every NT server should have some kind of tape backup strategy. Windows NT provides a tape backup utility that, while it does not have all the features of a more robust third-party backup solution, is at least guaranteed to be present on all installations of Windows NT Server. To see the utility, double-click on the My Computer icon on the Windows NT desktop, then double-click on the Control Panels Folder, then on the Tape Devices icon. The uses and benefits of the built-in tape backup utility are covered in Chapter 4.

SUMMARY

Fault Tolerance and disaster recovery features have been added as native components of NT right from the start. Whether you are using NTFS or the Event Log or an Emergency Repair disk, these built-in features make your job as an administrator easier. Look for Microsoft to continue to add more fault tolerant enhancements as basic components of future versions of NT.

Professional
Library

CHAPTER 3

Storage Devices in Perspective

Data storage devices are the core of a network's integrity and the key feature of its disaster recovery and disaster prevention scheme. Choices made in regard to storage devices have far-reaching consequences throughout an NT system. When it comes to storage devices, the lowest price should not be the primary concern. What good is a high-end CPU that continuously has to wait for a disk bottleneck to clear? Also what good is that same high-end system if the storage devices fail? The purpose of this chapter is to examine storage devices from the simple to the complex. In the process, we will describe several types of multi-drive configurations. Finally, we will look at some new bus designs whose impact on storage performance in both reads and writes is bound to be substantial.

MASS STORAGE DEVICES

Storage devices have changed profoundly in the past several years. They have gone from floppy drives through MFM into ESDI and IDE/EIDE, from SCSI-1 through SCSI-3 and into UltraSCSI-1 and 2, and are now moving into Fibre Channel and other relatively exotic systems. Drive sizes have grown from 5MB to over 20GB. Numerous generations of storage devices have come and gone in the last decade and a half.

NT can be extremely demanding on its storage subsystems. Windows NT's relatively large hardware requirements, including system RAM and hard drive space, confuse more and more users. What constitutes decent or even excellent drive choices for Windows NT? Arguments for EIDE versus SCSI are easy to start. However, when it comes down to making a decision, the way in which the Windows NT machine is used is what dictates its storage and bus requirements. One type of drive might be sufficient for a simple notebook computer, while a server that runs a database might need an entirely different storage configuration.

From the inception of Windows NT, Microsoft pushed SCSI on NT users. Microsoft hailed the way that SCSI systems remove much of the processing overhead and move it to the controller. In addition, EIDE lacks multitasking and simultaneous input/output. EIDE simply does not meet the requirements of a high-end server, such as an SQL or other server that must process many simultaneous queries.

So what are the rules of thumb? The answer is obvious: Purchase SCSI systems for most NT servers and high-performance workstations or whenever you are not sure. Purchase low-end storage systems for normal workstations and low-disk-use servers. For example, most companies opt for hardware RAID controllers on SCSI buses for servers, and fast SCSI systems for CAD and other common tasks of high-performance workstations. On servers that mainly run memory-resident processes (a firewall, for instance), companies load up the system with RAM and stick with a basic storage system. This chapter looks at this argument in much more detail in the following sections.

Storage devices are often misunderstood. They include, but are not limited to, hard drives, magneto-optical (MO) drives, tape drives, CD-ROMs, and drives that use jukebox libraries. In recent years, RAID (Redundant Array of Independent Disks or, originally, Redundant Array of Inexpensive Disks) has become very popular, as has clustering. In clustering, redundancy is carried to the extreme (e.g., two computers can share the same hard drives).

A hard drive is nothing more than a permanent repository for data. "Permanent" simply means that when the computer is turned off, the files are still present for retrieval later on. The basic mechanism by which a drive works is actually very simple. The drive consists of a platter (or multiple platters) that spin. A read/write head travels across distinct concentric circles that travel from the center to the periphery of the platter (which is rigid and accounts for the name "hard drive"). An electrical current that is sent to the read/write head conveys information. The current magnetizes particles on the platter tracks. During a read phase, the head passes over the magnetic fields, resulting in inductive currents in the head coils. Such currents are the actual binary stored bits of data. All read/writes occur in a sealed, dust-free environment. When the computer is turned off, the magnetic changes to the drive are maintained.

You have just been given a simple view of hard drive mechanics. Certain factors rapidly become evident:

▼ Because the disk is a spinning media, the faster the rotation speed of the platters, the faster reads and writes occur.

■ The location of information on the drive has to be cataloged so it can be quickly retrieved.

■ The way in which the drive acts on a bus and is seen by an OS is dictated by the electrical components on the drive (this actually accounts for much of the overhead of a drive; the more components that can be controlled, the greater the overhead).

▲ The number of platters and the data density dictate the size of the drive.

These elements are related to developments in many fields. To give you a comparison of some devices, a standard floppy drive rotates at 360 rpm; fast UltraSCSI drives rotate at 10,000 rpm (and will probably soon get faster), an incredible drive speed that was unthinkable in the past. Most laypeople are aware of the relatively slow transfer speed of a floppy drive. In comparison, the 10,000 rpm drives, simply based upon rotation speed, are 10000/360, or nearly 30 times, faster than a floppy drive!

NOTE: The hard drive was first developed in 1973 by IBM. (The first drives were called Winchester drives because their two 30MB disks reminded folks of the Winchester 30/30 rifle). Not until the development of the XT in 1983 did hard drives start appearing in the basic PC. Safe to say, hard drives are an idea that caught on.

MASS STORAGE INTERFACES

For all practical purposes, only two drive types should be considered today: IDE/EIDE (Intelligent Drive Electronics or Enhanced IDE) and SCSI (Small Computer System Interface). Three new bus designs are also starting to appear and are worth discussing: Fibre Channel (Fibre Channel Arbitrated Loop or FC-AL), FireWire, and Intelligent IO or I₂O. No purpose is gained by discussing the older MFM/RLL/ESDI drives, so the following pages discuss IDE and EIDE, SCSI, and two new buses, Fibre Channel and FireWire.

IDE and EIDE

IDE started as part of the CAM (Common Access Method) specification in the mid-1980s and was submitted for formal approval to ANSI in 1990. The CAM standard was adopted in 1994 as the X3.221-1994 specification. The IDE drive requires a very inexpensive controller and is set from the factory with specific settings that should not be changed. IDE drives were introduced at a very low price to begin with, and the price has been dropping ever since. IDEs are commodity drives and, with their low price, have seriously compromised the use of the other drive types. In fact, several major computer stores only stock IDE/EIDE drives and require you to special-order other drives.

As implemented originally, the IDE drive was controlled by a PIO (programmed I/O) card. In this design, the CPU handled all data transfers. Because no handshaking occurs in such transfers, the transfers were not synchronized. Data was transferred in 512-byte sectors and the CPU was tied up until the transfer completed, which had an obvious impact on system performance. The serious limitations to IDE became very evident early on and resulted in the Enhanced IDE (EIDE) drive.

The original controller by Western Digital, the WD1003, was widely adopted in the industry. It is controlled by the INT13 BIOS call. Such BIOS calls have a limitation of 1024 cylinders, 16 heads (although supposedly 255, the task file registers are limited to 16), and 63 sectors, effectively placing a 528MB limit on drive size. (The size of a drive is actually limited by DOS. DOS 4 supported 128MB hard drives. DOS 5 and higher allowed the use of a larger cluster size, 8192 bytes, which raised the 128MB limit on the early drives to 536MB, or 528MB in real size). There were only primary/secondary configurations and the ability to add more than two components simply was not present. This was clearly a major limitation.

Western Digital introduced the Enhanced IDE specification in 1994. EIDE circumvents many of the problems of IDE. First and foremost, EIDE uses LBA (Logical Block Address) to translate the cylinder, head, and sector information into a 28-bit block, much as is done in SCSI translation schemes. For example, instead of a 1.2MB drive with 450 cylinders and 16 heads, it now could have 64 heads and 610 cylinders.

The other major changes included faster transfer rates via mode changes in PIO, and even faster ones yet using the Mode 4 PIO or Mode 2 DMA transfers. To be practical, EIDE drives need to be connected to a fast bus. Intel realized this and started supplying on-board PCI chipsets that contained EIDE control in 1994, which led to a major industry acceptance of the EIDE specification. All in all, the EIDE standard has done much to increase performance with a minimum increase in cost.

The EIDE standard also incorporates support for up to four devices—a welcome change to EIDE users. The primary channel is designated for hard drives and the secondary for slower devices such as CD-ROMs and tape devices. In each situation, a device is either *slave* or *master*. The primary channel uses IRQ14 and the secondary uses IRQ15. With this device limit expansion, the use of the backward-compatible 40-pin ribbon connectors and the speed of the transfer via the EIDE cable is limited to 18 inches. Longer cables can cause data loss and retransmission that can adversely affect system performance.

As far as Windows NT is concerned, the most dramatic change in EIDE support is the incorporation of the ATAPI (Advanced Technology Attachment Packet Interface) standard. In Windows NT 4.0, all EIDE devices are incorporated into the ATAPI driver, whereas prior versions used ATAPI for CD-ROMs but ATDISK for EIDE hard drives. Currently, built-in support is limited to hard drives and CD-ROMs. Tape device support is vendor-specific and requires a driver from the outside source. From a technical perspective, the major change in ATAPI is the incorporation of packet-based transport rather than the computer architecture that was seen in IDE. In other words, ATAPI runs SCSI-2 commands over an IDE interface (there is no support for command queuing, multiple LUNs [logical units], or disconnect features found in SCSI-2). The advantage of this SCSI on the IDE model will be future standardized drivers that address ATAPI as well as SCSI. Such drivers and applications are currently in development. EIDE drives are nearly as fast as UltraSCSI drives on a single drive/single task machine, which gives EIDE proponents great ammunition in the SCSI vs. EIDE debate. The basic IDE commands are described in Table 3-1.

Command	Opcode	Description
Execute drive diagnostic	90_H	Perform internal diagnostics on the drive
Format track	50_H	Format a track to eliminate bad sectors (few drives have full format commands)
Identify drive	EC_H	Display information on the drive, including make and parameters
Initialize drive parameters	91_H	Set up head switch and cylinder increment points for multisector ops

Table 3-1.   The Standard Opcodes and Commands of IDE

Command	Opcode	Description
Physical seek	$F2_H$	Seek to a given head and cylinder
Power	$E5_H$	Set a drive to sleep, idle, or standby mode
Read DMA (direct memory access)	$C8_H$	Read data and enable Type B DMA mode transfers
Read multiple	$C4_H$	Read multiple sectors with one command
Read sector buffer	$E4_H$	Read contents of the drive's buffer
Read sector(s)	$2X_H$	Read data from the drive
Read verify sectors	$4X_H$	Verify that the sectors are error-free
Recalibrate	10_H	Move read/write head to cylinder 0
Retry count	$F4_H$	Return number of retries attempted after a Read, Read Verify, or Read multiple command
Seek	70_H	Seek to the selected track
Set features	EF_H	Enable features on the drive such as read or write cache and transfer mode
Set multiple mode	$C6_H$	Enable the drive to perform multisector reads and writes (multiples of 2)
Translate	$F1_H$	Translate head, cylinder, sector to physical location
Vendor-specific	$9A_H$	Vendors specify as needed
Write DMA	CA_H, CB_H	Write data and enable Type B DMA mode transfers
Write multiple	$C5_H$	Write multiple sectors with one command
Write sector buffer	$E8_H$	Write data to the drive's cache
Write sector(s)	$3X_H$	Write data to the drive

Table 3-1.   The Standard Opcodes and Commands of IDE *(continued)*

With ATAPI standards, optional Opcodes were added for packet transfers. Three important ATAPI additions are as follows:

Command	Opcode	Description
ATAPI soft reset	08_H	Perform soft reset of device
Packet	$A0_H$	Perform a SCSI command
ATAPI identify device	$A1_H$	Locate ATAPI devices

In 1995, the ATA-3 (Advanced Technology Attachment) improvement to the EIDE standard was begun. Improvements include the handing of large drive sizes (137GB to be exact), fast transfer rates via mode 4 or more likely DMA 2, and the inclusion of tape and CD recorders. As this technology matures, it will be interesting to see the outcome and the impact on the industry. Such concepts as terminators to reduce noise and echo are being considered (showing the SCSI heritage). More importantly, the specification will allow multitasking to occur, which is particularly important on NT systems.

It is apparent that IDE has come a long way. No doubt it will suffice for small servers. For instance, it works fine on small file servers that get few simultaneous queries. However, because it currently lacks multitasking and simultaneous I/Os, EIDE simply does not meet the requirements of a high-end server, such as a SQL or other server that can handle many simultaneous queries. Be prepared, however, for an onslaught of cheaper devices for use on servers. In fact, IDE will probably soon be replaced by FireWire, a topic that is discussed later in this chapter.

SCSI

SCSI began in 1980 as the Shugart Associates System Interface (SASI). The entire concept was based on an inexpensive interface to handle drives. In 1982, the ANSI committee started working on the first SCSI specifications (SCSI-1). Following are descriptions of SCSI-1, SCSI-2, SCSI-3, SCSI and NT, SCSI terminology, and EIDE vs. SCSI.

SCSI-1

As the name implies, SCSI-1 was the initial attempt to define the standard. The adoption of the SCSI hard drive by Apple brought about wide SCSI-1 acceptance. Today we have the SCSI-1, SCSI-2, and SCSI-3 specifications. The basic SCSI-1 control signals are shown in Table 3-2.

Signal	Description
Acknowledge (ACK)	The initiator asserts Acknowledge to let the target know that it has complied with the request. This handshake occurs after every information transfer.
Attention (ATN)	The initiator asserts Attention to let the target know a message is available.
Busy (BSY)	The initiator and competing targets assert Busy during the arbitration phase. During the Selection phase, the selected target asserts Busy and the remaining devices withdraw.
Control/Data	The target uses the signal to determine if data or control information is being sent. If the signal is positive, it is control; if negative, it is data.
Input/Output (I/O)	The target uses this signal to determine the direction of transfer. If the signal is positive, the transfer is from initiator to target; if negative, it is from target to initiator.
Message (MSG)	The target asserts Message to indicate that a message is being sent over the data bus.
Request (REQ)	The target asserts Request to initiate a data transfer. If the bus is in an Information-In-Phase, the initiator accepts the data from the bus. If the bus is in an Information-Out-Phase, the initiator places data on the bus.
Reset (RST)	A signal that clears the bus. Normally, only set at boot, but the initiator can use reset to treat a device that is not responding.
Select (SEL)	The initiator asserts a SEL command (with related SCSI ID) to select the target it wishes to perform a command. (If the target can disconnect, the target then passes a SEL to reconnect to the initiator.)

Table 3-2.   The Basic SCSI Instruction Set

SCSI-2

SCSI-2 built upon SCSI-1. Various commands, including enhanced SCSI-1 commands, were added. The important changes include the following:

▼ More device models were added (CD-ROM, scanners, libraries, and communication).

■ Extended sense and inquiry data were expanded.

■ Pages for mode select and mode sense were detailed for all devices.

■ Improved defect handling and cache management was added.

■ Specific required features were set in place.

■ Required features were mandated. These include a Common Command Set (CCS), Initiator provision for termination power, parity checking, and bus arbitration.

■ Tagged command queuing was added. This allows up to 256 commands to be placed in a queue so that the device can complete many requests without asking the initiator. The ability to tag the commands allows priorities to be assigned to commands. All of this was designed to enhance SCSI I/O.

■ Fast SCSI was added. This allows a standard 50-pin cable to pass data at rates up to 10MB per second. This is accomplished by cutting synchronous transfer timings in half.

▲ Wide SCSI was added. This increases data transfers to 16 lines. In theory, wide SCSI can handle 20MB per second transfers.

SCSI-3

Before SCSI-2 was fully developed, engineers began to work on SCSI-3. SCSI-3 is a logical enhancement to SCSI-2. The goal of SCSI-3 was to develop higher performance characteristics and still maintain backward-compatibility, but the standard evolved into a discrete set of specifications, including the following:

▼ **Fast20 or UltraSCSI (F20)**   This entails a further cutting of synchronous negotiation times, allowing 40MB transfers over sixteen wires and 20MB transfers over eight wires. Cable lengths with Fast20 devices are very short. There is a 3-meter maximum with four devices and a 1.5–meter maximum with five to eight devices on single-ended systems. Cables can be up to 25 meters long with differential SCSI (see below). Fast20 was developed to allow a transition to serial SCSI. For several reasons, serial SCSI has been slow to appear. Consequently, work is continuing on Ultra2SCSI, which will presumably be the Low Voltage Differential SCSI (LVDS). LDVS will further increase performance and also allow cables to be longer. As of this writing, it is unclear how LDVS will be accepted in the marketplace.

■ **SCSI-3 Fibre Channel Protocol**   This covers the SCSI protocols as implemented over Fibre Channel, which is described next.

▲ **SCSI-3 FireWire (1394) Protocol**   As is evident in its name, this is the SCSI implementation for FireWire. It is not clear how SCSI will be used with FireWire. The industry consensus is that FireWire will replace EIDE, while Fibre Channel will replace SCSI.

All the basic commands have been improved and many new features added. Because much of this specification is still in progress and the volume of material is very substantial, we do not detail the specification here.

SCSI and NT

It should be apparent by now that SCSI is nothing more than a communication standard. Signals are sent to specific devices on the bus and the hallmark of the bus is the negotiation of devices and signals. Because the standard SCSI bus can have seven devices on it, SCSI is truly a multi-tasking design and, in fact, is a client (target)/server (initiator) model. A side-effect of the design is the constant communication on the bus, known as "SCSI overhead." SCSI overhead is used by many EIDE users as an argument not to use SCSI.

Why the big push from Microsoft to use SCSI systems with Windows NT? The reason is the fact that SCSI is device-independent and allows arbitration and queuing to occur. The computer to which the controller is attached does not need to know anything about attached devices or the SCSI controller. The SCSI specification provides the above language to communicate across the bus, and all devices are treated as logical units. Each device can have eight logical unit numbers (LUNs), which allows devices to have many "sub-devices" within them. For example, a CD-ROM jukebox can have an ID of 4 and have eight CD readers in it.

Although the design of SCSI is Client/Server, the implementation is peer-to-peer, which allows devices to communicate with all other devices. Unfortunately, many special devices need special drivers to fully utilize all device functions. These drivers (called "device drivers" in NT-speak) are essential to Windows NT.

How does SCSI free up the CPU on an NT box? The entire SCSI system is based on a controller that uses an onboard processor. Most of these processors are RISC-based and assist in the transfer of information from devices to the parent system. (Remember that devices on a SCSI bus are system-independent. They are not reported to the system BIOS and indeed are controlled solely by the SCSI card.) If a file is needed, the NT system (the *initiator*) informs the controller, and a request is sent over the bus to the appropriate *responder*. This device acknowledges the request and fills it. During this process, the device can go offline to find the file and then inform the controller that the file is found. The ability to go offline is called *disconnection*. During the time of disconnection, a different request can go over the control lines. Thus, the basic nature of SCSI is a multiprocessing one, so it stands to reason that servers in general have all been SCSI-based on sophisticated operating systems like Windows NT.

SCSI Terminology

Unfortunately, many SCSI terms are confusing and tend to scare away people who lack familiarity with these systems. The following list defines important SCSI terms.

▼ **Single-ended SCSI** In single-ended SCSI (by far the most popular), the signals are determined by voltage relative to a common ground. The signal can be 5 volts but typically is considered present if it exceeds 2.5 volts relative to a ground of 0. A signal is considered negative if the voltage on the bus falls below 0.4 to 0.5 volts. As is easily seen, the crucial step in setting up a SCSI bus is the control of proper voltages on the bus. Because the bus is voltage-related, all cables must meet the SCSI specifications and length limits. The specification states 19 feet as the cable limit, but in reality fast SCSI and fast wide SCSI should be limited to about 10 feet for best performance and stability.

■ **Differential SCSI** The major difference between differential and single-ended SCSI is the manner in which signals are determined. Instead of a comparison to ground, all voltage is read by contrasting the voltage between two lines. This provides better control of the signal; as a consequence, cables can be longer (up to 80 feet or so). Differential SCSI is not very popular and devices are hard to find. Do not mix differential and single-ended SCSI devices, as mixing them can cause severe device and system damage. Be sure to clearly mark differential devices.

■ **Termination** Termination simply refers to stopping the signal at a certain point and also providing a good ratio between low and high signals. Having proper termination on the bus is mandatory. Some users consider termination the most complex issue with SCSI devices. In reality, termination is straight-forward. Always use active terminators, since they're specified in SCSI-2 and they provide the control of bus voltage. Most devices have onboard terminators and they can be disabled/enabled with jumpers or by removing the resistor packs These flat, inline resistors are typically found just behind and parallel to the SCSI connector. The bus or the device can also provide the power to the terminator. Wherever possible, have the bus provide termination power. A properly terminated bus has a termination at each end. If you use both internal and external devices, the last physical device (both internal and external) needs to be terminated, and termination needs to be removed from the controller card. Figure 3-1 better explains the possible scenarios. With most modern controllers, this is all set in firmware. For example, the options on Adaptec controllers are all set up by using their configuration utility. Pressing CTRL-A during the boot sequence (while the particular card is initialized) accesses this utility. Newer cards actually provide automatic determination of termination. With SCSI-2, terminator resistance was reduced from 132 ohms to 100 ohms because most cables did not match the 132 ohm resistance. Unfortunately, cable manufacturers continue to make cables that are not actually to SCSI-2 specifications and some adapters (for example, early 1542Cs from Adaptec) had serious problems with the inexpensive cables.

▲ **SCSI ID** Each SCSI device needs a unique identifier (ID). The higher the ID, the greater the priority given to the device. For this reason, most SCSI cards have an ID of 7. Drives are given the lowest priority in part because they are faster than other components on the bus. The boot drive is 0 and the next drive is usually 1. Tape drives are in between, typically 3 or 4, and CD-ROMs are given the highest priorities. All these IDs are set with jumpers. The first block (0) is 1, the second is 2, and the third is 4. Combinations are easily determined by simply adding the jumper numbers.

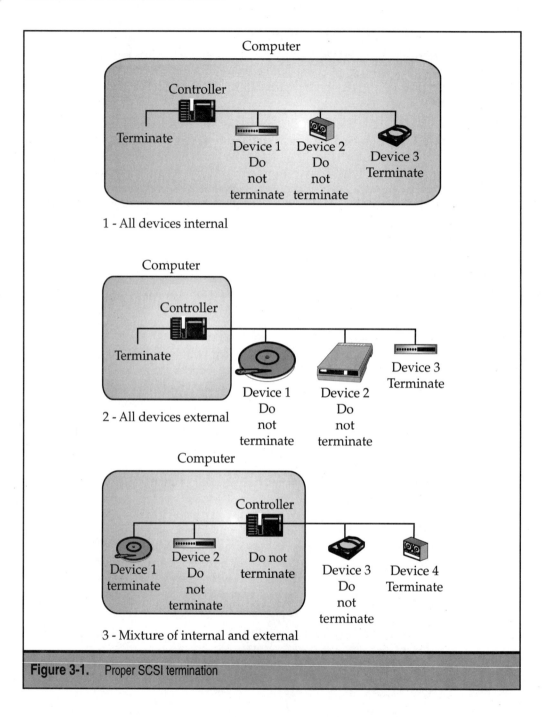

1 - All devices internal

2 - All devices external

3 - Mixture of internal and external

Figure 3-1.   Proper SCSI termination

The last items to cover on SCSI buses are the possible SCSI bus states. They are sometimes encountered when debugging the SCSI devices. The bus states include

1. *Bus free.* Nothing is on the bus. This is the state that happens when all commands are finished.

2. *Arbitration.* The situation in which multiple requests are being handled and the system must decide which has priority. As mentioned previously, priority is determined by the ID. After arbitration, the system enters the selection or re-selection phase.

3. *Selection.* The system selects the appropriate device and then chooses what information, when it will be sent, and where it's going. In all cases, the initiator and the target communicate based on ID. When all is selected, the target asserts a busy signal on the bus and then occupies the bus until the task is finished.

4. *Re-selection.* After a target goes offline, it is replaced on the line by this process.

5. *Command phase.* The target requests a command from the initiator. The command byte is sent, and the device can go offline to complete the task. The target interprets the command and finds the data block. The command phase is followed by the data in phase.

6. *Data in/Data out.* For data in, the target asks for data to be transferred to the initiator. In data out, the target receives information from the initiator.

7. *Status phase.* A complex phase in which the status of the ongoing task is described. This is usually "success" or "failure," but also includes "busy," "command completed," and others.

8. *Message in/Message out.* In this optional phase, messages are sent between the initiator and the target. In all cases, the command complete is sent at the end of a job.

EIDE vs. SCSI

No one doubts that drives are going to change dramatically in the next few years. We will see FC-AL replace SCSI and FireWire replace EIDE. The move to FireWire will occur on workstations and the move to FC-AL will occur on servers. Obviously, the transition will take place over several years. Full support for both technologies will occur with Windows NT 5.0. For now, EIDE is the choice for low-end workstations and SCSI for servers. Systems in between can go either way unless scanners, CD-ROMs, and so on are placed online; in that case, SCSI is the logical choice. Most NT experts prefer SCSI because it is faster with high-end drives and NT clearly functions more smoothly than it does with EIDE. NT was built with SCSI in mind.

The New Buses: FC-AL and FireWire

It is well known that the current bus designs have very serious speed limitations. Unless a drastic change is made in their fundamental design, only very serious RAID configurations will be able to supply needed I/O to such new systems as Pentium Pro/Pentium II or fast Alphas. These faster systems beg for relief from disk bottlenecks. Fortunately, faster designs are in the works. The following pages describe two faster designs: Fibre Channel-Arbitrated Loop (FC-AL) and FireWire.

Fibre Channel Arbitrated Loop (FC-AL)

Fiber Channel Arbitrated Loop (FC-AL) is a recent addition that stems from the Fiber Channel Specification Initiative started in 1993. Unlike the standard SCSI, the FC-AL is actually a loop connected to the backplane in two separate places. This allows data to be transferred quickly from device to device. In a single-channel design, FC-AL can send information at 100MB/sec (half duplex); in dual channel (full duplex), 200MB/sec. Such bandwidth eliminates most of the complaints having to do with SCSI overhead. In addition, FC-AL supports up to 126 devices. Early implementations of FC-AL include UltraSCSI drives all maintained on the FC-AL architecture. These systems are very efficient and fast.

Two serial cables make the basic connection to a Fibre Channel device, one carrying in-bound data and the other carrying out-bound data. These cables can be fiber optic or twin-axial copper. How the devices are connected is a question of system topology. Several topologies are defined for Fibre Channel, including Fabric, Point-to-Point, and Arbitrated Loop. Of all the available options, Arbitrated Loop using twin-axial copper offers the lowest cost per device and is thus the logical choice for use as a disk drive interface.

In a typical Arbitrated Loop with a single initiator and several target devices, the out-bound cable from each device becomes the in-bound cable for the next device in the loop. This efficient use of cabling (and the associated receivers and transmitters) is partly responsible for making Arbitrated Loop the lowest cost topology.

FC-AL contrasts significantly with SCSI in several ways. First, there is no common bus along which all the devices communicate. Instead, communication between two devices relies upon any other devices that fall between the two. These other devices must be able to accurately propagate the information to the intended destination. Second, parallel SCSI is an interlocked protocol. As such, the two devices are required to propagate handshake signals back and forth, requesting and acknowledging each byte transferred. Fibre Channel transfers occur in frames of data, with request and acknowledge activity occurring no more often than on a frame basis.

Despite the significant differences between the physical characteristics of FC-AL and SCSI, Fibre Channel disk devices use a version of the SCSI protocol mapped into the frame structure of Fibre Channel, so the similarities to SCSI are significant. Most notably, all parallel SCSI commands and much of the message function remain intact in Fibre Channel. This fact allows most Fibre Channel SCSI implementations to be based upon a previous SCSI implementation, salvaging much of the earlier programming effort.

As mentioned above, FC-AL data is transmitted from one device to another in the form of frames. Each frame consists of a frame header of 24 bytes followed by a payload of up to 2048 bytes. The payload contains the data being transmitted, while the frame header contains context information regarding the payload's data, such as the IDs of the devices involved.

Communication between two FC-AL devices occurs as a sequence of primitives and frames sent from one device to another. A *primitive* is a series of four characters that are used to control the passage of data between two devices. As mentioned above, the frame is the actual carrier of the data (the data is its payload). For example, an arbitrate (ARB) primitive is used to negotiate for control of the loop, while an open (OPEN) primitive is used to open a connection to another device. The ARB primitive is sent by the initiator to gain control of the loop, much like arbitration in parallel SCSI is used to gain control of the bus. An OPEN primitive is likewise analogous to the parallel SCSI selection, in that a connection between the initiator and the specified target device is established.

After the connection is established, the "OPENed" device (target) sends one or more R_RDY primitives to the "OPENing" device (initiator). Each R_RDY primitive sent by the target grants one "credit" to the initiator, allowing one frame to be sent to the target. This is analogous to the command phase in parallel SCSI.

After sending the command frame, the initiator closes the connection by sending a CLOSE primitive. The target responds with its own CLOSE primitive, freeing the loop for other activity, which is analogous to a disconnect on a SCSI system.

When the target is ready to send the requested data to the initiator, the process is similar to that described above, except that the roles are reversed. The target ARBs for the loop and then OPENs a connection to the initiator. One or more R-RDY primitives from the initiator give the target credit to send one or more data frames, after which the target and initiators exchange CLOSE primitives, again freeing the loop.

Command execution is completed when the target sends a response frame to the initiator. The sequence of primitives immediately before and after transmission of the response frame is the same as outlined above for the data frame.

Having completed the command, the initiator can process the data and response information the same way that it would for a parallel SCSI command execution. This is possible because every important aspect of SCSI command execution is mapped into a Fibre Channel frame.

The SCSI Access Model (SAM) describes command execution in terms of four functions: Command Service Request, Data Delivery Request, Data Delivery Action, and Command Service Response. Each of these functions is mapped into a Fibre Channel frame type, allowing an entire SCSI command execution to be mapped into frames.

A Command Service Request is transmitted from an initiator to a target by sending a command frame. The command frame payload contains the SCSI Command Descriptor Block, as well as the Logical Unit Number, the expected data transfer length, and a control field.

A Data Delivery is the transfer of actual data from one device to another. It occurs within one or more data frames, depending upon the length of the transfer. The Command Service Response is transmitted from the target to the initiator at the completion of command execution. It contains the SCSI status for the command, as well as any SCSI sense information that may have been generated for the command.

Prior to a Data Delivery Action, a Data Delivery Request may or may not be sent by the target to the initiator. If present, the Data Delivery Request is in the form of a transfer ready frame. The frame payload indicates the relative offset of the first data frame to follow and also the total number of bytes that can be transferred as a burst of one or more data frames. For disk drives, the transfer ready frames are typically used during write commands, but not read commands.

Even though the physical differences between Fibre Channel and Parallel SCSI are substantial, the mapping of SCSI functionality into Fibre Channel frames simplifies the migration dramatically. FC-AL devices can leverage existing parallel SCSI devices. Designers can learn Fibre Channel beginning with the parallel SCSI concepts that are already well known.

FireWire (or the 1394 Initiative)

FireWire was proposed as a low-cost serial bus. It was developed by Texas Instruments and Apple and was approved as an IEEE standard at the end of 1995. 1394 is the IEEE designation for this high-performance serial bus. This defines both a backplane (i.e., VME, FB+) physical layer and a point-to-point, cable-connected virtual bus. This backplane (the backplane is typically the motherboard in a PC) version operates at 12.5, 25, or 50 Mbits/sec, whereas the cable version supports data rates of 100, 200, and 400 Mbits/sec across the cable medium supported in the current standard. Both versions are totally compatible at the link layer and above. The interface standard includes definition for transmission method, media, and protocol.

The primary application of the FireWire cable version is the integration of I/O connectivity at the back panel of personal computers using a low-cost, scalable, high-speed serial interface. The 1394 standard also provides new services such as real-time UO and live (or hot) connect/disconnect capability for external devices, including disk drives, printers, and hand-held peripherals such as scanners and cameras.

FireWire or 1394 was designed to overcome many of the traditional problems of information storage and transfer. Typical EIDE and SCSI systems have serious issues with both bandwidth (speed) and distance allowed (cable length) between a system and the storage subsystem. The 1394 serial bus is basically a memory space situated between devices and interconnected with devices. All addressing is 64-bits-wide broken into 10 bits for network IDs, 6 bits for nodal Ids, and 48 bits for memory addresses. As a result, the 1394 standard can address an incredible amount of independent devices and nodes. All addressing is memory-based rather than channel addressing, and resources are viewed as registers or memory that can be accessed with processor-to-memory transactions. Each bus entity is termed a "node" to be individually addressed, reset, and identified. Multiple nodes may physically reside in a single module, and multiple ports may reside in a single node.

Interestingly, in FireWire each node also acts as a repeater that allows nodes to be chained together to form a tree topology. Due to the high speed of 1394, the distance between each node (or hop) should not exceed 4.5m (with 28 gauge cable) and the maximum number of hops in a chain is 16. Cable distance between each node is limited primarily by signal attenuation. Higher quality cables can be longer. For example, 24-gauge cable can be 14 feet long between nodes. The most widely separated nodes must have 16 or fewer cable hops between them. This gives an end-to-end distance of 72 (with lower quality cable) to 224 meters with the higher quality cable.

The main selling points of FireWire are its multi-master capabilities, live connect/disconnect (hot plugging) capability, and scalable transmission speed (from approximately 100 Mbits/sec to 400 Mbits/sec).

In addition, FireWire supports both asynchronous and isochronous data transfers. The asynchronous format transfers data and transaction layer information to an explicit address (point-to-point). The isochronous format broadcasts data based on channel numbers rather than specific addressing. Isochronous packets are issued on the average of each 125 microseconds support of time-sensitive applications. Providing both asynchronous and isochronous formats on the same interface allows both non-real-time critical applications, such as printers, STGTs, and scanners, and real-time-critical-applications, such as video and audio, to operate together on the same bus.

How can FireWire handle devices being removed and reconnected on the fly? Every time a new node is added or removed from the network, the tree topology is resolved and re-created. This provides a dynamic nodal network, which is true plug-and-play. The tree resolution starts with a bus reset phase wherein all previous information about a topology is cleared. The tree ID sequence determines the actual tree structure. During the tree ID process, each node is assigned an address and a root node is dynamically assigned, or it is possible to force a particular node to become the root. After the tree is formed, a self-ID phase allows each node on the network to identify itself to all other nodes. After all of the information has been gathered on each node, the bus goes into an idle state and waits for the beginning of the standard arbitration process.

Although set up originally with a high-speed backbone, FireWire has been somewhat disappointing in its actual throughput. Industry speculation to date is that FireWire will replace EIDE and be a viable option for the desktop or low-end servers. With the advent of Windows NT 5.0, FireWire is fully supported such that devices can be added to and removed from the bus while the system is live. It is clear that such an OS will save much rebooting, a traditional problem on NT systems.

Each of the discussed designs has advantages. FireWire is by far the cheapest. FC-AL has the fastest physical layer, but is the most expensive. In addition, FC-AL supports the longest cable length. Finally, Fiber Channel affords the greatest flexibility in mapping protocols to a common physical layer.

Intelligent I/O or I$_2$O

Recently, an add-on to the bus was standardized. This add-on is the I960 based I$_2$O. This new "bus" will dramatically influence drive and RAID performance. The most recent version of the I$_2$O specification is the 1.5 implementation. It calls for development of a communications "front-end"—an intelligent I/O subsystem (consisting of both hardware and software components)—that offloads much of the I/O communications processing task from the central processing unit. As a result, overall system efficiency will be improved by streamlining communications tasks and freeing processors to do real application work instead of I/O processing.

Following is a list of potential benefits to servers:

▼ Capability to increase the number of users (beyond current limitations) per server due to streamlined communications and increased bandwidth

■ Greater end-user productivity due to faster response times for data-intensive applications that depend on strong bandwidth performance

■ Greater ease of time-dependent tasks such as backup

▲ Effective use of I/O while application processing is occurring; parallel processing of I/O and applications

On the Intel platform, the CPU has vastly outgrown the bus. As a result, most Intel architecture-based servers are left underutilized, since they must wait for the bus to respond. These systems possess the CPU processing power needed to tackle more demanding tasks, ranging from high-volume transaction processing to complex decision support and analysis, through multimedia application creation and presentation. I_2O helps break this bottleneck.

The I_2O Architecture includes three parts:

▼ An I/O processor dedicated to handling I/O requests

■ A split-driver that features both operating system and device driver interfaces

▲ A peer-to-peer communications layer that will streamline the communication between hardware devices

Operating system suppliers will provide the split-driver architecture in current and future versions of their products. In the fall of 1997, server system manufacturers started installing I_2O-compatible I/O processors in their hardware, both on system systems boards and on some peripheral cards.

Other Standards

In addition to the standards mentioned above, others are emerging. Paramount among them is the Serial Storage Architecture (SSA) designed by IBM. SSA has an excellent design, but currently it is unclear how broadly its support will be implemented. Fast devices will emerge soon as UltraSCSI or fiberoptic. The first use of these drives in new technology will be SCSI over fiberoptic cable. In this case, FireWire is not currently a contender, as it does not support fiberoptic at present. In the near future, we'll see new generations of motherboards and components, probably developed as FC-AL (or related). Such devices will be fast and will in fact redefine server abilities.

CONFIGURING CONTROLLERS AND DEVICES

Optimizing the configurations of drives and controllers so that Windows NT runs properly and efficiently is important. Sometimes a poorly configured device does not run at all. For instance, people complain of CD-ROM recognition issues with EIDE and Windows NT. SCSI devices also require proper configuration, ID selection, and termination. Remember that Windows NT virtualizes its hardware, so all must be to specification. The following pages briefly summarize setup parameters and options.

EIDE

The safest way to set up EIDE drives is to place the disk drives on the primary channel of the system. This restricts the system to two hard drives, but in most cases two drives is plenty of space. Several large gigabyte drives have just been introduced and LBA enables their use in NT. Using EIDE on a server is not recommended, but clearly it can be done. It is best to save the secondary channel for CD-ROMs and be certain to obtain drives that are ATAPI 1.2-compliant.

Mixed Buses

Often you hear of people who use a small EIDE drive to boot into NT. They then add a SCSI drive for data. Again, this configuration works, but mixing buses can cause serious bus contention and so is not recommended. Without extremely compelling reasons, do not mix EIDE and SCSI hard drives on a Windows NT system.

SCSI

SCSI devices are getting easier to set up all the time. New controllers and devices are faster and somewhat self-configuring. If possible, avoid using legacy SCSI controllers in your systems (the disks already cause enough of a bottleneck). EISA controllers are acceptable if their use is required, but most of the better controllers use a PCI bus. A Fibre Channel may also be used, provided the proper adapter is present. Be sure to obtain a controller with onboard BIOS control. For example, the Adaptec 2940 and 3940 models are industry standard controllers. These cards can be configured by onboard SCSI utilities that can be accessed by simply pressing CTRL-A at post time. The Adaptec "U" series even allows multiple boards to be set up with a single utility. Always be sure to invest in quality controllers.

By convention, SCSI IDs should follow standards (IBM's Microchannel bus is somewhat different, but we exclude them because Microchannel is no longer supported). The controller should be the highest priority and by convention is assigned an ID of 7. The boot drive is assigned the lowest priority (ID 0) and subsequent drives start at 1. Tape drives (i.e., DAT) are given intermediate IDs, with 3 or 4 being the most common ID. CD-ROMs typically receive IDs of 5 or 6. However you decide to set up your SCSI IDs, it helps to be consistent across servers (again, this is only by convention, as no physical requirements prevent you from changing these orders).

Serious attention must be given to SCSI cables and termination. Some of the best products are currently offered by Granite Digital (**http://www.scsipro.com**), but they are expensive. On the other hand, cheaper cables that do not work can be more expensive in the end than the *more* expensive cables. Having a drive subsystem problem that turns out to be caused by a faulty cable is very frustrating. Keep the cable lengths to a minimum. If you doubt the integrity of SCSI cables, use diagnostic cables to deduce the problem. These cables are available from several companies, including Granite Digital. Be sure to minimize noise and echo on the bus or data corruption will occur.

Whenever possible, terminate the bus and not the device. For example, on an external chain, put a terminator on the connector and not on the device. This keeps additional noise from coming off the cable stub (the *stub* is the distance between the terminator and the "actual" end of the cable). Once more, buy a good active terminator. Some internal cables are also terminated, but they are relatively difficult to find. Compaq uses them in many of their high-end systems. Newer SCSI controllers automatically determine the best termination for the bus. In general, if a combined wide/narrow controller is used, only populate two of the ports at one time. Be sure to read the manufacturer's specifications if you want to stray from this policy.

NT SPECIFIC CONFIGURATIONS

After you have purchased drives, you can start working with them. Several NT applets and command line parameters can be of particular help. Among others, you can use the Disk Administrator and the format command. The following pages describe the Disk Administrator, as well as how to create and delete a partition.

Disk Administrator: Partitioning and Formatting

The Windows NT Disk Administrator is the major feature in Windows NT for manipulating partitions, formatting, handling drive and CD-ROM labels, handling volumes, and handling stripe sets. Understanding what it can and cannot do is key to the use of hard drives in Windows NT 4.0.

Partitioning drives is quite straightforward in Windows NT. All of the work is done at the command line (i.e., for special cluster sizes). Little has actually changed since version 3.51, but Disk Administrator does have a new interface and customization characteristics that make it more useful.

TIP: As a general rule, set up only one primary partition on a computer. If you add more drives, it's easier to maintain standard drive lettering without mixing drives and partitions in a confusing manner. In all cases, a letter is assigned to a primary partition before an extended partition. In such a situation, drive C could be the primary partition on drive 0 and drive D could be the primary partition on drive 3. Keeping drives and partitions as simple as possible is always good idea.

Creating and Deleting a Partition

Creating a partition and then formatting a drive is straightforward with NT's Disk Administrator. The hardest part is remembering to commit configuration changes before the drive is formatted.

The basic procedure for creating a partition is as follows:

1. Open Disk Administrator (it is an Administrative Tool).

2. Highlight the drive in question.

3. Select the Partition menu and choose Create or Create Extended (a drive can only have one extended partition). If an extended partition was created, logical drives must be created in the same manner.

4. Once the partitions are created, click on the Partition menu and select Commit Changes Now.

5. Run the format by selecting Tools | Format, as shown in Figure 3-2.

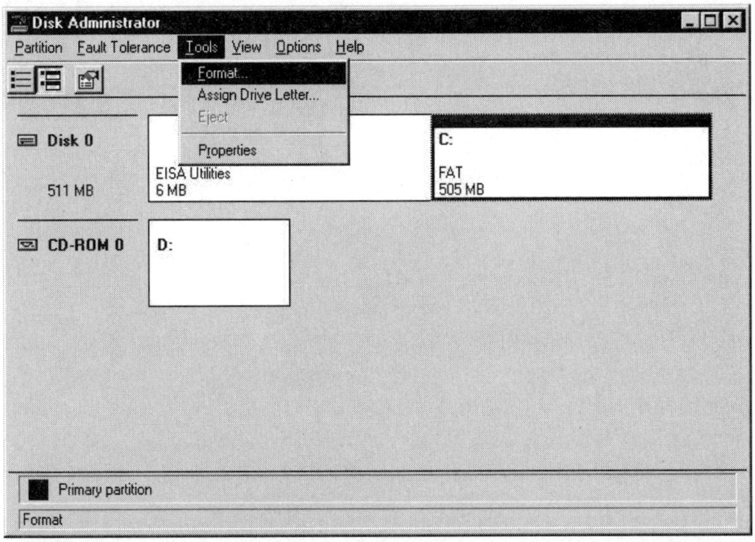

Figure 3-2.   Formatting a drive with Disk Administrator

Deleting a Partition

Deleting partitions is the exact opposite of creating them. In Disk Administrator, highlight the partition and choose Partition | Delete, as shown in Figure 3-3. You are informed that the drive and all its files will be deleted. If you select Yes, the partition is removed, but the removal is not permanent until the changes have been saved.

However, often you discover that you cannot delete a partition because it cannot be locked for exclusive use. When you attempt to delete the partition, a message appears that says that the partition cannot be removed because it cannot be locked for exclusive usage. If a pointer in the system is related to the drive in question, this indeed can be a troublesome problem. Make sure that no obvious pointer is directed to the drive. The obvious ones would include those in Explorer or File Manager.

If it is still apparently impossible to delete the partition, several options are available for remedying the problem. The FDISK.EXE program that ships with DOS 6.22 or higher will work. The DELPART.EXE utility that was released by Microsoft (and works similarly to FDISK) may also be used. This utility makes it easy to delete an NTFS partition. If the drive is a SCSI drive, a low-level format can be run on it to remove all traces of partition information.

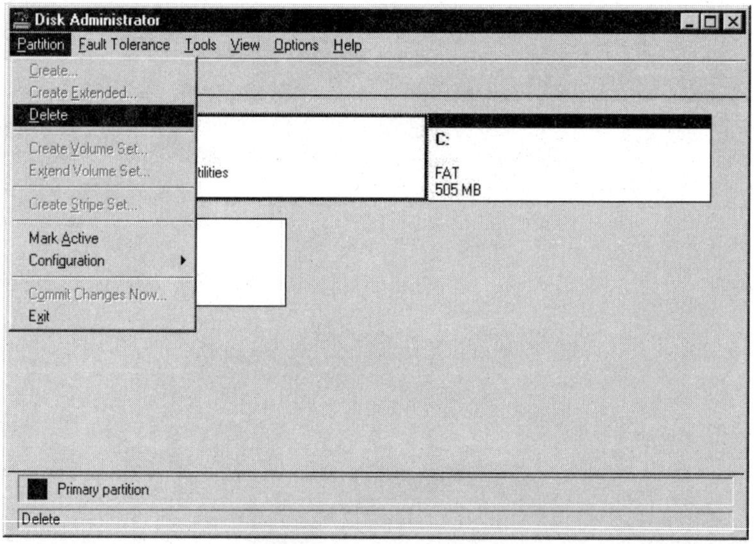

Figure 3-3.   Deleting a partition

Disk Administrator can also be used to change drive letters on partitions. Changing drive letters can be important if there is an older DOS user who wants CD-ROMs to be the last drives available on the system. Follow these steps to change a drive letter:

1. Select the partition in question.
2. Choose the Tools menu.
3. Select Assign Drive Letter.
4. Select the preferred letter assignment, as shown in Figure 3-4.

In the same way, drive letters can be moved around to reach the order that is desired.

Using the Format Command

If the system is likely to have unusually large files and you wish to optimize the cluster size, set the partition with Disk Administrator and then format the partition at the command line. The syntax is as follows:

FORMAT *drive*: [/FS:*file-system*] [/A:*size*]

Following is an explanation of the parts of the command line:

▼ /FS:*file-system* specifies the type of the file system (FAT or NTFS).

■ /A:*size* overrides the default allocation unit size. Default settings are used by Disk Administrator and should not be changed for normal use. (A drive formatted over 4096 cannot be compressed.)

■ *NTFS* supports 512, 1024, 2048, 4096, 8192, 16K, 32K, 64K.

▲ *FAT* supports 8192, 16K, 32K, 64K, 128K, 256K.

For example, if the drive will store large video files, small clusters will increase the amount of fragmentation on the drive. The cluster size should be increased accordingly. If the files are large TIF or CAD files, use the largest allocation unit. In general, staying with the default size of 4096 is best.

One additional role is played by these utilities: the establishment of fault-tolerant or RAID drive sets. These configurations are discussed in the next section.

FAULT TOLERANCE

Fault tolerance is a very complex issue. It involves configuring hard drives, configuring hardware in general, and planning for disaster recovery and prevention. This section examines the issue of hard drive redundancies and their value in Windows NT.

Several independent sources estimate that the amount of data storage is increasing 50 to 100 percent per year. These estimates are alarming. Not that many years ago everyone used a 40MB hard drive and the amount of storage used then seemed massive. Today

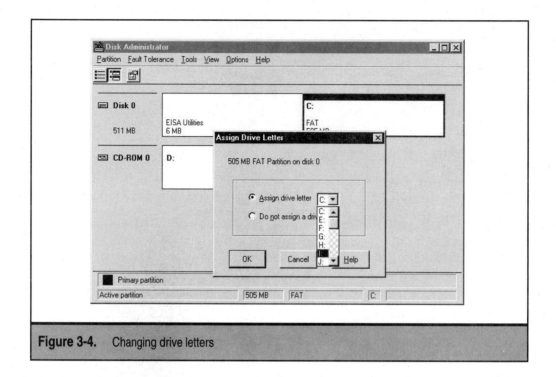

Figure 3-4. Changing drive letters

we're worrying about multi-gigabyte data files. In addition, the new emphasis on Network Computers (NCs) and Network PCs (NetPCs) has placed even more importance on safe storage. With the explosion in storage size, disk arrays have become more and more prominent. Simply put, a *disk array* is a logical grouping of drives that is designed to be faster, fault-tolerant, or both. The most common type of disk array is RAID (Redundant Array of Independent Disks).

Fault tolerance, as the name suggests, is the capability of a system to handle disasters in such a way that continuous operation is maintained. It denotes almost instantaneous recovery from hardware or software anomalies. Needless to say, considerable effort is required to provide such capability in RAID drive subsystem.

RAID can be discussed in several ways. One is the classic, almost ten-year-old configuration of hard drives only; the other consists of drives and other accessories (i.e., power supplies). The latter is the one that truly starts providing fault tolerance, although no single entity can provide complete crash resistance.

Almost every book that discusses RAID assumes that all you need to know are the levels of RAID and the discussion ends there. The major concern should be not what RAID *is* but how to *use* it. For completeness, however, various terms need to be defined, including the basic RAID levels.

The following list briefly describes the levels of RAID. We will consider RAID Levels 0, 1, and 5 in some detail in the rest of this chapter.

▼   **Just a bunch of drives (JBOD)**   This is nothing more than placing drives together for convenience. There is no implied fault tolerance in this level. In Windows NT, JBOD is called a *volume set*.

■   **RAID Level 0**   In RAID 0, the data is striped across drives, allowing for simultaneous I/Os to all the drives. As the number of drives increases, so does the speed of the array and the risk of data loss.

■   **RAID Level 1**   RAID 1 is considered the best of all levels. All data writes occur onto at least two drives. When both drives are on the same controller, this process is termed *mirroring*. When the drives are on separate controllers, the process is called *duplexing*.

■   **RAID Level 2**   RAID 2 is very seldom used. Striping is accomplished at the bit level, bringing about serious overhead.

■   **RAID Level 3**   Like RAID 2, RAID 3 is seldom used. All correction data is maintained on a single drive, and information is striped across the remaining drives a byte at a time. For this level to function properly and at optimal speed, drive spindles need to be synchronized. There is no need to consider Level 3.

■   **RAID Level 4**   This level is similar to RAID 3, except data is striped at the block level. Like RAID 3, there is no compelling reason to use it.

▲   **RAID Level 5**   RAID 5 is actually a compromise level. Striping is at the block level, and error correction is distributed across all drives. This level uses the simultaneous writes seen in levels 0 and 1, but parity data is distributed across all drives, which results in an increased overhead.

RAID Level 0

RAID 0 is used mostly in systems that require very fast reads and writes. No attempt is made to provide a parity bit for any fault tolerance. You expand level 0 by simply adding drives (generally, the number of drives must be set up initially; you cannot add drives after the fact). As the number of drives increases, so does the performance of the set.

In general, the addition of a drive increases throughput by a factor of 1.8. However, this increase depends on the bus and it must be remembered that large numbers of drives can rapidly saturate a bus. With the new Fibre Channel implementations, sustained throughputs of 100Mbits/sec have been recorded. One factor here is very important: as the number of drives increases, so does the probability of a drive failure. If the failure occurs, two choices are available: restore from a backup or send the drives to a data recovery specialty shop (very expensive). RAID 0 is much closer to "Just a bunch of drives" than to the other RAID levels and should not be considered on important data drives. Only use RAID 0 when you consistently back up your data and speed is your basic desire.

RAID Level 1

In RAID 1, disks are essentially mirrored. That is to say that writes to drive 1 are written at the same time directly to drive 2. To maximize I/O speed and fault tolerance, place the drives on separate controllers, a process called duplexing. Duplexing offers a modest improvement in performance over a single drive, particularly in reads. It also provides fault tolerance in the case of both drive and controller failure. Write performance is comparable to that of a single drive.

The concept behind all RAID 1 arrays is that if one drive fails, the other will take over its functions. This may or may not be the case. In hardware RAID 1, the automatic fall over is almost always straightforward. In software RAID, the fall over may not occur at all (see "Hardware vs. Software RAID" later in this chapter). Ideally, RAID 1 is the RAID of choice. It is also one of the most expensive types of RAID implementation because half of the drive space is committed to fault tolerance.

RAID Level 5

RAID Level 5 is the most common RAID level found on modern server systems. It is a convenient compromise between performance, cost, and fault tolerance. RAID 5 is very similar to RAID 3, but parity and data are spread over all drives. In general, writes occur to more than one drive at a time and small writes are faster than those in RAID 3. There are no dedicated parity drives and additional drives are easy to add to the array.

From the NT operating system perspective, RAID 5 is seen as a single volume of large size. Data is striped from storage device to storage device in sequence and by sectors. As far as Windows NT is concerned, the data is read from successive sectors but the sectors are actually on sequential drives.

The confusing issue of parity data should be examined as well. How is this feat accomplished? The parity information is created by comparing the data from one disk to the data on the others one bit at a time. This comparison is done across all the data disks of the array and uses the "Exclusive Or" Boolean function. The advantage of this arrangement is that every bit on the array can be determined by simple algebra.

An easy way to think of parity and regeneration is to consider an array of four drives with 1-bit sectors, as in Table 3-3. In actual RAID 5 arrays, the parity information is spread out, but the table keeps it on one drive for simplification.

Start at Data Stream 1. Add up all of the stream one bits from Disk 1, Disk 2, and Disk 3 and you get the parity result (in binary 1+0+0=1). For Data Stream 2 (1+0+1=0, drop the carry bit). For Data Stream 3 (0+1+1=0). Continue on for streams 4 and 5.

Now remove one of the disks (disk 2, for instance). You are now relegated to doing binary algebra to regenerate the missing disk's data in each individual data stream. For Data Stream 1:

$1+X+0=1. X=0$

Data Stream Number	Disk 1	Disk 2	Disk 3	Parity Disk
Data 1	1	0	0	1
Data 2	1	0	1	0
Data 3	0	1	1	0
Data 4	1	1	1	1
Data 5	0	0	0	0

Table 3-3. Parity Example

For Data Stream 2:

$1+X+1=0. X=0$

For Data Stream 3:

$0+X+1=0. X=1$

When one drive fails in RAID 5, it can be recovered by replacing the bad drive and allowing the array to regenerate itself with this parity information. If you are using hardware RAID with a hot spare, this is done automatically whenever the controller detects a drive failure. Of course, it must be remembered that in all of the RAID levels mentioned the data is lost if two drives fail at the same time.

Hardware vs. Software RAID

If budgets permit, using hardware RAID over a software RAID configuration is strongly recommended. Hardware RAID arrays place much of the system overhead on the controller, which frees precious processor time. Hardware RAID arrays are almost always faster and more stable than the software solution. In addition, the high-end hardware arrays offer hot-swappable drives and online array expansion capabilities, so you can expand your array without having to back up your data and wipe the drives clean. Most hardware arrays come with monitoring software that runs in NT and keeps tabs on the array. This is certainly a required feature.

So what is the bottom line? Use hardware RAID wherever possible. If you have no other choice, by all means use the software version of RAID 1. Do not use software RAID Level 5. These software levels of RAID are discussed in the "Creating Software RAID Arrays in Windows NT" section later in this chapter. Meanwhile, the following pages discuss hardware RAID supplies, some basic RAID facts, and some practical solutions.

Hardware RAID Supplies

Hardware RAID exists in several configurations. RAID controllers can be purchased from Mylex, DPT, AMI, and IBM. Complete NT servers with hardware RAID controllers are available from Dell, IBM, Digital Equipment, Compaq, and Hewlett Packard, among others. The Mylex, DPT, and AMI systems allow you to attach drives and build your own RAID enclosure. RAID enclosures come in several different configurations. Most of these systems also support some form of *Auto-RAID* software that asks several questions of the administrator and then offers the best RAID configuration for a particular situation.

Preconfigured RAID enclosures may also be purchased. These configurations consist of an external enclosure with a power supply, drives, and SCSI controller. Many enclosures are quite adequate for small LANs, but they do not offer much fault tolerance to an enclosure crash. The second level is a redundant level. There are two power supplies and the system is designed to handle an enclosure disaster. The upper-level RAID arrays offer internal power supplies to the bus, which allows data to be written to the drives.

Unfortunately, the IS budget becomes the major issue in selecting a RAID solution for a particular company. The top tier of hardware support is found in the clustering now provided by Digital Equipment and other companies. This clustering consists of RAID enclosures with dual controllers that can be attached to two separate computers. Failure of one brings about an automatic switch to the other. Clusters are discussed in detail in Chapter 5.

Some Basic RAID Facts

Table 3-4 shows a comparison of the performance of RAID levels 1 and 5 based on the use of 4GB Barracuda drives from Seagate. All calculations are based on standard formulas.

Factor	RAID 1	RAID 5
Capacity for use	16GB	16GB
Number of drives	8	5
Overhead	50%	20%
Concurrent reads	8	5
Concurrent writes	4	2.5
Maximum random reads	575	360
Maximum random writes	285	135

Table 3-4. Summary of Performance with Wide SCSI Hard Drives

Most discussions of RAID use mean time values to better quantify fault tolerance and drive integrity. The common mean time values used to discuss RAID functionality are the following:

▼   **MTBF**   Mean time between failures (before any component in the system fails). In general, this value predicts the frequency with which a system or system component needs to be repaired.

■   **MTRF**   Mean time to reduced function. This reflects a loss of a component that causes a reduced functionality in the array. Data can still be accessed but at noticeably inferior levels of performance.

■   **MTDA**   Mean time of data availability. This is the mean time to failure of nonredundant components that cause data to simply become unavailable.

▲   **MTBDL**   Mean time between data loss. The average time before components fail, resulting in loss of both data and error correction.

Following are MTBF (mean time between failures) values for common system components (all numbers are based on standard industry figures):

Hard drive	300,000–500,000 hours
Adapter	200,000–300,000 hours
Array controller	300,000–1,000,000 hours
Power supply	50,000–300,000 hours

This list demonstrates that the parts that one would not expect to fail (for example, the power supply) are perhaps the first to fail. As might be expected, as the number of components increases, a corresponding decrease occurs in the MTBF. As a conservative estimate, four hard drives in an independent array might log 100,000 operation hours of actual use. Five drives configured as RAID 5 (same storage space as the four independent drives) might log 75,000, and eight drives configured as RAID 1 would log only 50,000 operation hours. Conversely, the time to data loss would be the exact opposite. The independent drives would get 100,000 hours of use. In a RAID 5 array, two drives would have to be lost at the same time. These redundancies provide great data protection, but eventually they require more repairs. These factors weigh very heavily in determining a plan for drive system fault tolerance.

The main performance issues to consider are the time intervals between the loss of data availability and the time for return of system function. If a power supply (high-risk) is lost, you lose access to the data until the power is restored. Clearly, redundant power supplies are a good first step toward eliminating a common failure source. The optimal design would be dual power supplies with full power redundancy.

The use of software RAID dramatically increases the time between failure and repair. In some cases, the repair simply cannot be made. In such cases, a new installation of the OS must be completed and the data contained on the RAID drives restored from tape. In such cases, there is always a gap between the backup and the restore. Therefore, the data is never up-to-date. In hardware configurations, the RAID array can actually regenerate itself if spare drives are present. The parity information is used to fix the missing drive, as mentioned above. It is important to note that, at the time of regeneration, a corresponding system slowdown occurs.

The latest high-end RAID configurations actually allow real-time configuration, storage expansion, and repair. Drives can be added and RAID levels switched totally independently of the operating system. One such example of this type of enclosure is the SuperFlex 3000/DRG system from Storage Dimensions. Obviously, you pay a premium for such a system. On the other hand, being able to dynamically expand and configure might be very important to a business that cannot afford downtime.

A word of caution should be given to the use of cached controllers: Typically, NT does not operate well with RAM on controllers. In the case of array controllers, however, the RAM is being used to handle the RAID overhead. The latest array controllers like the Mylex DAC960PD use 15 nanoseconds SRAM (Static RAM). Generally speaking, 16MB RAM on the controller should be adequate.

Practical Solutions

When the various service parameter and times are examined (as above), the first thing that should come to mind is that every disk manufacturer expects every one of their drives to eventually fail. That is what parameters like MTBF (mean time between failures) are all about. The bottom line is that all administrators should design their systems with this assumption in mind: the disks will fail.

Assuming that money is limited, some measures can be taken to keep system downtime to a minimum. First of all, obtain a dual-channel SCSI controller and mirror the boot drive. Prepare a boot floppy as described in the "Creating a Software RAID Level 1 Array (Mirror or Duplex)" section of this chapter. This floppy will allow the system to be booted to either the primary or the secondary drive. The floppy will provide a means of booting into a viable copy of NT and then accessing an external RAID array. Some overhead is present, but that is acceptable.

If mirroring is not a satisfactory option, there are other alternatives. First of all, data can still be maintained on a RAID 5 enclosure. Data can be protected by using a real-time data replicator such as the Octopus Family of products from Qualix; information can be found on the Web at **http://www.qualix.com**. The top-of-the-line Octopus product even supports automatic switchovers. If the first system fails, the second system simply takes its place.

Ideally, the server should be designed in such a manner that the operating system is on a hardware mirror and the database is on a separate hardware RAID 5 enclosure. This design would maximize redundancy. It is possible with some devices to do a three-way mirror, but generally three-way mirrors are to be avoided.

If money is no object, the dual controller configurations allow system 1 and system 2 to share the same hard drives. Using clustering, you are protected locally, and, combined with Octopus, you can actually replicate the system to a distant cluster. Cluster solutions are discussed in Chapter 5.

Creating Software RAID Arrays in Windows NT

Windows NT server allows you to enable pre-RAID (volume set), RAID 0 (striping), RAID 1 (mirroring), and RAID 5 (striping with parity) via the operating system. RAID 0 and 1 are acceptable, but using RAID 5 at the NT operating system level is foolish and asking for serious disaster-recovery problems. If any file or process is locked onto the drive, you cannot repair it. Windows NT does not allow you to replace the drive, which is never the case with hardware-based RAID.

Volume Sets

Volume sets are termed "just-a-bunch-of-drives" (JBOD) by many RAID vendors. To create a volume set within NT, the Disk Administrator Tool is used, as follows:

1. Highlight the unpartitioned drives to be combined.

2. Select Create a Volume set from the Partition menu.

3. Select OK when prompted to do so.

4. Select Partition | Commit Changes Now to save the configuration.

5. Format the drive as required by selecting Tools | Format.

NOTE: Hold down the CTRL key to select more than one drive. Unlike the other arrays within NT, a volume set can be expanded at any time by adding an unpartitioned drive to the set.

A volume is really nothing more than a design of convenience. Remember that it offers no fault tolerance at all.

Creating a Software RAID Level 1 Array (Mirror or Duplex)

One of the nice features about RAID 1 sets in Windows NT is that you can include the system partition in the array. The procedure is the same whether you will have two drives on one controller (mirroring) or two drives on two separate controllers (duplexing). The following steps describe the procedure for building a RAID 1 set with NT's Disk Administrator tool:

1. Without establishing any partitions on the drives, highlight the first drive to be included in the set.

2. Press the CTRL key and highlight the second drive. Both drives should now be highlighted.

3. Under the Fault Tolerance menu, choose Establish Mirror.

4. Under the Partition Menu, choose Commit Changes Now.

5. Format the drive by selecting Tools | Format.

6. Save the RAID set information by selecting Partition | Configuration | Save.

If the mirrored set includes the system partition, a fault-tolerant boot floppy should be created. This floppy allows the system to boot to the working drive in case one of the mirrored disks fails. Follow these steps to create this floppy:

1. Place a floppy in the NT system's drive and run format.

2. Copy the NT startup files from the NT system partition. Include the following files: BOOT.INI, NTLDR, and NTDETECT.COM.

3. Label and store the diskette for future use.

To use this floppy to boot to the second disk in a mirror, simply edit the BOOT.INI file to include an option to point to the second disk. The top of Figure 3-5 shows a typical BOOT.INI file. To add the mirrored disk option to your boot menu, change the BOOT.INI file as shown in the lower half of Figure 3-5. In this case, the RAID 1 set is a true mirror (both disks on one controller).

The line multi(0)disk(0)rdisk(1)partition(1)\WINNT40="NT Svr From Mirrored Disk" has been added:

▼ Multi denotes the controller number, with 0 being the first controller.

■ Disk is always zero if the multi syntax is used.

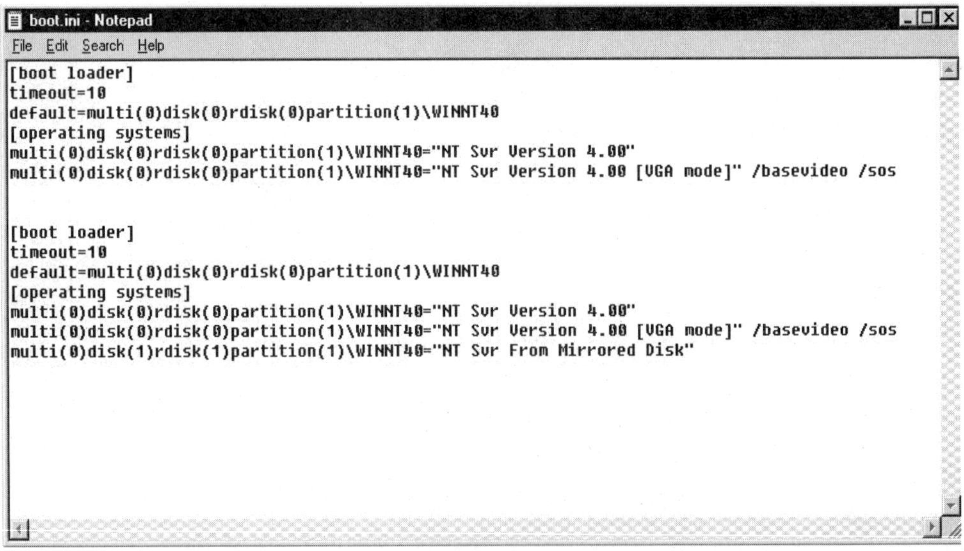

```
boot.ini - Notepad

File  Edit  Search  Help

[boot loader]
timeout=10
default=multi(0)disk(0)rdisk(0)partition(1)\WINNT40
[operating systems]
multi(0)disk(0)rdisk(0)partition(1)\WINNT40="NT Svr Version 4.00"
multi(0)disk(0)rdisk(0)partition(1)\WINNT40="NT Svr Version 4.00 [VGA mode]" /basevideo /sos


[boot loader]
timeout=10
default=multi(0)disk(0)rdisk(0)partition(1)\WINNT40
[operating systems]
multi(0)disk(0)rdisk(0)partition(1)\WINNT40="NT Svr Version 4.00"
multi(0)disk(0)rdisk(0)partition(1)\WINNT40="NT Svr Version 4.00 [VGA mode]" /basevideo /sos
multi(0)disk(1)rdisk(1)partition(1)\WINNT40="NT Svr From Mirrored Disk"
```

Figure 3-5. The BOOT.INI file

- rdisk denotes the disk number and starts at zero as well (i.e., the second disk is 1). Therefore, to make NT boot to the second disk on the controller, simply change the rdisk value to 1.

▲ The partition number always starts at 1 and should not be changed when creating the boot floppy.

Creating a Software RAID Level 0 Array (Stripe Set)

A stripe set is slightly better than a JBOD set because it offers an increase in speed. To create the stripe set under NT, use Disk Administrator as follows:

1. Without establishing any partitions on the drives, highlight the first drive to be included in the set.

2. Press the CTRL key and highlight the second drive so that both drives are highlighted (two is the minimum number).

3. Select all remaining drives in the set.

4. Under the Partition menu, choose Create Stripe Set.

5. After the set is created, go to the Partition menu and choose Commit Changes Now.

6. The drive set may now be formatted by selecting Tools | Format.

7. Save the RAID set information by selecting Partition | Configuration | Save.

Creating a Software RAID Level 5 Array

Disk Administrator is the simplest way to create a fault-tolerant RAID 5 array in NT. The following describes the procedure for building a RAID 5 set:

1. Be sure you have at least three hard drives installed in the system. It is recommended that they be the same model and geometry.

2. Without establishing any partitions on the drives, highlight the first drive.

3. Press the CTRL key and highlight each successive drive. When you have chosen all the drives, the whole set is highlighted.

4. Under the Fault Tolerance menu, choose Create Stripe Set with Parity.

5. Under the Partition menu, choose Commit Changes Now.

6. The drive set may now be formatted by selecting Tools | Format as NTFS (FAT will fail).

7. Save the RAID set information by selecting Partition | Configuration | Save.

Figure 3-6 shows an example of a RAID 5 and a RAID 0 set on the same system. Note that the RAID 5 set (F:) is composed of the same drives. The NT system partition cannot be part of a RAID or RAID 5 array. It can only be part of a RAID 1 array (mirror or duplex).

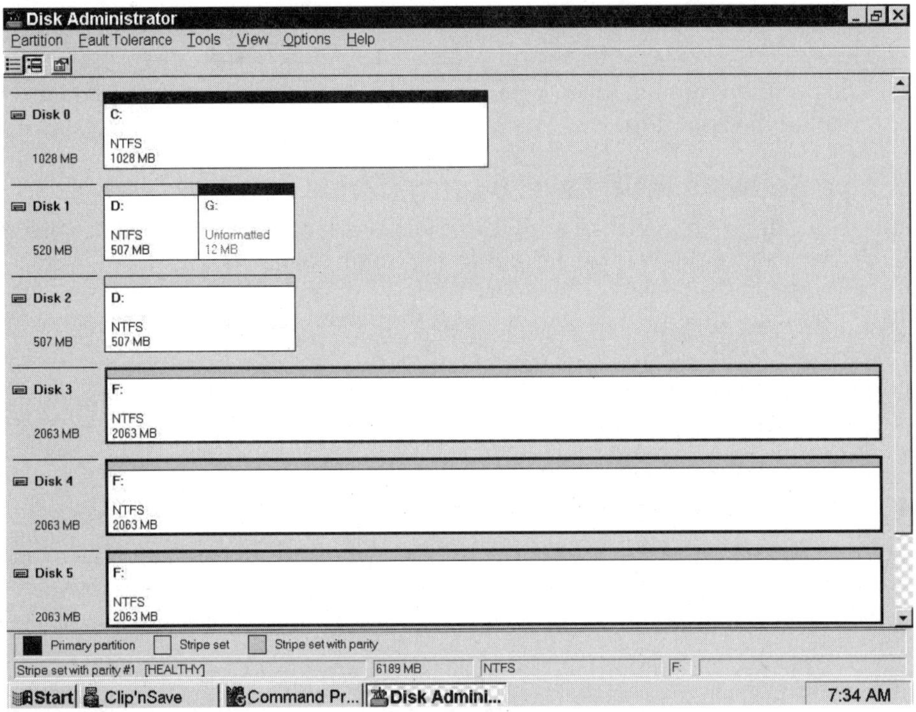

Figure 3-6.   RAID sets as seen in Disk Administrator

The FTEDIT.EXE program in the Windows NT Resource Kit can also be used to create and manipulate RAID sets. Figure 3-7 shows the same drive sets that are shown in Figure 3-6. FTEDIT.EXE is a very powerful program and can be useful for diagnosing and fixing array problems. For the most part, Disk Administrator should be the tool of choice because it is a more intuitive tool.

OPTIMIZING DISK PERFORMANCE

In any system, a balance must always be struck between cost, performance, and risk. If speed is the main concern, RAID 0 becomes an option, but the data on the RAID will be in serious jeopardy of being lost. The best overall strategy to optimize performance is to separate drives and devices based on speed and function.

Windows NT functions to a large extent via thread and thread handling. Each thread is assigned a priority; a thread with a higher priority can interrupt a thread with a lower

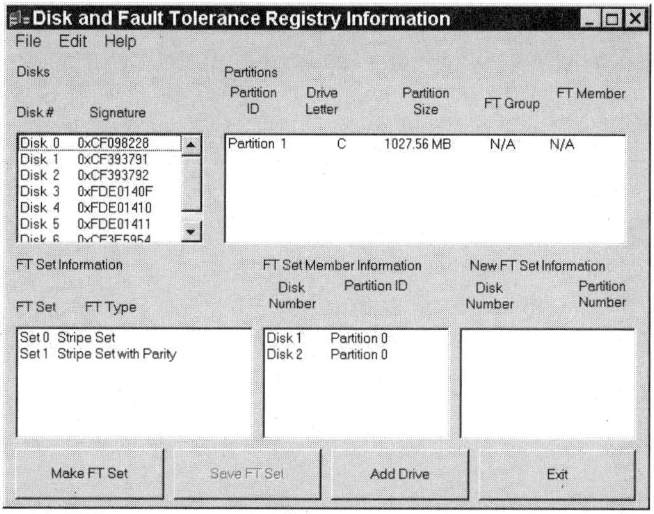

Figure 3-7.   FTEdit shows the RAID sets but in a different manner than Disk Administrator

priority. In fact, a client thread that spawns a server thread is preempted by that server thread. This was why video and printer drivers were moved to ring 0 in NT Version 4.0—to avoid unnecessary thread disruption. To optimize NT performance, the trick then is to provide separate paths for disruptive threads (threads that interrupt normal processing).

So what steps should be taken? First, place the operating system and its page file on a controller or channel by itself. Place any NT utilities and related applications on this drive. Only include applications that are not speed-sensitive.

Second, place all data and applications on a separate drive on a different controller or controller channel. For example, a convenient entry-level server would have a 2GB boot drive on channel A of an Adaptec 3940uw and all applications on a larger drive (maybe 4GB) on channel B. Because this card allows multiplexing, both channels can be active at nearly the same time. In this manner, activating the page file on channel A will not be very preemptive (destructive) to tasks on B.

Finally, place all slow devices on a separate controller. For this configuration, you can use a 3940u and put tape drives, scanners, and CD-ROMs on one channel, and devices such as a CD-R on the other channel. Setting up systems with hardware as described here can dramatically improve NT performance.

STORAGE DEVICES COMPANIES

Several companies supply storage devices, controllers, and computers that are compatible with Windows NT. Many of the computer companies use repackaged versions of the hardware RAID offerings shown on the following list in their own servers. This list includes several of the major players:

- ▼ Compaq (**http://www.compaq.com**)
- ■ Dell (**http://www.dell.com**)
- ■ Digital Equipment (**http://www.digital.com**)
- ■ Granite Digital (**http://www.scsipro.com**)
- ■ Hewlett Packard (**http://www.hp.com**)
- ▲ IBM (**http://www.ibm.com**)

Following is a list of hardware RAID controller manufacturers:

- ▼ AMI (**http://www.ami.com**)
- ■ DPT (**http://www.dpt.com**)
- ▲ Mylex (**http://www.mylex.com**)

Here are hard drive manufacturers:

- ▼ IBM (**http://www.ibm.com**)
- ■ Seagate (**http://www.seagate.com**)
- ▲ Western Digital (**http://www.wdc.com**)

SUMMARY

Decisions made in the data storage area have far-reaching consequences throughout an NT system. This chapter talked about many kinds of storage systems and their bus structures. It mentioned how newer technologies will revolutionize storage and retrieval speeds. It discussed how RAID arrays provide a layer of fault tolerance to a company's NT servers. However, the most important issue that was discussed was the fact that all of these devices eventually fail. That is why manufacturers place MTBF, MTRF, and MTDA values on their products. Storage devices will become points of failures. This entire book stresses seeking out and finding single points of failure. This chapter discussed many devices that fall into that category.

Data storage is an area where the lowest price should never be the primary concern. Most administrators would rather have a Pentium 90 server with a solid SCSI hardware RAID array than a Pentium Pro-300 with a single large EIDE drive. The bottom line is that stability in the storage systems goes a long way toward providing an NT platform that is both fault tolerant and, more importantly, recoverable.

**WINDOWS
NT**
Professional
Library

CHAPTER 4

Backing Up Data

Tape backup devices are considered a staple of any network's disaster recovery plan. They have been used for decades to back up computer data. The devices are a proven, easy-to-use technology and are reasonably cost-effective. Today, tape backup devices remain the most popular choice for small and large backup jobs. The tape devices available currently are more advanced than ever before. The speed of the tape systems has increased dramatically, and the number of media choices available to administrators has increased as well. Software used to drive the new devices with Windows NT ranges in capability from the simple (NTBackup) to the advanced (third-party vendors).

This chapter begins by presenting NT's built-in backup software, NTBackup, and showing you how to create scripts to configure NTBackup for scheduled backups. Third-party software solutions coupled with tape libraries can meet the requirements of the most demanding environments, so this chapter also outlines these. In addition, special problems associated with tape backup software, such as what to do with open files, are discussed. This chapter considers the most popular types of tape media, as well as alternatives to tape devices that offer additional versatility and features to a backup plan.

CREATING A TAPE BACKUP PLAN

Before you purchase a tape backup device, you should assess your needs and create a plan. By completing this legwork ahead of time, you can make an intelligent purchase. What's more, you end up with an operational product that meets your needs.

The following pages explain how to select and put together a backup system. You also learn the ins and outs of a disaster recovery plan for your data.

Selecting a Backup System

You have to consider several things as you select a tape backup device. You need to inventory how much data you have to back up, find out the rate at which data increases, note the times at which the backup system is in use, and take into account the relative location in terms of bandwidth distance from the tape device. These factors play an important role in determining your backup needs.

Location of Data

The location of data is an important consideration. Location is used here in terms of bandwidth distance from the tape device. If your tape device is internal to the machine that needs to be backed up, you can make use of the relatively large bandwidth of your subsystem. However, if most of your data is located remotely, you have to bring the data across the network, which means you have relatively small bandwidth to work with. Pulling large amounts of data across a network has serious implications for the available network bandwidth. On a typical 10Mb Ethernet link, expect an actual throughput of

.5MB per second (30MB/minute). If you are limited in bandwidth, consider adding additional tape drives or placing the data servers on a separate high-speed LAN segment such as 100Mb Ethernet or Fiber Distributed Data Interface (FDDI).

CAUTION: Above all, do not even consider backing up over a WAN connection. Not only will you clog the pipe, the small amount of data you get into the computer controlling the tape device is not worth the trouble.

Nature and Size of Data

The nature and size of the data drives should also be considered so you can purchase a tape system of the correct size. Look for data trends that give you an idea about what to expect in terms of drive usage in the future. For example, if a drive seems to be increasing in size at a rate of 100MB per day, you need to plan your backup strategy accordingly. You have to utilize a much larger backup system to accommodate this growth. If the capacity requirements are extensive, you may have to purchase a robotic auto-loader device or assign staff to periodically change the tape cartridges. These tasks are discussed in more detail later in the chapter.

Backup Types

Which type of backup you use is an important factor in determining capacity requirements. There are three basic methods of backing up data files:

▼   The empirical, or full backup, method

■   The partial backup method (incremental or differential)

▲   The Hierarchical Storage Management (HSM) method

EMPIRICAL METHOD   The empirical method is the traditional backup method. With this method, the entire contents of a drive are backed up file by file. Periodically, it is necessary to back up data this way, but on most occasions only a small portion of the data actually changes from the previous backup, which makes this method less than efficient.

PARTIAL BACKUP METHOD (INCREMENTAL OR DIFFERENTIAL)   Backup software can check the archive bit on each file to determine which files have never been backed up. The *archive bit* is simply a flag that can be set to on or off. When the flag is set to off, backup software recognizes that the file has been backed up and leaves it alone. In new or modified files, the archive bit is set to on, so these files are backed up the next time an incremental backup is executed. With the incremental backup method, only data that has changed since the last backup is backed up. After the incremental backup is completed, the archive bit is set to off so that backup software can tell that the file has been backed up. Of course, for an incremental backup to work, you must start with a full backup to compare the files against.

A differential backup is similar to an incremental backup except it does not affect the archive bit. With a differential backup, every file since the last full backup is backed up. In the real world, incremental backups tend to stay constant in size, whereas differential backups tend to grow in size as the time from the last full backup increases.

HIERARCHICAL STORAGE MANAGEMENT (HSM) METHOD   With the HSM method, the least-used files are stored on tape or another medium. This more sophisticated system was designed when hard drive space was expensive and tape space was inexpensive. The basic premise is that relatively unused files are transferred from hard drives to cheaper (and slower) media such as tape. HSM works well in environments in which the files that are relatively unused must still be accessed occasionally.

You are still required to have an alternative means for backing up the more accessed files on the hard drive. In fact most HSM products require that backup devices are installed. They will not even migrate a file onto the low cost media unless a file has been included in a traditional backup set. NT 5.0 offers some interesting built-in support for HSM.

FILE-BY-FILE VS. IMAGE COPY BACKUPS   There are two basic methods of creating a backup of an NT operating system, the file-by-file method and the image copy method. Most software programs use the file-by-file method whereby each file is read from the hard drive and subsequently copied to the tape. This method operates at the operating system level and is how data files are backed up in the methods outlined here.

The alternative method is to make an image copy of the disk. With this method, each cluster on the disk is copied to the tape with no regard for what is contained in the clusters. The image copy backup method operates at the level of the disk drive, not the operating system, and is thus faster than the file-by-file backup method. Typically, the entire disk must be copied to make an image.

In the past, when it came time to restore a file from the tape, image copies had to be restored in their entirety all at once to the same type of drive as the original. With today's more intelligent software, you can restore individual files within the image in the same way that you can restore individual files from file-by-file backup copies. You should be aware that some of these "intelligent" programs do not actually perform a true image backup. Be sure to read the fine print with any product that claims to run an image backup that can restore a file independent of the entire image.

Backup Time

You also need to consider the amount of time you have to back up the drives. If you are fortunate, you can find a window of time for running backups in which your systems are not in use. How "big" the window is determines the number of tape drives you need and the technologies you employ.

With 7-by-24 systems like mail and Web servers, you may have to search for a time when usage is reasonably low. In these instances, you may consider using an open file handling product like Stac's Replica or St. Bernard's Open File Manager to do online backups.

Most vendors that sell backup programs also offer plug-in software components called *agents* for extending and customizing their products so that they support online backups. For example, a typical agent might back up files that are open in another application without disrupting ongoing transactions or jeopardizing data integrity. Traditionally, open files are simply ignored during the backup process. However, open files may be mission-critical databases or e-mail communications. Unless you can back up open files, your only alternative is to shut down the database or e-mail server and cut off all users until the files are backed up, which isn't a viable proposition. Agents are specially designed to work with certain applications and back up data while the applications are still running. Backing up data this way can be a real lifesaver if your only alternative is to shut out all user activity from an application. Common agents include those for databases, e-mail applications, and Microsoft BackOffice Suite.

Selecting the Hardware

Once you know the nature of your data, you select the tape technologies that best meet your requirements. As you select the hardware, remember that you have to consider the speed of the tape systems as well as the speed of disk subsystems and the network links that the data is being moved over. On a tape device that supports compression, expect a 40 to 60 percent increase in capacity. As mentioned earlier in this chapter, expect a maximum throughput of 30MB per minute if you are pulling your data across a 10Mb Ethernet link.

For local disk drives, consider a top disk-to-tape transfer rate of 160MB per minute with Ultra SCSI configurations. If your local disks are on a RAID system, expect the maximum data rate to be around 300MB per minute. If you use one of the high-end tape systems (DLT or Mammoth) mentioned in the devices section of this chapter, expect a maximum throughput of 130MB per minute. As you can see, the speed of the tape system is extremely important. One last thing to consider is that 20 percent of the data changes on any given day. This fact becomes important if you are considering running differential or incremental backups.

Using the above assumptions, you can get a basic understanding of your requirements. For example, if you must back up 40GB of data in six hours and you want to put the data on a single tape cartridge, you will be forced to go with a Digital Linear Tape (DLT) format due to the storage requirements. The native capacity of a DLT cartridge is 35GB. With compression, you can reasonable expect up to 50GB per tape, using this formula:

35GB + (35GB × 40%) = 50GB

130MB per minute × 360 minutes (or 6 hours) = 48.6GB

This value falls within the requirements. You could also use an Exabyte Mammoth drive, but you would be required to manually change tapes or use an autoloader. Another solution would be to set up a network dump over a fast topology. In this case you would dump the data to a large hard drive and then back it up from there to a large tape capacity device tape (such as the DLT 7000 format). These systems are discussed in detail in the devices section of this chapter.

The Backup Scheme

Once you work out the details of your tape backup requirements, you have to decide on a backup scheme. Several different schemes go by several different names. By "scheme," we mean the method that you use to rotate backup tapes through your system. Most third-party tape backup offerings support automatic tape rotations and scheming. Following is a description of the most common scheme.

The most common scheme is known as the *grandfather-father-son scheme*. In this scheme, 21 tapes are used to back up data for up to 12 months. The process is quite simple. First, take twelve tapes and label each with the name of a month. Next, label four tapes with the numbers 1 through 5, with one tape for each week in the month. Finally, assuming a five day/week operation, label four tapes with the names of the first four days of the workweek.

On the first day of the scheme (assuming a calendar year), run a full backup on the first weekday tape. On each day of the week, run a differential or incremental backup. On Friday night, put in the Week 1 tape and run a full backup. On the second Monday, return the original Monday tape to the drive and run a differential backup. Repeat this procedure through the second week until Friday, when you place the Week 2 tape in the drive and run a full backup. On the following Monday, repeat the differential backups during the week and run a full backup on Friday to the Week 3 tape. Continue until the last day of the month, when you run a full backup on the January tape. Archive the January tape and set the write protection tab. Repeat this procedure every week and every month of the year.

To make the backup scheme work, you need to clean the tape drives weekly. And sticking to the scheme and analyzing your backup reports for errors is imperative if the scheme is to work. If a tape shows an error on two or more consecutive backup dates, replace it and clean the drive.

If you work the scheme correctly, you end up with day-to-day backups of the current week, week-to-week backups of the current month, and month-to-month backups of the current year. You can restore files as old as one year. Of course, at the end of the year you simply archive the month and year tapes and start again with fresh tapes.

Working Out a Disaster Recovery Plan

Although doing so isn't any fun, you should define a tape backup disaster recovery plan early on. Prioritize the most essential drives and systems to back up. Take the time to consider the minimal acceptable level of service you need to return a server. Some servers must be up and running as soon as possible, but others may be the repository for old files and so do not require the same attention.

In the case of a server that must be up and running soon, you need to be able to rebuild the server from scratch in hours. In the case of servers that hold old files, you may have the luxury of taking days to rebuild the server from files on archived tapes. In any event, a plan must be created and priorities established.

Once the disaster recovery process is in place, test it. By testing your plan, you gain insight into the backup and recovery process. If possible, use a test server or perhaps a new server to emulate the downed machine. Rebuild the system from the tapes you have created and see if you meet the minimal criteria outlined in your disaster recovery plan.

The tape backups you create should be stored in a secure, data-friendly environment. Some administrators boast about the security of their systems but keep tape backups of critical server data in a cabinet or even on a table easily accessible for others. The entire system, including user account information, is on that tape, so it should be protected and secured in the same manner as the machine that houses the data. Keeping a copy of your data off-site or in a protected area is imperative. If a disaster strikes, you won't know where it will stop. Some companies use fireproof vaults as an alternative to off-site storage. These vaults are typically kept in a secure sever room where they are safe from disasters and intruders.

NT'S BUILT-IN FEATURES

NTBackup is a simple yet powerful application that can serve many backup needs. It supports a variety of tape devices and offers important backup software options. Unfortunately, it is only marginally useful for network backups. The following pages explain how to install a tape device, back up files manually, restore files manually, recover a system from tape, and use backup scripts to automate NTBackup.

Installing a Tape Device

For NT's built-in backup software or any other tape backup software to run, you must install an NT-compatible tape device. Microsoft provides a list of tape devices that are compatible with NT. The HCL is updated frequently and can be found at **http://www. microsoft.com/hwtest**. A myriad of choices are available for serving both the ISA and SCSI bus technology. You may also download updated drivers from the site.

Once you have obtained a tape device and attached it to your computer, you install the device and load the driver for it. Both tasks are accomplished using the Tape Devices Applet in the Control Panel. You need Administrator privileges to install a tape backup device on an NT machine.

Figure 4-1 illustrates a tape device that is correctly configured. In this example, the Windows NT operating system has detected a Hewlett Packard JetStore 6000 4mm DAT drive and listed it here as the SCSI adapter card has identified it. NT can detect many types of tape devices on bootup, if they are present, and the devices are listed here. You must load the correct driver for each device. To do so, use files found on the NT installation CD-ROM or on a disk provided by the tape device vendor.

Make sure your tape device is installed and functioning correctly; otherwise, no backup software can be used. If your tape device does not appear to be operating, get information about its installation status by clicking the Properties button. You see a dialog box that lists the device's current status and offers details about the driver and firmware. An ill-configured device means wasting many hours troubleshooting backup software that does not appear to be working. A typical error produced by backup software under these conditions is "No tape device detected…" If the view of your Tape Devices window resembles that of Figure 4-1 (with your device listed with "Driver loaded" status, you are ready to use the NTBackup software.

Backing Up Files Manually

The shortcut to start NTBackup is located under Administrative Tools and is called Backup, whereas the executable is called NTBACKUP.EXE. It is located in the %SYSTEMROOT%\SYSTEM32 directory. Figure 4-2 illustrates the layout for NTBackup.

The user interface for NTBackup is a single window that contains several floating windows. Typically, the floating windows are minimized and are found at the bottom of

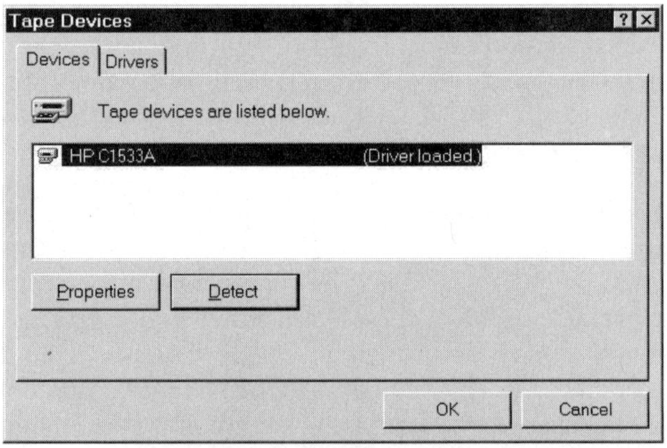

Figure 4-1. Installing and configuring a new tape device

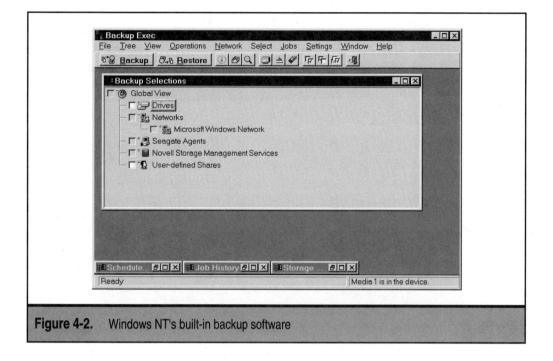

Figure 4-2.   Windows NT's built-in backup software

the NTBackup program area. The uppermost window is called Drives. This window lists the drives, either local or remote, that have been mounted by the local machine. You select files or whole drives from the Drives window for backup. If you double-click on one of the drives, another window with more details appears, as shown in Figure 4-3. In the figure, E: drive has been double-clicked and an X appears ahead of the entire drive. All files in E: drive are selected for backup. You can unclick the entire drive, subtrees, or individual files and decide for yourself which files to back up. In this manner, you proceed through all drives until only the files you want to back up are selected.

The drop-down menus can assist you in the file selection process. By choosing commands on the Tree menu, you can expand or collapse the hierarchical tree structure and see only the files you need. Similar to the tree menu, the View menu to shows varying degrees of file detail. By choosing commands on the Select menu, you can select or deselect files and directories just as you do with the mouse.

When the files you want to back up have been selected, put a tape in the drive and click the Backup button. You next see a window that prompts you to enter the details of the backup, as shown in Figure 4-4. Although most users do not routinely use all the options listed, you should know what each does because the options are powerful and have serious ramifications.

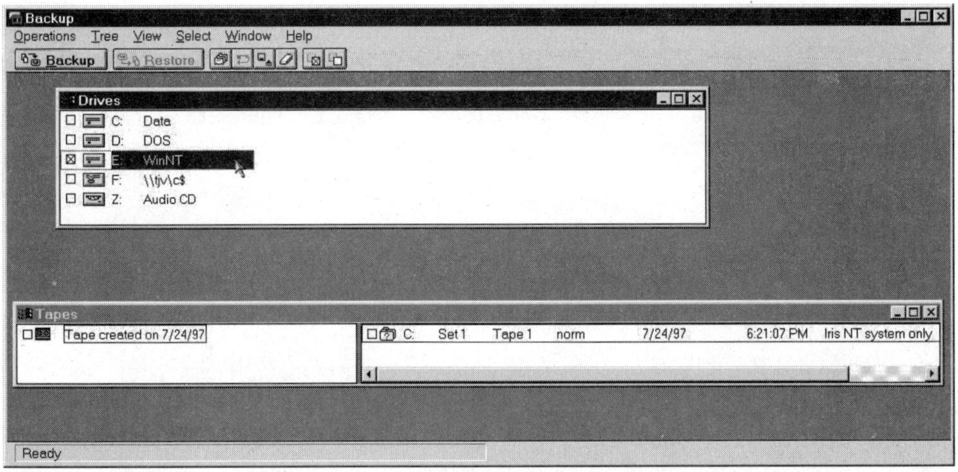

Figure 4-3.   Selecting files for backup in NTBackup

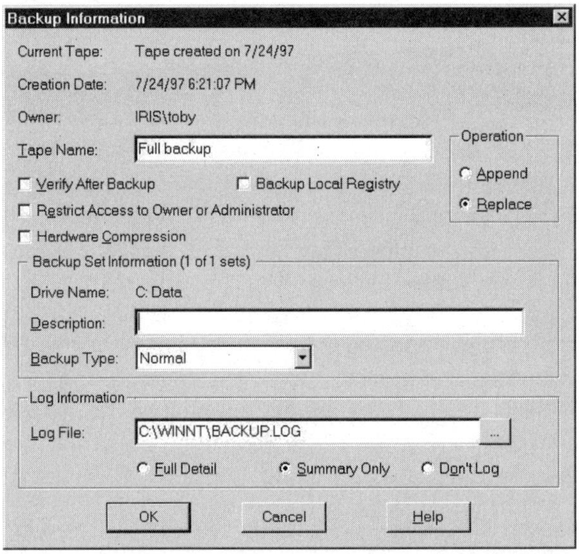

Figure 4-4.   Selecting backup parameters

Following are the backup options:

▼ **Append/Replace**   Perhaps the most important parameter is the Append or Replace option. The Append option creates a backup set that is added to the other sets on the tape; the Replace option erases all other sets and writes the backup copy to the tape.

■ **Verify After Backup**   When this box is checked, NT compares each file on the tape to the original after the backup is complete. The process naturally takes time to complete and thus should only be used when file validity is absolutely essential.

■ **Backup Local Registry**   This option is highlighted only if the drive you are backing up is the current NT system partition. Backing up the local Registry is essential if you would like to restore an NT system from tape. It is a short-coming of NTBackup that Registries on remote NT systems cannot be backed up. You can create an Emergency Repair Disk (see Chapter 2) to back up the remote registry. This disk would have to be created before each remote backup if you want to restore the entire operating system.

■ **Hardware Compression**   This option is only available if your tape device offers compression. If you plan to switch tapes among different tape drives, do not check this box because the other drives may not support the same compression algorithms. You can achieve up to 100 percent increase in capacity when this box is checked, depending on your hardware and data. Using realistic data (a mixture of text and binary files), the actual number is probably between 40 and 65 percent.

▲ **Restrict Access to Owner or Administrator**   This option allows limited security on the tape. Only the tape's owner or an administrator can read, write, or erase the tape. Remember to store your tapes in a secure location.

You are able to perform five types of backup using NTBackup. They are described in Table 4-1.

NOTE: When the archive bit property of a file is set to on, backup software backs up the file. You can see how a file's archive bit is set under File Manager or Explorer by highlighting a file and choosing Properties from the File menu.

You are given three levels of detail to choose from when you log backup information. Depending on your needs, you may not require any log files or you may require details concerning every file that is backed up. By using the Summary Only option, you can capture the name of each file that is backed up, but log files can grow to many megabytes in size even with the Summary Only option.

Backup Type	Description
Normal	All selected files are backed up; resets archive bit
Copy	All selected files are backed up; archive bit is unchanged
Differential	Backs up only selected files that have an archive bit set to on; archive bit unchanged
Incremental	Backs up only selected files that have an archive bit set to on; resets archive bit
Daily	Backs up only selected files that have been modified today; does not reset archive bit

Table 4-1.   Options for Backup Types

CAUTION: Not only can log files be cumbersome, they also can be a security risk. You probably don't want everyone to know the names, dates, and sizes of all the files on your servers. Place your log files in a secure directory by themselves so they can be quickly located, viewed, and deleted, as necessary.

When you have established the desired parameters and filled in the text boxes, simply click OK to start the backup process. The files are backed up to the tape using the Microsoft Tape Format (MTF) and can be read by software that is compatible with this format, such as Seagate BackupExec.

Dealing with Open Files with NTBackup

Many people ask about NT's native ability to back up open files. A registry value allows Windows NT to back up files that are in use: HKEY_CURRENT_USER\SOFTWARE\ MICROSOFT\NTBACKUP\BACKUP ENGINE\BACKUP files in use.

By default, the registry value is turned off and set to 0 (do not back up open files). This means NTBackup only tries to reopen a file that is in use for the normal retry interval of 30 seconds. The file must close within that window in order to be backed up. If the file is still in use after the 30 seconds, NTBackup moves on to the next file. Setting the value to 1 forces NTBackup to back up an open file regardless of its status (i.e. it will not even check for status).

Some third-party software makes this change automatically. Most of the time, making the change works fine and does not cause trouble in an NT system. However, problems have been associated with making the change. In particular, some open files are backed up in an inconsistent state and are found to be corrupt when they are restored. Having corrupted files is clearly unacceptable and making this change is not recommended.

Then how should you back up open files? You have a few options. The first and probably the best method is to close the files. Sometimes closing files is easier said than done and sometimes it is downright impossible. However, you can shut down an open file for a relatively short period of time in several different ways. We will use Microsoft Exchange Server as an example.

It is an easy task to stop Exchange services, run a copy or backup command, and restart the services all in an NT batch file. Stopping services requires knowledge of what each service does and whether or not other services depend on it to run. Stopping services that have no dependencies first is important. Otherwise, a prompt appears and tells you that other services depend on the service you want to shut down. The script pauses for user input and the application likely shuts down until you come to the rescue. Use the NET STOP and NET START command to start and stop services. Following is example code that stops all Exchange services:

```
net stop MSExchangeMSMI /Y
net stop MSExchangePCMTA /Y
net stop MSExchangeFB /Y
net stop MSExchangeDX /Y
net stop MSExchangeIMC /Y
net stop MSExchangeMTA /Y
net stop MSExchangeIS /Y
net stop MSExchangeDS /Y
net stop MSExchangeSA /Y
```

You would next insert your backup command. Because all services are stopped, the files should be available for exclusive-read access. Another procedure you can use is to quickly copy the open files to another location and allow the backup job to back them up from there. In the case of Exchange, the database files (*.EDB) may be too large for this to be practical. Ether way, the process is reversed to start the services back up:

```
net start MSExchangeSA
net start MSExchangeDS
net start MSExchangeIS
net start MSExchangeMTA
net start MSExchangeIMC
net start MSExchangeDX
net start MSExchangeFB
net start MSExchangePCMTA
net start MSExchangeMSMI
```

These commands allow you to back up Microsoft Exchange. However you can easily modify them so that they start and stop other services that control software. Be sure to test scripts at the command line first before scheduling them to run on their own.

A second way to back up open files is to wait for Microsoft to add the support to NTBackup. Microsoft did just this in the case of Exchange Server. When Exchange server is added to a Windows NT Server machine, it updates the NTBackup program with a new feature that allows you to back up Exchange's message stores while the system is online.

The third method of backing up open files is to use a third-party product such as Stac's Replica or Open File Manager (OFM) by St. Bernard Software. OFM works wonderfully in conjunction with NTBackup. These products are discussed in later in this chapter.

Restoring Files Manually

Let's say you created a backup and now you want to retrieve a file, a directory, or an entire drive (restoring the Microsoft Windows NT operating system is not discussed here, as that topic is covered in the next section of this book). Assuming that the cartridge is in the tape device, open the Tapes window (this window is usually minimized and found at the bottom of the NTBackup program area). Inside the Tapes window is information pertaining to the header of the current tape. Double-clicking on the description of the tape causes the catalog on the tape to be read and printed to the screen, a process that can take several minutes, as the tape may have to be repositioned.

Once the catalog has been read, another window appears to show the directory structure of the drive that was backed up. Selecting the files that you want to restore is done the same way as selecting the files that you want to back up—click on the boxes in front of the directories or files. You may also use the Tree, View, or Select menus. When the files are selected, click the Restore button. You see another window with restoring options, as shown in Figure 4-5.

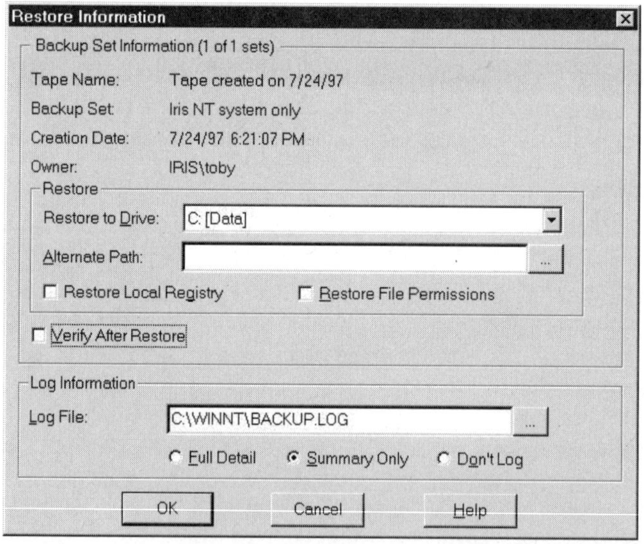

Figure 4-5. Restoring files using NTBackup

The options include choosing a location to restore the files. If you intend to restore network files to their initial location, make sure that the original network connections are reestablished. Unless another drive or alternative location is selected, the files are placed in the locations from which they were backed up originally. Of course, restoring files overwrites the files currently on the drive.

Following are descriptions of the other location options:

▼ **Restore Local Registry**   Choosing this option is essential for restoring a damaged NT system. (This option is only available if the backup set includes a Registry from an NT system.)

■ **Restore File Permissions**   Choose this option if the file system was NTFS and you want to restore the original permissions. This will not work if the system to which you are restoring the files does not have the same users as the original system.

▲ **Verify After Restore**   This option is similar to the same option in the backup process. NTBackup checks each file against the tape after all files have been restored, a time-consuming process that almost doubles the restore time. Choosing this option is worthwhile if data integrity is paramount and you cannot test data integrity by other means.

The criteria for choosing the level of logging information is the same as for the restoration process and the backup process. Detailed log files are obviously more informative but are also much larger.

Recovering a System from Tape

Restoring drives containing a Windows NT operating system requires more work than just retrieving files on a tape, mainly because you are required to overwrite the operating system's registry files during the restore. Obviously, overwriting the registry files would fail without some additional intervention. If the drive you want to restore was local to the NT system that created the backup and you backed up that system's Registry to the tape, you can completely recover the machine.

NOTE: Remember that the Registry is not backed up by default with NTBackup. You must have checked the Backup Local Registry option when you ran the backup. You can check for registry files on the tape by cataloging it and looking for the following SYSTEM, SOFTWARE, SAM, and SECURITY files in the %SYSTEMROOT%\SYSTEM32\CONFIG DIRECTORY. If they do not exist, the registry was not backed up onto the tape. You will have to reinstall all of the original systems applications and change your system information manually.

Following are four methods for recovering a system from tape.

Method 1: Using a Parallel NT Installation

Using a parallel NT installation is the most convenient and solid way to recover a downed NT system. Use this method after you have replaced the drive that houses the

NT system files or when you want to completely restore an NT system to a backed up copy:

1. Install NT into a temporary directory (i.e. C:\NT-TEMP).
2. Install the tape device drivers on the temporary copy.
3. Run NTBackup and open up the Tapes window.
4. Catalog the tape and select the directories to be restored.
5. Select Restore.
6. Enter the restore information and select OK. Be sure *not* to select the Restore Local Registry check box.
7. Modify the C:\BOOT.INI file to include the restored copy of NT.
8. Restart the system and your original configuration is restored.

NOTE: One common practice that can make this process easier is to have two drives with separate copies of NT on each one. If one drive fails you simply use a boot floppy to point to the other drive and restore following the steps above.

Method 2: Overwriting an Existing NT Installation

Overwrite an existing NT installation when you want to roll back an existing NT installation from a good backup. First, you must restore the Registry and then the remaining NT files.

1. Run NTBackup and open up the Tapes window.
2. Catalog the tape.
3. Select %SYSTEMROOT%\SYSTEM32\CONFIG directory to be restored.
4. Choose Restore.
5. In the Restore dialog box, select the Restore Local Registry check box and click OK.
6. When the restore is complete, quit NTBackup and restart NT.
7. Restart NTBackup and select the Tapes window.
8. Catalog the tape and select all directories necessary to restore NT.
9. Select Restore.
10. Enter the restore information and click OK. Be sure that you do not select the Restore Local Registry check box.
11. Restart the system and your original configuration will be restored.

Method 3: Installing to a Remote Drive

If the drive you want to restore contains an NT system and was a remote drive, an emergency repair disk is required to return the system to its previous state. The repair disk is needed because NTBackup does not support remote registry backups. First restore the operating system files and directories:

1. Install NT into a temporary directory (i.e. C:\NT-TEMP).
2. Install the tape device drivers on this temporary copy.
3. Run NTBackup and open up the Tapes window.
4. Catalog the tape and select the directories to be restored.
5. Select Restore.
6. Enter the restore information and select OK.
7. Modify the C:\BOOT.INI file to include the restored copy of NT.

Now you need to recover the registry files from an emergency repair disk:

1. Insert the first NT installation disk into the floppy drive and restart the system.
2. When prompted, choose to repair the NT installation and click OK.
3. When prompted, insert the emergency repair disk.
4. Select Inspect Registry Files and continue.
5. When the program presents you with a list of Registry keys that the system can restore, select all of them.
6. When the program has successfully restored the Registry, reboot your system.

NOTE: This method assumes a relatively small SAM on the machine. Remember that an Emergency Repair Disk does may not always repair all of your registry. If the registry is over 1.44M (the size of the floppy) you will not be able to use this method. The Emergency Repair Disk must be created with the RDISK /S parameter.

Method 4: Recovering a System to a Different Hardware Configuration

The previous solutions work for restoring an NT system to a hardware configuration that is the same as the original, but sometimes you have to restore an NT system to a computer that is not identical to the original. In this situation, special steps are required to erase the hardware configuration files but still maintain the files that control other aspects of the system, such as files that control users and network functionality. Follow these steps:

1. When configuring the new system, set the drive partition information to that of the original system. Start by setting up all partitions to the FAT type. You can convert them later to NTFS by using the "convert" utility, as explained below.
2. Install Windows NT onto the primary FAT partition and use the same computer name and domain name as the original computer.
3. Once the NT system is up and running, install the tape device drivers.
4. Run NTBackup and open up the Tapes window.

5. Catalog the tape.

6. Create a directory off the root and give it a temporary name (C:\NT-TEMP).

7. From the backup set, copy the registry files (%SYSTEMROOT%\ SYSTEM32\CONFIG directory) to C:\NT-TEMP.

8. Delete the SYSTEM.* and *.EVT files from C:\NT-TEMP. You have now copied the configuration information from your downed system into a temporary directory on your new system. Deleting the SYSTEM.* and *.EVI files removes the hardware-specific information from these files.

9. Boot to DOS and copy the remaining files from C:\NT-TEMP to the %SYSTEMROOT%\SYSTEM32\CONFIG directory for the current Windows NT installation. This is done from DOS because SAM or Security hives of the registry cannot be replaced while NT is running.

10. After the machine is restarted, NT should come up with restored user accounts and configuration files in place.

11. At this point, you should convert drive partitions over to NTFS if they were NTFS in the original system. To use the "convert" utility, type the following at the command prompt: **convert** *<drive letter>* **fs:ntfs**. Reboot the machine so that the conversion can take place.

12. Restore user data and applications from the tape backup as required.

NOTE: If you use TCP/IP with DHCP and/or WINS, restore the %SYSTEMROOT%\ SYSTEM32\DHCP and the %SYSTEMROOT%\SYSTEM32\WINS directories from the backup tape, although it may be necessary to reestablish the DHCP scope. You can also restore the %SYSTEMROOT%\SYSTEM32\ SPOOL and %SYSTEMROOT%\SYSTEM32\REPL directories if you were using TCP/IP printing. Unfortunately, printer queues have to be re-created and IP addresses reassigned.

Using Backup Scripts to Automate NTBackup

Using the GUI for NTBackup, as described above, is easy and straightforward. However, the limitations of the manual backup process are obvious. For example, suppose you need to back up many file systems at regular intervals or back up files in the middle of the night. Fortunately, NTBackup supports the command line mode. In addition, Windows NT comes with a scheduling solution—the AT Command Scheduler. The AT command is a command line program that allows you to schedule the execution of programs or batch files at regular intervals. If you prefer a GUI interface, the Command Scheduler (WinAT) is provided with the NT Resource Kit. Both of these tools are covered in this section.

To automate the backup of drives, a script (batch file) is required. The script contains commands to mount necessary network drives as well as NTBackup commands that instruct NTBackup to add each drive to a tape backup. The NT Command Scheduler is then used to designate when the scripts run. By using these tools, you can perform unattended, scheduled backups of any network drive to which you can connect, including shared drives on Windows 95, Windows 3.11 machines, and NT systems.

The following pages explain the things you must do to prepare to write the script, how to create the backup script, and how to schedule the script.

Preparing to Write a Script

The same requirements must be met to run NTBackup from commands in a script as must be met to back up drives manually. The account must have Administrator privileges and a tape backup device must be installed on the NT machine on which the backup script will be run.

The script is a simple list of commands that are sent to the NT system to connect with (i.e. map to) a remote drive, back up the mapped drive, and disconnect from the mapped drive. Here is the basic plan:

1. Map or mount a remote drive on an NT, Win95, or Win 3.11 machine or other supported system by using the **net use** command.

2. Use the NTBackup command parameters to back up the mounted drive to tape.

3. Use the **net use** command again to unmount this connection.

Make sure that you can map shared drives on the machines you want to back up. In a workgroup environment, in which every system has a separate user database, you must have an account with sufficient privileges on each machine. Creating an account for the sole purpose of backing up the systems is usually a good idea. Give this user a name, such as Backer, and assign it to the Users and Backup Operator groups only. If you are working in a domain environment, create a user on a domain controller with the group settings mentioned previously, and use this account to connect to all shared drives.

Many problems associated with permissions can be avoided simply by checking to make sure that the user who will be used to map to the drives has sufficient privileges. An easy way to test whether a user has sufficient privileges is to try to connect to the shared drive under File Manager while substituting the new user in the Connect As box in the Connect Network Drive menu option. If you receive the "Network path was not found" error, the share is unreachable and you need to verify that the share is present. If you receive the "Access denied" error, you probably don't have sufficient privileges. To correct this at the share, include access to the user who was created to conduct the backup operations.

Another important consideration is the question of where to keep the log files. Log files should be placed in a secure location on the server that is doing the backup. For instance, place the log files in a directory called LOGFILES in a subdirectory of the NT system directory. If you choose to store the log files on a network drive, make sure that your connection will be stable for the duration of the backup.

It is now time to organize a list of the names of machines that will be backed up, the share names on those systems, and the passwords required to connect to those systems or drives. Different types of Windows systems require different pieces of information to mount their shares. Table 4-2 lists those requirements. Again, remember to check whether you can connect to the shared drives and whether you have authority to back up all appropriate files.

Creating the Backup Script

It is now time to create the actual scripts. The following list shows the commands for a sample backup script (BACKUP.BAT). The script can be written using any text editor.

The sample script includes *net send* messages at the beginning and the end to let the operator know that the script started and ended successfully. By default, the messages also include the times that the system sent the messages. Because these times correspond to the start and end times of the script, it is easy to calculate how long the entire script took to run.

The script follows a basic format. First, a connection is made to a shared drive on a remote NT machine and a drive letter is assigned. Next, the NTBackup command is used to copy the contents of the drive to tape. When NTBackup has finished copying the drive, the drive mappings are deleted (i.e., by disconnecting from the share) and the process moves to the next shared drive. In this way, all shared drives are backed up sequentially. NT adds each shared drive's contents (i.e., backup set) in turn to the backup tape, and each backup set has a section in the backup log.

Following is a sample network backup script:

1. net send <operator> backup started

2. rem The next line backs up the local C drive.

	Required to Mount	Permissions Set At
Win 3.11	Share password	Win 3.11 machine
Win 95	Share password	Win 95 machine
NT FAT	User permissions to access share	User rights on NT FAT system if using workgroup, or user rights on PDC if using domain model
NT NTFS	User permissions to access share and user permissions to access files in the share	User rights on NT NTFS system if using workgroup, or user rights on PDC if using domain model

Table 4-2.   Required Information to Mount Shared Drives in Different Environments

3. NTBACKUP BACKUP C: /D "COMMENT HERE"/B/HC:ON/T NORMAL/L "%WINDIR%\ LOGFILES\BACKUP.LOG"/TAPE:0

4. rem The next line mounts and backs up a shared drive on a remote NT system

5. NET USE X: \\<WORKSTATION>\<SHARENAME> <PASSWORD> /USER:<DOMAINNAME>\BACKER

6. NTBACKUP BACKUP X: /A/D "COMMENT HERE"/HC:ON/T NORMAL/L "%WINDIR%\ LOGFILES\BACKUP.LOG"/TAPE:0

7. NET USE X: /DELETE

8. rem The next line mounts and backs up a share on a Win 3.11 machine.

9. NET USE X: \\<WIN3.11MACHINE>\<SHARENAME> <PASSWORD>

10. NTBACKUP BACKUP X: /A/D "COMMENT HERE"/HC:ON/T NORMAL/L "%WINDIR%\ LOGFILES\BACKUP.LOG"/TAPE:0

11. NET USE X: /DELETE

12. rem The next line mounts and backs up a share on a Win 95 machine.

13. NET USE X: \\<WIN95MACHINE>\<SHARENAME> <PASSWORD>

14. NTBACKUP BACKUP X: /A/D "COMMENT HERE"/HC:ON/T NORMAL/L "%WINDIR%\ LOGFILES\BACKUP.LOG"/TAPE:0

15. NET USE X: /DELETE

16. net send user Backup Finished

NOTE: For NT shares, a user name and a password must be supplied for a user that has sufficient privileges; for Win 3.11 and Win95 shares, only the password for the share is required.

The first line sends the user a message saying that the backup has started. The second line and all subsequent lines beginning with *rem* are not executed and serve only as remarks. The first real backup command, found in line 3, tells the system to perform several tasks: back up the local C: drive, include a comment (/D), include the local Registry in the backup (/B), use hardware compression (/HC:ON), perform a particular backup type (/T), write the results to a log file called BACKUP.LOG (/L), and designate which tape drive you want to use (/TAPE). You set the /tape switch to 0 to indicate that you're using the first tape drive installed. A value of 1 indicates the second tape drive, 2 the third, and so forth. Note that the /T switch can be followed by *normal*, *copy*, *incremental*, *differential*, or *daily*, depending on the type of backup you want to do (see Table 4-2). You can obtain more information about the switches for the NTBackup command by entering **NTBACKUP /?** at the command prompt.

Notice also that the full path to the log file is included starting with the environmental variable %WINDIR%. This variable lets the script be used on other machines with little modification.

Lines 5 through 7 tell the system to back up a network shared drive on an NT system. First, you connect to the share and assign it a local drive letter (X in this case). In this line, you used the authority of user Backer in domain *domainname* to connect a share on a workstation. You must include this user's password in the script. Because the program saves this script as ASCII text and anyone with sufficient privileges can read the script, a security risk exists. This risk is one reason to create a user with limited authority simply for the purpose of backing up shares.

Next, the script issues an NTBackup command to back up the X: drive. This line differs from the previous backup command (line 3) in two ways. First, NT appends this backup set to the previous one (/A) so that the previous backup sets aren't erased. Second, this line has no /B switch that tells the program to include the Registry with the backup. The current version of NTBackup lets you back up the Registry of the local machine only. To safely back up the Registry, including the user database (/S), a repair disk must be made at the console for each machine. Of course, the same emergency repair disk can be used (see Chapter 2) for identically configured systems. The disk is required if you have to restore a network drive that contained a functional NT system.

The number of shares that are backed up could easily exceed the number of available drive letters on the system, so always disconnect the share after they have been backed up. Doing so cleanly terminates the session with the network share and lets the drive letter be reused. The following command disconnects the share and frees the X drive letter:

NET USE X: /DELETE /Y

The sample script also includes commands (lines 9-11) for backing up a share that resides on a Windows 3.11 machine or a Win95 machine (lines 13-15). These systems need not be in a workgroup or domain, although its name must be able to be resolved with the Universal Naming Convention (UNC) (e.g., you must be able to access them by using *computername* in the script). Assuming that a password protects the shared drive, connect to the share by executing the command in line 11 or 13. These statements do not include usernames because only passwords, not user authorization, protect Win 3.11 and Win95 shares. However, the command to back up the share is the same as that used for the NT workstation. The NET USE X:/DELETE command disconnects the share.

NTBackup includes two useful arguments for tape management, although they cannot be used in batch files because they require user input. The first is the /NOPOLL argument. It is used to erase a tape regardless of what its contents are. The /NOPOLL argument should be used carefully and without other arguments:

NTBACKUP /NOPOLL

The second useful argument is used to tell NTBackup that the backup spanned several tapes and one or more have been lost. Typically, losing a tape in a series renders the set useless. With the /MISSINGTAPE argument, the files on each tape are made accessible. Again, no other arguments are used:

NTBACKUP /MISSINGTAPE

The NT Resource Kit includes commands that let a script pause in its execution or pause for user input. The SLEEP command simply pauses the script for a set amount of seconds, as in this example, in which the script pauses for one minute:

SLEEP 60

The TIMEOUT command is slightly different. It pauses the script for a given amount of seconds, although a user can press any key to bypass the delay. A text line is displayed on the command window that shows the remaining seconds before the script will resume. For example, to pause the script for ten minutes unless the user presses any key, use this command:

TIMEOUT 600

Scheduling the Script

Now the backup script for automated network backup should be tested by entering the commands one line at a time at the command prompt. If the commands execute as planned, run the entire script from the command prompt by entering the script name. If the script works as intended, then it can be scheduled to run automatically using either the Command Scheduler or the AT command. The Command Scheduler (WinAT) is a graphical interface for the AT command. The basic AT command isn't as elegant, but it is just as useful for all of your scheduling requirements. In either case, by default only Administrators can submit commands with these utilities.

To use either the Command Scheduler or the AT command, start the Scheduler service from Control Panel, Services. You need Administrator privileges to start this service. Note, however, that AT jobs don't run under the security context of the user who requests the job. Rather, they use the security context of the Schedule service, which is typically in the context of the operating system. If your batch file seems to work as intended when you run it from the command line but fails when it is scheduled, you most likely did not give sufficient privileges to the users you placed in the script to act on your behalf. Also make sure you set the startup mode of the Scheduler to Automatic so your scheduled jobs will survive a system restart.

As mentioned, the NT Resource Kit includes the Command Scheduler in the Configuration menu. Once this program is started, it asks whether you want to start the Scheduler service if the service isn't already started. Answer yes, and then select Edit | Add to schedule your new script. You see a window similar to Figure 4-6. Enter your script filename (use the full path if the script isn't in a directory listed in the path variable) and parameters that describe when you want it to run. Check the Interactive box only if you want to require a user to enter information during the script execution. For example, you may wish to run in Interactive mode if your data will not fit on one tape. In this situation or others that require user input, you must run the script in Interactive mode or the NTBackup process will hang and you'll have to reboot and restart the script.

After you click OK, you see the Command Scheduler window shown in Figure 4-7. It lists AT jobs, including your script file with the appropriate times. If an error appears in

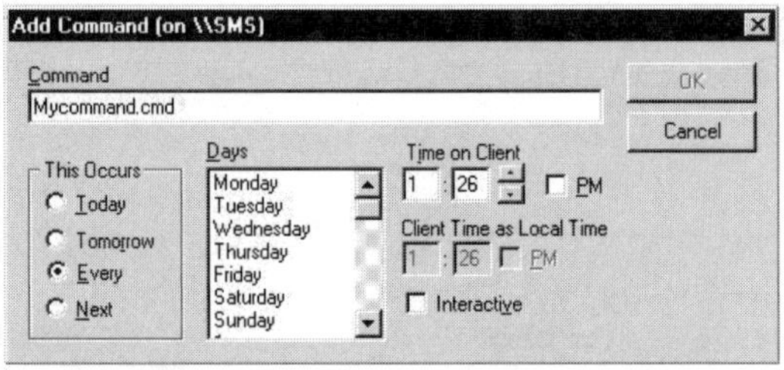

Figure 4-6. Scheduling a batch file in the Command Scheduler

the Error column after the time scheduled for your AT job to execute, make sure you've placed the script file in a directory listed in the path, or provide the full path to the script file. When you're sure the scheduling information is correct, simply close the Command Scheduler. Your script file is ready to go. If the script tries to connect to a share on a machine that is turned off or otherwise debilitated, the script will skip this command, move to the next one, and back up other shares.

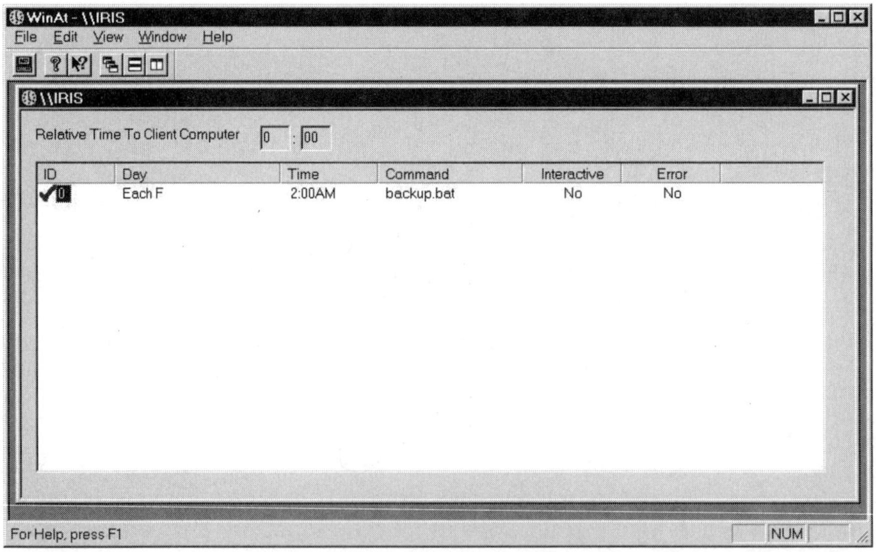

Figure 4-7. Command Scheduler showing a batch file that is correctly configured

If you don't have the Resource Kit, you can still use the AT command to schedule the backup script. Enter AT /? at the command prompt to learn more about the AT command's switches and arguments. At the command line enter a line similar to the following:

AT \\<MACHINENAME> 2:00 /EVERY:FRIDAY "BACKUP.BAT"

This command schedules the script file for the same settings you used for the Command Scheduler.

Although writing a script and using the AT command or Command Scheduler meets many backup requirements, it is not perfect. One of the most obvious shortcomings is the inability to back up Registries on remote systems. In addition, although NTBackup supports hardware compression, it does not support software compression, which would presumably enhance storage capacity. Another pitfall is that all shares you back up must fit on one tape; otherwise you must manually change tapes, which defeats the purpose of an unattended, scheduled backup. These limitations are addressed by commercial software packages, the topic of the next section of this chapter.

THIRD-PARTY SOFTWARE

When your backup demands exceed the abilities of NTBackup, you should consider third-party software. Perhaps you require more speed or flexibility. Perhaps you have special applications such as an e-mail server that requires an agent to back up its files while it is running. Whatever your needs, you ought to consider the special issues that relate to tape backups before purchasing third-party software.

The following pages explore three third-party software alternatives to NTBackup: Cheyenne ARCserve, Backup Exec, and Replica.

Cheyenne ARCserve

Cheyenne (a Computer Associates Company) promotes its ARCserve backup software as a data-management software solution. ARCserve can back up and restore all Windows NT file systems, including NTFS (NT File System), HPFS (High Performance File System), and FAT (File Allocation Table). The software can perform a full or partial backup and restore of the Registry as well. Not only does ARCserve back up and restore data across the wire in a Windows NT domain, it offers advanced capabilities such as centralized administration, remote management, and intelligent alert notification. It also supports tape-drive RAID, virus scanning, image backups and restores, file pruning, and automatic backup scheming. To match the needs of users' NT environments, ARCserve comes in three different levels of capability: Enterprise, Single Server, and Workstation.

You probably want to consider the Single Server and Enterprise editions, as the Workstation edition is made for stand-alone systems and offers little that can't be done with NTBackup. The other two editions install on NT Server or Workstation, although only the Enterprise version backs up remote systems and supports all of the client agents offered by Cheyenne. The Single Server edition supports only Windows 3.11, Windows 95, and Windows NT workstation client agents. The Enterprise edition adds clients for OS/2, Macintosh, UNIX, and NetWare.

One look at ARCserve's GUI and you realize that ARCserve is a serious backup program. Regardless of which edition you choose, you get an abundance of features and tools. The GUI is comprised of separate tabbed windows for every aspect of the program. For instance, there are separate windows for backup, restore, job queue, devices, databases, and reports. You can open as many of these windows as space on your screen allows. Figure 4-8 shows the backup and report windows open in the program area. Because each window pertains to a specific function of the program, the windows are not cluttered with countless options as a way to keep things organized and easier conceptually to operate.

ARCserve employs what it calls "client agents" and "application agents." Client agents are small executables that run on remote machines so that ARCserve can back up data on remote machines without having to make a direct network connection to the machine. By using a client, backup speed and performance is enhanced and you can back up the security properties of files.

Application agents extend the capabilities of ARCserve. One example is the Backup Agent for Open Files, an open file manager agent that works with ARCserve to back up

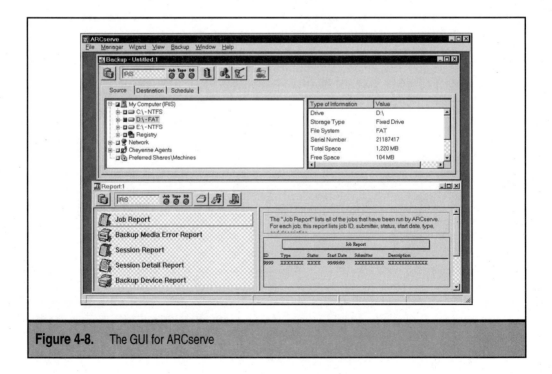

Figure 4-8. The GUI for ARCserve

all open files, even files that are locked or opened in deny read or write mode by another application. The BackOffice agents allow you to back up Microsoft SQL Server and Microsoft Exchange Server online while those applications are running. Other application agents support Lotus Notes and Oracle Server.

ARCserve also provides centralized management of ARCserve host servers so you can manage host machines from another NT system. If you use the manager, you can control and monitor all ARCserve activities in the enterprise, including initiating backup/restore jobs and viewing the real-time status of each job. Administrative functions are even accessible from remote locations via Remote Access Services (RAS). If you prefer, you can bypass the GUI altogether and schedule backup and copy operations through the command line.

In the event of full system disaster, you want to get your server up and functioning in the shortest time possible. ARCserve has addressed this need with the Disaster Recovery agent. Before disaster strikes, you use the Disaster Recovery wizard to create several diskettes. Using the diskettes, ARCserve can restore the server quickly without installing the operating system first, as long as you created a backup tape of the hard drive *image*. If you made a file-by-file copy of the system, you need the recovery disks, the NT installation CD, and your last full backup tape to completely restore your system.

Backup Exec

Seagate designed the first backup solution that was built into NT and still maintains 100 percent Microsoft Tape Format (MTF) compatibility. In fact, you can use NTBackup to read a tape that was backed up with Backup Exec as long as compression was not used. Seagate has since made a more comprehensive backup program called Backup Exec, now in its fifth generation. Backup Exec, like its predecessor NTBackup, shares a similar user interface and is closely tied to the NT operating system. The GUI resembles the NTBackup interface—it uses the same floating windows for tapes and drives; however, the Backup Exec GUI has more menus for controlling features such as network connections and scheduling, as Figure 4-9 shows. As the developer of the Microsoft Exchange Server and Windows NT versions of NTBackup, Seagate can boast 100 percent compatibility with Microsoft BackOffice.

Similar to ARCserve, Backup Exec offers central management, including 24-hour network-wide scheduling, administration, monitoring, and device and media management. Some of the more advanced features of the centralized management include dynamic load balancing, drive cascading, fault-tolerant processing, media overwrite protection, and maximizing backup performance with drive pooling. Users can generate predefined or user-defined reports with Crystal Reports, a reporting tool found throughout the Microsoft product line. Like ARCserve, Seagate incorporates agents for performance optimization at the client level and a Disaster Recovery agent that minimizes recovery time. Agents for SQL Server and NetWare are two of many widely available agents.

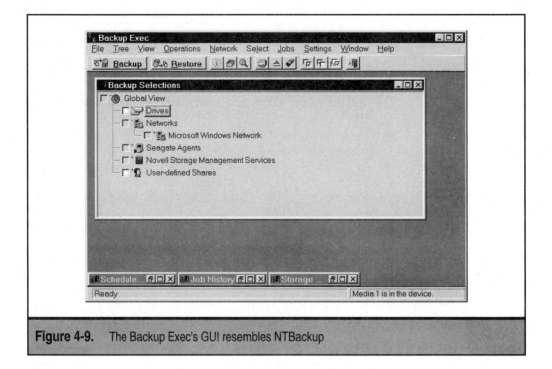

Figure 4-9. The Backup Exec's GUI resembles NTBackup

Replica

Stac's Replica has been providing service for NetWare servers for many years. Now Stac offers an NT version. Replica is different from the more traditional file-by-file backup programs in that it copies the entire disk image, including the boot volume, disk partitions, the NT Registry, the NT operating system, and all data as well as open files. Because you can recover your system from the tape without having to manually rebuild disk partitions or reinstall NT, restoring the system is quick and easy. To create your disaster recovery disks, you modify a copy of the NT installation disks and store the information on one additional floppy. You use these disks to get the system up, then feed the image copy of the disk to the system, and be on your way. An average 2GB server downtime is reduced from about ten hours to around two hours.

Replica uses a technology called *instant volume replication* to capture the entire disk volume at one instance in time. The technology saves you from having to resynchronize files and rebuild servers after a crash. Replica captures the volume at a single instance by flushing the server cache. It steps in and captures the volume directory information and then replicates the volume to tape. No matter how long the replication process takes, the tape backup consists of a copy of the volume at the instant the replication began.

Previously, using image copies meant that, to retrieve a single file, you had to restore the *entire* image to a disk that was identical to the original. Replica includes Direct Media Access, a feature that mounts tapes as NT volumes. Users can recover their own individual files by using File Manager or Explorer to connect to the Replica tape and mount their own drives. Because all security objects (NT Registry and ACLs) are replicated, users can only see the files to which they had access on the original volume.

Replica's GUI is light on menus and heavy on buttons that call up floating windows. These buttons cover major program areas such as duplication, recovery, and utilities. Each window is tabular in design for compact, intuitive control over the program, as shown in Figure 4-10.

To keep users informed of latest revisions and other news, Replica has built in a connection to their servers. You tell Replica how often you want to connect to Stac's Internet Central and only news you haven't seen yet is pushed to your desktop.

For more information about these products, connect to the following Web sites:

Cheyenne—ARCserve	**http:\\www.cheyenne.com**
Seagate—Backup Exec	**http:\\www.seagatesoftware.com**
Stac—Replica	**http:\\www.stac.com**

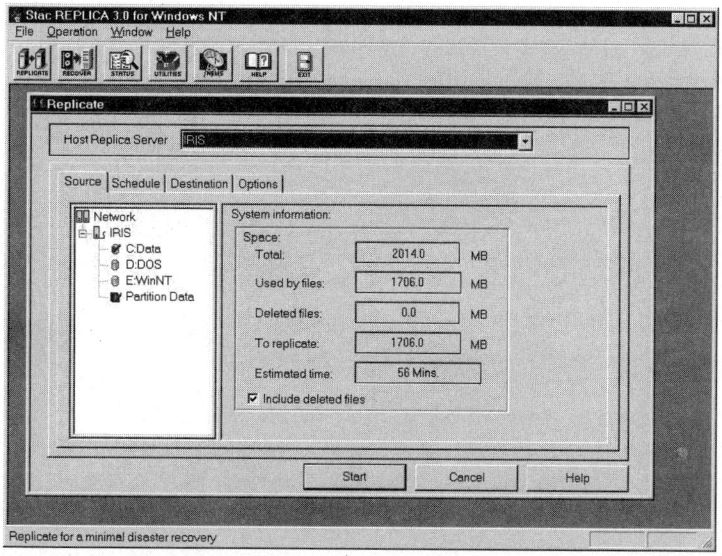

Figure 4-10. Replica's GUI is button-rich and tabular in design

In addition to the software discussed in this section, there are several other vendors of backup related software for NT. They include the following:

Legato Systems—Networker	**http:\\www.legato.com**
High Ground Systems—Media Mirror	**http:\\www.highground.com**
St. Bernard Software—Open File Manager	**http:\\www.stbernard.com**
Software Moguls—SM-arch	**http:\\www.moguls.com**
Barratt Edwards—UltraBac	**http:\\www.bei.co.uk**
Yosemite Technologies—Tapeware	**http:\\www.tapeware.com**
Columbia Data Products—SNAPBACK!	**http:\\www.cdp.com**
IBM—ADSTAR Distributed Storage Manager	**http:\\www.ibm.com**

HARDWARE OPTIONS

Almost as many hardware options are available for tape backups as are available for computer systems and networks. Although machines differ in media type and format, the main differences have to do with data transfer speeds, total storage size, and cost. Naturally, you pay more for a 250GB tape library than you do a simple 4mm DAT drive. At present DAT drives hover around $1000, whereas a basic 8mm drive costs slightly more. In the pages that follow is an overview of popular media types and the advantages and disadvantages of each one.

As more and more users work remotely, and given the fact that many corporations maintain offices in different time zones, servers are being used at all hours, not just between 8:00 and 5:00. Therefore, you need a backup solution that can deal efficiently with open files and applications that cannot be brought down. The backup solution you choose must put the data to the tape as quickly as possible. Because downtime caused by a crashed server can be very costly, you need a backup solution that can restore a system to a usable state in short order.

Tape Formats

There are a large variety of tape formats available for use with Windows NT. The following pages explain the advantages and disadvantages of the most prominent formats on the market: 4mm Digital Audio Tape (DAT), Digital Linear Tape (DLT), 8mm tape format, and Advanced Intelligent Tape (AIT).

4mm Digital Audiotape (DAT)

The 4mm Digital Audiotape (DAT) format is one of the most widely used formats. It has been around a long while and been accepted the longest. It now comes in three flavors: DDS-1, DDS-2, and DDS-3.

The DDS-1 format offered only 2GB of capacity. When the DDS-2 tapes came out, it seemed impossible to fill the 8GB of native storage space that the tapes offered. Today, with the DDS-3 technology, a single tape can hold up to 12GB (up to 24GB with compression) of data and tape drives can transfer data at a rate of 2.4 MB/sec using a Fast-Wide SCSI-2 interface. DDS-3 technology is still the favorite for systems that have a total backup demand that is less than the capacity of the tape, which makes changing the tape manually unnecessary.

One disadvantage of the 4mm DAT format is the limited life span. Although the format fully supports several hundred backups, the header on the tape gets read at every backup operation. A quick read of one small file wears the tape as much as a full backup because the header receives the same amount of wear in each case. The tape header presents the most likely point of failure for this format.

Digital Linear Tape (DLT)

Quantum introduced the Digital Linear Tape (DLT) format to compete against 4mm DAT drives. DLT uses a half-inch tape and has proven faster and more reliable than the DAT format. Each tape can store between 15 and 35GB (30/70GB compressed) and DLT drives support data rates up to 5MB/sec. Traditional DAT technology stores data in diagonal stripes along the tape, using helical scan technology. DLT places information along the horizontal surface of the tape in tracks. This technology records data by running the tape past a stationary head at 100 to 150 inches per second, whereas helical scan technology records the diagonal stripes using a rotation drumhead.

DLT delivers performance advantages over DAT systems because it records and reads multiple channels simultaneously. Although the helical scan technology increases capacity, it is not suited for quickly reading or writing to tape. To increase performance and total capacity, libraries exist that support multiple drives and hundreds of tapes.

8mm Tape Format

Exabyte introduced the 8mm tape format and promoted it as a larger and faster alternative to the 4mm format. It caught on quickly, especially with UNIX systems, and has dominated the upper end of the tape device market. The latest incarnation of the Exabyte 8mm format is called the Exabyte Mammoth. The format uses Sony's AME tapes to enhance reliability and capacity. One of the biggest advantages of the Mammoth system is that it is backward-compatible with all Exabyte 8mm tapes, which represent most of the 8mm tape drives in use. Another advantage is its capacity. The Mammoth is capable of fitting 40GB (with 2:1 compression) on a single tape at a rate of up to 360 MB/min.

Advanced Intelligent Tape (AIT)

The Advanced Intelligent Tape (AIT) is another 8mm format created by Sony. It differs from the original 8mm format from Exabyte in that it is more reliable, sustaining 300 copies per tape. AIT uses what Sony calls the Advanced Metal Evaporated (AME) method. Essentially, the tape has a super-tough, carbon protective layer that helps the tape hold up under the higher speeds of the new drives. Meanwhile, a magnetic layer composed of 100 percent cobalt doubles the magnetic flux density of the media, which allows more data to be stored on the tape. Each tape can hold 25GB, or about 50GB with compression.

Perhaps the most advanced feature of the new tape is that an EEPROM chip, called the Memory In Cassette (MIC), is embedded on each tape. The MIC contains user-definable information and the system's log. Sony has promised that the MIC technology will allow the tape's capacity to be doubled. The Exabyte Mammoth tape systems use the AME tapes, but not with the embedded MIC architecture. Drives that use the AITs with MIC are not backward-compatible with many of the tapes in use and therefore are limited to newer tapes. Tape libraries from Qualstar support 2 to 6 AIT drives to provide capacities from 250GB to over 6TB, depending on the number of tapes in the library.

Other Media

The following pages look at some of the less traditional ways to store backed up data. Included is a discussion of compact disk recordable (CD-R) units, compact disk rewritable (CD-RW) technology, Digital Versatile Disks (DVD), and magneto-optical (MO) drives.

Compact Disk Recordable (CD-R)

A regular compact disk (CD) is composed of a polycarbonate substrate, a recording layer, a reflective layer, and the uppermost protective layer. Data is pressed onto the recording layer by a mold at the manufacturing plant and cannot be altered after production. Unlike regular CDs, in recordable CD-ROMs (CD-Rs) a recording layer composed of an organic dye is sandwiched between the substrate and reflective layer. A laser is used to create a series of pits in the dye layer. The space between pits is called *lands* and the pattern of pits and lands encodes the binary information.

Recordable CD-ROM technology has been around since 1990. The units cost hundreds of thousands of dollars and were mainly found in large corporations and specialty shops. Affordable units have only been on the market since 1995. CD-Rs offer several advantages over tape devices for backing up data. The units can be accessed randomly and have a very long shelf life. However, each CD can only store about 650MB of data. Actually data takes up a bit more room on the CD, because data is written in blocks to the CD. The block size is 512, 1024, or 2048 bytes, and data fits into a multiple of the block size (MSCDEX uses the 2048-byte size block, for example.)

Another limitation of the CD is that the directory structure must conform to the International Standards Organization (ISO) 9660 file format, which ensures that the disk can be read by DOS, Macintosh, and UNIX systems. You are limited to eight subdirectory levels. Only uppercase letters, numbers, and underscores can be used in filenames. The RockRidge extensions to the ISO 9660 specifications allow for long, mixed-case filenames, as well as symbolic links. But perhaps the biggest limitation of CD-Rs is that they can only be written once.

Compact Disk Rewritable (CD-RW)

Several years ago, the rewritable CD-ROM (CD-RW) was developed to address the limitations of write-once CD-ROMs. Although these devices came through on their promise and could be written to more than once, they were relatively slow, had a limited storage capacity, and were offered at an increased price per disk. Rewritable CD-ROM drives were announced by manufacturers in 1996 and began shipping in late 1996.

The basic technology is the same for CD-RWs as CD-ROMs, except the drives do not create deformations in the recording dye layer. Instead, the dye in the recording layer is changed from a crystalline form to an amorphous form. To erase data, the crystalline form is altered and turned back into the amorphous form. Because the optical difference between the crystalline and amorphous form is small, a special automatic gain control is required to read the disk. Therefore, disks created using CD-RW drives are unreadable by most CD-ROM drives.

Digital Versatile Disk (DVD)

Recent technological advances have transformed the CD-ROM into a massive storage media that is capable of storing 17GB of data per disk. The new CD-ROMs promise to hold video games, data, and movies with soundtracks in four languages on one disk. Manufacturers have accomplished this in part by decreasing the size of the pits, thus packing more pits on a single CD and using a shorter wavelength laser to read the media. Where 650MB used to reside, now a disk can hold 4GB of data. In addition, the new technology has allowed for two layers of data per side, which has increased the amount of data to about 8.5GB per side. Just flip it over to add two more layers and you have a whopping 17GB of total storage on a standard CD.

The Digital Versatile Disk (DVD) drives have a higher constant linear velocity (i.e., they spin faster) compared to standard CD-ROM readers, which allows for greater throughput. Because the devices spin at three times the rate of normal CD-ROMs and a shorter wavelength of light is used to read the disk's surface, DVDs are capable of a transfer rate of about 10 MB/sec. Unfortunately, the shorter wavelength of light also makes CD-R-created disks unreadable, although backward-compatibility has been promised for standard CD-ROMs and possibly CD-RW-created media. Currently, the DVD drive is read-only, but manufacturers have hinted at rewritable versions in the future.

Magneto-Optical (MO)

When magneto-optical (MO) drives appeared on the market in 1989, they only had a capacity of 650MB in the larger $5\frac{1}{4}$ inch form. The smaller versions (slightly larger than a $3\frac{1}{2}$ inch floppy disk) can hold about 650MB, while the larger platters ($5\frac{1}{4}$ inches) can store a total of 2.6GB. MO drives offer a data throughput rate of 6MB/sec and a shelf life of many decades.

MO drives are rewritable and use a different technology than CD-ROMs. The data layer is composed of a magnetic film that can have a magnetic field up or down for very small regions on the disk. This magnetic film has one other special property: at room temperature, it is very difficult to change the magnetic field associated with the small regions of the disk. However, if heated to about 300°C, the magnetic field can be changed easily by applying a small magnetic field. A laser is pulsed on to heat the medium in just the right location as a magnetic field is applied. This creates regions of up and down magnetic fields representing the 0s and 1s in the binary code. To erase a disk, the magnetic field is applied continuously with the laser as the disk is spinning. The same laser is used to read the disk, although the intensity is reduced so as not to heat up the magnetic film.

Although the drives are expensive, a platter can be placed in the drive and accessed in the same way as a hard drive, albeit at slightly slower speeds. The devices are commonly used as working drives for large files that are only accessed occasionally but are too big to remain on the hard drive. You can use them safely as backup devices, but the cost of the platters may prove prohibitive. Look for these drives to be used instead of hard drives, in some instances, as their cost and access speeds decrease. Magneto-optical drives are compared to other optical media in Table 4-3.

Autoloaders and Tape Libraries

When you have to back up more data than can fit on a single tape, you have to manually change tapes yourself or use machines called *autoloaders* or *tape libraries* to change tapes for you. Tape autoloaders are the first step in the direction of tape automation. They have one tape drive and usually less than a dozen tapes. Typically, autoloaders are used to access the tapes about once a day in a sequential fashion. Performance over a single tape drive does not increase because only one drive is being accessed. However, autoloaders do relieve you of the burden of changing tapes.

	Access Time (avg.)	Max Space	Cost ($US)
CD-R	6–350	600–680MB	320–840
CD-RW	290–450	650MB	450–700
DVD	180	17GB	450
Magneto-Optical	19–200	1.3–2.6GB	400–1700

Table 4-3.   Basic Specifications for the Most Common Optical Storage Systems

For more serious demands, you require a tape library. These devices house more than one drive and many tapes (more than 100). Each drive is capable of reading every tape, and tape libraries are designed for simultaneous reading and writing to multiple drives. Because more drives are being used in parallel, throughput is increased. In addition, you get the benefit of redundancy, because if one drive fails, the others continue to function.

As you can imagine, keeping track of hundreds of tapes is a nightmare. Fortunately, many tape libraries make use of bar code scanning. Each tape has a small bar code placed on it. A scanner is used to quickly take inventory of the stock and evaluate each tape for content and age. Most backup software has a built-in database for tracking tapes. Unfortunately, hidden costs are associated with purchasing a tape library system. For example, you may need to buy a new interface card and uninterruptible power supply (UPS), as these devices are external.

For those interested in even greater redundancy, RAID technology has been combined with tape drives into tape RAID systems. In its simplest incarnation, data is simultaneously written to two or more identical tape drives to provide mirroring of the data. Although all tapes contain the same data, you get multiple copies in the time that it takes to write a single tape. Advanced tape RAID systems use striping to simultaneously write data to up to four tape devices and a parity tape. A failed tape can be reconstructed by using the remaining tapes and the parity tape. Moreover, writing to five drives simultaneously has speed advantages, because often the slowest point in the process is the time it takes to write the data to the tape.

A library of recordable CD-ROMs or magneto-optical platters is called a *jukebox*. Jukeboxes have the advantage of having random access. These devices offer faster access on a highly reliable media. However, the cost per megabyte is more when compared to tapes. A partial list of tape and optical vendors is provided in Table 4-4.

Vendor	Phone	Web	Tape Formats	Drives	Autoloaders	Libraries
Box Hill Systems	800-727-3863	http:\\www.boxhill.com	4mm DAT, 8mm, DLT	x	x	
Digital Equipment	800-STOREWORK	http:\\www.storage.digital.com	4mm DAT, DLT	x		x
Exabyte	800-EXABYTE	http:\\www.exabyte.com	4mm DAT, 8mm, DLT	x	x	x
Hewlett-Packard	800-826-4111	http:\\www.hp.com/go/storage	4mm DAT, DLT	x	x	x
IBM	800-IBM-3333	http:\\www.storage.ibm.com	4mm DAT, 8mm, MO		x	x
Iomega	800-MYSTUFF	http:\\www.iomega.com	Quarter Inch Tape	x		

Table 4-4.   Partial Vendor List for Tape and Optical Systems

Vendor	Phone	Web	Tape Formats	Drives	Autoloaders	Libraries
nStor	800-724-3511	http:\\www.nstor.com	4mm DAT, 8mm, DLT, AIT	X		X
Pinnacle Micro	800-553-7070	http:\\www.pinaclemicro.com	MO	X		
Qualstar	818-592-0061	http:\\www.qualstar.com	4mm DAT, AIT			X
Quantum	408-894-4000	http:\\www.quantum.com	DLT	X	X	
Seagate Technology	800-626-6637	http:\\www.seagate.com	4mm DAT, AIT	X	X	
Sony	800-352-7669	http:\\www.sony.com	4mm DAT, AIT, MO	X		

Table 4-4. Partial Vendor List for Tape and Optical Systems (*continued*)

SUMMARY

The disaster recovery plan of any network must include a tape backup system. You need to consider many options when choosing a system that is right for you. This chapter considered many of these options including backup devices, formats and software. Of course, you must balance your budget with your need for tape backup capacity and speed. A good backup procedure can make or break a disaster recovery plan.

Mirroring, Clustering, and Parallelism

There is no doubt that the personal computer has come a long way from its humble beginnings. Just imagine, 15 years ago we were dealing with systems so slow they defy imagination in today's world. We have seen the 286, the 386, the 486, the Pentium, the Pentium Pro, the Pentium II, and now the Pentium II Slot I for the workstation and the Pentium II Slot II for the server. With these changes in CPUs there have also been dramatic changes in storage devices, memory, video cards, and bus architecture, and even performance-enhancing symmetrical processing systems have been released.

The fascinating issue with the these changes is that all of them have already been done on mainframes and large host systems. We now talk about SMP machines and how they scale versus UNIX machines, and how multiple processor machines seem to have limitations. For example, when SMP machines became available for NT, most people ran out and got one. To most users chagrin, these boxes were slower on some applications than a comparable single-process machine. The software running on them had no knowledge of how to take advantage of the extra processors. It became apparent that software had to be written to take advantage of the SMP architecture. This simply meant that program threads had to be properly managed so as to include the other processor instances. This SMP architecture was an early attempt on PCs to provide parallelism and provides an important point that needs to be understood: these high-end systems need both hardware and software implementations to allow true scalability to occur. But, the die had been cast; businesses and IS managers were getting caught up in a mixture of hype and reality.

As the above changes were being accomplished, users and network IS managers began demanding more out of their systems. Buzzwords began running rampant, and the rhetoric has been awesome. The entire concept of clustering and related topics is actually very complex, and that is what this chapter tries to explain. The subject will be approached by examining three levels of clustering or cluster-like products. These three are

- ▼ Mirroring
- ■ Clustering as defined by Microsoft's Phase 1 Cluster product
- ▲ Parallelism

TERMINOLOGY

Any discussion of NT clustering cannot be complete without examining the other major topics of this book. Clustering basically presupposes multiple servers. These servers all need to fit certain criteria discussed elsewhere. Simply put, the servers need access to the following:

- ▼ RAID enclosures for storage
- ■ UPS protection
- ■ Network protection

■   Emergency power, if necessary

▲   Other protections (virus, security, etc.)

Several terms need defining in the context of this chapter. When discussing mirroring, it is meant to examine mirroring as in mirroring all aspects of a system or designated components to a standby or remote server. Obviously, this configuration has been around for some time, but as will be shown, NT handles it a bit differently. Distributed processing refers to a situation in which all systems in a cluster are active and applications are distributed across all servers, with no server simply being a standby server. (This is a different concept than distributed computing in which an application or its threads can be distributed across multiple CPUs.) Clustering is defined as that software and hardware solution being presented by Microsoft. Parallelism is the clustering solution in which all processors of the cluster are tied together to function as one unit. This latter approach, which is the common clustering configuration on UNIX systems, is designed to increase processing power within the cluster.

All four of these alternatives provide fallover (or failover) capabilities. Fallover is simply the action of processes on one system falling over to another system. This provides high availability of data or an application. On the other hand, mature clustering will allow network increases in the availability and capacity of servers (scalability). You will simply combine the processing power and storage resources of multiple servers into a single virtual system; that is, a parallel processing system. All should provide (in full form) the following:

▼   **High availability**   A server or servers can take over function for a fallen node and thus allow processing to continue. All failures are isolated and the remaining nodes can continue functioning, but clearly with less capacity. In practice, failure of isolated components can also be rolled over in the cluster.

■   **Scalability**   If the cluster is set up to take advantage of all components, you can increase capacity and performance by simply adding more nodes into the system (this is the basic concept of ServerNet from Tandem). In this circumstance, the software must be able to take advantage of the cluster architecture. For example, imagine a SQL server running in parallel on multiple nodes, concurrently accessing data from shared disks. (This scalability, or lack thereof in NT, is the basic criticism given by UNIX folks to current clustering in NT.)

▲   **Manageability**   Clustering can assist in managing a network by allowing only certain systems to be configured for new software or updates without bringing down the entire network.

MIRRORING

Mirroring in NT systems provides only data protection and high availability. There is typically no (or very little static) scalability in these systems. It can be thought of as having a hot-spare system (the spare does not add to the overall system until fallover). Two examples of mirroring software will be considered. One is the Octopus group of products from Qualix (**http://www.qualix.com**) and the other is the Vinca (**http://www. vinca.com**) product line. Both function by mirroring data to a second server, or in some cases many servers.

Octopus

The Octopus line consists of three products including one for high availability and the other two for data protection. Each will be treated separately, but all have a simple common structure. Any changes in designated files are mirrored across a network to virtually any other location. All that is required is a continual network connection of moderate bandwidth. Because only changes (deltas) are mirrored, bandwidth requirements are minimal.

Octopus DP (Desktop Protection)

This is actually an interesting version of Octopus. When discussing backup and backup strategies earlier in this book, one of the concerns was the issue of backing up workstations. This product does exactly that (at least in part). Changes to files can be replicated to any workstation in a network. The obvious place to use this product is in peer-to-peer networks, but it could also be used to mirror files on segments of client/server networks. You simply install Octopus DP on the designated systems on your network and the replication and mirroring of data becomes almost automatic. The installation and setup is very straightforward.

Octopus DataStar

Like the DP version, DataStar captures changes in files and transfers them across the network. In essence, any user application that has files that go through the I/O manager are written to the sender Octopus log and then sent across the LAN/WAN to an Octopus receiver. This receiver writes the event in the log and then basically routes the files to the appropriate user file. This sequence of events is fast and places little overhead on the system.

The installation of the software is easy, as is the setup. Certain customizable features of the software are very useful. You can mirror data from one NT system to another, from one NT system to many, from many NT systems to one, and from many to many. Obviously, each system requires a licensed copy of Octopus, but the flexibility in setup is beneficial. In fact, Octopus enables more than two-node failover.

Octopus HA+ (High Availability and Real-Time Data Protection)

This version of Octopus is very much like the DataStar, but also adds automatic switchover (Super Automatic Switch Over—SASO) capabilities. SASO simply allows a target machine to automatically assume the role of a source machine (or machines) without human intervention. To understand how this is done, some fundamental concepts at work here (and in all clustering applications) must be examined.

In a standard network, machines are connected to a server via a simple set of network cards, hubs/switches, and network protocols. This configuration can be referred to as a public network. In a clustering situation, machines communicate with each other in a manner commonly known as a heartbeat; that is, a server machine lets a target machine know it is present by sending a signal (the heartbeat) at set intervals. By definition, this communication is known as a private network. Although Octopus is usually set up without special NICs, you can indeed set up Octopus to communicate over designated NICs on a private network.

The automatic switchover feature in Octopus is not difficult to enable. Most of the configuration is automatic. In simple terms, you configure both the source and the target machines, and then set the wait time. This is the time between heartbeats. If the source machine does not respond within the wait time, the target machine takes over the function of the source machine. You can configure the target machine to start certain services on switchover or all of the services. Likewise, you can configure the switchover of the IP address and subnet mask. You can even add batch files rules that are applied before or after the switchover. Finally, you specify which machines on the network are notified of the switchover. Octopus HA+ is a powerful application that provides availability of data by mirroring and it also has automatic fallover capabilities. This application's architecture is shown in Figure 5-1.

It is not the purpose of this chapter to discuss complete details of the Octopus product line, but certain features deserve mentioning:

▼ A monitoring toolbar enables you to monitor all the important aspects of sites, mirroring, and synchronization of sites. This feature is a great administrative addition.

■ Only users in the administrative group can administer Octopus. This feature adds security to the application.

■ SNMP add-ons allow notifications to be to an SNMP console (trap monitor), or sent via e-mail or even to pagers.

■ Hidden shares can be mirrored.

▲ You can configure forwarding for individual targets.

Numerous other features are built into the product that make it a solid application. There are, however, certain situations that can create difficulties. If you use the SASO feature and the target takes over, synchronizing the system when the primary source is brought back online is cumbersome. In this circumstance, doing a manual fallover might be better. The Octopus folks are aware of this problem. In fact, the problem may not be considered a major issue by many users as the backup system can usually suffice until a downtime window can be arranged.

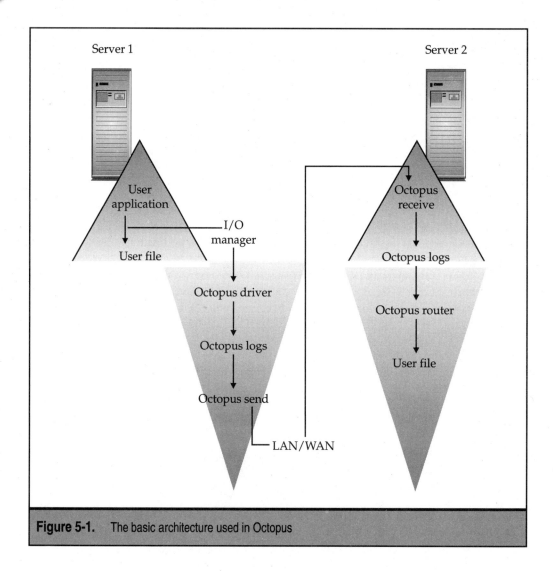

Figure 5-1. The basic architecture used in Octopus

Vinca

Vinca Corporation enables mirroring in their Co-StandbyServer product in a different way than Octopus. This NT application is a server-mirroring solution that allows system administrators to define cluster resources on two servers, creating high availability for both servers. The product, unlike Octopus, is designed to mirror servers bidirectionally. This can allow you to add some basic static scalability to the overall system.

Co-StandbyServer is designed to work on any supported servers that run Windows NT and to be independent of any single point of failure. If one server goes down, the other takes over its function very rapidly. The application installs easily and is also straightforward in configuration. Its basic architecture is shown in Figure 5-2.

Like Octopus, Co-StandbyServer is based on capturing files at the I/O level, but Vinca designed their product to write to both servers simultaneously. This is very similar in concept to the way software-based drive mirroring works in NT. This simultaneous write allows both servers to always be synchronized. In its design, Vinca incorporated the assumption that important tasks would be balanced across both servers. Many tasks can be balanced in this regard. Only upon fallover would the one server provide all applications.

Vinca, also like Octopus, includes remote administration in their Co-StandbyServer. All server pairs can be seen as ActiveX documents across the Web. This means that all functions of a mirrored pair are accessible via most standard Web browsers. Obviously, this function allows very easy remote control of the servers.

Unlike Octopus, Vinca uses a private network for mirror communications by design. This allows all mirroring to be done outside the public network, and also provides a separate link to listen for the pair heartbeat. Interestingly, any pair of servers can function in the mirror. There is no hardware dependence at all. Likewise, Co-StandbyServer can function in any LAN or WAN environment.

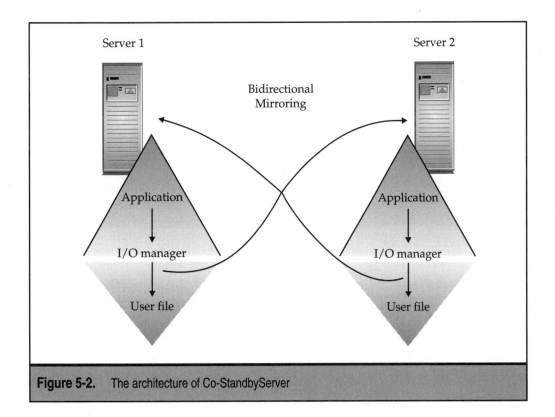

Figure 5-2.   The architecture of Co-StandbyServer

When a server fails, the remaining server assumes the identity of both machines. Whatever services were running under the failed server's IP address are now running on the remaining machine. This failover setup is customizable and is a fast and many times seamless failover from the pair to the remaining machine.

Vinca provides an interesting adjunct to the standard registry. If a system is a print server, obviously only it alone can have the registry settings for the printers. When the server fails, the registry on the remaining server is updated immediately, thus assuring a smooth transition of resources.

Mirroring in Summary

As should be obvious, both Vinca and Octopus have gone to great lengths to provide a failover redundancy that will allow rapid access to data and services should one of the servers go offline. These products become extremely important in large-scale data center mirroring projects over LAN links. By using mirroring, both applications provide certain advantages and disadvantages to users, as summarized in the following table:

Advantages	Disadvantages
Hardware independence	CPU utilization in mirroring
No reliance on a common set of storage devices	Error replication
Can mirror standard clusters remotely	Can have synchronization problems when old server is brought back online
Easy to configure	Requires multiple copies of storage
From one to many nodes are easily supported	Synchronization can cause slowdown

Clustering by Sharing Hardware

When Microsoft was doing original market research for clustering on NT, nearly 85 percent of large customers questioned stated that availability, not performance, was their key concern. Naturally, Microsoft developed their first server cluster to provide this failover capability. Veritas, during the same time period, ported their UNIX-based FirstWatch product to NT. These products will both be examined in this section. They provide a failover approach that is quite different than mirroring.

The key difference between this type of clustering and that provided by Octopus and Vinca is that servers in the cluster have access to a common RAID driveset. Imagine a computer booting NT off its own drive but sharing a common dataset with another computer. This scenario is exactly what clustering provides. Immediately, it should be apparent that certain basic drive features are necessary. SCSI is the required type of drive, and specifically, the multi-initiator SCSI specification built into SCSI-2 is used to allow multiple nodes to access and initiate the drives (actually, up to four cluster nodes can be supported by this specification). Multi-initiator simply means that the device supports two separate controllers (one in each node server). It is also mandatory that the drive array be external and have connectors to both machines. Obviously, one major difference between this type of failover support and simple mirroring is the basic nature of the hardware; NT clustering is indeed hardware dependent.

What constitutes a cluster? As pointed out earlier, a cluster is a parallel or distributed system that appears as a virtual system to users. Clusters, in general, are comprised of separate servers or nodes. Each node has its own version of the operating system and is connected to a common set of hard drives typically configured as RAID 5. It is actually quite interesting that this hardware that runs most clusters has been available for some time. What has been lacking is the software to control the cluster. Using Microsoft's terminology, the software on each node that manages all cluster activity is known as the cluster service. Cluster resources are those physical and logical devices that when online provide a service to a node. In a broad sense, resources include hard drives, NICs, databases, IP addresses, or applications. Groups of resources refer to collections of resources seen as a single entity. Typically, users see groups rather than individual resources.

In a management situation, various aspects of NT need to be supplemented. In the first place, the software really needs to be as separate from the NT kernel and HAL as possible. If changes were added that directly affected the OS, then many other aspects of NT would be compromised. Since failover is a key component, provision has to be made to allow for dynamic changes of network addresses and names. In addition, transaction monitoring must be added to allow cluster-aware applications to fall over to the same place on system A as on system B. This means locked or open files need to be copied from A to B. Finally, the I/O subsystem must allow shared access to the common RAID storage system. Both Veritas FirstWatch and Microsoft Cluster Server provide these software capabilities.

FirstWatch from Veritas

FirstWatch is a well-developed product that is used on many UNIX systems. Veritas has ported FirstWatch to NT and added many needed components. FirstWatch is designed to eliminate all single points of failure. For this reason, FirstWatch uses redundant NICs for heartbeat monitoring. If one NIC stops functioning, the other will assume the monitoring function. You can argue that this design is overkill, as most NICs are fairly robust. However, it does eliminate a possible point of failure.

FirstWatch is designed by Veritas to provide the following features:

▼   FirstWatch installs easily and is nondisruptive (e.g., CPU nonintensive) to normal system functioning.

■   FirstWatch is compatible with multiple types of hardware and operating systems.

■   FirstWatch is expandable.

■   Failures are detected and corrected automatically.

▲   FirstWatch is nonobtrusive to the user.

For the most part, Veritas has succeeded in their design goals. FirstWatch is an application that runs on the systems or nodes of the cluster. Being an application, there are no alterations of HALs or kernels and the downtime at installation is minimal. Importantly, the design of FirstWatch supports a symmetric environment; that is, a two-node system can run applications on both nodes. This helps ensure a distributed computing environment, if needed. Finally, Veritas has provided a fairly open architecture of FirstWatch, thus making it very flexible in configuration.

Veritas designed FirstWatch to monitor services to provide rapid switchover. Unlike Microsoft's concept of a service, Veritas defines a service as anything that can be monitored. The monitoring aspect of a particular software product is called an agent, and the following are available:

▼ Microsoft SQL Server

■ Oracle

■ IISWeb

■ NSWeb

■ Mshare (NetBIOS resolution for sharing files and printers)

■ FTP

▲ Gopher

As part of its attempt to provide an open architecture, Veritas has provided a programmable interface called the High Availability (HA) API. This allows custom DLLs to be written for specific purposes. Nearly any standard programming language can be used, including Visual Basic, C++ or Visual C, or PERL. Documentation is shipped with each copy of FirstWatch.

When a system running FirstWatch is started, two status-monitoring processes start on each server. This means that each FirstWatch server monitors itself as well as its failover partner. This architecture, as shown in Figure 5-3, implies that heartbeats are being examined locally as well as across the cluster. The actual state of a FirstWatch machine is dictated, in part, by the manner in which it is set up. For example, if one node of the cluster is designated as a standby machine, the cluster is asymmetric and only the primary node is considered to be online as a primary node. The second node in this configuration is considered to be in a takeover-ready mode. If both nodes are designated as active, the system is symmetric and both are operational. If one node of a symmetric cluster goes offline, the server left running is designated as a dual service machine.

The manner in which FirstWatch switches from one machine to another is interesting. Let us assume that server 1 has an IP address of 192.168.1.111 and server 2 has an IP address of 192.168.1.222. When server 1 goes offline, server 2 activates a second Ethernet card and gives it an address of 192.168.1.111. Server 2 thus impersonates server 1 on the network and is able to access the data of server 1. Likewise, multiple NetBIOS names can

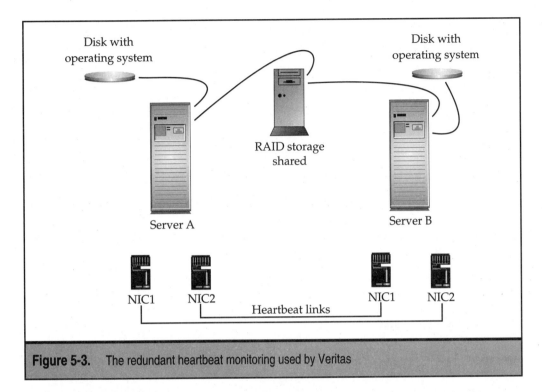

Figure 5-3. The redundant heartbeat monitoring used by Veritas

be assigned to each server so all file and print functions can continue as well. It is easy to see why the symmetric failover is called dual service.

Control of the FirstWatch cluster can be accomplished by means of a standard Web browser. There are important functions that can be controlled by the Web browser. You can manually switch a server to a dual services mode and effectively remove one server from a cluster. In doing this switchover, you can then add service packs or other repair processes to the offline server. Once the repair is done, you can bring the server back online. This cluster is easy to configure and maintain. If you need batch file control of the cluster, a command line interface is also available.

To summarize, the various sequences used by FirstWatch are as follows:

1. Startup

   ■ Makes certain that the secondary NIC is offline

   ■ Puts primary NIC online

   ■ Makes certain that the file systems are Okay (actually, not that necessary with NTFS)

   ■ Mounts the primary shared data disk

   ■ Starts all the specified primary applications

2. Takeover sequence

- Takes control of the failed server's disks
- Impersonates the failed server's IP addresses and names
- Starts secondary applications on takeover server

3. Surrender sequence

- Shuts down secondary applications
- Removes secondary NIC from network
- Unmounts secondary data disks

4. Shutdown sequence

- Shuts down primary applications
- Removes primary NIC from network
- Unmounts its data shares

The above represent nearly every possible state that a server can function in as part of a Veritas cluster. As you can see, FirstWatch has been designed to be a high-availability cluster solution.

Cluster Server from Microsoft

Unlike Veritas, which simply ported FirstWatch to NT, Microsoft started from scratch in designing their cluster server. As pointed out earlier, Microsoft asked their partners and other independent software vendors (ISVs) about the most important direction of clustering and the primary response was failover capability rather than scalability. With this in mind, Microsoft set out to design their cluster server with four basic design concepts or goals:

▼ Use a wide partner participation to increase development speed. In this regard, a consortium assembled that included over 60 companies (some are the other cluster product manufacturers discussed in this chapter). The end goal here was to develop an open process and specification.

■ Support standard hardware (mainly SCSI) rather than proprietary hardware as found in many other existing cluster products. Although this did not happen with many SCSI enclosures, the attempt to accept most hardware is laudable. In fact, Cluster Server already supports the largest variety of hardware for any true cluster system available today.

■ Develop strong application support, including the easy creation of cluster-exploitative (cluster-aware) applications and allowing basic support for programs out of box.

▲ Develop an ease of use for administrators and programmers, and do this through a standard Windows GUI.

The cluster server is a high-availability cluster product much like FirstWatch. The product is a two-node cluster in its phase-1 stage, while the phase-2 stage (in development) will allow more nodes and will be more scalable.

All nodes in the cluster act through a cluster service that is resident on each node, as shown in Figure 5-4. This cluster service is composed of six major, closely related components, as follows:

▼ The node manager, which handles membership in the cluster and also monitors the heartbeat of cluster nodes.

■ The configuration database manager, which maintains the cluster configuration.

■ The resource manager/failover manager, which makes resource and group decisions and initiates startup, restart and failover.

■ The event processor, which connects all components of the cluster service, maintains the initialization of the cluster service, and handles common operations.

■ The communication manager, which controls communication with all nodes.

▲ The global update manager, which provides a global update service and is used by all components in the cluster service.

When a cluster node is booted, the cluster service is started and is under the control of the event processor. When all is initialized, the event processor tells the node manager to either create or join the cluster. Although this sounds simple, the node manager must form a constant and consistent view of the state of the membership by monitoring the nodal heartbeats. The information about the membership of cluster is maintained in the configuration database (actually part of the registry). The node will attempt to join the cluster through cluster authentication. Assuming all is well, the node is now part of the cluster. If a cluster is not found, the node manager will attempt to form a new cluster. To do so, the node must gain access to a special resource, called a *quorum resource*. This resource is actually a tiebreaker when booting a cluster and also assures that each node will not form new clusters when communication between the nodes is broken.

The quorum resource is the first single point of failure component of a Microsoft cluster. The resource is typically a disk. Such a device obviously can fail very easily; therefore, the disk must be mirrored or made fault tolerant one way or another. The quorum resource must maintain at least three qualities:

▼ It has to be able to store data across system failures.

■ It has to be accessible by all nodes in the cluster.

▲ Any node must be able to seize the resource to the exclusion of all others. The node then defines, in a unique manner, all aspects of the cluster.

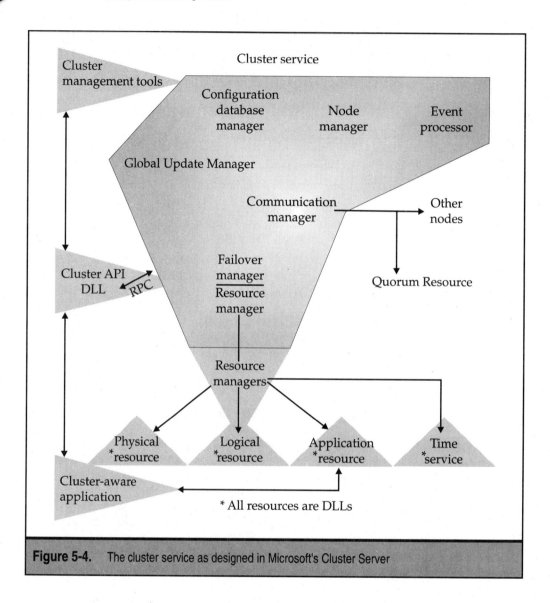

Figure 5-4.   The cluster service as designed in Microsoft's Cluster Server

Currently, only SCSI and FC-AL meet all these requirements.

There is an interesting aspect to the quorum resource. Ownership is always up for contention (sort of reminds you of browser contention, does it not?). If you own the quorum resource, you own the cluster. If a node joins the cluster, it must update its configuration database. This is usually done by maintaining a log of all changes stored on the quorum resource. These changes are obviously stored in a global transactional log on the quorum resource. If any node fails, once that node rejoins the cluster, the transactional update to the node's registry allows it to start where it finished when it left the cluster. This transactional design is similar in concept to the rollback ability of most high-end database products. Not a bad design!

Let's assume a node has left the cluster due to a failure. What must the remaining node do to keep things running? Certain events must occur. There must be a transfer of:

▼ IP addresses

■ Disk ownership

■ Name services

▲ Registry values

In addition, NTFS must be reinitiated via software, on the fly.

Where is all the appropriate data maintained? In the configuration database, of course. This configuration database maintains a list of data, including what node it prefers to be on. For example, the data may list an application, an IP address, and a file share as one part of the data—in other words, a group resource.

Several additional services or monitors contribute to the cluster. The resource monitor runs in a separate process and communicates with the cluster service via standard remote procedure calls (RPCs). This monitor constantly checks on the status of each resource in the cluster. The time service maintains the time within the cluster. This obviously creates a consistent time across the cluster.

The last aspects of the Cluster Server we need to examine are the resources of the cluster. A resource is basically a DLL that is loaded into the resource manager memory space. As might be expected, resources might depend upon other resources. If this is the case, no resource will load until all dependent resources are loaded. Importantly, each resource has a restart contingency that defines the appropriate action if the resource cannot continue functioning on its current node. The standard resources provided as part of the standard Cluster Server are as follows:

▼ Physical disk

■ Logical volume (more than one physical disk in an array)

■ File and print services (NetBIOS control)

■ Network addresses and names

■ Generic service or application

▲ Internet Server service

These resource DLLs are very important because they allow the failover of specific components rather than a whole application. For example, if a DLL is not present, an application and its databases would all failover to another node. If the DLL were present, this would allow only the database itself to failover. In other words, the resource DLL allows an application to be cluster aware.

> **NOTE:** Resource DLLs can actually be customized with a Cluster Wizard that ships with Cluster Server.

Unlike FirstWatch, there are only three states that a node may be in at any one time. These states are as follows:

▼ **Offline**   Simply stated, the system or its cluster service is not running.

■ **Online**   The system is a fully functional member of a cluster, contributes heartbeats, and can own or run groups. All time, database updating, and related events are done through the virtual cluster rather than an individual node.

▲ **Paused**   This nodal state is similar to the Online state, but the node cannot own or run groups.

Cluster Server is similar in function to FirstWatch, but the design is different. Microsoft did an excellent job of developing Cluster Server. Its job was made somewhat difficult by the stated design goal of making future cluster implementations scalable. Many of the needed aspects of scalability are built in to this first release. Certain aspects of beta testing of Cluster Server need to be emphasized. First of all, it became evident that not all systems could carry the stress of the cluster; that is, some systems simply would crash. Because of this, Microsoft states that Cluster Server must be run on systems that carry a BackOffice logo. This implies that the system has been certified to run Cluster Server. In reality, Cluster Server will run on many systems—but only certified ones will be supported by Microsoft.

As this is written, Cluster Server phase 2 is undergoing testing. Unlike phase 1, phase 2 requires NT 5.0. Changes will include the following:

▼ Support for more than two servers (at least up to eight)

■ Newer types of hardware will be supported (FC-AL, for example)

■ Enhanced application support

■ Scalability

■ Adoption of industry standards such as the Virtual Interface Architecture, which is proposed by Intel (see below)

▲ Support for both corporate use and third-party programers will be available. For corporate use, MS Transaction Server can be used. It has full cluster support built into it. For high-end third-party applications, new APIs will be available.

It is very clear that Microsoft is building significant features into Cluster Server, and this will include scalability.

The Move to a Standard—Virtual Interface Architecture (VIA)

This will be our first look at a solution to what is referred to as a system area network, or SAN. In this particular example, VIA is a low-level software interface to facilitate communication on a cluster (actually, it is referred to as an intracluster network). The basic premises of VIA are spelled out very well, as outlined here from the VIA architectural paper (for more information go to **http:// www.viaarch.org**.)

Distributed applications require the rapid and reliable exchange of information across a network to synchronize operations and/or to share data. The performance and scalability of these applications depend upon an efficient communication facility.

Traditional network architectures do not provide the performance required by these applications, largely due to the host-processing overhead of kernel-based transport stacks. This processing overhead has a negative performance impact in several ways:

- **Bandwidth** The overhead limits the actual bandwidth that a given network can deliver. Network hardware bandwidths are increasing by orders of magnitude, while software overhead in available networking stacks remains relatively constant.

- **Latency and Synchronization** Efficient synchronization is a major scalability factor for distributed and network-based applications. The overhead directly contributes to end-to-end latency of messages used for synchronization.

- **Host processing load** The overhead consumes CPU cycles that could be used for other processing.

The above quotation shows the purpose of the VIA SAN. The architecture can be laid upon a high-level protocol like TCP/IP. VIA is designed to offer software and hardware control that is very small and efficient. In essence, the VI architecture eliminates the system-processing overhead of the traditional OSs by providing each consumer process with a protected, directly accessible interface to the network hardware; that is, a virtual interface, or VI. Each VI represents a communication endpoint that can be logically connected to support bidirectional, point-to-point data transfer. In this design, the network adapter will enable the endpoint virtualization directly and perform the multiplexing/demultiplexing and data transfer scheduling.

Three basic factors are used to eliminate communication overhead in VIA. These are as follows:

▼ Elimination of conventional interrupts and setting up efficient polling in their place

■ Zero copying of messages in message transfer

▲ User-mode or virtualized communication

Each of these components deserves some comment. It might not seem a big deal that interrupts are present on networks. Most messaging over networks deals with small file transfers. In such situations, the interrupt overhead may actually be quite significant. Removal of interrupts may help more than you think.

Unlike the interrupt issue, copying of files before message transfer can be deadly with large files. We have seen this all too often with file transfer from the Internet. VIA eliminates this copying and thus can dramatically facilitate large-file transfer over the cluster nodes.

The third mode change is one that deals with user-mode or virtual communication. In many ways, this reminds one of logical address networks or LANs in ATM. Quite simply, virtual communication adapters are set up and can be addressed directly by applications. In essence, this will move internode communication to direct memory access.

While the argument can be made that SANs should be a hardware issue and not a software one (see next section), Intel, Microsoft, and Compaq are attempting to work out an inexpensive solution to bandwidth demands. As nodes function in scalable ways, the communication bandwidth has to be increased. VIA goes a long way in providing this increase in a standardized manner.

Parallelism

If you look at the general architecture of a PC, you should be aghast at the cheap construction of the bus. Nowhere is this more obvious than on an SMP machine where the number of CPUs jumps from two to four and higher. Quite frankly, the cost-conscious PC gets "bogged" down with the additional CPUs. The memory structure, cache implementation, and system buses cannot handle these large SMP boxes.

Let us take PCI as an example. There simply are not enough slots available to provide sufficient cards for many cluster nodes. Remember, there have to be both private and public networks on many cluster systems. No problem, right? We will simply add bridging to handle multiple PCI buses. Well, this is a good idea but adds significant bottlenecks to bus communication. An obvious way to solve this dilemma is to have hardware that simply opens bandwidth for intranodal communication. This is exactly the tact taken by Tandem with ServerNet and their own implementation of a SAN. Unlike, VIA, the ServerNet SAN is a hardware solution.

ServerNet—Parallel Processing for Large Data Processing

Suppose we are trying to use data mining to examine our shipments or products across numerous stores in the United States. We know that stores on the West Coast sell different products than do the same stores in Maine. How do we address such large and complex questions? The standard database queries simply will not suffice. The answer, of course, is to use the scalability of clusters to provide parallel processing of the queries (which are in this case somewhat the equivalent to the statistical procedures known as factor analysis).

ServerNet uses a shared nothing design. This means of course that there are no common components such as drive arrays that are shared across machines, as seen in both FirstWatch and Cluster Server. The basic principle behind this type of design is to break down a large query into a series of smaller ones and then parcel the smaller queries to multiple nodes where the queries are processed in parallel. When all queries are finished, they are joined (typically on a single node). There are, in fact, some advantages to this approach. First of all, there is no need for a lock mechanism that prevents systems from writing to the same file at the same time (preventing data corruption). Secondly, a properly designed database management system can scale massively in this design.

There are, however, certain factors that must be maintained. As the number of nodes increases, the backbone connection of the nodes (so-called interconnect) must scale with the increasing number of nodes. At the same time, there has to be low overhead on this interconnecting backbone. These two features are the exact design of ServerNet.

Tandem defines the SAN as the central nervous system of clusters and, in fact, this is not a bad definition. The SeverNet SAN provides the following:

▼ High bandwidth

■ Low overhead and the elimination of LAN/WAN stacks

■ Scalability

■ Fault tolerance

■ Transparent utilization

▲ Ability to use low-priced PC components

Tandem has designed hardware that will provide all the above. As you might expect, ServerNet is a hardware solution, and not a software solution, to the SAN. Tandem used their six-way ASIC (application-specific integrated circuit) from UNIX with NT. They have also moved their fabric switch technology to NT. According to Tandem, they are ready to provide scalable clustering in Windows NT.

In the typical SAN setup, as outlined in Figure 5-5, communication goes from a system bus (memory) to the SAN and then to another node's system bus (memory). Obviously, it is the intranodal backbone that has to expand to provide necessary bandwidth. With ServerNet, this typically means the addition of some more hardware. Most importantly, this addition is to the backbone and not to individual nodes. To add more nodes, simply increase the SAN backbone. While clearly this is overkill for many businesses, data mining and the use of data warehouses can benefit significantly from this design.

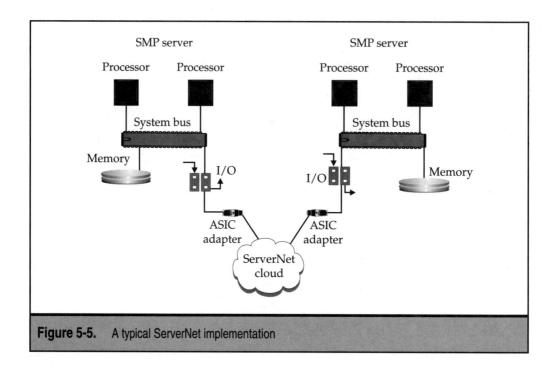

Figure 5-5. A typical ServerNet implementation

SUMMARY

There is no doubt that clustering will propel Windows NT into a scalable enterprise environment solution. No longer will we worry about thread affinity and related SMP issues in the same way as we did before. The scalability and fault tolerance of clustering will be of enormous value. There is, however, a potential downside to this new technology. Now, more than ever before, planning will be critical for designing your networks.

In many small businesses, a mirrored approach is more than adequate. In larger businesses with large inventories and data queries routine, clustering is the only reasonable option available. Hopefully, this clustering can be provided sufficiently transparently that most software can take advantage of the benefits. It is certainly clear that the next few years will be very exciting, with NT at the high end of many enterprises.

CHAPTER 6

Protecting Your NT System from Viruses

There is no question that a system running Microsoft Windows NT is susceptible to computer viruses. Therefore, antivirus considerations are paramount to providing fault tolerance to your NT enterprise. This chapter will examine the effects of viruses in an NT environment. In addition, this chapter will discuss types of viruses, antivirus corporate policy and the most commonly occurring computer viruses. It will also examine some well-known third-party antivirus products.

WHAT IS A VIRUS?

A *virus* is a self-replicating piece of code designed to affect your computer without your knowledge or permission. Computer viruses do not spontaneously generate. They must be written and usually have a specific purpose. In the technical sense, a computer virus is any undesired file that has the ability to replicate itself. It is a common misconception that a virus is any type of malicious code. It is actually the automatic replication characteristic that classifies a piece of code as a virus.

NOTE: In this chapter, a loose definition of the term "virus" will be used. A virus will be considered any code, malicious or otherwise, that had been introduced into a computer system without the knowledge of the user.

Viruses can be defined within two categories: they can be malignant or benign. Malignant, or malicious, viruses cause damage within a PC. This damage can be intentional or not. Benign viruses are nondamaging, or innocuous. A program that waits until a specific date and then displays some sort of harmless message is considered benign. In reality, most viruses are benign.

The action a virus takes—the symptom or damage planned by the perpetrator—is known as the *payload*. Possible actions include erasing a disk, corrupting your programs, or just wreaking havoc on your system. A payload could also be a Trojan horse (described later in this chapter) or another virus.

Common Problems Caused by Viruses

There are many ways in which a virus can effect your systems. They range from performance degradation to complete system crashes. A solitary virus on a single PC can cause hundreds of dollars in lost man-hours, with both the user and the technician being affected. A good example is the AntiEXE virus, a very common memory-resident, boot sector virus. One of our customers had a Microsoft Windows 3.*x* machine that crashed every time Windows 3.*x* tried to start. It was on a vice president's machine, so two technicians were sent to repair the "memory" problem. After 20 man-hours and immeasurable amounts of bad public relations, the company decided to run an antivirus scanner. Problem solved.

On a Windows NT system, viruses can have varying affects. With certain viruses, Windows NT will crash with a blue screen or just stop running. This will normally occur during start-up, when the NT disk drivers take control from the system BIOS. If a blue screen shows Inaccessible_boot_device, then you should immediately check for viruses. With other viruses, NT will actually boot, but the data on the hard disk will become corrupted. The following lists some common symptoms that may indicate a viral infection:

▼　An NT blue screen shows Inaccessible_boot_device

■　NT fails to boot for no apparent reason

■　NT fails to install for no apparent reason

■　Reduced memory or disk space

■　Unexpected writes

■　Changes in the file date or time

■　Failed program execution

■　Bad sectors on your floppy

■　Slower system operation

■　Longer program load times

■　Changes in the file length

▲　Unusual error messages

If you encounter a virus, there is a good chance that an antivirus utility will remove it. Unfortunately, some viruses will force you to format the drive and do a complete install.

Generally speaking, more attention must be paid to the damaging forms of viruses. Viral infections can lead to server and workstation downtime, lost productivity, and bad public relations. They can cause a great deal of frustration at the end user level. The monetary costs of viruses can be staggering. The reaction to the threat of virus infection alone results in a great deal of capital outlay, both for antivirus software and for man-hours. A recent study at NCSA (National Computer Security Association) showed that the worldwide costs of detecting and recovering from computer virus incidents amount to over a billion dollars annually. This translates to approximately $800 per infected computer per year and does not include the cost of data loss!

Does this mean that viruses that cause no apparent damage should be ignored? The answer is obvious. The problem with some of these innocuous viruses is that they often cause damage their designers never expected. There are very few pieces of bug-free code in the world, and with viruses this is even more apparent. Viruses can install themselves over existing data and into portions of the boot sector the operating system is trying to utilize. This can result in both data loss and a complete operating system failure. This is an especially aggravating problem with NT's file system, NTFS.

An example of an accidentally malicious virus is the Denzuko virus (a.k.a. Den Zuk). The Denzuko payload is shown in Figure 6-1. It is a resident DOS virus that mainly infects 360K floppies. On a computer infected with this virus, pressing CTRL-ALT-DEL will not result in a simple reboot. Instead, the payload will appear on the screen for a fraction of a second. The computer will appear to reboot, but the virus will remain in memory. The problem is that most people do not have 360K floppy drives. When a higher-capacity floppy is accessed, Den Zuk can cause data loss.

There are several different types of viruses, including boot track viruses, file infecting viruses, and Trojan horses. To date, between 12,000 and 15,000 computer viruses are known to exist. This number includes several viruses that are very close to being duplicates; in some cases, a minor change has resulted in a newly classified virus. The number of viruses continues to grow at an alarming rate. In companies with over 500 computers, unique virus detections occur at a rate of approximately one per month. This number is expected to triple in the next few years, coinciding with the explosive growth of the Internet. Each month, over 100 new computer viruses are created. It is amazing that so many people seem to have so much time on their hands. It is also incredible that an entire industry is based on the bad intentions of others.

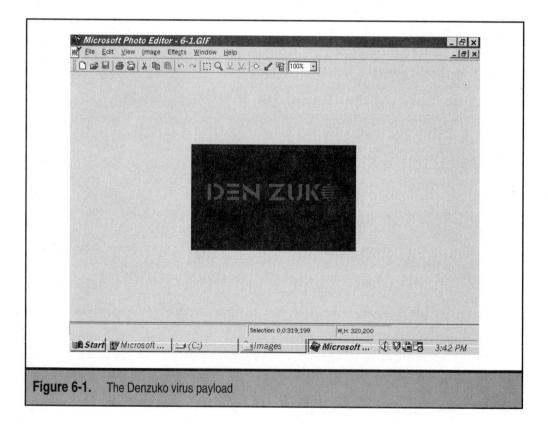

Figure 6-1.   The Denzuko virus payload

The majority of viruses are created by young people looking for a way to pass their time. Usually the intent is to see how far their creations can go. Information on creating the older DOS-type viruses is readily available in books and on the Internet. In fact, menu-driven virus creation programs and engines are available for these older viruses: the person just enters in the desired characteristics, a name, and a new virus is created—with no programming necessary. The new 32-bit viral programs are more difficult to create. It is this fact that keeps the number of true 32-bit viruses so low. To create 32-bit viruses requires a decent knowledge of Win32 programming. One would think that people with that kind of knowledge are too busy making bags full of money to have time to create computer viruses. The lack of 32-bit viruses does not seem to matter, however, as the old-style viruses are troublesome enough for Windows NT.

Of the thousands of known viruses, almost all are of the old DOS type. There are about a dozen Windows 3.*x* viruses, a handful of Windows 95 viruses, and no known true NT viruses. One well-known 95 virus, Boza, was a 32-bit virus but did not affect NT machines. It first appeared in January 1996. Boza has no destructive routines. Like many viruses, it contains a bug that can automatically enlarge an infected EXE file's size by several megabytes. The virus also has an activation routine that displays text, such as "The taste of fame just got tastier!" and "From the old school to the new." This screen appears if the virus is run on the 31st day of the month. Figure 6-2 shows a Boza payload screen.

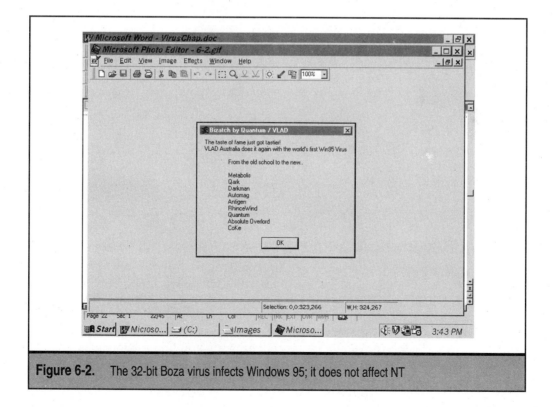

Figure 6-2.   The 32-bit Boza virus infects Windows 95; it does not affect NT

The computer industry is still waiting to see the impact of malicious Java and ActiveX applets. The automatic nature and new complexities of Web pages make these threats especially frightening. As Web browsers become more functional, their virus hosting capabilities will only increase.

In the fast-growing macro virus arena, there are already around 500 known viruses. This number has basically doubled in the last year. Their prevalence in the corporate world is nothing short of amazing. Macro viruses have been found in almost every country in the world. In the United States they have been found in almost every company site with over 100 computers. This is an incredible statistic.

▼ There are no known viruses that can damage or infect computer hardware (only software).

■ Viruses must be executed in order to infect your system.

■ Viruses don't infect compressed files.

▲ Computer viruses don't infect files on write-protected disks.

In an effort to quash the number of computer viruses, many countries have joined the United States in outlawing the creation of computer viruses. A kind of hit team, called the Computer Emergency Response Team (CERT), has also been set up to abate virus proliferation. In the United States, creating or knowingly distributing a virus is considered a federal offense. On the international side, the Computer Anti-Virus Research Organization (CARO) is made up of many of the leading antivirus experts. CARO studies viruses and issues the names that are used as standards throughout the industry.

TYPES OF VIRUSES

There are several different types of viruses that can infect and affect a Windows NT system. They range from the commonly encountered boot record viruses to the seldom seen Trojan horse programs. This section will also examine some of the more common hoaxes that have appeared in the last few years.

Master Boot Record/Boot Sector Viruses

Boot track viruses are the most common form of computer viruses in terms of numbers of individual viruses. They account for approximately ten thousand of the twelve to fifteen thousand known viruses. The two basic forms are master boot record and partition boot record. Essentially, every physical drive has in its first sector (Side 0, Track 0, Sector 1) the disk's master boot record and partition table. Similarly, every logical drive has a partition boot record. This boot record contains the boot program and information relating to the formatting and data on the disk. Figure 6-3 shows a symbolic picture of a hard drive that illustrates these different areas.

The interesting thing about boot track viruses is that most of them could not possibly be either loaded to or downloaded from a bulletin board or the Internet (however, the Internet presents more serious problems with other forms of viruses, as you'll see later). Boot track viruses usually come from infected floppies, but they can also come from dropper programs. A *dropper program* is simply a virus that drops another program, usually a virus, onto your system.

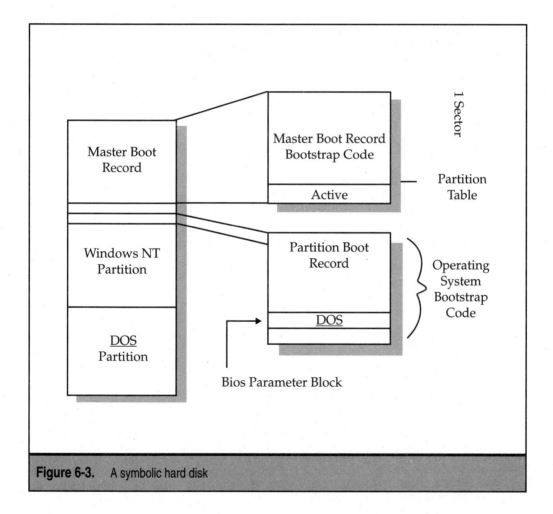

Figure 6-3. A symbolic hard disk

As mentioned, every physical drive has in its first sector the disk's master boot record and partition table. When a PC is turned on, the BIOS reads the master boot record. It has a small program in it, called the master boot program, that looks up the values in the partition table for the starting location of the active partition. It then tells the system to go there and load the active partition's boot record. The master bootstrap executes the partition bootstrap, which in turn loads the operating system.

The usual vector of infection of a master boot record virus is the same as a boot sector virus: an infected floppy is left in the drive. Windows NT is completely susceptible to this form of viral infection, even on an NTFS partition. When NT boots up, it first uses the BIOS disk drivers to access the hard disk. At this point, it can be affected. Eventually, the NT loader takes control of the boot process and switches to protected mode. NT does not rely upon the computer's ROM BIOS disk drivers beyond this point. It also does not rely upon a resident DOS kernel for system services. NT uses its own protected-mode disk drivers for all disk operations, which renders a DOS virus useless. It is impossible for boot sector viruses to replicate once NT is fully loaded. This is due to the fact that NT does not support a compatibility mode as in 95. NT will not allow direct hardware access through the old BIOS drivers.

The other way to pick up a master boot record virus is from a dropper program. Dropper programs infect the master boot record of the hard drive by using BIOS services to write directly to the hard drive. As has been shown, NT prevents all such direct writes from within a DOS box. Thus, this type of infection will be prevented while NT is running.

This then begs the question, what if the machine dual boots to 95 or some other traditional OS? In that case, these viruses will act normally. They can even affect the system in such a way as to make it incapable of booting back to NT. For this reason, you should not dual boot any critical server machines.

How do master boot record viruses cause infected drives to be inaccessible when NT attempts to start up? NT examines the partition table from the master boot record to determine what logical drive is active. Since NT reads this information using the protected-mode drivers, the stealth mechanism of the virus is bypassed. This means the virus is unable to pass back the original partition table. NT will then see a mixed-up partition table and will be unable to identify the logical drives on the system. If the virus does not modify the partition table, then Windows NT should boot up normally.

Partition boot record viruses affect NT a little differently. As mentioned above, this boot record contains the operating system boot program and information relating to the formatting and data on the disk. It is this boot program that gets infected by viruses. Like master boot viruses, the usual transmission mechanism of a partition boot record virus is through dropper programs and through floppies accidentally left in a computer when the machine is turned off or rebooted. Floppy drives are very similar to hard drives. They contain code that tells them whether they are bootable, and it is this code that becomes infected. You should note that a floppy boot attempt does not need to be successful in order to infect the hard drive. The virus simply overwrites the existing boot sector with its own infected boot code before it displays the nonsystem disk message.

The dropper programs are easy to deal with on an NT system. As with master boot record viruses, they are basically prevented from infecting a Windows NT machine due to NT's protected-mode disk drivers. They do not allow the direct hardware access the programs require.

Now the question to ask is, why should NT administrators worry about these viruses? Boot record viruses infect hard drive boot records by relocating the original boot record to a new location of the drive. They then replace the original boot record with the viral boot record. Usually, boot record viruses hide the original, uninfected boot record at the end of the infected drive. You can only hope that this space is not being used for data. If it is overwritten after start-up, it will destroy the original record. The actual problems you will have depend on the type of file system.

First, let's look at the FAT file system. If the virus places the original boot record at the end of the drive, then Windows NT may inadvertently overwrite the saved boot record. This will cause the system to crash during boot-up, as the boot record will be destroyed. NT may or may not start, depending on where the original boot record is placed.

NTFS drives are much more likely to cause a system crash in the presence of boot sector viruses. On bootable NTFS partitions, NT places its operating system loader program on the sectors immediately following the boot record. When the Windows NT boot record is loaded and executed by the master boot record, it immediately reads these additional sectors and itself into memory and transfers control to them. This then loads the rest of the NT operating system.

If a boot record virus infects the NTFS boot record, it effectively overwrites the first sector of the multisector loader program. In this case, an important part of the NTFS program will be lost and NT will crash. If the virus has well-written stealthing capabilities, it may be able to work even on an NTFS drive. As stated previously, once the protected-mode drivers kick in, the virus will no longer be effective in terms of propagation. Remember that NTFS is more prone to crashes from boot record viruses than FAT.

What if you install NT on a partition with a boot record infection? If you decide to make NT dual boot back to a DOS-based system, NT will make a copy of the old infected boot record. It saves it in a file called BOOTSEC.DOS. NT will then replace the old boot sector with its own. When the machine boots, NT will give you the opportunity to select which system to boot with the BOOT.INI menu. If the old DOS-based system is selected, then the NT loader loads the original boot record from the BOOTSEC.DOS file—this is the one infected with the virus! The worst part is that the virus will never be cleaned from the BOOTSEC.DOS file unless the virus tools are aware of the swapping trick.

What is the bottom line with boot sector viruses? Although Windows NT does not allow them to propagate, it is still very susceptible to problems from them. Both FAT and NTFS partitions should boot fine with a master boot record infection, unless there is damage to the partition table. NTFS will usually fail in the presence of partition boot record viruses. Therefore, if your server is in a secure place, make the system partition FAT. You'll have less of a chance of a virus crashing your system. Disable floppy booting in your system's BIOS to prevent boot sector infections. Emergency repair disks can sometimes be used to repair the damage caused by these viruses, so be sure to keep them up-to-date. Be sure to keep a DOS boot disk handy as well. The DOS fdisk command (fdisk /mbr) can help repair the boot record if a virus corrupts it. Lastly, when installing NT on a previously-used machine, be sure to scan for viruses.

It should be noted that the question of making the system partition FAT or NTFS has been debated for years now. In the other chapters of this book you will see many statements calling for NTFS on the system partition. Why the apparent conflict? It will depend on your circumstances. If your primary goal is performance, security, and fault tolerance, you will want to make the system partition NTFS. You can then boot to the NT using a boot floppy or through a parallel installation of NT. If you are mainly worried about viruses, make it FAT. If you are not sure, make it NTFS!

▼ NT does not allow boot sector viruses to propagate.

■ FAT file systems on the boot-up drives are less prone to damage from boot sector viruses.

■ Bootable NTFS will usually fail in the presence of a partition boot record virus.

■ Disabling floppy booting on servers can help prevent these viruses.

■ Be sure to make Emergency Repair Disks.

▲ Scan older machines for viruses before upgrading to or installing NT.

File Infecting Viruses

File infecting viruses are another form of the old DOS viruses. The two most common types are EXE and COM infectors. These viruses attach themselves to their host programs and gain control before their host does. They then try to emulate the action the host program was attempting, in an effort to hide themselves.

Here is an example of how a simple file virus works

1. User tries to execute a DOS program.

2. Virus intercepts execute request and infects the program.

3. Virus then passes the original execute request to the operating system.

The user has no idea the infection took place. After the infection has occurred, several things can happen, depending on the virus. It can execute a payload the next time the program is accessed, or it can infect other programs and continue to spread throughout a system.

Do these viruses work under NT? It turns out that upwards of 80 percent of DOS file viruses work fine under NT DOS boxes. The ones that don't work correctly are those that take advantage of some undocumented or CPU-specific functionality. Windows NT may not be able to emulate this specific behavior in DOS boxes. The whole idea of a DOS box is to emulate a true DOS session. Therefore, the better the DOS box that NT presents, the greater the chance of DOS file infections. The main difference between an NT DOS box and a DOS booted machine is that NT does not allow DOS boxes to have direct hardware access. This turns out to be an excellent way to abate virus propagation.

Another anti–file virus feature of NT turns out to be the NTFS file system. DOS file viruses are subject to the increased file and directory level protection offered by NTFS. Files stored on NTFS drives can be made read-only in such a way that DOS programs are completely unable to modify them or change their attributes. It takes more than a simple ATTRIB.EXE to modify file permissions. The administrator, or someone with specific rights, can completely deny access to certain files and directories. Of course, it can sometimes be difficult to go through your entire NT system to determine which files can be marked read-only.

One exception to the effectiveness of setting the file permissions to control file viruses is the slow virus that can infect files at their creation. A slow virus works by infecting only files it thinks you are going to change anyway. If you are going to change a file, it stands to reason that you are not going to make it read-only. In addition, if you are running an antivirus program that works by detecting changes, you will be expecting changes in those files, and the virus will be overlooked.

You must also be aware of resident DOS viruses. On NT, resident DOS viruses can only infect those files accessed or executed from within the affected DOS box. They cannot infect files accessed or executed in other DOS boxes. Such a resident file virus cannot spread from one DOS box to another; it stays in the box it was introduced into. Also, programs executed from the Windows shell are not susceptible to viral infection by a resident DOS virus. Only in the case of an infected command shell will more than one DOS box be affected by a particular virus.

Even with the limitations NT places on DOS file viruses, they can still do serious damage. They can damage unprotected programs and data and can cause the DOS box they affect to crash.

Trojan Horses

Trojan horses, or Trojans, are generally damaging programs that are hidden within another program. Probably the most famous Trojan is the AIDS Information Diskette. Back in 1989, some 20,000 diskettes were sent out claiming to be a program that teaches about AIDS. After you installed it and rebooted your computer 90 times, it hid all the files on your hard disk and demanded you pay for the license. What a marketing plan!

There are also several Trojans written in the Word macro language. These typically delete data as soon as the Trojan document is open. Again, since these do not spread by themselves, they are not widespread and are not considered to be a significant threat. Some known macro Trojans are Concept.M.Drp, FormatC, and WeideroffnenC.

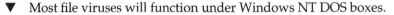

▼ Most file viruses will function under Windows NT DOS boxes.

■ Resident file viruses can only infect those files accessed or executed within the affected DOS box.

■ No DOS file viruses can override Windows NT's NTFS file protection. Slow viruses can bypass this protection during new file creation only.

■ Viruses cannot directly write to the hard drive. (This stops many multipartite viruses and droppers.)

▲ DOS file viruses can still cause serious corruption to unprotected data and program files.

Trojan horses normally lack the ability to automatically propagate and are relatively rare. They are usually difficult to detect. In fact, most virus scanners do not search for Trojans. They are not considered a high enough threat. The only time they are a threat is when they are an "inside job" or when they are sent to a large number of people.

Polymorphic Viruses

With complex encryption, polymorphic viruses are often the most difficult to detect using conventional antivirus programs. When you execute an infected program, the virus unencrypts the main body of the virus. Each time it infects a new program, the virus encrypts itself using a different encryption scheme. If you take two instances of the virus, they will be of different. Polymorphic viruses accomplish this by creating engines and varying encryption and code generation techniques. Polymorphic viruses have infinite ways to conceal themselves. The standard method of virus detection—identifying a particular sequence of code known as a signature—is not efficient. This chameleon-like camouflaging can often beat the traditional scanners. Most third-party products have had to continually enhance their technologies to battle these viruses. DAME, Boxbox, PC-Flu, and HARE are all examples of polymorphic viruses.

HARE is an especially nasty virus, as it employs several techniques to fool antivirus software. It is a resident, stealth, multipartite virus incorporating antiheuristics and antiemulation techniques. Moreover, it is encrypted with a slow polymorphic encryption layer. HARE commonly infects COM and EXE files, master boot records of hard drives, and floppy boot sectors. Infected files and boot sectors are encrypted with a slowly changing polymorphic encryption layer. When HARE infects files, it marks them by setting the seconds field of the time stamp to 34. Another neat feature of HARE is that it will not infect files starting with "TB" or "F-". It also ignores files that have the letter *V* in their name. This is an attempt to avoid infecting any antivirus program that uses a self-checking routine.

Polymorphic viruses are among the most dangerous. They force you to continually update your virus definition files and put third-party products to the test.

Stealth Viruses

Stealth is more a characteristic than a virus form. This virus characteristic is usually a component of one of the other types of viruses. Most successful viruses survive on their ability to avoid detection. There are several ways viruses can stealth themselves. If a virus were to change the date stamp, it would be easy to detect. Savvy virus writers find a way to preserve the exiting stamp. The file size is another area were stealth helps to hide a virus. A stealthy virus might adjust a file's size to hide itself. It might also affect the DIR utility so that it correctly subtracts the size of the virus from the new file size and effectively hides itself. Viruses that stealth their file sizes usually cause inconsistencies in the file sizes as reported by the FAT table and a DIR command, which means that running CHKDSK.EXE would expose the virus. To prevent this type of detection, some viruses actually disable their stealth capabilities when a CHKDSK.EXE command is detected!

Boot sector viruses almost have to be stealthy. If they did not pass disk activity to the original boot sector, the machine would not boot and they would be found out. This is similar to successful file viruses that attach themselves to a program but still allow the program to run normally. Most stealth viruses are unable to function properly once Windows NT has completely loaded, because the virus routines are never given control.

Multipartite Viruses

Multipartite viruses are viruses that infect both files and boot sectors. They often use a dropper program to drop a virus or malicious program onto the system. The virus that is dropped is typically some form of a boot virus. Multipartite viruses use this boot sector virus characteristic as their vector of infection. Under NT, multipartite viruses are almost completely useless. The boot record portion of these viruses is effectively disabled under Windows NT once the real-mode disk drives have taken control. In addition, DOS programs cannot write directly to the hard drive, and this is the only way droppers and some multipartite viruses can spread. These types of viruses are currently rare, but the number of cases is growing steadily.

Mail-Borne and Macro Viruses

With the continuing growth of the Internet and with e-mail addresses being as common as phone numbers, viruses carried on e-mail are going to be an ever more urgent problem. Macro viruses have become the most prevalent form of viruses in terms of infected machines. Consequently, it is important to understand how these viruses are spread.

In common PC mail systems, viruses cannot be "in" a piece of mail. Most mail is encrypted into an envelope, and when you read it, no execution takes place. The mail reader simply brings up the data and presents it in the viewer. The file attachments cause the problems. If an attachment is an executable or (in the case of Microsoft Word) it contains macros, it will be activated after being launched.

These viruses are interesting, because the "operating system" is the program in which they are meant to launch. They are generally independent of the underlying hardware platform. That means that Windows NT is just as susceptible as Windows 95 or Windows 3.*x*. These viruses operate perfectly under any of these operating systems.

The first macro viruses appeared in the summer of 1995. Today, as we stated earlier, there are already over 500 macro viruses. End user infections are up tenfold due to the advent of the macro virus. Macro viruses have been discovered in Microsoft Word, Microsoft Excel, and Lotus Ami Pro (now Lotus Word Pro). In no way are macro viruses a new concept. Their feasibility was predicted in the early nineties, and they quickly came to fruition.

It really should not be surprising that Microsoft Word seems to get the brunt of the macro viruses. It has such a powerful macro language and advanced template system that it almost makes virus creation easy. As far as infections go, a word processor is an excellent host—people are much more likely to exchange documents than executables. The other problem is that word processing documents are the most common form of e-mail attachment. A single infected document can be sent simultaneously to thousands of people on an e-mail distribution list. Microsoft even sent out a Concept-infected Word document on one of its sample CDs! This helps to account for the unbelievable infection rate of macro viruses.

The first credited macro virus, called DMV, was more of a test virus. It was written by someone named Joel McNamara to study macro virus behavior. DMV was no real threat, as it did nothing and announced itself immediately.

The first widespread macro virus was the Concept virus. It is also known as the WW6Macro or Word Prank Macro. It was written with the Microsoft Word 6.X macro language. The Concept virus macro list is shown in Figure 6-4. It has been reported in almost every country of the world and has shown an amazing ability to propagate. Concept was originally discovered in the middle of 1995.

About a year after the Concept macro virus first appeared, the first real Microsoft Excel macro virus was found. This macro virus was named Laroux. Once an Excel environment has been infected by Laroux, the virus will always be active when Excel is loaded and will infect any new Excel workbooks that are created. It will also infect old workbooks when they are accessed.

The first Ami Pro macro virus was discovered in early 1996. This virus, called Green Stripe, works by creating a .SMM file for every .SAM file in the default docs directory. It then modifies the existing .SAM files to use the new macros. The name of the virus comes from its main macro procedure, Green_Stripe_virus. With Microsoft Word, a document and all macros related to it are stored in a single file; for example, a file called SOMEFILE.DOC contains both the text and any macros it utilizes. With Ami Pro, macros are stored in a separate file with a .SMM extension; so, for example, the SOMEFILE.SMM file relates to the SOMEFILE.SAM document. This feature abates the ability of Green Stripe to propagate. Most users don't include the .SMM file when they exchange documents.

The majority of the current macro viruses do not cause major destruction. What they do cause is major embarrassment. Imagine sending the president of your company a virus in the same e-mail in which you ask for a raise! Imagine sending a virus in the multimillion-dollar proposal you just e-mailed to your best client.

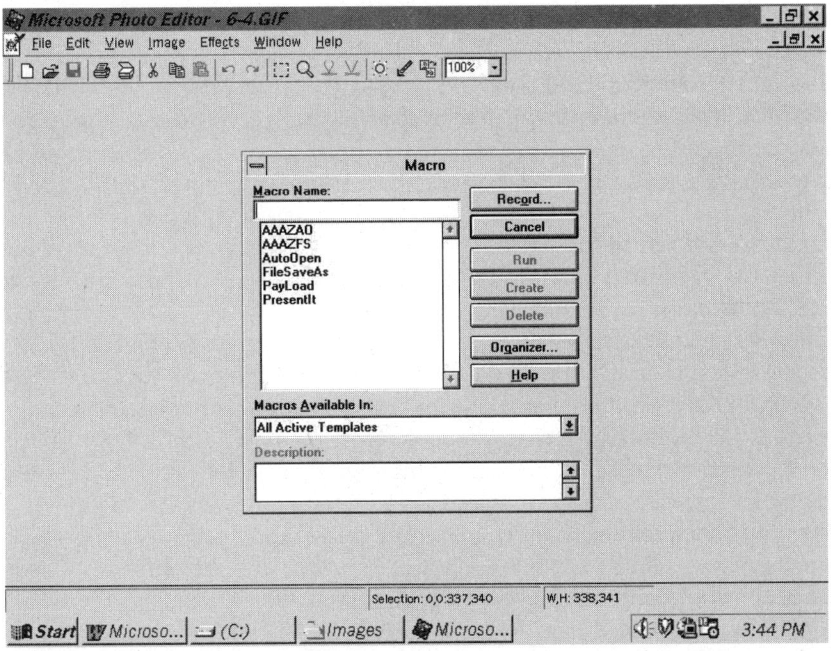

Figure 6-4.   The Concept virus macro list as shown in Word

Not all macro viruses are benign. Some even try to infect the entire host system by deleting files and dropping other viruses. The Nuclear macro virus is a good example. It attempts to delete system files, especially in older versions of Windows. The Word macro Trojan FormatC actually attempts to format the C drive! Others in the malicious class of macro viruses erase documents and do quick saves. This can obviously be a very serious problem. Remember that any program that supports macros embedded in its data files is at potential risk.

Here's an example of how a Microsoft Word for Windows macro virus works

1. The user loads an infected file into Word.

2. The viral macros are activated as soon as the file is opened.

3. The macros copy themselves to the Word global macro area.

4. The user later opens an uninfected document.

5. The global macro area macros activate and copy themselves to the new document.

6. When the user saves the file, Word for Windows automatically saves the viral macros.

The virus does not exhibit any abnormal or detectable behavior. When that user sends the virus as an e-mail attachment or gives it to a coworker on a disk, the virus is transferred to the new machine.

There are many ways around the macro virus problem. Many of the latest versions of antivirus products have the capability to examine attachments to mail messages as they sit in the post office. These so-called mail-aware applications can go a long way to solving this embarrassing issue. They have agents running on the mail server machine that understand the mail storage structure. A good example is the Cheyenne Innoculan agent, which analyzes the Microsoft Exchange data store. Microsoft now adds additional protection in the 95 and 97 versions of Word for Windows that prevent infection from some of the earlier macro viruses.

There are also virus scanners that can work in conjunction with your Internet firewall to search incoming mail for viruses. Check Point, a leading manufacturer of firewall products (Firewall-1), has a product that supports e-mail shunting and scanning. When a piece of SMTP mail is received, the firewall shunts the e-mail off to a third-party e-mail scanning server for analysis. The interesting thing is that if a virus is found in an attachment, it can, in some cases, reattach the cleaned version of the attachment. The user never even knows a virus problem was encountered and solved.

Another way to avoid e-mail-borne viruses is to make it policy to save all attachments to a drive that is autoscanned for viruses every time a file is written to it. In the case of some companies, this would simply be the local hard drive on a desktop machine. In other cases, it might be a server drive. You could also have users save the attachment locally and have them run their local virus scanner against the file. Again, the problem with these manual solutions is that you must depend on your users to follow corporate computer policy.

One interesting Word macro virus is the ShareFun virus. It is also known as "You have GOT to see this" and "Share The Fun." It is a macro virus that affects Word version 7 and version 8 documents and appears to be based on the Wazzu macro virus. The virus attempts to spread itself over e-mail attachments. Every time an infected attachment is opened, there is a chance the virus will activate. This is the part that makes network administrators nervous. If Microsoft Mail is running, the virus will attempt to send e-mail messages to three random people in the local MSMail alias list. The subject line will be "You have GOT to see this!" The message will contain no text but will have a file attachment called DOC1.DOC, which is, of course, infected by the virus. The document will be the one that the user happened to have open when the virus activated. If the recipient double-clicks on the attachment, the infection will spread further. This assumes that the recipients have Microsoft Mail. It is important to notice that this is not an e-mail virus. You will not get infected by simply reading your e-mail. You activate the virus by clicking on the infected attachment.

This brings us back to the end user training issue. Warning your users of the dangers of mail attachments should be a priority in your antivirus training. Tell them that opening an attachment is just as dangerous as downloading a file from the Internet and assuming it is virus-free. A few years ago, when computer bulletin boards were the rage, users had no problem being cautious about viruses. People should use this same cautious attitude toward files from the Internet, regardless of the method of transfer.

Macro viruses should not be taken lightly. They are expected to account for the largest growth of end user infections, since macro viruses attack the way people work. The advent of global e-mail will only add to the problem. Furthermore, the files that macro viruses infect are the files that cannot be feasibly write-protected, because they are constantly being changed.

World Wide Web Viruses

The Internet has become a primary source of computer viruses. E-mail-based viruses and viruses contracted from file downloads are trouble enough. Now the threat of malicious ActiveX controls or Java applets must be taken into consideration. Workstations can experience all of the normal viral problems from these applets. It has already been mentioned that viruses need to be executed in order to infect a system. One of the nice features of World Wide Web pages is that simply accessing them starts the applets automatically, and herein lies the problem. The user is even less aware of the potential trouble than with other, more traditional virus attacks. There is a similar security concern with some of the more complex Web products.

An ActiveX component is a fully functional Windows programs, like any other DLL or EXE file. ActiveX components, along with Java applets, are what bring the Internet alive. They will usher in a new level of Web-based products. Such a component has the same access to the computer as its user. It doesn't take long to realize the viral threat of these controls. One answer to the threat is code signing. Code signing will verify that an applet has not changed in transit but says nothing about its functionality. You are not told anything about the capabilities of the virus.

A Java applet is an interpreted program that runs in a protected Java virtual machine. Java applets are limited in their functionality and theoretically cannot access files, the registry, or other critical areas of the computer. As Java has been maturing there have been news reports of holes that have been found in the virtual machine implementations. At one site, researchers created a Java applet that can breach the VM and execute instructions on the host processor. As these holes in browser security have appeared, they have been quickly plugged. This basically means you are okay as long as you keep up with the latest bug fixes. In addition, browser manufacturers have been furiously enhancing browser functionality and security. Upcoming versions of popular Web browsers will allow signed Java applets to have a greater system access. This will make Java applets as dangerous as ActiveX components.

At the time of this writing, McAfee, the antivirus market share leader, is offering its antivirus products free to Web masters through its Safe Surf'n program (**http:// www.mcafee.com**). This program is designed to help sysops and Webmasters slow the growth of electronically transmitted computer viruses by providing them free use of McAfee's antivirus products. One nice thing about McAfee is that it offers virus scanners for an impressive number of computer OSs, including Solaris, DOS OS/2, and Linux.

So now what should a company do? Turn off all Internet connections? That would be ridiculous. There needs to be a combination of proper user education with some of the newer Web scanning software. New intelligent Web scanning products can search for applets and at the very least notify the user that an applet is being executed. This type of technology is already being built into several of the third-party applications.

The Java/ActiveX issue is relatively minor, but that is only because the Java and ActiveX market penetration is fairly new. It will be interesting to watch the future of Web-based viruses. The Internet is quickly becoming the number one source of external computer viruses.

Hoaxes

Hoaxes are basically just annoying e-mail messages claiming to do one thing or another, but they actually do no harm. They are included here because they are so widespread. They also tend to cause great embarrassment to the well-meaning but somewhat naïve people who pass them on. There are two things to keep in mind when trying to determine if an alert is a hoax. First, viruses do not cause damage to hardware. Second, mail-borne viruses are contained in the attachments. If you are concerned about a particular file attachment, save it directly to disk. Then run a virus scan on it before you open it.

Following are some of the latest hoaxes.

AOLFREE.COM

AOLFREE.COM was spread via e-mail in early April 1997. The original message was as follows:

> Anyone who receives this must send it to as many people as you can. It is essential that this problem be reconciled as soon as possible. A few hours ago, I opened an E-mail that had the subject heading of aol4free.com.
>
> Within seconds of opening it, a window appeared and began to display my files that were being deleted. I immediately shut down my computer, but it was too late. This virus wiped me out. It ate the Anti-Virus Software that comes with the Windows 95 Program along with F-Prot AVS. Neither was able to detect it. Please be careful and send this to as many people as possible, so maybe this new virus can be eliminated.

You can see this is a hoax, as it claims to activate simply by opening the e-mail.

Matra R-440 Crotale April Fools' Day

There is no virus by the name Matra R-440 Crotale. However, a widespread April Fool's Day joke was distributed discussing a hypothetical virus by this name. The actual message was posted to several newsgroups in March 1997:

From: Kenhert
Subject: !!!!!!!! VIRUS ALERT !!!!!!!!!!
Date: Sat, 29 Mar 1997 06:16:23 GMT
!!! Virus Alert!!!
Matra R-440 Crotale Virus
The Virus (or Viruses, rather)

The world's first multi-platform, multi-environment, and multi-systems virus surfaced in Missouri on March 14, 1997. It was written in Pakistan by a group called Intolerant I-Rads. It seems to have been written by some extremely talented people. The extraordinary thing about it is it can infect any system and any OS and any chipset. It is not just one virus, but rather a series of them with an identical purpose.

The first virus was sent [to] about 3,000 people world wide via e-mail. It is not a self-starting Trojan as some people believe these types of things are, but rather a document attached to the e-mail. This version of the virus is a macro Trojan. It was sent to people using Netscape Navigator Mail and because Netscape's mail supports HTML tags they just used a simple tag that would autoload the DOC. The document contains the macros AARTS0, NTYAAA, PayLoad, and AutoOpen. When the document is opened the virus becomes active and infects all other documents opened after [that] the original. It then writes its code to the boot sector so it automatically loads with any type of reboot. From then it infects any COM/EXE file opened. Also, the next time you send someone e-mail the virus uses the Netscape address book to send itself to anyone you've ever sent e-mail to.

The second virus distributes itself on the modem sub-carrier present in all newer modems. The sub-carrier is used for ROM and register debugging purposes only, and otherwise serves no other purpose. The virus sets a bit pattern in one of the internal modem registers. A modem that has been "infected" with this virus will then transmit the virus to other modems that use a subcarrier. The virus then attaches itself to all binary incoming data and infects the host computer's hard disk. The only way to get rid of this virus is to completely reset all the modem registers by hand.

The third virus is the last known version of this virus. This virus works on the same principles of the second version instead it travels through power lines. It gets into the line by traveling on the 60 Hz sub-carrier. It works by reversing the I/O port pin-outs thus achieving control over the CPU and the rest is history.

Sole Purpose

It seems that this is a rather, actually, extremely destructive virus. Although it may enter you[r] system differently, once inside it behaves the exact same way. The virus contains the text "(c)1997 by Intolerant I-Rads. All rights reserved. Unauthorized reproduction is prohibited by law." and "Matra R-440 Virus, the Almighty!". The virus has a self-changing encryption algorithm, so every time it is written to disk it appears differently, making it nearly impossible to detect. When a computer is booted up the virus automatically loads before command.com trapping 13h disabling any virus scanner that might be loaded after command.com. It then checks the real time clock using 17Ah, if it returns that the date is Jan. 6 then the virus becomes activated. Any time after Jan. 6 the virus will become active if the computer is left idle for 30 minutes. The virus then displays the message, "Do not turn off your computer until this virus is finished working on your hard drive or you will lose everything." What the virus is doing is encrypting all the data on the drive with XOR. While it is encrypting the data this virus does one of two things. It either focuses part of the cathode ray beam in your monitor, burning a hole in your screen, or it modifies the horizontal scan frequency of your Multisync CRT so that the monitor begins to overheat. This in turn causes the monitor case to melt! The next thing the virus does is gain access to the basic functions of your IDE controller and reversing the spin of your hard disk.

Solution

We have yet to discover a solution for this virus and we are working around the clock at it. But PLEASE! Before you do anything else. Send this message to everyone you know, so that they may take whatever precautions they feel necessary.

Dr. Kenhert, Cambridge University

There are several reasons this is a hoax. It makes many claims that are just not possible. You have to admire the ingenuity!

YUKON3U.MP JPG Hoax

The YUKON3U.MP JPG hoax was posted to dozens of Usenet newsgroups in early 1997. Of course, it is not possible to get infected by downloading and viewing GIF or JPG pictures. Here is the text:

From: SammyT32@shorty.com (Sammy T.)
Subject: VIRUS WARNING!!: YUKON3U will strike!
Date: Sun, 23 Mar 1997 04:37:37 GMT
Organization: MDM Communications, Inc.

YUKON3U.mp VIRUS IS ABOUT TO STRIKE THE NEWSGROUPS!

As many of you know, the amount of viruses that have been posted within the past couple of months are tremendous—now we have 2 new threats to contend with.

To continue... a medium amount of the recent posts in some of the Alt.Binaries have contained a time-bomb Trojan virus called YUKON3U.mp which is a derivative of a 2nd generation Mutating Engine developed by the Dark Avenger—a self-described "King" of viruses from Bulgaria. The only difference is that this strain has a stealth capability beyond the reach of Norton or McAfee Anti-Virus programs latest updates, with the possible, but not probable exception of Dr. Solomon's Anti-Virus version 7.69. The encryption technique is incredible.

The YUKON3U.mp virus is somehow compiled within the UUE code of the JPG itself, and when decoded will install the virus onto the boot sector of the hard drive, and lie in wait for the trigger date sometime in April (changing your internal system clock won't help since the trigger day changes with each infection). The only constant is the month itself. The simple fact of decoding the file via a newsreader or third-party decoder such as Wincode automatically runs and installs the virus without detection, thereby eliminating the wait for somebody actually launching the file by accident (we all know viruses do nothing unless they're launched).

For all intents and purposes, the JPG is viewable without any problems and normal in every way, but there is a second file hiding within your boot sector without detection. One of the effects carries a nasty manipulation task which damages hardware—an interrupt call set to a track value beyond 39, which will cause the drive heads to move past the inner track of the hard drive, causing the heads to stick on some models.

That isn't the worst of it. Untitled posts which contain special BOTS that are basically invisible and cannot be seen or read by newsgroup readers have also been recently posted according to Dr. Solomon's Web-site.

These BOTS are capable of replacing ASCII characters within all posts in the Alt. Binaries newsgroups (i.e. H becomes S, G becomes F, and so on). The BOTS are triggered to alter other user posts by certain words contained in the post, or by calling upon the Cancel Date of the article (probably some time in April).

It's very possible that the same group who posted the KILL-BOTS last July are behind this second posting along with the YUKON3U.mp virus.

There actually is a Yukon.151 virus. The e-mail is the hoax.

Join the Crew

This is a variation of the famous Good Times hoax (see next):

Hey, just to let you guys know one of my friends received an e-mail called "Join the Crew," and it erased her entire hard drive. This is that new virus that is going around. Just be careful of what mail you read. Just trying to be helpful...

Cancer Chain Letter

This widespread chain letter asks people to send e-mail messages to benefit a cancer patient. There are several different versions of this chain letter. By the way, the acs@aol.com address does not exist.

Here's one example:

Please forward this message to EVERYONE you know. The American Cancer Society gets 3 cents every time this message is forwarded. Please make sure that you cc: American Cancer Society...acs@aol.com

For more information, check the America Cancer Society Web site.

Hacker Riot

Hacker Riot is another widespread hoax:

> Date: Sun, 9 Feb 1997 21:35:59 -0500 (EST)
> Subject: Fwd: This is serious guys Fw: Important Please Read!!! VIRUS
> ALERT!!!!!!!!!!!...
> THERE IS GOING TO BE A RIOT FEB 14 OF HACKERS SO I WOULD NOT GET
> ON
> THAT WHOLE DAY. I AM TELLING YOU THIS BECAUSE YOU ARE MY
> FRIENDS AND I DON'T WANT YOUR COMPANY TO GET INFECTED FROM A
> HACKERS IDEA OF A FUN TIME. SOME THINGS THEY ARE GOING TO DO IS
> MAIL BOMBS AND GIVE VIRUSES AND TOSS PEOPLE OFF SO IF I WERE YOU
> I WOULD TELL ALL OF YOUR FRIENDS AND FORWARD THIS TO AS MANY
> PEOPLE AS POSSIBLE AND CLEAR OUT YOUR MAIL BOXES THE DAY
> BEFORE AND DONT READ ANYTHING THE DAY AFTER JUST DELETE IT
> ALL. THIS IS NOT A JOKE PLESES [sic] SEND IT TO AS MANY PEOPLE AS
> SOON AS YOU CAN!

NaughtyRobot

Here's the text of this hoax:

> Subject: EMERGENCY—security breached by NaughtyRobot. This message was
> sent to you by NaughtyRobot, an Internet spider that crawls into your server
> through a tiny hole in the World Wide Web. NaughtyRobot exploits a security bug
> in HTTP and has visited your host system to collect personal, private, and sensitive
> information. It has captured your E-mail and physical addresses, as well as your
> phone and credit card numbers. To protect yourself against the misuse of this
> information, do the following:
>
> 1. alert your server SysOp,
> 2. contact your local police,
> 3. disconnect your telephone, and
> 4. report your credit cards as lost.
>
> Act at once. Remember: only YOU can prevent DATA fires. This has been a public
> service announcement from the makers of NaughtyRobot—CarJacking its way onto
> the Information SuperHighway.

Good Times, Bad Times

The Good Times hoax warning has been going around for several years already. It just
seems to keep coming back. There have been several versions of this hoax, including

Irina, Penpal Greetings, PKZIP300, and Deeyenda Maddick. This is an example of an authentic Deeyenda Maddick hoax warning, which has been passed on via e-mail:

> ******* VIRUS ALERT ******
> VERY IMPORTANT INFORMATION: PLEASE READ!
>
> There is a computer virus that is being sent across the Internet. If you receive an e-mail message with the subject line "Deeyenda", DO NOT read the message, DELETE it immediately. Please read the messages below. Some miscreant is sending e-mail under the title "Deeyenda" nationwide, if you get anything like this DON'T DOWNLOAD THE FILE! It has a virus that rewrites your hard drive, obliterating anything on it. Please be careful and forward this mail to anyone you care about.
>
> FCC WARNING !!!!! ----- DEEYENDA PLAGUES INTERNET ----
>
> The Internet community has again been plagued by another computer virus. This message is being spread throughout the Internet, including USENET posting, E-MAIL, and other Internet activities. The reason for all the attention is because of the nature of this virus and the potential security risks it makes. Instead of a destructive Trojan virus (most viruses!), this virus, referred to as Deeyenda Maddick, performs a comprehensive search on your computer, looking for valuable information, such as e-mail and login passwords, credit cards, personal info, etc. The Deeyenda virus also has the capability to stay memory resident while running a host of applications and operation systems, such as Windows 3.11 and Windows 95. What this means to Internet users is that when a login and PASSWORD are sent to the server, this virus can COPY this information and SEND IT OUT TO AN UNKNOWN ADDRESS (varies).
>
> The reason for this warning is because the Deeyenda virus is virtually undetectable. Once attacked, your computer will be unsecure. Although it can attack any O/S, this virus is most likely to attack those users viewing Java enhanced Web Pages (Netscape 2.0+ and Microsoft Internet Explorer 3.0+ which are running on Windows 95). Researchers at Princeton University have found this virus on a number of World Wide Web pages and fear its spread. Please pass this on, for we must alert the general public at the security risks.

NOTE: These hoaxes do no harm to your computers. We have included them because they can be added to your company's virus training package. The prevalence of the hoaxes on the Internet illustrates the geometric properties of viral infections.

THE TEN MOST COMMON COMPUTER VIRUSES

The information in this section is condensed from the McAfee Virus Information Library (**http://www.mcafee.com**) with permission. The following are examples of the types of viruses that are most prevalent. While you should be wary of all types of viruses, these are the ten you most likely will encounter.

AntiEXE

The AntiEXE virus overwrites the master boot record of your hard drive. The virus contains all of the standard information of a normal master boot record. The virus is destructive in one circumstance, if the user presses the key combination of CTRL-BREAK while the virus is accessing the disk. If this happens, the virus overwrites the first eight sectors of every head and track on the drive starting at Side 0, Sector 4.

AntiEXE is a memory-resident, stealth, master boot record/boot sector infector. When a user attempts to boot from an AntiEXE-infected diskette, the virus activates itself in memory and overwrites the system hard disk master boot record without saving a copy. The boot does not need to be successful. When AntiEXE infects a diskette, it moves the original boot sector of the diskette to the last sector in the root directory. AntiEXE attempts to hide from antivirus software by displaying an uninfected sector when an attempt is made to access the hard drive (stealth techniques). Thus, detection of AntiEXE is difficult. When AntiEXE is installed, total system memory decreases by 1,024 bytes. AntiEXE also targets and corrupts files of 200,256 bytes in length.

The primary vector of infection of a master boot record/boot sector virus is through booting from an infected floppy diskette. The boot sector of the diskette has the code to determine if the diskette is bootable and to display the "Non-system disk or disk error" message. It is this code that contains the infection. By the time the nonsystem disk error message comes up, the infection has occurred. Once the virus is executed, it will infect the hard drive's master boot record and may become memory-resident. With every subsequent boot, the virus will be loaded into memory and will attempt to infect any floppy diskettes accessed by the machine, thus propagating itself.

Prevention:

▼ Disable Floppy Booting unless absolutely necessary.

■ Scan often with a third party antivirus utility.

▲ Always scan floppy drives as they are accessed.

NYB

NYB is a memory-resident, master boot record/boot sector infector. It is a stealth virus. Master boot record/boot sector viruses are some of the most successful viruses. They are fairly easy to write, and they take control of the computer at a low level. The first time a system is booted from a diskette infected with the NYB virus, NYB will become memory-resident at the top of system memory but below the 640K boundary. Also at this time, the virus will infect the master boot record. Once NYB is memory-resident, it will infect diskettes when they are accessed on the infected system.

On double-density, 5.25-inch diskettes, the original boot sector will have been relocated to Sector 11. On high-density, 5.25-inch diskettes, the original boot sector will have been relocated to Sector 28. In both cases, these sectors are the last sector of the root directory of the diskette; any files whose directory entries were in these sectors will be lost.

NYB uses stealth techniques to avoid detection on the system hard disk as well as on diskettes. If you suspect that you have the NYB virus, power off the system and reboot from a clean write-protected diskette, then check the system hard disk for the virus. Total system memory, as indicated by the DOS CHKDSK.EXE program, decreases by 1,024 bytes. NYB does not contain any messages that are displayed on boot. Infected systems may experience intermittent seek errors upon disk accesses.

The primary vector of infection of a master boot record/boot sector virus is through booting from an infected floppy diskette. The boot sector of the diskette has the code to determine if the diskette is bootable and to display the "Non-system disk or disk error" message. It is this code that contains the infection. By the time the nonsystem disk error message comes up, the infection has occurred. Once the virus is executed, it will infect the hard drive's master boot record and may become memory-resident. With every subsequent boot, the virus will be loaded into memory and will attempt to infect any floppy diskettes accessed by the machine, thus propagating itself.

Prevention:

▼ Disable Floppy Booting unless absolutely necessary.

■ Scan often with a third-party antivirus utility.

▲ Always scan floppy drives as they are accessed.

Monkey

Monkey is a memory-resident infector of the hard disk master boot record and the boot sector of diskettes. It is a stealth virus, hiding the infection of the hard disk and diskettes when it is memory-resident.

The first time the system is booted with a diskette infected with the Monkey virus, the virus becomes memory-resident and also infects the hard disk MBR. The virus moves interrupt 12's return to 9FC0. On the system hard disk, the virus will write one sector of viral code at Side 0, Cylinder 0, Sector 3, and then alters the MBR to point to this sector. Monkey also encrypts the MBR and relocates it to the third sector of the hard disk. Once the Monkey virus is memory-resident, it will infect non-write-protected diskettes as they are accessed on the system. Total system and available free memory decreases by 1,024 bytes. On 360K, 5.25-inch diskettes, the virus will write a sector of code at Sector 11, the last sector of the root directory, and then alter the boot sector. On 1.2M, 6.25-inch diskettes, the sector of viral code is at Sector 28 (also the last sector of the root directory). If directory entries were originally located in the directory sectors overwritten, the corresponding files are inaccessible.

Accessing the C: drive after booting from a noninfected system diskette results in the message:

Invalid drive specification
Diskette directories may also be corrupted.

The primary vector of infection of a master boot record/boot sector virus is through booting from an infected floppy diskette. The boot sector of the diskette has the code to determine if the diskette is bootable and to display the "Non-system disk or disk error" message. It is this code that contains the infection. By the time the nonsystem disk error message comes up, the infection has occurred. Once the virus is executed, it will infect the hard drive's master boot record and may become memory-resident. With every subsequent boot, the virus will be loaded into memory and will attempt to infect any floppy diskettes accessed by the machine, thus propagating itself.

Prevention:

▼   Disable Floppy Booting unless absolutely necessary.

■   Scan often with a third-party antivirus utility.

▲   Always scan floppy drives as they are accessed.

Concept

Concept is a small yet sophisticated program that attaches itself to Word documents. Concept is a macro virus. It is not particularly destructive, but it can be annoying. The Concept virus creates a change with the Save As function. The user will not be able to choose the drive or the type of file when saving documents. The TEMPLATES radio button will be grayed. The macro will cause the document to behave as a template file.

Upon infection, the virus searches for the macros Payload and FileSaveAs among NORMAL.DOT templates. If either of these macros exist, Concept assumes that the system is already infected and aborts. If neither of these files exist, it begins its infection process by copying its viral macros to the template and displaying a dialog box, which contains the number 1.

Once a macro virus is running, it can copy itself to other documents, delete files, and create general problems in a system. These things occur without the user explicitly running the macro. Once Concept is active on a system, it adds the following macros: AAAZAO, AAAZFS, and Payload. Two additional macros appear, called AutoOpen and FileSaveAs. These macros can be viewed in the TOOLS | MACRO menu.

Concept.H is a variant of the Concept virus. The macro names have changed. The AAA* macros are now CRYPTIC and CITPYRC.

The following macros also exist:

▼   AutoOpen

■   FileSaveAs

▲   PayLoad

The Payload macro contains the message:

```
Sub MAIN
REM That's enough to prove my point
End Sub
```

Macro viruses spread by having one or more macros in a document. Opening or closing the document or any activity that invokes the viral macros activates the virus. When the macro is activated, it copies itself and any other macros it needs, sometimes to the global macro file NORMAL.DOT. If they are stored in NORMAL.DOT they are available in all open documents.

At this point, the macro viruses try to spread themselves to other documents. Macro viruses spread easily through e-mail packages. The ability of these packages to send and quickly launch documents can infect hundreds of users at a time. Documents are much more mobile than executable files, passing from machine to machine as different people write, edit, or access them. Macro viruses can therefore spread very quickly through business offices and corporations.

Prevention:

▼ Mark NORMAL.DOT as read-only. This prevents NORMAL.DOT from being infected.

■ Continue to vigilantly scan with an antivirus scanner.

■ Use Office 95A from Microsoft (**http://www.microsoft.com**) or Office 97.

▲ Install MVTools from Microsoft.

Wazzu

Wazzu is a small program that attaches itself to Word documents. It is a macro virus. Wazzu contains one macro, AutoOpen, which it uses to infect and spread throughout the Word environment. When Wazzu is active in Word, it infects documents as they are opened.

The following differences apply to shown variants:

▼ Wazzu.B is Wazzu.A with an extra comment in the macro.

■ Wazzu.C is Wazzu.A without the call to the payload.

▲ Wazzu.D is a different rendition of Wazzu.A without the payload.

Infected documents may have the word "wazzu" inserted in the document and up to three words rearranged. All infected documents insist on being saved in the template directory.

Wazzu.F, a variant of Wazzu, displays the following text string:

EAT THIS: This one's for you, BOSCO.

Once active on a system, Wazzu infects documents using an AutoOpen macro as the documents are opened.

Macro viruses spread easily through e-mail packages used under Windows. The ability of these packages to send and quickly launch documents can infect hundreds of users at a time. Documents are much more mobile than executable files, passing from machine to machine as different people write, edit, or access them. Macro viruses can therefore spread very quickly through business offices and corporations.

Prevention:

▼ Mark NORMAL.DOT as read-only. This prevents NORMAL.DOT from being infected.

■ Continue to vigilantly scan with an antivirus scanner.

■ Use Office 95A from Microsoft (**http://www.microsoft.com**) or Office 97.

▲ Install MVTools from Microsoft.

AntiCMOS

AntiCMOS is capable of erasing the system's CMOS or setup information but does not infect files on the system. Additionally, because this virus makes changes to the system's master boot record, the user may experience problems during the boot-up process. AntiCMOS is a master boot record/boot sector infector. When a user attempts to boot from an AntiCMOS-infected diskette, the virus will infect the system's hard disk master boot record; however, it does not become memory-resident at this time. Note that the boot does not need to be successful for infection to occur. AntiCMOS becomes memory-resident the next time the system is booted from the newly infected hard drive.

When the AntiCMOS virus is memory-resident, total system and available free memory decreases by approximately 2,048 bytes. The payload for AntiCMOS is the erasure of CMOS and system setup information.

The primary vector of infection of a master boot record/boot sector virus is through booting from an infected floppy diskette. The boot sector of the diskette has the code to determine if the diskette is bootable and to display the "Non-system disk or disk error" message. It is this code that contains the infection. By the time the nonsystem disk error message comes up, the infection has occurred. Once the virus is executed, it will infect the hard drive's master boot record and may become memory-resident. With every subsequent boot, the virus will be loaded into memory and will attempt to infect any floppy diskettes accessed by the machine, thus propagating itself.

Prevention:

▼ Disable Floppy Booting unless absolutely necessary.

■ Scan often with a third party antivirus utility.

▲ Always scan floppy drives as they are accessed.

FORM

FORM is a boot sector, memory-resident virus. The FORM virus inhabits both a portion of high DOS memory and also the last two sectors on the hard drive. The virus does not infect files. Usually no damage is done to data on the hard drive. However, it may corrupt the contents of infected diskettes. On the hard drive, FORM moves the original boot sector and a portion of itself and stores it in the last two sectors of the infected hard drive.

If these sectors are overwritten by data at a later date, the system may hang during the boot-up process. However, you may still access the drive. FORM creates bad sectors on floppy diskettes. The virus is stored in the second sector of the diskette and relocates the original data into the unused section of the File Allocation Table (FAT). The area of the FAT where the code is stored is marked as bad, so that the information will be preserved and remain undamaged.

One indication of the FORM virus is a clicking noise produced when any key on the keyboard is pressed on the 18th day of any month. Please note that if a keyboard driver is used, the clicking noise is undetectable. Another symptom of infection is that your system will hang on a failed disk read. Form consumes 2K of memory. The DOS MEM command will report 2K less memory. On a floppy diskette, CHKDSK.EXE reports 1,024 bytes of bad sectors. In the binary code of the virus is a message that identifies the virus, states that it does not destroy data, and includes an expletive to Corrine:

The FORM-Virus sends greetings to everyone who's reading this text. FORM doesn't destroy data! Don't panic! (Expletive) go to Corrine.

This message is not displayed but can be found using a disk editor.

The primary vector of infection of a master boot record/boot sector virus is through booting from an infected floppy diskette. The boot sector of the diskette has the code to determine if the diskette is bootable and to display the "Non-system disk or disk error" message. It is this code that contains the infection. By the time the nonsystem disk error message comes up, the infection has occurred. Once the virus is executed, it will infect the hard drive's master boot record and may become memory-resident. With every subsequent boot, the virus will be loaded into memory and will attempt to infect any floppy diskettes accessed by the machine, thus propagating itself.

Prevention:

▼ Disable Floppy Booting unless absolutely necessary.

■ Scan often with a third party antivirus utility.

▲ Always scan floppy drives as they are accessed.

Stealth_C

Stealth_C is a memory-resident stealth virus that infects the system's master boot record and diskette boot sectors. Upon infection, Stealth_C will become memory-resident at the top of system memory but below the 640K DOS boundary. Stealth_C will also infect the master boot record at this time. Once the Stealth_C virus is memory-resident, it will infect diskette boot sectors when non-write-protected diskettes are accessed. Upon infection, Stealth_C will move the original boot sector to the last sector on the diskette.

This virus is a full stealth virus, hiding the infection on the system's hard disk and diskette boot sectors when the virus is memory-resident. Therefore, it is important to be sure that the virus is not memory-resident before attempting to scan a possibly infected system or diskette(s). Systems infected with Stealth_C may experience difficulty loading some drivers and memory management software into memory, resulting in operational difficulties with programs that access upper memory blocks, such as Windows 3.*x*. It may also cause 32-bit disk or file access to be disabled.

Stealth_C causes the total system and available free memory to decrease by 4,096 bytes.

The primary vector of infection of a master boot record/boot sector virus is through booting from an infected floppy diskette. The boot sector of the diskette has the code to determine if the diskette is bootable and to display the "Non-system disk or disk error" message. It is this code that contains the infection. By the time the nonsystem disk error message comes up, the infection has occurred. Once the virus is executed, it will infect the hard drive's master boot record and may become memory-resident. With every subsequent boot, the virus will be loaded into memory and will attempt to infect any floppy diskettes accessed by the machine, thus propagating itself.

Prevention:

▼   Disable Floppy Booting unless absolutely necessary.

■   Scan often with a third party antivirus utility.

▲   Always scan floppy drives as they are accessed.

NPAD

NPAD is a macro virus. It infects .DOC and .DOT files in the Microsoft Word environment. NPAD claims to be from Indonesia. After 23 infection iterations, NPAD announces itself with a series of message boxes declaring its origin and a simple copyright message. The NPAD macro virus contains the following macro when it infects a DOC file:

AutoOpen

This macro maintains the variable named "NPAD328" in the WIN.INI file to count the number of times you open documents in Microsoft Word. Regardless of when you open a document, when the counter reaches 24 the virus will display this message banner:

DOEUNPAD94, V.2.21, (C) Maret 1996, Bandung Indonesia

The message banner moves back and forth quickly in the lower-left corner of the monitor.

Macro viruses spread by having one or more macros in a document. Opening or closing the document or any activity that invokes the viral macros activates the virus. When the macro is activated, it copies itself and any other macros it needs, sometimes to the global macro file NORMAL.DOT. If they are stored in NORMAL.DOT they are available in all open documents. At this point, the macro viruses try to spread themselves to other documents. Macro viruses spread easily through e-mail packages. The ability of these packages to send and quickly launch documents can infect hundreds of users at a time. Documents are much more mobile than executable files, passing from machine to machine as different people write, edit, or access them. Macro viruses can therefore spread very quickly through business offices and corporations.

Prevention:

▼ Mark NORMAL.DOT as read-only. This prevents NORMAL.DOT from being infected.

■ Continue to vigilantly scan with an antivirus scanner.

■ Use Office 95A from Microsoft (**http://www.microsoft.com**) or Office 97.

▲ Install MVTools from Microsoft.

Junkie

Junkie is a multipartite, memory-resident, encrypting virus. Junkie specifically targets .COM files, the DOS boot sector on floppy diskettes, and the master boot record. When initial infection is in the form of a file infecting virus, Junkie infects the master boot record or floppy boot sector, disables VSafe (an antivirus terminate-and-stay-resident program, which is included with MS-DOS 6.X) and loads itself at Side 0, Cylinder 0, Sectors 4 and 5. The virus does not become memory-resident or infect files at this time. Later, when the system is booted from the system hard disk, the Junkie virus becomes memory-resident at the top of system memory but below the 640K DOS boundary, moving interrupt 12's returns. Once memory resident, Junkie begins infecting .COM files as they are executed and corrupts .COM files.

The Junkie virus infects diskette boot sectors as they are accessed. The virus will write a copy of itself to the last track of the diskette, and then alter the boot sector to point to this code. On high-density, 5.25-inch diskettes, the viral code will be located on Cylinder 79, Side 1, Sectors 8 and 9.

This virus will cause .COM and .EXE files to grow in length by 1,030 to 1,042 bytes, with the virus inserted at the end of the file. CHKDSK.EXE also reports a decrease of 3,072 bytes of total system and available free memory. This decrease may cause memory conflicts.

Junkie contains two encrypted messages:

Dr White—Sweden 1994

Junkie Virus—Written in Malmo...MO1D

These messages are not visible in files but can be viewed in memory.

Multipartite viruses have two main routes of infection; either as a master boot record/boot sector virus or as a file infecting virus. Most infections occur when a computer attempts to boot from an infected floppy diskette. The boot sector of the diskette has the code to determine if the diskette is bootable and to display the "Non-system disk or disk error" message. It is this code that harbors the infection. By the time the nonsystem disk error message comes up, the infection has occurred. Once the virus is executed, it will infect the hard drive's MBR and may become memory-resident. With every subsequent boot, the virus will be loaded into memory and will attempt to infect floppy diskettes accessed by the machine.

The second route of infection is by receiving an infected file through a multitude of sources, including floppy diskettes, Internet downloads, and network and various modem connections. Once the infected file is executed, the virus may activate.

CORPORATE VIRUS POLICY

After examining the many different types of viruses that can infect your Windows NT computers, the obvious next step is to look at the policies and procedures that will protect your systems. Of all of the policies that should be enforced in an organization, antivirus policies should be near the top. As much of a problem that viruses can be, they are extremely controllable with a few simple steps.

▼ Include antivirus training in normal training programs.

■ Scan for viruses at both workstations and servers.

■ Set up nonnetworked computers for testing new programs.

■ Run NT to take advantage of its security features.

■ Do not dual boot.

■ Require locked screen savers to prevent internal Trojan horses.

■ Assign at least one IS person to keep up-to-date on the latest virus attacks.

▲ Download the latest virus information files regularly.

This last step is extremely important. Your virus protection plan is worthless unless you regularly download the latest virus definition files. The major thing to keep in mind is that you cannot overstate to your employees the importance of good virus policy.

One example of good policy we have run into was at a medium-size company we worked with. This company had the most virus-conscious receptionist we have ever seen. Every time an outsider would show up with software, she would test it for viruses. She took the brunt of jokes from the entire company, including the IS department—that is, until she started finding an amazing number of viruses. Again, the point is that you are better off being overly cautious when it comes to viruses.

It is amazing to see the number of computer professionals who ignore the threat of viruses. Sections of some major companies still feel immune to the threat. Others simply feel that the costs of prevention are not offset by the potential threats. Using virus scanning software is as important as following tape backup procedure. If you do not implement these procedures, you are exposing your corporate data to a grave risk. It is not a matter of *if* you will get a virus, it is simply a matter of *when* you will get it and how bad it will be. Viruses have been found in banking networks, in secure, encrypted Pentagon networks, and throughout the Internet. One great story on the Internet claims that the United States military's network was infected with a virus during the Desert Storm operation. It was a completely encrypted network. The problem was that when files were unencrypted, so was the virus. Nobody is immune.

THIRD-PARTY ANTIVIRUS PRODUCTS

After the antivirus corporate policy has been considered, it becomes time to decide on a third-party antivirus product to use. Microsoft does not bundle antivirus software with NT. Luckily, a large number of excellent third-party products service this need.

▼ Data Fellows Limited (**http://www.datafellows.com**)

■ Trend Micro (**http://www.antivirus.com**)

■ Symantec (**http://www.symantec.com**)

■ Cheyenne Computer Associates (**http://www.cheyenne.com**)

■ McAfee Associates, Inc. (**http://www.mcaffe.com**)

■ Dr. Solomon's Software Limited (**http://www.drsolomon.com**)

■ IBM (**http://www.ibm.com**)

▲ ThunderByte, Inc. (**http://www.thunderbyte.com**)

Also, several shareware utilities are available to scan and remove DOS viruses. A couple of examples are ALERT!, BOOTCOMP, and CRC CHECK. These and many other shareware utilities can be found at your favorite Internet download site. One well-organized site is at Simtel (**http://simtel.coast.net/SimTel/msdos/virus.html**). In addition, many of the companies listed offer free 30-day evaluation copies either via Internet download or by requesting a CD-ROM.

All "NCSA certified" antivirus products are tested and certified to have virus scanners that detect 100 percent of all computer viruses known to have recently infected any computers worldwide.

Many of the commercial third-party products run as services on an NT system. These can provide real-time scanning of files on your system. Others are simply a one-time scan that can be run automatically during start-up or scheduled with an NT internal scheduler server (see Appendix C for more information on using Windows NT AT jobs). The real-time virus scanners provided by many of the third-party providers seem to vary greatly in their stability. Most interfere with at least one other program running on Windows NT servers. Others actually cause unexpected system crashes. This is not to say that you should not use real-time scanning. You simply need to be aware of the possible complications with these products.

Microsoft sent real-time virus scanners into a bit of a whirl with NT 4.0 Service Pack 2 (SP2). SP2 interfered with these products' capability to autoscan removable disks. The end result was that the NT system would crash with a blue screen almost every time the user accessed a floppy drive. This problem proved to be particularly embarrassing for network administrators. The Internet was full of interesting anecdotes about this problem. The most common story seemed to be about people using NT's built-in ability to create network installed floppies. Imagine the administrator's surprise when the floppy write activity caused a blue screen right before his or her eyes. Be careful with real-time scanners. Test before you leap!

Most of the third-party products use a virus definition file to search for viruses. Some use heuristics to detect for the presence of malignant code. Some use a bit of both. The heuristic approach is analytical or investigative attempt to detect new and unknown viruses without having ever seen them before. These systems try to sense patterns and common behaviors associated with viruses. Poor detection rates and an unacceptably high level of false alarms have traditionally hampered this approach. The heuristics in Dr. Solomon's Anti-Virus Toolkit are considered some of the best on the market. They are combined with the traditional virus information file technique. Some companies are even promoting a pure heuristic solution that never needs updating. Unfortunately, the technology has not progressed to the point that you can count on heuristics as the only form of virus protection.

The bottom line on third-party virus scanners is that you should be using at least one of them. They install relatively easily and, with the exception of the real-time components, tend to run bug-free. The antivirus market leader, McAfee, holds an over 50 percent share. Another major antivirus scanner, Norton AntiVirus, is described in the next section. It provides a good example, as it has several of the standard antivirus features.

Symantec Norton AntiVirus

Norton has been a player in the antivirus market for some time. Norton AntiVirus protects Windows NT workstations and servers from viruses incoming from the Internet, floppy disks, hard drives, CD-ROMs, in e-mail attachments, shared files, network drives, and drives shared between peer machines. It can even protect Windows NT-based FTP and Web servers. Norton AntiVirus also uses its Symantecs Striker technology to detect and eradicate most polymorphic viruses. Figure 6-5 shows the Norton AntiVirus main screen.

Symantec offers free virus definition updates. You can receive them on CD-ROM, download them from the Symantec Web site, or use the built-in, automatic download tool. This tool called LiveUpdate automates the definition update process via modem or through the Internet. This makes it easy to ensure that your virus definition files always stay current. Figure 6-6 shows the LiveUpdate feature.

Norton AntiVirus also has an autoprotect service for Windows NT that loads at the kernel level of the operating system. It is quite good at providing continuous, automatic protection with minimal impact on performance. This was one of the products affected by Microsoft NT 4.0 Service Pack 2. As previously mentioned, NT crashed on floppy access due to SP2. Norton AntiVirus gives you the option of disabling the autoprotect service if it is a problem. The Norton AntiVirus autoprotect service is highly regarded in the industry.

Norton AntiVirus is a full-featured product. It uses the NT scheduler and an event log, and it can scan network drives. It is extremely configurable through its options screen, shown in Figure 6-7. It allows toggling through different types of scans (master boot record, boot record) and allows scanning within compressed files. It allows you to choose the types of files to scan or exclude and gives you several options when a virus is

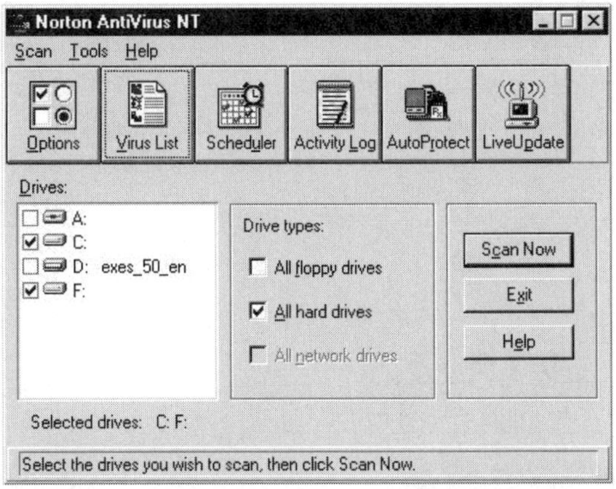

Figure 6-5.   The Norton AntiVirus main screen

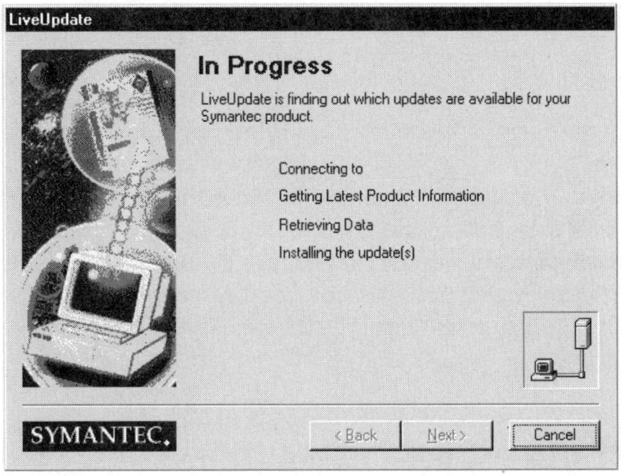

Figure 6-6.   Norton uses its LiveUpdate feature to quickly get the latest virus definitions

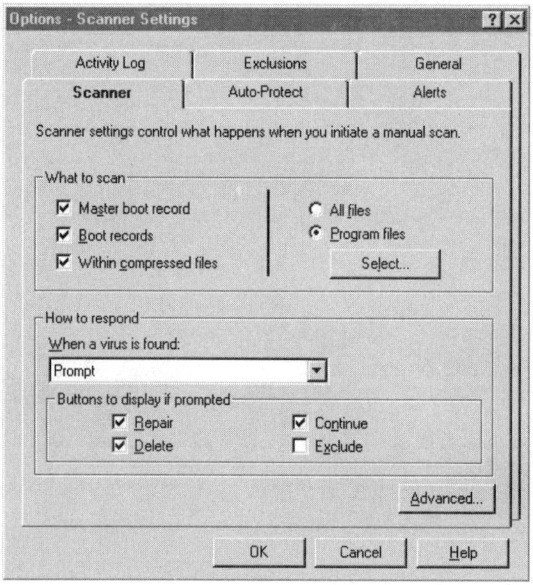

Figure 6-7. The Norton AntiVirus options screen

found. It currently does not support e-mail alerting, relying instead on console messages and audible sounds.

Norton also offers the Norton AntiVirus for Internet E-mail Gateways. This product sits on the SMTP gateway, automatically intercepting and destroying viruses hidden in e-mail attachments. Separate scanning policies can even be set for incoming and outgoing files of several different file types. It scans compressed and encoded files and can be administered from any location via an HTML interface. This product also supports the LiveUpdate function.

SOURCES FOR VIRUS INFORMATION

There are many fine places to get information on the latest virus alerts on the World Wide Web. Almost all of the third-party providers mentioned in this chapter have an area on their Web site specifically dedicated to providing information on a variety of viruses. Three of my favorite places to get virus information are the Symantec AntiVirus Research Center (SARC—**http://www.symantec.com**), National Computer Security

Association (NCSA—**http://ncsa.com**) and the McAfee Virus Information Library (**http://www.mcafee.com**). Dr. Solomon also ships an informative *Virus Encyclopedia* with each copy of its software. The makers of F-Prot have an easy-to-navigate Web site located at **http://www.datafellows.com**. All of these resources provide a vast array of virus information, and possible viruses can be submitted for analysis.

SUMMARY

This chapter analyzed the threat of viruses to your NT network. At first glance, it may seem a bit alarming, however, the hard truth is that ignoring the threat of viruses has caused unpleasant surprises at too many companies. Virus policy must be a part of any disaster recovery plan. There is no question that an NT system is susceptible to computer viruses. In the best case, the virus will simply be an annoyance. In the worst case, a virus can destroy data or even render your system unbootable. Since NT does not use BIOS-based disk drivers, it will prevent the propagation of many of the traditional boot sector viruses.

By far, the two types of infections you are most likely to encounter are from infected floppies (boot sector viruses) and infected e-mail (macro viruses). These can be prevented with good corporate policy and a good third-party antivirus product.

CHAPTER 7

Windows NT Security

As Windows NT becomes the preeminent network operating system, it is under an enormous amount of pressure from outside developers who are trying to break through its security scheme. NT networks are now used to store and share critical information among many users throughout all levels of an organization. A security disaster is among the most costly type of problem that can hit your enterprise network. The ability to prevent or monitor unauthorized access to these systems can be crucial to the security and even the survival of an organization. It is easy to understand why security is one of the most important areas to consider in your plan for corporate fault tolerance and disaster prevention.

There are several areas that an NT administrator must consider when designing an NT security policy. Security threats can come from outside sources, like hackers, but they are just as likely to come from within your own organization. This chapter is meant as an NT security overview and explains the basics of NT security and the steps required for protecting your NT environment. For a more comprehensive look into NT security, see the *Windows NT Security Handbook*, (Osborne/McGraw-Hill), by Tom Sheldon.

SECURITY

Many people have an "It will never happen to me" attitude about security. This naïve attitude is fine as long as one understands the ramifications of such an attitude. There are not, and never will be, any completely secure networks. The best you can hope to do is to secure your systems to make unauthorized entry as difficult as possible or at least not worth the effort. You need to plan your security policy and take the necessary precautions with this in mind. Flaws in the security of network operating systems and protocols are bad enough, but you also must consider the "people factor." Security professionals use the term *social engineering* to describe the art of manipulating people in such a way as to gain control of critical data, usernames, and passwords. This can be through investigation or even casual conversation. There are some great examples of hackers gaining access by trying a person's birth date or anniversary as the password.

Lack of encryption in today's networks can be a major security problem. Much of your data, usernames, and even passwords cross your network in unencrypted form. An inexpensive network analyzer can be used to collect and read this unencrypted data with very little chance of being detected. There are an enormous number of software and hardware-based network analyzers available in the market. Microsoft ships a software-based network monitor with the Systems Management Server (SMS) component of BackOffice. This network analyzer can be installed from the SMS installation program without actually installing the entire SMS product. It also can be purchased separately for around $900. A limited version of the same product ships with Microsoft Windows NT 4.0 Server. You should take the time to install this product or one of the third-party versions to locate and understand the vulnerable areas of your network. Understanding your weaknesses is a large part of the solution to network security problems.

NT SECURITY

Microsoft has made great strides in making Windows NT a secure operating system. They have also worked to make its security scheme easy to understand. They use common schemes and interfaces to set security on a wide variety of objects from files and directories to printers and the Registry.

C2

No discussion of Windows NT security would be complete without talking about the C2 security level. C2 is one of several Orange Book security levels developed by the United States government for operating systems. The real name of the Orange Book is the *Trusted Computer System Evaluation Criteria*. C2 is used as a baseline measurement for security and applies to a stand-alone PC only. In fact, if your machine is connected to a network, it cannot be Orange Book C2 secure! That gets into the Red Book and Blue Book interpretations of the Orange Book levels. NT is currently being evaluated for these designations, because Microsoft has gone beyond C2 in many ways to protect an NT system from unauthorized access. A properly configured Windows NT server is one of the most secure network operating systems available. NT protects data not only on system hard drives but also while that data is in memory. Even with this secure design, it is necessary to keep up to date with the latest security information pertaining to NT networks. Microsoft maintains a list of known security issues and solutions on its Web site at **http://www.microsoft.com/security**.

Security Accounts Manager (SAM)

All Windows NT machines have a Security Accounts Manager (SAM). The SAM is the database of user, group, and computer accounts that are authorized to access the NT system. In the case of domains, a single SAM is shared among the domain controllers. This SAM database file is located in the NT Registry directory (%SYSTEMROOT%\ SYSTEM32\CONFIG\). Only NT servers and workstations have SAMs, which is the reason that Windows 95 and other machines cannot actually "join" a domain.

The maximum size of the NT SAM is 40MB, which has ramifications on the maximum size of an NT domain. Each user account requires 1K. Each computer account requires 0.5K. Each group account requires 4K. Therefore, a domain with 10,000 users, 10,000 computers, and 50 groups would require 15.2MB of SAM space. You can break up domains into smaller entities using the models shown in the "Domain Models" section of this chapter. Be sure to plan for future organizational growth.

The Logon Process

There are two ways you can log on to an NT machine: locally or remotely. Logging on locally implies you are logging directly on to the machine in question. Remote logon refers to an "over the network" logon to some shared resource that requires a valid username and password.

When logging on locally to an NT workstation or server, you are presented with the NT Security dialog box. You are prompted for your username, password, and domain name. The domain name could be the local machine, the local domain, or a trusted domain. Note that it is possible to have an account in all three account databases. To avoid confusion, administrators should try to give each user only one account. Your choice for domain tells the Local Security Authority (LSA) in which SAM your account will be located.

The LSA is the main security broker of the NT security subsystem. It compares account information from the logon process to the SAM. The LSA also manages the security and audit policies and passes audit messages to the event log.

If your username/password combination is found to be authentic, the LSA creates a security access token. This token contains your unique user account security ID (SID), any applicable group ID (GID), and your specific user rights. Each process you start during your NT session gets passed this token so that it operates with your specific privileges. This prevents you from having to keep entering your information each time you open a network resource or execute a local program.

The Security Reference Monitor (SRM) is the enforcer of the access and audit policies established by the LSA. All attempts to access objects go through the SRM. Objects can be files, shares, ports, printers, and directories, among others. Even a process is an object in NT. When a process tries to access an object, the SRM steps in and examines the object's access control list (ACL). The SRM bases the decision to grant access on the ACL of the object. You can edit the ACL using the Properties dialog box of most common objects or through other programs, like CACLS.EXE from Microsoft.

The ACL is basically a list of access control entries (ACEs). The ACEs are normally organized so that entries that deny access precede those that allow it. If the information in your token matches any of the deny access ACEs, you are immediately refused access. If you are entitled to have access to the object, a handle is generated. The *handle* contains a list of the rights granted. The information is then stored in the process table for subsequent object access.

Share and File Level Security

There are two ways to give access to NTFS files and directories with Microsoft networking: through the ACL for the network share or through the ACL on the files or directories. Your access will be controlled by a specific combination of the permissions of the two ACLs. If you are running the FAT file system, you will only be able to control the share's ACL.

Share Security

The first part of this discussion assumes the file system is FAT, which implies that the only access control is through the share.

NOTE: FAT is a violation of C2 security. For maximum NT file system security, it is recommended to make ALL drives NTFS.

The network *share* indicates how you are gaining access to the drive. It can be considered a pointer that maintains certain rights. Your rights to a file or directory can never exceed the rights of the share you used to access it. You also cannot move above the share point through which you gained access. Consider the NT Explorer view of a directory tree, shown in Figure 7-1. Again, assume the file system is FAT.

If you access the drive through the i386 share as read-only, you will have read-only rights on all files and folders in the tree from the i386 directory downward. Your rights cascade throughout the lower directories. Your apparent root will be the i386 directory. You will not be able to see any files above it. The only way to see any of those files would be to gain access through a different share (in this case, the share of the root drive). In addition, the only way to increase your permissions to the i386 tree is to change the share-level ACL. Remember that this is a FAT formatted drive.

Figure 7-2 shows the Access Through Share Permissions dialog box for the i386 share. You can access this page through the Permissions button on the Sharing tab of the directory's property page. Notice the four choices for share-level ACLs: No Access, Read, Change, and Full Control. Table 7-1 explains the different access levels. If you are a member of several groups with varying share-level access, the permissions will be cumulative. The highest level of access will be granted. This changes in the case of No Access. If your access token contains a group identification (GID) or account identification (SID) that matches a No Access ACE, you will have no access.

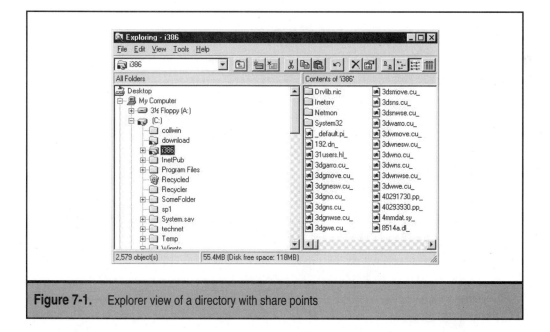

Figure 7-1.   Explorer view of a directory with share points

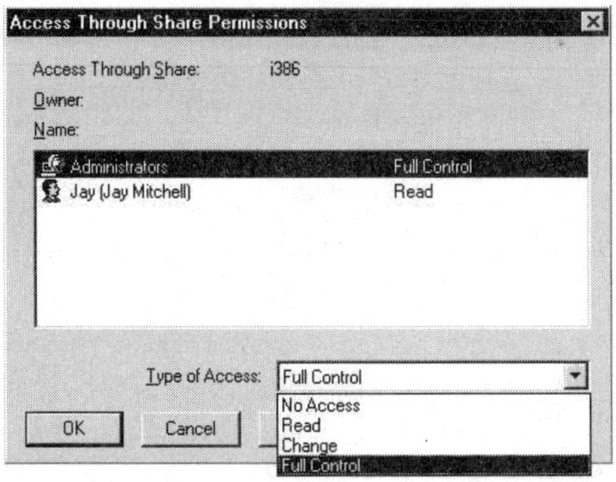

Figure 7-2.　i386 folder share ACL settings

NTFS Security

What happens if the drive is formatted as an NTFS partition? The permissions work in unison, and the more restrictive ACL takes precedence. This means that if you gain entrance through a share that has read-only permissions and you are accessing an NTFS

Type of Access	Permissions
No Access	Prevents access to files and subdirectories. If you belong to a group with this right, it overrides all other permissions, including NTFS.
Read	View file and subdirectory names. View data in files and executing programs. Change to subdirectories.
Change	View file and subdirectory names. View data in files and executing programs. Change to subdirectories. Change file and subdirectory names. Change file data. Add and delete files and subdirectories. Change file and subdirectory permissions (NTFS).
Full Control	Same as Change but can also take ownership of the file or subdirectory.

Table 7-1.　Share-Level Permissions

drive in which you have full control, you will have read-only rights. The only way to increase your rights is by changing the share's ACL or changing your point of entry. Conversely, if you gain access to a drive through a share that allows you full control, your permissions will be completely based on the NTFS permissions of the drive.

To change the ACL of an NTFS partition, you can go to the security page of the particular object's properties. Figure 7-3 shows the Directory Permissions dialog box for the i386 directory. You can access this page through the Permissions button on the Security tab of the directory's property page. In Figure 7-4, the associated ACL is shown using the SHOWACL.EXE utility from the NT Resource Kit. Notice the direct correlation in the entries for the i386 directory in these figures.

There are several different access levels you can assign to an NTFS object. These make up the basic permissions and are shown in Table 7-2.

To make assigning permissions easier, NT has a set of standard permissions that you can assign to accounts. They are made up of assortments of the basic permissions set. The standard permissions for directories are listed in Table 7-3. In the example using the i386 directory (Figure 7-3), the permissions were all assigned using the standard permissions. Notice that Figure 7-3 shows two sets of cumulative permission designators in parentheses to the right of the standard permissions for the directory. The first set contains the permissions on the directory, and the second set is for the files in the directory.

When the object's cumulative permission designator is set to Not Specified, the account cannot access any files unless permission is specifically granted elsewhere. A designation of None means the account will have no access. An asterisk following a directory designation means that subdirectories do not inherit the indicated permissions. In addition, any account with full control of a directory can delete files in a directory no matter what permissions are on the files! If you want to apply a custom set of permissions

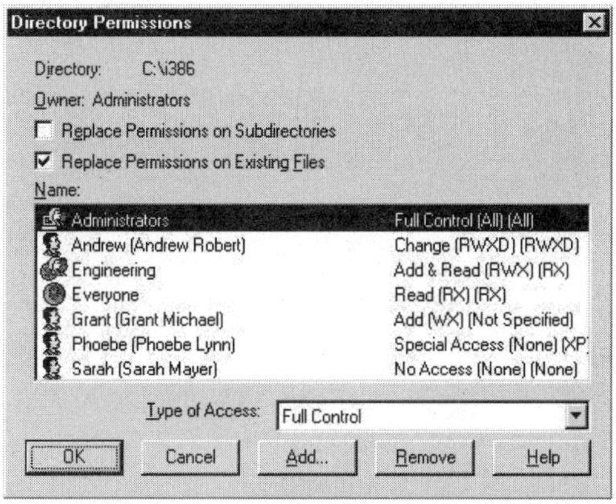

Figure 7-3.   NTFS permissions for the i386 directory

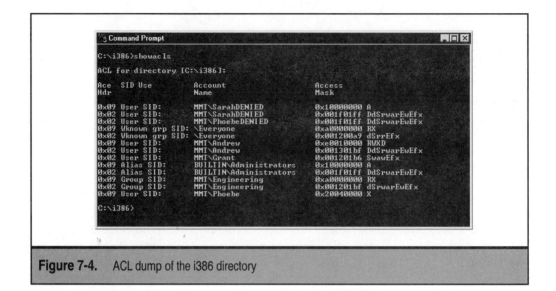

Figure 7-4.   ACL dump of the i386 directory

to a file or directory, you use the Special Access dialog box, which is accessed from the Type of Access drop-down list. Special Access is some combination of the basic permissions shown in Table 7-2.

The standard permissions for files have the same meanings as the permissions for directories. They are simply a smaller subset of the directory permissions and include

NTFS Permission	Permissions on the Directory	Permissions on the Files in the Directory
Read (R)	View file and subdirectory names in the folder	View the file's data
Write (W)	Add files or subdirectories	Change the file's data
Execute (X)	Change to subdirectories	Run the file (if it can execute)
Delete (D)	Remove the directory	Remove the file
Change Permissions (P)	Change the directory's permissions	Change the file's permissions
Take Ownership (O)	Assume ownership of the directory	Assume ownership of the file

Table 7-2.   NTFS Basic Permissions Set

NTFS Permission	Permission on the Directory	Permissions on the Files in the Directory
No Access	None	None
List	RX	Not Specified
Read	RX	RX
Add	WX	Not Specified
Add & Read	RWX	RX
Change	RWXD	RWXD
Full Control	All (RWXDPO)	All (RWXDPO)

Table 7-3.   Standard Permissions for Directories

only No Access, Read, Change, and Full Control. If you set an individual file's NTFS permissions, be sure that you have checked the overall directory permissions. In some cases, the directory permissions take precedence. As mentioned above, full control of a directory allows a user to delete any files in the directory.

Ownership

The person who creates a directory or file becomes that object's owner. In order to change the access permissions for an object, you must be an owner or an administrator. In fact, the owner (or an administrator) can grant the permission to take ownership to other users. Note that you cannot transfer ownership to other users. You can only give them the right to *take ownership*. They must take ownership of the object themselves after they are granted the right to do so. Figure 7-5 shows the Owner dialog box. It is accessed through

Figure 7-5.   The Owner dialog box

the Auditing button on the security tab of an object's properties. Again note that your only option is to take ownership. You cannot give it away. This preserves security, as it allows the object to show any change in ownership even if it is done by an administrator.

Auditing

A secure operating system needs to be able to both restrict access and audit security events. NT offers a full-featured auditing capability that enhances your system's integrity. To turn auditing on for the entire NT system, you use the Audit Policy dialog box in the User Manager for Domains tool (Figure 7-6). You can access this page in the User Manager for Domains tool through the Policies menu by selecting the Audit option. Turning off auditing in this dialog box will disable all auditing on the system. This dialog box also allows you to make other system-wide audit policy changes, such as logon events, user rights changes, and system shutdowns.

Once auditing has been enabled, you can make changes to auditing through the property pages of a file, a directory, a printer, or even the Registry. A Directory Auditing dialog box is shown in Figure 7-7. Note that you can audit both successes and failures of several events, including write and delete attempts. To allow auditing modifications to propagate through any subdirectories of a folder, simply click the Replace Auditing on Subdirectories check box.

NOTE: Remember to consider that auditing does have an adverse affect on system performance.

You can also audit your printers. This allows tight control and monitoring of your print processes. Printer events include deleting, changing permissions, and, of course, printing. A Printer Auditing dialog box is shown in Figure 7-8. It is accessed from the Security tab of the printer property page.

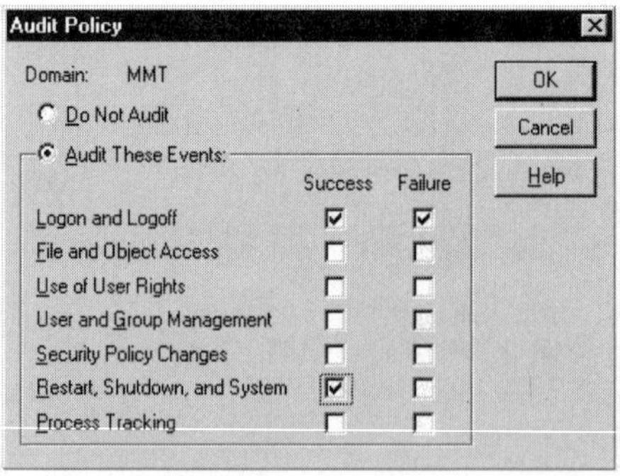

Figure 7-6.   The Audit Policy dialog box in the User Manager for Domains

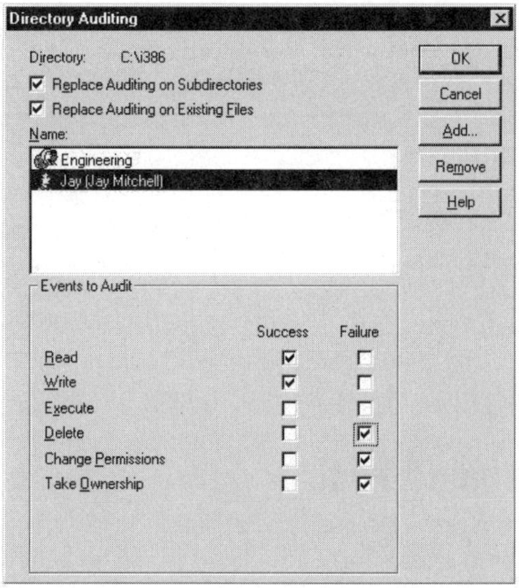

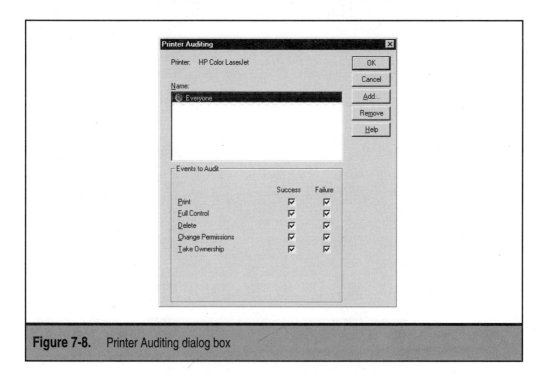

Figure 7-7.   Directory Auditing dialog box

Figure 7-8.   Printer Auditing dialog box

Audited events are saved in the Security Log of the NT Event Viewer. An example is shown in Figure 7-9. You double-click any event to see more details. Be sure to set the event log settings to not overwrite the events automatically. This is done in the Log Settings option under the Log menu. The event log can be dumped to a file using the DUMPEL.EXE tool in the NT Resource Kit or any similar tool. It can then be parsed and examined by a custom or third-party program. Note that NT's Event Viewer is also an excellent remote diagnostic tool. You can select a different NT machine to examine using the Select Computer option under the Log menu. This allows you to easily check on another machine's event status.

There is one important point to make about auditing events on your NT system. If you audit too many events, you can slow down your system's performance. Auditing adds overhead, as it uses processor time and needs time to write to the event log on the disk. You must choose carefully the areas you wish to monitor.

User Manager for Domains Tool

The User Manager for Domains administrative tool is the heart of NT security and control (Figure 7-10). It is an intuitive tool that allows you to create user and group accounts, set up trust relationships, and modify time restrictions, among other things. Remember that you can use this tool to modify settings on another domain's domain controllers and on remote workstations. To select different domains, go to the User menu, choose the Select

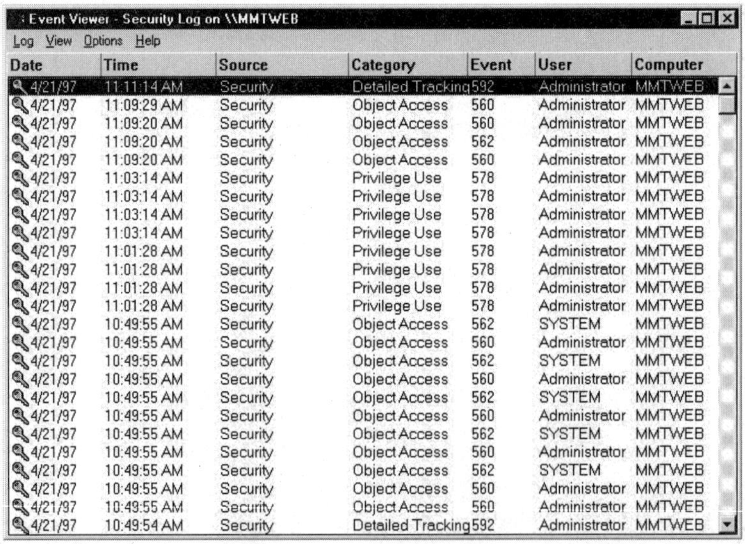

Figure 7-9. The Event Viewer Security Log

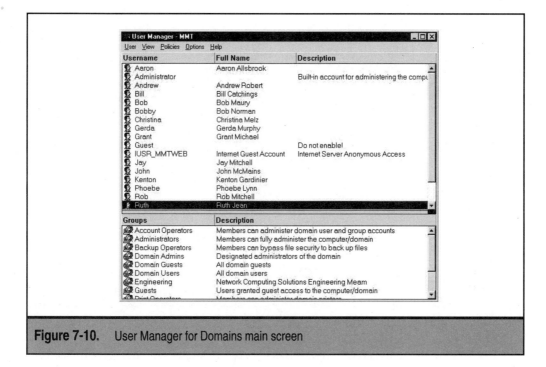

Figure 7-10. User Manager for Domains main screen

Domain item, and browse for the required domain. To select an individual server or workstation, again choose the Select Domain item on the User menu and manually enter in the universal naming convention (UNC) identity of the machine.

You can make several modifications to a user's environment with this tool. If you double-click a user on the main screen, the User Properties dialog box appears (Figure 7-11). The buttons at the bottom allow you to control group assignments (Groups), logon profile (Profile), time restrictions (Hours), workstation assignments (Logon To), account lifetime (Account), and remote access rights (Dialin). These check boxes override other user rights.

Domains and Workgroups

An understanding of domains and workgroups is central to planning a Microsoft network. They are Microsoft's answer to two network problems: browsing and security.

A *workgroup* is a peer-to-peer relationship between computers. Everyone is both a server and a workstation. Most computer users spend 95 percent of their time sharing data between a small number of people and servers. A workgroup enables them to not have to *see* the entire network. Instead, their browse lists only contain those servers pertinent to their department's function. Authentication is based on the local security policy of each workgroup member. Therefore, workgroup security is decentralized and quickly becomes confusing with ten or more machines.

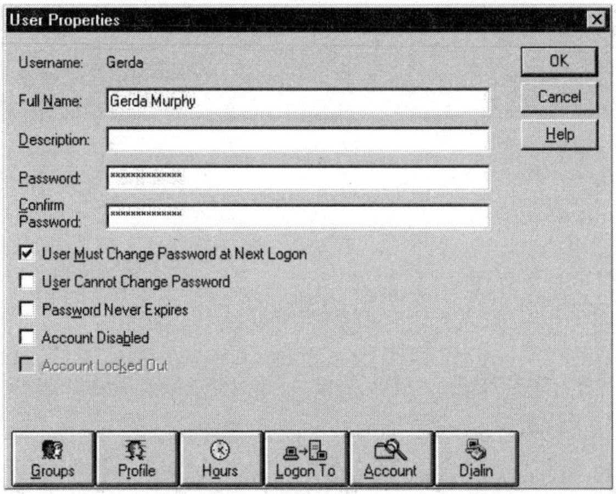

Figure 7-11.   User Properties dialog box

Domains, on the other hand, are the workhorses of Microsoft's pre–NT 5.0 security model. *Domains* are collections of users and computers that are managed by a central authority. This central authority is known as the primary domain controller (PDC). The primary domain controller maintains the accounts database for the entire domain. The User Manager for Domains utility is actually a front end to the accounts database on the PDC. To add fault tolerance and scalability to your domain authentication servers, you can add backup domain controllers (BCDs). All NT networks should have at least one BDC. Chapter 2 gives a more complete explanation of the domain controller relationship. In addition, the NT 5.0 section at the end of this chapter discusses the account structure of Windows NT 5.0.

Trusts

Interdomain security can be set up with the trust relationships. These relationships allow a user account in one domain to access the resources of another domain. The use of trust relationships is an integral part of the domain models discussed in the following section. Trusts must be carefully thought out, as they can pose a grave security risk if not properly administered. There are no implicit trust relationships. Everything must be explicitly defined in the User Manager for Domains Trust Relationships dialog box (Figure 7-12). A *trusting domain* is the domain that allows accounts in other domains to have rights to its resources. A *trusted domain* is the domain that supplies the accounts that can access the other domain's resources.

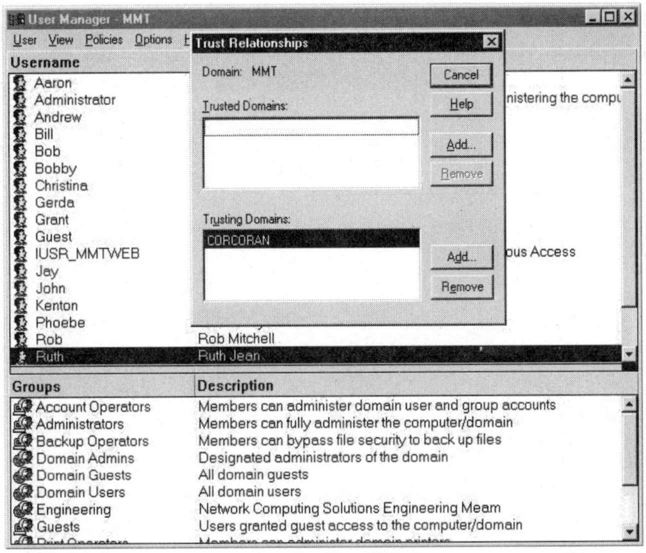

Figure 7-12. The Trust Relationships dialog box

The easiest way to set up a trust relationship is to start at the trusted domain's domain controller. Here are the steps:

1. Open the Trust Relationships dialog box in the User Manager for Domains.

2. Click the Add button. Think of this as the "who trusts me" entry. This is the domain that is going to be able to see *your* account lists. This enables the domain to add *your* users and groups to the access control lists of its resources.

3. Enter in the information for the trusting domain. The password is only used to set up the initial trust. It does not need to be an administrator password.

4. Be sure you have established NetBIOS connectivity with the other domain.

5. Have an administrator in the other domain enter in the information from your domain in the Trusted Domains box and click OK. The administrator should enter the same password used in step 3.

6. After a brief pause, NT will tell you that the trust is successfully established. If it does not, the problem is usually a typing error, a bad password, or a problem with NetBIOS connectivity.

Remember that a trust is a one-way relationship. If you want a two-way relationship, you must complete the previous steps in both directions.

Now that the trust is set up, what happens? Nothing. You must go into the access control list of your resources and give accounts in the other domain specific access.

Nothing is implied—you must add specific access rights. This becomes even more of an issue when you add more domains. For instance, if you have four domains and you want all four to trust each other, you will have to complete the previous steps 12 times (see Figure 7-13). This translates to (n*(n-1)), where n is the number of domains. You can imagine how messy this would be with 20 or 30 trusting domains! The relationship in which each domain trusts all others is referred to as the *complete trust model*.

Domain Models

There are four basic trust models that most NT networks tend to fall into: complete, single domain, single master, and multiple master. Your choice of which to use will depend on several factors, including the number of users, the layout of your network, and the security required. As mentioned, the maximum size of an NT SAM is 40MB. The SAM is made up of the accounts for users, groups, and computers. Each user account uses 1K, each computer 0.5K and each group account requires 4K.

COMPLETE TRUST   In the complete trust model, all domains trust all other domains. From a security point of view, the complete trust model is very close to having a single huge workgroup. Every domain administers its own resources, and there is no centralized control. This model quickly becomes confusing and should only be used when security is not a major concern.

SINGLE DOMAIN   The single domain model, as the name implies, has all servers, workstations, and resources in one domain. This model has excellent security, has centralized administration, and works well with small and medium-sized organizations up to 5,000 users.

SINGLE MASTER   In the single master domain model, there is a central management domain (the master) surrounded by one or more resource domains. The master domain is

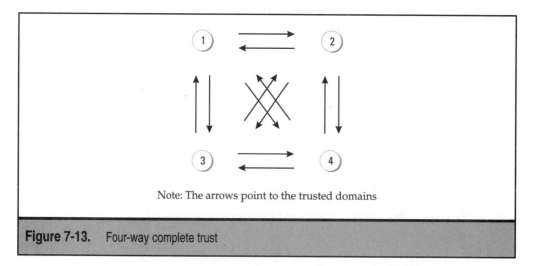

Note: The arrows point to the trusted domains

Figure 7-13.   Four-way complete trust

also called the account domain, as all users have an account in that domain. All resources appear in one of the lower level domains, and each of these domains trusts the master domain. Because account management is centralized, this model has excellent security.

Another practical feature of this model is that resources can be administered by a local resource domain administrator. For instance, if marketing wants to restrict access to its color printer, the marketing manager may assign rights, using user account or groups from the master domain. If you have remote offices connected by a slow link with this model, you would want to add a local backup domain controller to quickly authenticate those users. This model works well with large organizations up to 15,000 users but can be difficult to manage as the size of the master domain's accounts database grows large.

MULTIPLE MASTER   The multiple master domain model (Figure 7-14) is a tiered approach to account and resource management. It requires two or more single master

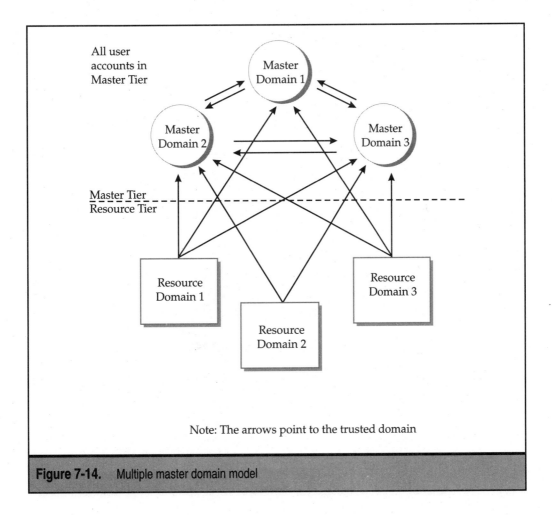

Figure 7-14.   Multiple master domain model

domains whose account domains all have two-way trust relationships with each other. Each master domain has one or more resource domains associated with it that contain computer accounts and network resources. Each of these resource domains has one-way trust relationships with all of the master domains. This allows accounts in any one domain to have access to the entire network. This model works well for large organizations with 15,000 or more user accounts. Organizations of that size tend to break up administrative groups into major geographical locations, which is reasonably analogous to this model. Microsoft uses this tiered approach to NT domains for its own worldwide network.

Account Rights

While permissions apply to specific objects, rights on an NT machine apply to specific actions. For instance, you may have the right to log on locally to an NT machine. This means you are allowed to enter your username and password and log on to that machine. You are only allowed to proceed if you have an account or are a member of a group that has that specific right.

You make modifications to rights in the User Rights option under the Policy menu of the User Manager for Domains tool. This is shown in Figure 7-15. NT rights are considered either standard or advanced. The list of standard rights is shown in Table 7-4.

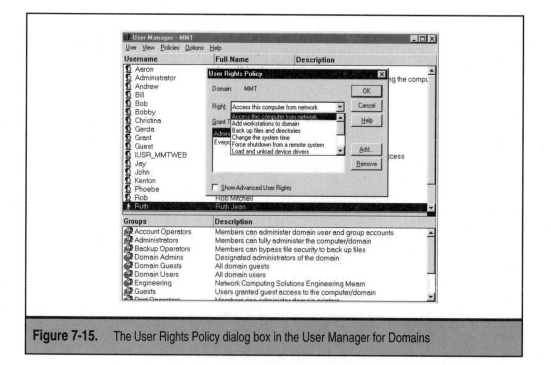

Figure 7-15. The User Rights Policy dialog box in the User Manager for Domains

NT Standard Right	Actions Allowed	Groups That Have This Right by Default
Access this computer from the network	Remote connections to resources on this machine over the network	Administrators, Everyone
Add workstations to domain	Add computer accounts to the domain	This right is inalienable to the Administrators and Account Operators groups
Back up files and directories	Back up files and directories, regardless of the object's permissions	Administrators, Backup Operators, Server Operators
Change the system time	Modify system date and time	Administrators, Server Operators
Force shutdown from a remote system	Not currently implemented	Administrators, Server Operators
Load and unload device drivers	Dynamically install and remove device drivers	Administrators
Log on locally	Log on directly to this computer's console	Administrators, Account Operators, Print Operators, Server Operators
Manage auditing and security log	Modify the auditing on a specific object, view and clear security log	Administrators
Restore files and directories	Restore files and directories from backup, regardless of the object's permissions	Administrators, Backup Operators, Server Operators
Shut down the system	Initiate a system shutdown	Administrators, Account Operators, Backup Operators, Print Operators, Server Operators
Take ownership of files and other objects	Allows the account to assume ownership of an object	Administrators

Table 7-4.   NT User Rights

NT Standard Right Selected Advanced Rights	Actions Allowed	Groups That Have This Right by Default
Bypass traverse checking	Navigate through the directory trees of the system, regardless of directory permissions	Everyone
Log on as a service	Register with the system as a service and log on	None by default

Table 7-4.   NT User Rights (*continued*)

This table also includes some of the advanced rights you are most likely to encounter. The advanced right called Log on as a service is probably the most commonly applied custom right, as it is required for the service accounts that are used in programs such as Microsoft Exchange, SMS, and third-party backup software. Remember that the rights applied to a domain controller affect all domain controllers in a given domain.

You need to be very careful with rights, as they can sometimes override the NTFS permissions. For instance, the right to back up files and directories gives you the ability to read any file, regardless of the NTFS permissions.

Groups in NT

Groups in Windows NT are simply sets of accounts that make administration easier. The group system in NT allows you to customize and control your NT network. NT also includes some built-in groups to get you started, such as Administrators, Guests, and Users.

NT groups come in two flavors: local and global. To make it even more confusing, global groups can be members of local groups but not vice versa. Either group can be added to an access control list. However, local groups are only seen on the local security entity (LSE). Global groups can appear both inside and outside of the LSE. The LSE can be a workstation, a stand-alone member server, or most commonly a set of NT domain controllers. Figure 7-16 illustrates this point. The Users local group will only appear on other domain controllers, as they are all within the same LSE. The Domain Users global group will appear both inside and outside of the domain controller LSE. What this means is that the member server or workstation will be able to assign access control entries using the domain controllers' global groups but will *never* see the domain controllers' local

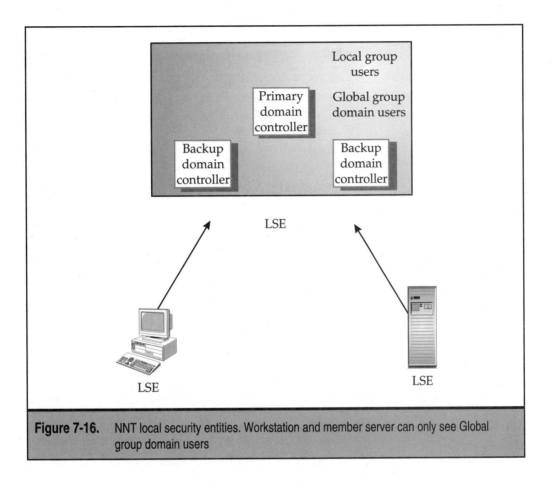

Figure 7-16. NNT local security entities. Workstation and member server can only see Global group domain users

groups. Note that the same is true if you add a second domain. The second domain will only see the global groups of the first domain and will never see its local groups.

Which type of group should you use? In an enterprise environment with several domains, the easiest procedure to follow is to use local groups for changing access control lists and use global groups only as members of local groups. This means that even if you just want to add a single global group to a resource, you will first have to create a local group. This sounds like a great deal of extra work, but it can actually make security administration easier in a large environment. If you stick to this procedure, adding another group to access a resource is as simple as opening up the User Manager for Domains tool and making group-level changes.

In addition to the built-in groups on an NT machine, you may notice the special groups: CREATOR OWNER, Everyone, INTERACTIVE, NETWORK, and SYSTEM. They are a convenient way NT denotes particular types of accounts on the machine and network. Table 7-5 explains their functions.

Special Group	Definition
CREATOR OWNER	The account that created the file or last took ownership.
Everyone	Everyone who accesses the computer both locally and over the network, including guest users. By default, NT assigns a surprising number of permissions to the group Everyone
INTERACTIVE	Users logged on to the local console.
NETWORK	Users logged on remotely over the network.
SYSTEM	The NT operating system itself. In general, leave assignments to the SYSTEM group as they are.

Table 7-5.   NT Special Groups

Be especially careful to understand the ramifications of the special group Everyone. It includes not only accounts in your domains and any trusted domains but literally everyone. To truly lock down your system, you would want to remove as many rights from this account as possible. Using the built-in Users or the Authenticated Users group as an alternative to the Everyone group is an excellent solution. More information on removing rights to the Everyone account can be found on the Microsoft security page (**http:// www.microsoft.com/ security**). There is also a shareware utility written by a gentleman named David LeBlanc called EVERYONE2USER.EXE that makes these changes for you on the specified directory tree. NT's CACLS.EXE tool can also make this job easier by allowing ACL changes from the command line using wildcards and even scripts.

Printer Security

Windows NT allows you to control access to and audit a shared printer. Printer permissions are assigned on the security tab of the printer's property page, as shown in Figure 7-17. The permission options for printers are explained in Table 7-6.

Notice that you can also take ownership of a printer. This works in the same way as ownership of a file or directory. You cannot assign ownership; your only option is to take it over. In addition, NT also allows printer auditing. This gives you the option to tightly control and monitor the use of your printers.

Registry Security

The Registry is a database containing information and settings for your entire NT system. It is a hierarchical structure of keys and values. Like printers, files, and directories, you

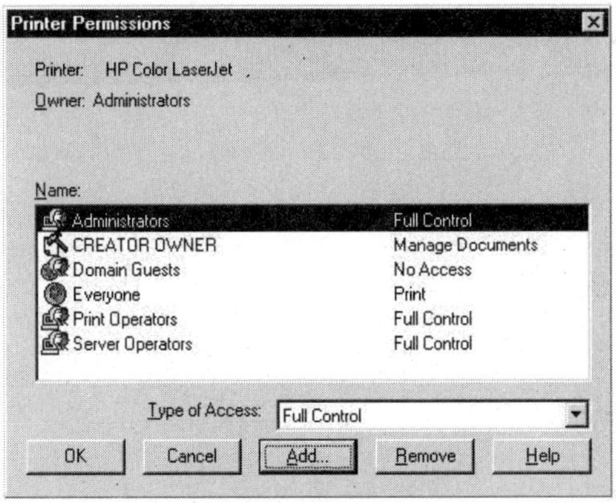

Figure 7-17. Printer Permissions dialog box

can limit access to all or parts of your Registry keys. Remember also that the Registry is basically a set of files found in the %SYSTEMROOT%\SYSTEM32\CONFIG directory. If your system partition is NTFS, you can modify the ACL of these files. By default, the Everyone group has full control of the Registry files.

To modify internal Registry security, use the REGEDT32.EXE tool that is native to all versions of NT. Figure 7-18 shows the Security menu of the Registry Editor tool. It allows you to make permission changes, take ownership, and audit in a manner very similar to

Type of Access	Permissions
No Access	Prevents any access
Print	Send a print job to the printer
Manage Documents	Control documents and delete, pause, resume, restart specific jobs
Full Control	Manage document permissions plus change printer properties, permissions, ownership, delete printers, delete, pause, resume, restart entire queue, and adjust printing order

Table 7-6. Printer Permissions

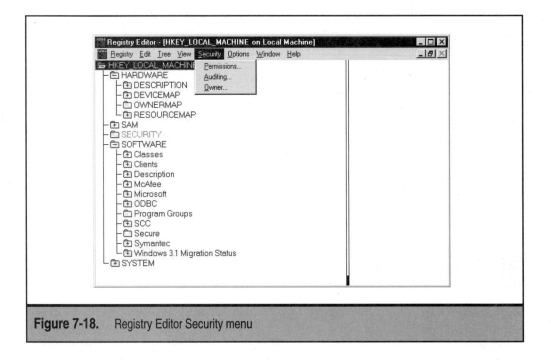

Figure 7-18. Registry Editor Security menu

the file and directory security menu. Figure 7-19 shows the special permissions that can be assigned in the Registry.

If you are worried about some of the "password and Registry key attacking" utilities that are popping up on the Internet, you may want to consider setting up auditing on the password Registry keys. By default, you do not have rights to make these modifications. In fact, you will see that the SAM key is actually grayed out on the REGEDT32 screen. To enable password key security, you must change administrator permissions on the keys or start the Registry Editor with the SYSTEM security context. The SYSTEM security context has full rights to the entire Registry.

To start the REGEDT32.EXE program with the SYSTEM security context in order to change auditing, you use NT's built-in Schedule service. Follow these steps:

NOTE: This procedure will not work on a remote system.

1. Go to the control panel. Under Services, ensure that the start-up settings for the Scheduler service are set to Log On As SYSTEM.

2. Stop and start the Schedule service.

3. Open a DOS prompt and type the following to get your current system time:

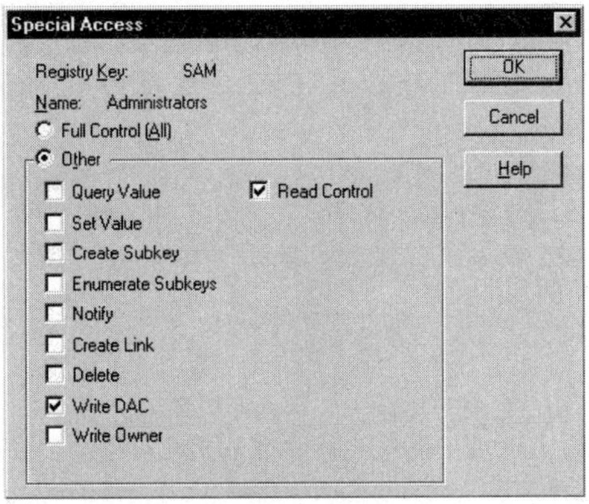

Figure 7-19. Registry's Special Access dialog box

TIME
Press ENTER.

4. Now type:

   AT 8:00 /INTERACTIVE "REGEDT32.EXE"
   Press ENTER. Of course, change the time entered here (8:00) to two or three minutes ahead of your current system time.

5. The Registry Editor tool will start using the SYSTEM security context at the appointed time. You will notice that the SAM and SECURITY hives are no longer grayed out.

6. Select the HKEY_LOCAL_MACHINE window within the Registry Editor.

7. Highlight the SAM key. Select Auditing from the Security menu.

8. Click Add.

9. Add the Administrators, Backup Operators, Domain Admins, and SYSTEM groups and any other users or groups that have any of the following rights and select OK:

   ■ Add workstations to domain

   ■ Back up files and directories

   ■ Manage auditing and security log

   ■ Replace a process level token

- Restore files and directories
- Take ownership of files or other objects

10. Check Audit Permission on Existing Subkeys to allow subkeys to inherit the modifications

11. Select the Success and Failure check boxes for the following entries and click OK:
    - Query Value
    - Read Control
    - Set Value
    - Write DAC

12. Click Yes and exit from the Registry Editor.

13. Return the Schedule service to its previous state.

At this point, logging for the password keys will be enabled. The last important step will be to add event log checking to your routine security procedures. Look for any entries in the log that indicate tampering with these keys.

User Profiles and System Policies

User profiles and system policies can make the life of your users easier as well as provide some security. Do not be lulled into thinking that this is good security. Profiles or policies do allow control over the client workstations but can generally be overridden by a moderately technical user.

User Profiles

The user profiles hold personal configuration preferences for each user's desktop. One useful feature is that they allow several people who use the same workstation to still have their *own* desktop. Profiles also allow roving users to always "see" the same desktop. Profiles can be made mandatory so that administrators can control exactly how a user's desktop will look. Mandatory profiles are stored on the server so that they take effect each time a user logs on. If a user makes changes during a particular session, those changes will be ignored the next time the user logs on.

You can assign profiles using the User Manager for Domains tool. Under the User menu, select Properties, then select Profile and User Profile Path and enter in the appropriate path and profile name (see Figure 7-20). NT will automatically create the file if one does not exist. If you wish to create a profile for a user, you can set up a desktop the way you like it for the user, log out, log back in as an administrator equivalent and copy the profile for the user. You can copy profiles using the System applet in the Control Panel on the User Profile tab. Generally speaking, if you are looking for a more secure environment, go with system policies. If you are looking for user convenience, profiles will work fine.

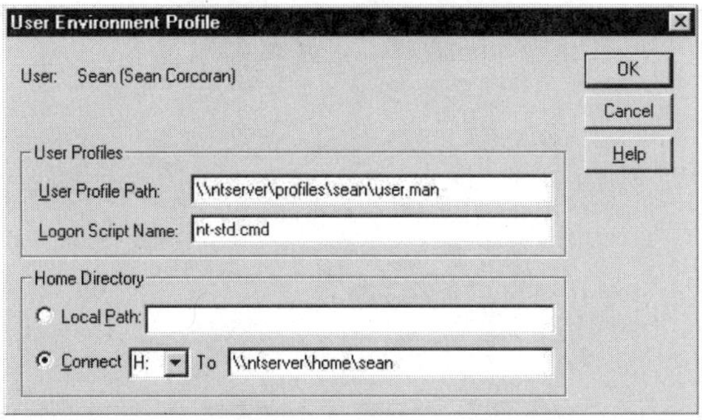

Figure 7-20.   User Environment Profile dialog box

Policies

Policies offer more networkwide control of what users can and cannot do on their desktops. When you create a policy, you save it to the netlogon share on your domain controllers (%SYSTEMROOT%\SYSTEM32\REPL\EXPORT\SCRIPTS). On NT machines, the profile file NTCONFIG.POL is accessed each time the user logs in. It is then "merged" with the information in the user profile to set up the desktop and control what the user does. It essentially makes changes to the user's Registry entries. Note that if there is a conflict between the profile and the policy, the policy takes precedence.

The System Policy Editor in the Administrative Tools folder is used to manage NT profiles (Figure 7-21).

Following are some examples of the policies you may want to consider setting with a system policy.

Under Computer:

▼   Windows NT System:Logon:Banner

▲   Windows NT Network:Create hidden drive shares (server and workstation)

Under User:

▼   Control Panel:Display:Restrict display

■   System:Restrictions:Run only allowed Windows Applications

■   System:Restrictions:Disable Registry editing tools

■   Shell:Restrictions:Hide Network Neighborhood

■   Shell:Restrictions:Hide drives in Network neighborhood

■   Shell:Restrictions:Remove Run command from Start menu

▲   Shell:Restrictions:Don't save settings at exit

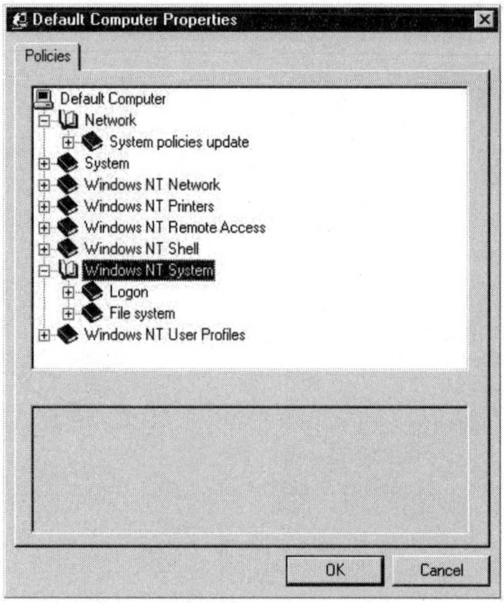

Figure 7-21.   System Policy Editor

Remember that policies and profiles do not really offer much security, because they can be easily bypassed. However, they can make for a consistent, convenient network desktop.

NT SECURITY WEAKNESSES

As Windows NT becomes the prominent network operating system, it continues to be the main target of hackers trying to break down its security scheme. Each time this occurs, the solution from Microsoft seems to be one of two messages:

▼   Protect your passwords

▲   Secure your servers

Most criticisms people have had about NT security can be fixed simply following both of the above suggestions; protect your passwords and secure your servers. It is interesting to note that every other operating system is just as vulnerable if these two procedures are not followed.

Strong Passwords

Username and password combinations are usually the first thing a would-be hacker tries to determine. In a typical hacking scenario, a hacker breaks into your networks via the Internet or some other connected network or a phone line or by just walking into your building.

The part of the logon process hackers first attempt to determine is the username. Unfortunately, it is very difficult to prevent hackers from figuring out usernames. Usernames are vulnerable for many reasons. To start with, most companies use some form of an employee's name for the username. Employee names can be very easy to come by. One can obtain them from a variety of sources, including printed company literature, voice mail systems, and newspaper articles. In addition, by looking at a company's Web site, one can quickly grab three or four usernames without effort, as it is a common practice for e-mail names to be the same as logon names. E-mail names are available from many other sources as well, such as online directories and business cards.

Another way to grab usernames is by physical access. A laptop-based network analyzer can yield many valid usernames, machine names, and IP addresses in clear text. There are also utilities built into Windows NT that can be used to obtain user information. For instance, a Microsoft NT network running TCP/IP is usually running NetBIOS over TCP/IP. A hacker can run the NetBIOS over TCP/IP Statistics utility (NBTSTAT.EXE) or the FINGER utility to gather usernames. Figure 7-22 shows the result of the NBTSTAT.EXE

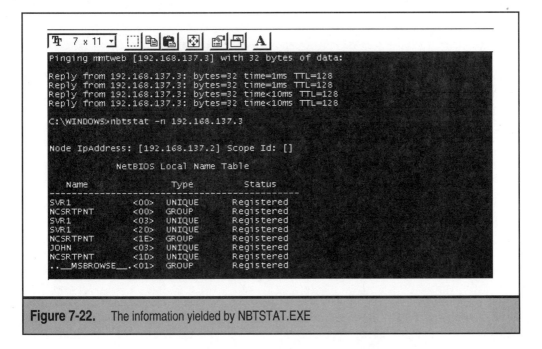

Figure 7-22.   The information yielded by NBTSTAT.EXE

command. Once an IP address is known, NBTSTAT.EXE is impressive in its ability to give out information on remote machines. The first half of a valid username/password combination is now known as well as the domain name, without using any special programs. You can see why you would not want to use NetBIOS bound on your Internet-connected machines! Note that you can also block NBTSTAT by disabling ports 137, 138, and 139.

The hacker now takes the usernames and attempts to determine passwords. One possibility is to use a "dictionary attack" program to guess passwords. These programs use common words and other custom information to try to determine passwords. SCANNT from MWC, Inc. (**http://www.ntsecurity.com**) is a good example of this type of program. Figure 7-23 shows the results of a dictionary attack using the demo version of SCANNT. Another way to determine passwords is to use an analyzer to "sniff" for an FTP or Telnet session. The passwords for FTP and Telnet are sent in clear text and can easily be searched out by would-be hackers.

So how do you protect passwords? This once again comes down to good corporate policy. Two areas should be examined: users' responsibilities and network administrators' responsibilities.

Users are the weakest link in any security scheme. They need to understand the ramifications of being flippant with their passwords. In any corporation, probably 5 percent of users have their passwords on a piece of paper beneath the keyboard. This

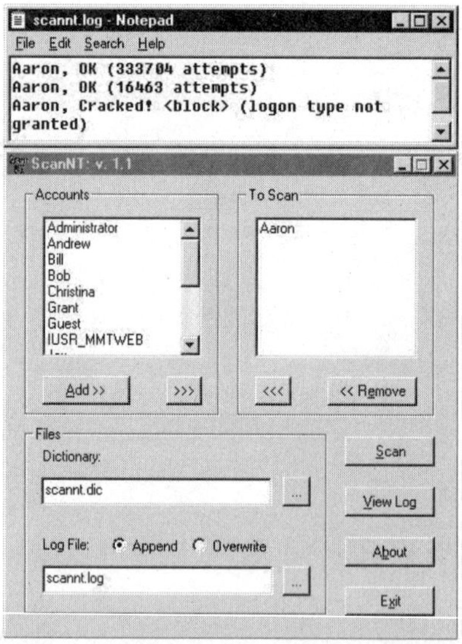

Figure 7-23.   SCANNT results

percentage may even be a low approximation! It is amusing to follow help desk personnel to a typical corporate desk. It can be very frustrating to arrive at a computer only to find a screen saver or BIOS password enabled, and since help desk people are short on time, which means they don't have time to track every person down, they try to guess the password. They look for the telltale "yellow sticky." If that doesn't work, they look for family names on the desktop. A child's signed picture will often suffice. The point is that most IS people are very good at guessing poor passwords. Be sure to train users on the importance and value of good passwords.

Another common password problem is actually caused by IS staff, which usually creates a default password. This password is used for first-time logons and when account passwords need to be reset. The IS people will use common terms, like ABCDE or 12345. We have seen the same default passwords used at some companies for years. Users will pick up on this and make their password the same or very close to it. Obviously, this completely destroys password-based security.

Here are some guidelines for dealing with users to help improve the strength of their passwords:

▼   Users should never write a password down.

■   Users should never disclose passwords to others.

■   Users should never reuse passwords (especially outside of work).

■   Teach users the basic structure of a good password.

■   NT users should use the NT Security dialog box (CTRL-ALT-DEL) to log on.

■   Require locked screen savers.

■   Require BIOS passwords.

▲   Require Locks on all system cases if complete security is required (this prevents deletion of the BIOS passwords via motherboard jumpers).

There are also several precautions the network administrators can take on the Windows NT server side. They need to understand which programs pass unencrypted passwords over the network. Be particularly careful with FTP or Telnet servers connected to the Internet. If you must use these utilities, consider possible encryption-enhanced versions. Here are some recommendations for network administrators to secure their systems from unauthorized access:

▼   Set a minimum password length (NT passwords can be up to 14 characters in length).

■   Enforce password rotation (extremely unpopular with users but effective).

■   Enforce account lockout (can render dictionary attack programs useless).

■   Remove unnecessary usernames and groups (check for account inactivity).

■   Do not allow automatic (scripted) logons to the domain.

- Disable the NT Guest account (it is disabled on servers by default).
- Rename the Administrator account.
▲ Require strong passwords.

By default, the NT Administrator account does not have the account lockout feature that other user accounts do. If the Administrator account is allowed to log on from the network, access to a share can be attempted with password guessing without fear of account lockout. This attack can easily go unnoticed. You can set the Administrator account to allow locking out with the PASSPROP.EXE utility in the Windows NT Resource Kit.

Password rotation is also extremely important. The shorter the password life, the more secure your security plan will be. The idea is that you want the password lifetime to be shorter than the time it would take to crack the password. This would make password discovery almost useless. Password expirations also abate the propagation of valid passwords among users who give out their passwords to coworkers for convenience. Figure 7-24 shows the Account Policy dialog box in the User Manager for Domains tool. Use this dialog box to make domain-wide password policy.

To increase the integrity of corporate passwords, Microsoft has come up with two utilities, PASSPROP.EXE and PASSFLT.DLL. They are meant to protect NT systems from

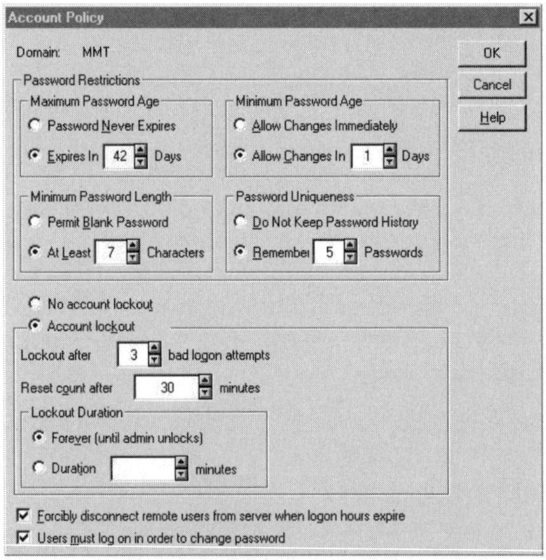

Figure 7-24.   Account Policy dialog box in the User Manager for Domains

dictionary attacks and other forms of password guessing. These programs consider a complex or strong password to be one that meets the following criteria:

▼ Passwords must be a minimum of six characters long

■ Passwords may not contain your user name or any part of your full name

▲ Passwords must be made up of characters from three of the four classes listed in Table 7-7

PASSPROP.EXE is a Windows NT Resource Kit utility. It is run from the command prompt and gives you the options to force complex passwords and to allow Administrator account lockout. Remember that by default the Administrator account cannot be locked out.

PASSFLT.DLL was an addition to NT 4.0 with Service Pack 2. The requirements for complex passwords are hard-coded into the .DLL and cannot be changed through the Registry. To enable strong passwords with PASSFLT.DLL, follow these steps on all domain controllers and stand-alone member servers:

1. Install Windows NT 4.0 Service Pack 2 or later.

2. Copy PASSFLT.DLL to the %SYSTEMROOT%\SYSTEM32 folder.

3. Open up the Registry Editor (REGEDT32)

4. Go to the LSA key under HKEY_LOCAL_MACHINE\SYSTEM\CURRENTCONTROLSET\CONTROL\LSA.

5. Add the value Notification Packages to the LSA key. Make it of type REG_MULTI_SZ.

6. Now double-click the Notification Packages key and add the following value: PASSFILT

7. Click OK and exit the Registry Editor.

8. Shut down and restart.

Character Class	Example
Uppercase letters	A, B, C…Z
Lowercase letters	a, b, c…z
Numbers	0, 1, 2, 3…9
Nonalphanumeric symbols	`~!@#$%^&*()=+,"<>.?\	[]{}

Table 7-7. Password Character Classes

Lock Up Your Servers

In addition to good password policy, there needs to be a policy for protecting servers from unauthorized physical access. Servers should always be kept behind locked doors. Direct access to a server is the easiest way to get control of sensitive data. Even an NTFS-formatted drive is at risk because of utilities like NTFSDOS. This utility allows read-only access to any NTFS drive regardless of the access control lists. It requires booting to an NTFSDOS floppy. It obviously caused quite a stir when it was introduced in 1996. Microsoft was quick to respond with the following: "Although the assertion that one could break the ACL protection was true, the break required physical access to the server." All organizational security plans should stress the importance of securing server locations.

Other Server Security Problems

Another NT server security "problem" came in the spring of 1997. An article in a major trade publication asserted that one could use a utility called PWDUMP to retrieve usernames and encrypted passwords from an NT system. The attacker could then use another utility, NTCRACK, to try to guess the passwords using a dictionary attack. Shortly thereafter, another article was published, asserting that one could do the same thing with a program called L0phtcrack. Microsoft responded to both with the following statement:

NOTE: This statement was published by Microsoft on its security page at **http://www.microsoft.com/security** and was written by Russ Cooper of R. C. Consulting, Inc. Russ Cooper maintains the NTBugTraq mailing list and can be found at **http://www.ntbugtraq.com**. This list has been the first to notify users of many security bugs and their applicable work-arounds. The page also has some excellent sources for NT security-related information.

The *EE Times* published an article, "'Hack' Punches Hole in Microsoft NT Security," on March 31, 1997, asserting that user passwords could be compromised in the Windows NT operating system. The issue raised by the article relies on getting access to Administrator accounts and guessing user passwords by looking for common words. The reported problem is not a security flaw in Windows NT, but highlights the importance of protecting the Administrator accounts from unauthorized access. It also reinforces the importance of following basic security guidelines. Therefore, customers who want a secure solution on Windows NT should implement proper security policies.

All operating systems, including UNIX or Windows NT, are susceptible to attacks anytime the Administrator accounts are compromised. The article states that this alleged security problem could enable a remote user to unscramble encrypted information, like a user password, and display it as plain text. The article refers to the existence of two utilities, PWDUMP and NTCRACK, that enable the uncovering of this flaw. Here's how each utility works:

PWDUMP. You can log onto the system and retrieve a user name and encrypted password only if you have administrator privileges.

NTCRACK. You can run the second utility to try to guess passwords using dictionary lookup only after you run PWDUMP under administrator privileges.

Microsoft has ascertained that the reported problem does not represent a security flaw in Windows NT. The issue relies on the existence of an Administrator account that has been rendered vulnerable by neglecting basic security guidelines.

What Should Customers Do?

Every computer operating system is susceptible to security issues if basic security guidelines are not followed. Security is achieved through a combination of technology and policy. In order to maintain a highly secure environment, standard security practices should be followed, including:

Only trusted individuals should be granted Administrator privileges on the system.

The Administrator account should not be used for casual use.

The Administrator account should only be used to administer the network/domain.

The Domain controllers should be physically secured.

Maintain a strong password policy.

Rename the Administrator account.

Never run untrusted programs while logged in as Administrator.

The point here is that even Microsoft admits the importance of strong passwords and of locking down server machines. What about the SAMs and other critical information on backup tapes, Emergency Repair Disks, and in the repair directory? Are they susceptible to these utilities? The answer is yes. Individuals who have access to backup tapes can obtain the Windows NT password database from the tapes. However, these passwords are encrypted, and the attacker would again need to mount a dictionary attack in an attempt to crack the passwords. A strong password policy is necessary to stop this form of intrusion. This also points to the fact that you must be very wary about the storage of your backup tapes.

The repair directory information is a similar problem. Anyone with rights to the repair directory (%SYSTEMROOT%\REPAIR) can obtain the encrypted password list. By default, the group Everyone has read rights to the folder. This would imply that a dictionary attack could also work here. Again, it can be stopped with strong passwords.

You can also set permissions on the repair directory so nobody has access to it. Then you can just restore access to the Administrator account when you want to update the repair information.

Another issue with NT security is the built-in Schedule service (AT). It can be extremely useful to administrators, but it also has security issues. In the "Registry Security" section of this chapter, you learned how to use the Schedule service to start the Registry Editor with the SYSTEM security context, not as the person logged on to the machine. This should concern you, because even with Registry auditing turned on, you won't know who made the changes.

There is another issue with the job scheduler. The Schedule service stores the commands that are scheduled to run in clear text in the Windows NT Registry. In Figure 7-25, the program to be run is called ZAP.EXE, as is clearly shown. Server operators and other users with the appropriate permissions can modify the Registry key to run a different program of their choice. This program could potentially cause harm or even provide access to the password database. You can prevent this problem by changing the Registry access control lists to remove access to the scheduler keys for most people. Set it to allow only administrator access (see the "Registry Security" section of this chapter).

Midwestern Commerce, Inc. (**http://www.ntsecurity.com**) released a security program called RedButton in April 1997. This tool allows anyone with remote IP access to an NT server to connect with a username, read the Registry, and create a new share through Registry editing that is accessible to the Everyone group. RedButton accesses the resources available to the group Everyone and can even determine the current name of a renamed built-in Administrator account.

To prevent attacks similar to RedButton, administrators should disable NetBIOS over TCP/IP access either by blocking access to ports 137, 138, and 139 on Internet-exposed

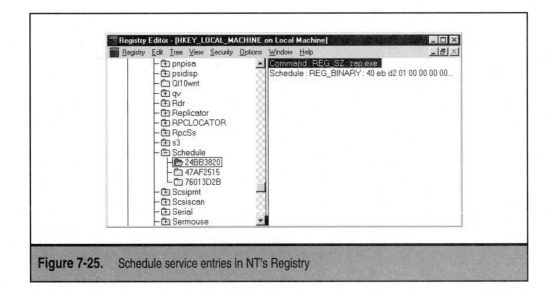

Figure 7-25.   Schedule service entries in NT's Registry

machines or by unbinding NetBIOS from TCP/IP. You can also unbind the Server service from Internet servers and NT workstation computers if they do not require it. Replacing the Everyone group throughout your Registry tree with the Users group will partially stop RedButton. You could also disable your built-in Administrator account or tightly audit it and create a new account to be used for administrative purposes.

Microsoft built protection against RedButton and similar attacks into NT 4.0 Service Pack 3.

Security Suggestions Checklist

The steps you take to secure your NT system will vary depending on environment and security needs. Following is a checklist of suggestions that you should consider for your network.

General Suggestions

▼ Do not bind NetBIOS to your network cards on TCP/IP networks unless there is a reason. This is especially true for machines directly connected to the Internet.

■ Block access to the NetBIOS over TCP/IP Ports 137,138, and 139 (same result as previous suggestion).

■ Put servers in locked, secure rooms.

■ Keep up to date with Service Packs and Hot Fixes.

■ If you are using remote access software, be sure to invoke the security features.

■ Place backup tapes in a secure location.

■ Change the ACL of the repair directory to restrict access (%SYSTEMROOT%\ REPAIR).

■ Use NTFS on all drives.

■ Use strong passwords.

■ Review all network bindings and remove protocols and bindings you do not need.

■ Remove unnecessary NT services.

■ Be wary of the Backup Operators group.

■ Check user rights closely, especially backup and restore rights.

■ Remember default permissions on directories and shares is Everyone> Full Control.

■ Remove the group Everyone from ACLs and replace it with the group Users (carefully).

■ Remove unused computer entries from your domain server list.

■ Limit the number of users with full administrative privileges.

- Limit the number of people with the Administrator password.
- Log on to systems with your own personal account (not as Administrator).
- Enable auditing, especially of logon violations and security changes.
- Audit Registry password files.
- Enforce off-hours account lockout.
- Closely examine interdomain trust relationships.
- Do not allow the security log to be overwritten.
- Do not log on as Administrator through untrusted programs (only use CTRL-ALT-DEL).
- Do not log on as Administrator on untrusted operating systems (only on NT).
- Disable the right of the Administrator account to access the computer from the network (requires local access to use Administrator account).
- Rename the Administrator account or cripple it and use a separate account for administrator access.
- Create a dummy Administrator account and audit for logon failures.
- Keep the Guest account disabled.
- Be sure to stay abreast of group memberships. (This can be an especially daunting task in an enterprise with several domains).
- Periodically check your event logs, especially the security log.
- ▲ Regularly monitor the Microsoft security page (**http://www.microsoft.com/security**).

Dialup Security

- ▼ Use the Dial Back feature.
- Use security authentication products like Secure-ID.
- Only enable RAS for accounts that require it.
- Examine event logs regularly for improper RAS access.
- ▲ Turn on time restrictions for user accounts.

NOTE: One after-the-fact measure you can take is to enable legal notices on your workstations. On NT, the legal notice pops up before the Security dialog box when you press CTRL-ALT-DEL. You should use phrases like "Unauthorized access is prohibited" and state the purpose of the network. Words such as "Welcome" and "Greetings" should be avoided, as they imply a right to use. This is especially important on servers connected to the Internet. If you are not careful with your legal notices, you may find you have no legal recourse after a security breach, even if the perpetrator is known.

Problems with Other Versions of Windows

Be sure to understand the security ramifications of Window 3.*x*, Windows 95, and Windows 98 machines. It is completely possible to capture and replay logon information from these machines. This can enable unauthorized access to a valid NT account. Be especially careful to not use the Administrator's account on these untrusted systems. Another problem with earlier versions of Windows is that it offers no protection to the local data. Critical data should never be stored on these types of workstations. Consider upgrading all machines on extremely sensitive networks to Windows NT.

Network Issues

The equipment and protocols you select for your network will have an enormous effect on your overall security. For instance, a network analyzer's abilities are greatly restricted in the presence of switching hubs. They isolate the ports on the hub below the network layer, preventing sniffing in some cases. These hubs are more expensive but should always be considered for your server segments.

On the protocol side, Microsoft has been pushing TCP/IP as the protocol of choice. You must plan your IP security scheme carefully. One area to pay close attention to is IP address allocation. The Dynamic Host Configuration Protocol (DHCP) makes the life of any IP network administrator much easier. It automatically passes out IP addresses and other IP configuration information to a requesting machine. It maintains the list of allocated addresses for you. The problem with DHCP is that by default it does not attempt to determine the identity of the requesting machine. Any machine that plugs into a live jack is instantly assigned an address. In order to control IP address allocation, Microsoft NT's version of DHCP supports a reservation scheme based on a network card's unique MAC address. This is very similar to BOOTP, an address allocation scheme more commonly found on UNIX machines.

Figure 7-26 shows the Add Reserved Clients dialog box of the DHCP Manager tool. The NBTSTAT.EXE utility is a great way to remotely determine the MAC addresses

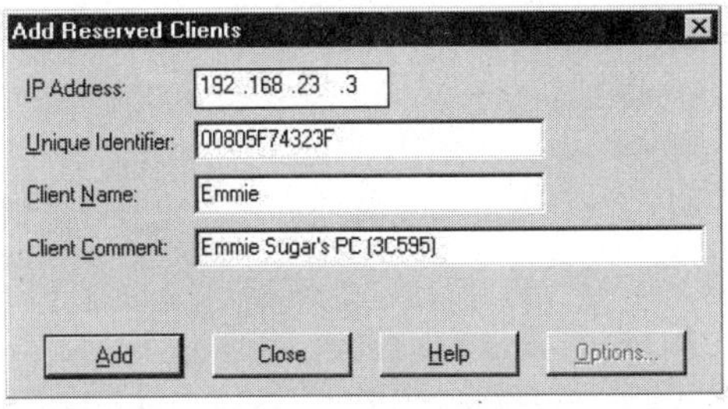

Figure 7-26.   DHCP Add Reserved Clients dialog box

needed for reservation configuration. Networks that require a high degree of security should use the DHCP reservation system or should stick to statically assigned IP addresses. It is a matter of balancing your security needs with your administration needs.

Another problem with DHCP is the potential for roving leases. This is mainly a problem on very secure networks that audit packets moving over their networks. If DHCP leases are very short, a person could possibly change leases every few days. The problem arises when you need to track historical lease data. For example, if your firewall reported that last Tuesday an internal user with IP address 192.168.4.55 tried to Telnet to your human resources department's Intranet server, you would not know who had that IP address at the specified time.

There are two ways to track this information. The first way takes advantage of the fact that NT audits address allocation in the event log. You can manually scan old event logs or parse the information using a separate utility. This assumes that your logs are not filling up (it would be a bad policy if they did). The second way to maintain historical lease data actually was contrived by a network engineer at a major utility company. It makes use of the Windows Internet Name Service (WINS) database. WINS is a utility that maintains lists of IP addresses for NetBIOS name resolution. You can dump this WINS database periodically throughout the day. You can then parse this information and put the output into a more readable format. The only problem with this method is that WINS is a passive tool. It does not attempt address resolution on its own. It is told of the existence of host names and their associated IP addresses by the hosts themselves. If a machine is set up to not use WINS, it simply will not report its IP address.

There is another important issue to understand about NT's use of TCP/IP, namely NBT. NetBIOS over TCP/IP (NBT) is only necessary for native Microsoft networking services like file sharing and printing. As the NBTSTAT.EXE command has clearly shown, NBT can yield a great deal of important information to would-be intruders. Windows NT binds NBT to the network adapters that are using TCP/IP automatically. You do not need to use NetBIOS over TCP/IP for Windows Sockets and other native TCP/IP services. Therefore, you should disable it in these cases. This is especially important if you have a full-time, unprotected connection to the Internet. If you have NBT installed in this scenario, it is possible for an outsider to gain access to your internal shared resources. If you need to allow NetBIOS connection from the Internet, consider NT's Point to Point Tunneling Protocol (PPTP) or the encryption packages that come with many commercial firewalls. Firewall-1 from CheckPoint (**http://www.checkpoint.com**) is one of the many firewall products that offer this useful capability.

It is important to understand that with NetBIOS Enhanced User Interface (NetBEUI) and with IPX\SPX you will have the same problem as a freely configured DHCP server. Anyone can walk up to a hot jack and start analyzing. The solution is obviously to eliminate unnecessary hot jacks, especially in remote areas of a building, vacant offices, or conference rooms. This can be done in several ways, from physically removing patch cables to implementing intelligent hubs. Intelligent hubs can be set up to only allow connections from specific MAC addresses.

INTERNET SECURITY

The Internet offers outsiders many interesting ways to affect your computer systems. Instead of worrying about the 20 or 30 thousand people on your corporate network, you now have to worry about the millions of Internet users and thousands of available Web sites. Internet security problems come in two classifications: servers and clients. You need to analyze what happens when *your* internal clients connect to Internet servers and when Internet clients connect to *your* servers.

Web Clients

Web clients include Internet utilities like Telnet and FTP, e-mail tools, and, of course, Web browsers. One major problem with most Internet utilities and e-mail tools is the amount of unencrypted information that they generate on the network. Be sure that users understand that other people can theoretically read passwords, usernames, and the e-mail they send over the Internet. Users need to be aware of the unsecured nature of the Internet. Chapter 6 discussed e-mail-borne viruses and viruses contained in Internet downloads, which will continue to be problematic.

Another Web client issue is ActiveX controls and Java applets. They are the driving forces behind the compelling, dynamic Web sites found on the Internet. It is their dynamic nature that presents the problem. They are run automatically, usually without user intervention, when a particular Web site is accessed.

A Java applet is supposed to operate within its own runtime space, the so-called sandbox. The applet should have no access to the underlying operating system and especially the disk drives. Developers have already found ways to breach the sandbox and gain access to the system. The browser manufacturers have quickly plugged these holes. The industry is waiting to see the effect of misbehaved or malicious Java applets. As Java applications become more complex, you can expect more of these types of problems.

In the case of ActiveX controls, there is even more potential for abuse. They are not confined to a sandbox. The usual method for assuring the authenticity of an ActiveX control is to have the code digitally signed. This allows a path of accountability back to the author or publisher. Be sure your browser has the ability to detect and verify this code. Microsoft's Internet Explorer also gives you the ability to preset your user's browser security settings. You can choose or decline to enable active downloads, enable ActiveX controls and scripts, and enable Java applets.

Internet Connected Servers

Another major Internet security problem is protecting your Windows NT servers that are directly connected to the Internet. This section does not talk about the security of Web server software in particular but can be generalized to all servers that are directly connected to the Internet.

The first step in protecting your servers that are accessible through the Internet is to put your servers into a control demilitarized zone (DMZ). Figure 7-27 shows a basic DMZ/firewall implementation. The objective of the DMZ is to allow some Internet access but in a very controlled manner. Notice that the list of Web servers in Figure 7-27 includes a separate database server. For added security, you can make the HTTP server communicate with the database server via some non-TCP/IP protocol (for example, IPX).

The most common way to create a DMZ is through the use of a firewall and a packet filtering router (Figure 7-27). There are several NT-based firewall products available today. The firewall can audit and control the well-known ports through which the Internet servers can receive and answer requests. Firewalls start by assuming that all packets to all ports on all machines should be dropped. You then specifically indicate which packets should be allowed to pass through to which machines. For instance, there

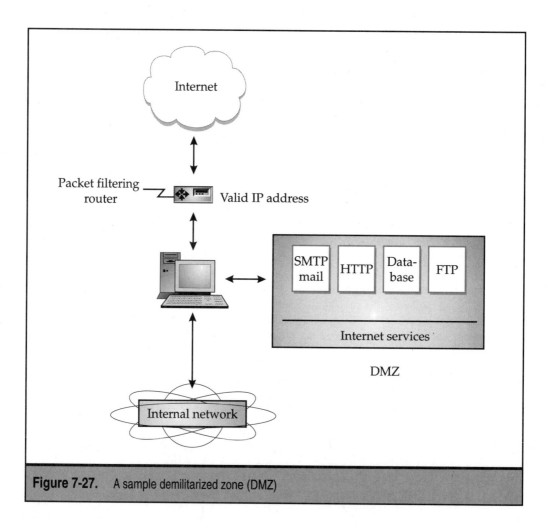

Figure 7-27.   A sample demilitarized zone (DMZ)

is no reason you would want any of these machines to receive NetBIOS requests. Therefore, you would want to be sure that no packets destined for ports 137, 138, and 139 are allowed through. On the firewall, you simply never specify these packets. In the same sense, you would not want your mail server to receive HTTP packets, so you would stop port 80 packets from going to the SMTP server. However, you would allow these port 80 packets to the HTTP server. With a firewall, you can specify what machines receive what packets and you can clearly audit any or all events. Some of the more commonly used IP ports are shown in Table 7-8. Port numbers are defined by RFC 1060 (tcp) and RFC 768 (udp). Port numbers over 1024 are generally user specified.

Obviously, the other important use of a firewall is to protect and control the packets going into your private network. Most firewalls include address translation, which *hides*

Port Number	Type	Keyword	Description
0	tcp, udp	Reserved	Reserved
1	tcp, udp	tcpmux	TCP Port Service Multiplexer
2	tcp, udp	compressnet	Management Utility
3	tcp, udp	compressnet	Compression Process
4	tcp, udp	Unassigned	Unassigned
5	tcp, udp	rje	Remote Job Entry
6	tcp, udp	Unassigned	Unassigned
7	tcp, udp	echo	Echo
8	tcp, udp	Unassigned	Unassigned
9	tcp, udp	discard	Discard
10	tcp, udp	Unassigned	Unassigned
11	udp	users	Active Users
12	tcp, udp	Unassigned	Unassigned
13	tcp, udp	daytime	Daytime
14	tcp, udp	Unassigned	Unassigned
15	tcp, udp	Unassigned	Unassigned
16	tcp, udp	Unassigned	Unassigned
17	tcp, udp	qotd	Quote of the Day
18	tcp, udp	msp	Message Send Protocol
19	tcp, udp	chargen	Character Generator

Table 7-8. TCP/IP Well-Known Ports

Port Number	Type	Keyword	Description
20	tcp, udp	ftp-data	File Transfer Protocol Data
21	tcp, udp	ftp	File Transfer Protocol Control
22	tcp, udp	Unassigned	Unassigned
23	tcp, udp	telnet	Telnet
24	tcp, udp	n/a	Any Private Mail
25	tcp, udp	smtp	Mail, Simple Mail Transport Protocol
26	tcp, udp	Unassigned	Unassigned
27	tcp, udp	nsw-fe	NSW User System FE
28	tcp, udp	Unassigned	Unassigned
29	tcp, udp	msg-icp	MSG ICP
30	tcp, udp	Unassigned	Unassigned
31	tcp, udp	msg-auth	MSG Authentication
32	tcp, udp	Unassigned	Unassigned
33	tcp, udp	dsp	Display Support Protocol
34	tcp, udp	Unassigned	Unassigned
35	tcp, udp	n/a	Any Private Print Server
36	tcp, udp	Unassigned	Unassigned
37	tcp, udp	time	timeserver
38	tcp, udp	Unassigned	Unassigned
39	tcp, udp	rlp	Resource Location Protocol
40	tcp, udp	Unassigned	Unassigned
41	tcp, udp	graphics	Graphics
42	tcp, udp	nameserver	Host Name Server
43	tcp, udp	nicname	Who Is/nickname
44	tcp, udp	mpm-flags	MPM FLAGS Protocol
45	tcp, udp	mpm	Message Processing Module
46	tcp, udp	mpm-snd	MPM (send)
47	tcp, udp	ni-ftp	NI FTP
48	tcp, udp	Unassigned	Unassigned

Table 7-8. TCP/IP Well-Known Ports (*continued*)

Port Number	Type	Keyword	Description
49	tcp, udp	login	Login Host Protocol
50	tcp, udp	re-mail-ck	Remote Mail Checking Protocol
51	tcp, udp	la-maint	IMP Logical Address Maintenance
52	tcp, udp	xns-time	XNS Time Protocol
53	tcp, udp	domain	Domain Name Server (DNS)
54	tcp, udp	xns-ch	XNS Clearinghouse
55	tcp, udp	isi-gl	ISI Graphics Language
56	tcp, udp	xns-auth	XNS Authentication
57	tcp, udp	n/a	Any Private Terminal Access
58	tcp, udp	xns-mail	XNS Mail
59	tcp, udp	n/a	Any Private File Service
60	tcp, udp	Unassigned	Unassigned
61	tcp, udp	ni-mail	NI MAIL
62	tcp, udp	acas	ACA Services
63	tcp, udp	via-ftp	VIA Systems—FTP
64	tcp, udp	covia	Communications Integrator (CI)
65	tcp, udp	tacacs-ds	TACACS-Database Service
66	tcp, udp	sql*net	Oracle SQL*NET
67	tcp, udp	bootpc	DHCP/BOOTP Protocol Server
68	tcp, udp	bootpc	DHCP/BOOTP Protocol Server
69	udp	tftp	Trivial File Transfer Protocol
70	tcp, udp	gopher	Gopher
71	tcp, udp	netrjs-1	Remote Job Service
72	tcp, udp	netrjs-2	Remote Job Service
73	tcp, udp	netrjs-3	Remote Job Service
74	tcp, udp	netrjs-4	Remote Job Service
75	udp	n/a	Any Private Dial Out Service
76	tcp, udp	Unassigned	Unassigned
77	tcp, udp	n/a	Any Private RJE Service

Table 7-8.   TCP/IP Well-Known Ports (*continued*)

Port Number	Type	Keyword	Description
78	tcp, udp	vettcp	Vettcp
79	tcp, udp	finger	Finger
80	tcp, udp	www	World Wide Web HTTP
81	tcp, udp	hosts2-ns	HOSTS2 Name Server
82	tcp, udp	xfer	XFER Utility
83	tcp, udp	mit-ml-dev	MIT ML Device
84	tcp, udp	ctf	Common Trace Facility
85	tcp, udp	mit-ml-dev	MIT ML Device
86	tcp, udp	mfcobol	Micro Focus Cobol
87	tcp, udp	n/a	Any Private Terminal Link, ttylink
88	tcp, udp	kerberos	Kerberos
89	tcp	su-mit-tg	SU/MIT Telnet Gateway
89	udp	su-mit-tg	SU/MIT Telnet Gateway
90	tcp, udp	DNSIX	Security Attribute Token Map
91	tcp, udp	mit-dov	MIT Dover Spooler
92	tcp, udp	npp	Network Printing Protocol
93	tcp, udp	dcp	Device Control Protocol
94	tcp, udp	objcall	Tivoli Object Dispatcher
95	tcp, udp	supdup	SUPDUP
96	tcp, udp	dixie	DIXIE Protocol Specification
97	tcp, udp	swift-rvf	Swift Remote Virtual File Protocol
98	tcp, udp	tacnews	TAC News
99	tcp, udp	metagram	Metagram Relay
100	tcp	newacct	(Unauthorized use)
101	tcp, udp	hostname	NIC Host Name Server
102	tcp, udp	iso-tsap	ISO-TSAP
103	tcp, udp	gppitnp	Genesis Point-to-Point Trans Net

Table 7-8.   TCP/IP Well-Known Ports (*continued*)

Port Number	Type	Keyword	Description
104	tcp, udp	acr-nema	Digital Imag. & Comm. 300
105	tcp, udp	csnet-ns	Mailbox Name Nameserver
106	tcp, udp	3com-tsmux	3COM-TSMUX
107	tcp, udp	rtelnet	Remote Telnet Service
108	tcp, udp	snagas	SNA Gateway Access Server
109	tcp, udp	pop2	Post Office Protocol, Version 2
110	tcp, udp	pop3	Post Office Protocol, Version 3
111	tcp, udp	sunrpc	SUN Remote Procedure Call
112	tcp, udp	mcidas	Data Transmission Protocol
113	tcp, udp	auth	Authentication Service
114	tcp, udp	audionews	Audio News Multicast
115	tcp, udp	sftp	Simple File Transfer Protocol
116	tcp, udp	ansanotify	ANSA REX Notify
117	tcp, udp	uucp-path	UUCP Path Service
118	tcp, udp	sqlserv	SQL Services
119	tcp, udp	nntp	Network News Transfer Protocol
120	tcp, udp	cfdptkt	CFDPTKT
121	tcp, udp	erpc	Encore Expedited Remote Proc. Call
122	tcp, udp	smakynet	SMAKYNET
123	tcp, udp	ntp	Network Time Protocol
124	tcp, udp	ansatrader	ANSA REX Trader
125	tcp, udp	locus-map	Locus PC-Interface Net Map Server
126	tcp, udp	unitary	Unisys Unitary Login
127	tcp, udp	locus-con	Locus PC-Interface Connect. Server
128	tcp, udp	gss-xlicen	GSS X License Verification
129	tcp, udp	pwdgen	Password Generator Protocol

Table 7-8.   TCP/IP Well-Known Ports (*continued*)

Port Number	Type	Keyword	Description
130	tcp, udp	cisco-fna	Cisco FNATIVE
131	tcp, udp	cisco-tna	Cisco TNATIVE
132	tcp, udp	cisco-sys	Cisco SYSMAINT
133	tcp, udp	statsrv	Statistics Service
134	tcp, udp	ingres-net	INGRES-NET Service
135	tcp, udp	loc-srv	Location Service
136	tcp, udp	profile	PROFILE Naming System
137	tcp, udp	netbios-ns	NetBIOS Name Service
138	tcp, udp	netbios-dgm	NetBIOS Datagram Service
139	tcp, udp	netbios-ssn	NetBIOS Session Service
140	tcp, udp	emfis-data	EMFIS Data Service
141	tcp, udp	emfis-cntl	EMFIS Control Service
142	tcp, udp	bl-idm	Britton-Lee IDM
143	tcp, udp	imap2	Interim Mail Access Protocol v2
144	tcp, udp	news	News
145	tcp, udp	uaac	UAAC Protocol
146	tcp, udp	iso-ip0	ISO-IP0
147	tcp, udp	iso-ip	ISO-IP
148	tcp, udp	cronus	CRONUS-SUPPORT
149	tcp, udp	aed-512	AED 512 Emulation Service
150	tcp, udp	sql-net	SQL-NET
151	tcp, udp	hems	HEMS
152	tcp, udp	bftp	Background File Transfer Program
153	tcp, udp	sgmp	SGMP
154	tcp, udp	netsc-prod	Netscape
155	tcp, udp	netsc-dev	Netscape
156	tcp, udp	sqlsrv	SQL Service
157	tcp, udp	knet-cmp	KNET/VM Command/Message Protocol
158	tcp, udp	pcmail-srv	PCMail Server

Table 7-8. TCP/IP Well-Known Ports (*continued*)

Port Number	Type	Keyword	Description
159	tcp, udp	nss-routing	NSS-Routing
160	tcp, udp	sgmp-traps	SGMP-TRAPS
161	tcp, udp	snmp	Simple Network Management Protocol (SNMP)
162	tcp, udp	snmptrap	SNMP Trap
163	tcp, udp	cmip-man	CMIP tcp Manager
164	tcp, udp	cmip-agent	CMIP tcp Agent
165	tcp, udp	xns-courier	Xerox
166	tcp, udp	s-net	Sirius Systems
167	tcp, udp	namp	NAMP
168	tcp, udp	rsvd	RSVD
169	tcp, udp	send	SEND
170	tcp, udp	print-srv	Network PostScript
171	tcp, udp	multiplex	Network Innovations Multiplex
172	tcp, udp	cl/1	Network Innovations CL/1
173	tcp, udp	xyplex-mux	Xyplex
174	tcp, udp	mailq	MAILQ
175	tcp, udp	vmnet	VMNET
176	tcp, udp	genrad-mux	GENRAD-MUX
177	tcp, udp	xdmcp	X Display Manager Control Protocol
178	tcp, udp	nextstep	NextStep Window Server
179	tcp, udp	bgp	Border Gateway Protocol
180	tcp, udp	ris	Intergraph
181	tcp, udp	unify	Unify
182	tcp, udp	audit	Unisys Audit SITP
183	tcp, udp	ocbinder	OCBinder
184	tcp, udp	ocserver	OCServer
185	tcp, udp	remote-kis	Remote-KIS
186	tcp, udp	kis	KIS

Table 7-8. TCP/IP Well-Known Ports (*continued*)

Port Number	Type	Keyword	Description
187	tcp, udp	aci	Application Communication Interface
188	tcp, udp	mumps	Plus Five's MUMPS
189	tcp, udp	qft	Queued File Transport
190	tcp, udp	gacp	Gateway Access Control Protocol
191	tcp, udp	prospero	Prospero
192	tcp, udp	osu-nms	OSU Network Monitoring System
193	tcp, udp	srmp	Spider Remote Monitoring Protocol
194	tcp, udp	irc	Internet Relay Chat Protocol
195	tcp, udp	dn6-nlm-aud	DNSIX Network Level Module Audit
196	tcp, udp	dn6-smm-red	DNSIX Session Mgt Module Audit Redir
197	tcp, udp	dls	Directory Location Service
198	tcp, udp	dls-mon	Directory Location Service Monitor
199	tcp, udp	smux	SMUX
200	tcp, udp	src	IBM System Resource Controller
201	tcp, udp	at-rtmp	AppleTalk Routing Maintenance
202	tcp, udp	at-nbp	AppleTalk Name Binding
203	tcp, udp	at-3	AppleTalk Unused
204	tcp, udp	at-echo	AppleTalk Echo
205	tcp, udp	at-	AppleTalk Unused
206	tcp, udp	at-zis	AppleTalk Zone Information
207	tcp, udp	at-7	AppleTalk Unused
208	tcp, udp	at-8	AppleTalk Unused
209	tcp, udp	tam	Trivial Authenticated Mail Protocol
210	tcp, udp	z39.50	ANSI Z39.50

Table 7-8.   TCP/IP Well-Known Ports (*continued*)

Port Number	Type	Keyword	Description
211	tcp, udp	914c/g	TI 914C/G Terminal
212	tcp, udp	anet	ATEXSSTR
213	tcp, udp	ipx	IPX
214	tcp, udp	vmpwscs	VM PWSCS
215	tcp, udp	softpc	Insignia Solutions
216	tcp, udp	atls	Access Technology License Server
217	tcp, udp	dbase	dBASE UNIX
218	tcp, udp	mpp	Netix Message Posting Protocol
219	tcp, udp	uarps	Unisys ARPs
220	tcp, udp	imap3	Interactive Mail Access Protocol v3
221	tcp, udp	fln-spx	Berkeley rlogind with SPX auth
222	tcp, udp	fsh-spx	Berkeley rshd with SPX auth
223	tcp, udp	cdc	Certificate Distribution Center
224-241	tcp, udp	Reserved	Reserved
243	tcp, udp	sur-meas	Survey Measurement
245	tcp, udp	link	LINK
246	tcp, udp	dsp3270	Display Systems Protocol
247-255	tcp, udp	Reserved	Reserved
345	tcp, udp	pawserv	Perf Analysis Workbench
346	tcp, udp	zserv	Zebra server
347	tcp, udp	fatserv	Fatmn. Server
371	tcp, udp	clearcase	Clearcase
372	tcp, udp	ulistserv	UNIX Listserv
373	tcp, udp	legent-1	Legent Corporation
374	tcp, udp	legent-2	Legent Corporation
512	tcp	print	NT LPD uses ports 512-1023, 721-731, alias exec
512	udp	biff	New Mail Notification

Table 7-8.   TCP/IP Well-Known Ports (*continued*)

Port Number	Type	Keyword	Description
513	tcp	login	Remote logon
513	udp	who	Whod
514	tcp	cmd	Cmd
514	udp	syslog	SYSLOG
515	tcp, udp	printer	Spooler
517	tcp, udp	talk	TALK
518	tcp, udp	ntalk	NTALK
519	tcp, udp	utime	Unixtime
520	tcp	efs	Extended file name server
520	udp	router	Routed
525	tcp, udp	timed	Timeserver
526	tcp, udp	tempo	Newdate
530	tcp, udp	courier	RPC
531	tcp	conference	Chat
531	udp	rvd-control	MIT disk
532	tcp, udp	netnews	Readnews
533	tcp, udp	netwall	For emergency broadcasts
540	tcp, udp	uucp	Uucpd
543	tcp, udp	klogin	Klogin
544	tcp, udp	kshell	Krcmd
550	tcp, udp	new-rwho	New-who
555	tcp, udp	dsf	DSF
556	tcp, udp	remotefs	Rfs server
560	tcp, udp	rmonitor	Rmonitord
561	tcp, udp	monitor	Monitor
562	tcp, udp	chshell	Chcmd
564	tcp, udp	9pfs	Plan 9 file service
565	tcp, udp	whoami	Whoami
570	tcp, udp	meter	Demon
571	tcp, udp	meter	Udemon

Table 7-8. TCP/IP Well-Known Ports (*continued*)

Port Number	Type	Keyword	Description
600	tcp, udp	ipcserver	Sun IPC Server
607	tcp, udp	nqs	NQS
666	tcp, udp	mdqs	MDQS
704	tcp, udp	elcsd	Errlog copy/server daemon
721	tcp	printer	Printer 721-731
731	tcp	printer	Printer 721-731
740	tcp, udp	netcp	NETscout Control Protocol
741	tcp, udp	netgw	NetGW
742	tcp, udp	netrcs	Network based Rev. Cont. Sys.
744	tcp, udp	flexlm	Flexible License Manager
747	tcp, udp	fujitsu-dev	Fujitsu Device Control
748	tcp, udp	ris-cm	Russell Info Sci Calendar Manager
749	tcp, udp	kerberos-adm	Kerberos administration
750	tcp	rfile	Kerberos authentication, kdc
750	udp	loadav	Loadav
751	tcp, udp	pump	Kerberos authentication
752	tcp, udp	qrh	Kerberos password server
753	tcp, udp	rrh	Kerberos userreg server
754	tcp, udp	tell	Send, Kerberos slave propagation
758	tcp, udp	nlogin	Nlogin
759	tcp, udp	con	Con
760	tcp, udp	ns	Ns
761	tcp, udp	rxe	Rxe
762	tcp, udp	quotad	Quotad
763	tcp, udp	cycleserv	Cycleserv
764	tcp, udp	omserv	Omserv
765	tcp, udp	webster	Webster
767	tcp, udp	phonebook	Phone
769	tcp, udp	vid	Vid

Table 7-8. TCP/IP Well-Known Ports (*continued*)

Port Number	Type	Keyword	Description
770	tcp, udp	cadlock	Cadlock
771	tcp, udp	rtip	Rtip
772	tcp, udp	cycleserv2	Cycleserv2
773	tcp	submit	Submit
773	udp	notify	Notify
774	tcp	rpasswd	Rpasswd
774	udp	acmaint_dbd	Acmaint_Dbd
775	tcp	entomb	Entomb
775	udp	acmaint_transd	Acmaint_Transd
776	tcp, udp	wpages	Wpages
780	tcp, udp	wpgs	Wpgs
781	tcp, udp	hp-collector	HP performance data collector
782	tcp, udp	hp-managed-node	HP performance data managed node
783	tcp, udp	hp-alarm-mgr	HP performance data alarm manager
800	tcp, udp	mdbs_daemon	Mdbs_Daemon
801	tcp, udp	device	Device
888	tcp	erlogin	Logon and environment passing
996	tcp, udp	xtreelic	XTREE License Server
997	tcp, udp	maitrd	Maitrd
998	tcp	busboy	Busboy
998	udp	puparp	Puparp
999	tcp	garcon	Garcon
999	udp	applix	Applix
999	tcp, udp	puprouter	Puprouter
1000	tcp	cadlock	Cadlock
1000	udp	ock	Ock

Table 7-8.   TCP/IP Well-Known Ports (*continued*)

Obviously, the other important use of a firewall is to protect and control the packets going into your private network. Most firewalls include address translation, which *hides* the actual internal network IP addresses. You can also use a proxy server to hide the internal addresses. At some large secure organizations, you may even find cascaded proxy servers being used in conjunction with a firewall to provide layered security.

If your budget does not allow a firewall or proxy server implementation, you can make changes directly to the NT servers to enhance security. You can set the TCP/IP advanced security options to only listen on certain ports. This is done with the Network applet in Control Panel under the Protocols tab. Open the Network applet and select TCP/IP Protocol. Next left-click on Properties, Advanced. When you check the Enable Security check box, the Configure button will appear. As Figure 7-28 shows, you can specify which ports you want to enable. You will also want to examine which services are running on the server and disable any services that are unnecessary. In addition, be sure to remove any NT servers directly connected to the Internet from your internal NT domain.

CAUTION: Directly connecting NT servers to the Internet can be a risky venture. Be sure you understand the security ramifications.

There are several different issues to consider when planning your Internet security scheme. The one you utilize will be based on security needs and budget restraints. These issues include the following:

▼   Firewall protection with address translation should be very seriously
    considered if you are connected to the Internet.

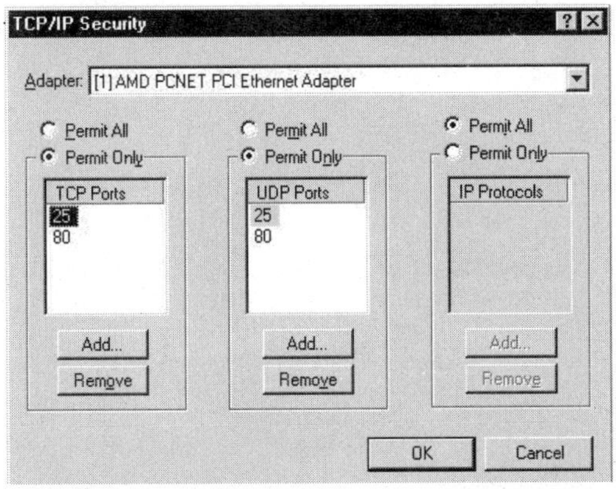

Figure 7-28.   NT TCP/IP Security dialog box

- If you have an unprotected connection to the Internet, disable NetBIOS over TCP/IP.
- If you require NetBIOS access, use the Point-to-Point Tunneling Protocol (PPTP).
- Know what services are running on your Internet-connected machines.
- For top security, use encryption when sending data over the Internet.
- Consider secure e-mail (ESMTP) instead of normal SMTP.
- Put your demilitarized zone (DMZ) behind a firewall, not in front of it.
- Connect to Data Sources (SQL Server) through a protocol other than NBT (NetBEUI or IPX).
- ▲ Do not include Internet-connected servers in your corporate domain. Make them stand-alone member servers or create a separate domain.

SECURITY PROGRAMS AND UTILITIES

There are several programs that can make configuring security on an NT machine easier.

NT Resource Kit and Built-in Tools

Table 7-9 shows the tools from the NT Resource Kit that can help you. Appendix A gives a more complete description of all of the utilities found in the Resource Kit.

Resource Kit Tool	Function
CACL.EXE	Commands utility to change ACLs, accepts wildcards (native NT utility)
C2CONFIG.EXE	C2 Configuration Manager
DELPROF.EXE	Deletes profiles
DUMPEL.EXE	Dumps event log to a file
FINDGRP.EXE	Finds the groups a user belongs to even if from a different domain
FLOPLOCK.EXE	Prevents floppy drive access except to members of the Administrators group
GETSID.EXE	Compares security identifications (SIDs)
GLOBAL.EXE	Displays members of global groups

Table 7-9.   Security-Related Resource Kit Tools

Resource Kit Tool	Function
GRPCOPY.EXE	Copies usernames from one group to another
LOCAL.EXE	Displays members of local groups
NLMON.EXE	Lists aspects of trust relationships
NLTEST	Performs several admin tasks including trusts
PASSPROP.EXE	Sets two password properties: Administrator account lockout and password complexity
PERMCOPY.EXE	Copies share-level ACLs from one share to another
PERMS.EXE	Shows a user's permissions for a file or group of files
POLEDIT.EXE	System policy editor: sets policies to override user selections
REGSEC.EXE	Removes the group Everyone from a Registry key
SCOPY.EXE	File copy that maintains security
SECADD.EXE	Adds permissions to a Registry key
SECEDIT.EXE	Allows modification and viewing of the security privileges of the logged on user
SHAREUI	An easy-to-use GUI for administering shares
SHOWACLS.EXE	Shows access control lists for files, folders, and trees
SHOWGRPS.EXE	Shows groups to which a user belongs
SHOWMBRS.EXE	Shows group membership
SRVCHECK.EXE	Shows nonhidden shares and associated ACLs
USRSTAT.EXE	Shows user statistics, such as names and last logon time
USRTOGRP.EXE	Adds users to a group
Web Administrator for NT Server	Allows NT server administration through a Web browser
WINEXIT.SCR	Screen saver that logs users out

Table 7-9. Security-Related Resource Kit Tools (*continued*)

Third-Party Products

There are many companies that offer third-party products that can help you secure your NT enterprise. Most of the companies offer several different security products for your use. In addition, many of these companies offer 30-day evaluation versions of their software.

Security Auditing/Monitoring/Checking Software Companies

▼ En Guard Systems (**http://www.engarde.com**)

■ Internet Security Systems (**http://www.iss.net**)

■ Intrusion Detection (**http://www.intrusion.com**)

▲ Somarsoft (**http://somarsoft.com**)

NT-Firewall Companies

▼ BorderWare (**http://www.border.com**)

■ CheckPoint (**http://www.checkpoint.com**)

■ Digital Equipment (**http://www.digital.com**)

■ Global Internet (**http://www.gi.com**)

■ IBM (**http://www.ibm.com**)

■ NetGuard (**http://www.netguard.com**)

■ Network-1 (**http://www.network-1.com**)

▲ Raptor (**http://www.raptor.com**)

Miscellaneous Security Companies

▼ MWC (**http://www.ntsecurity.com**)

▲ Verisign (**http://www.verisign.com**)

Network Encryption Software

▼ Data Fellows Limited (**http://www.datafellows.com**)

■ McAfee (**http://www.mcafee.com**)

▲ NetLock (**http://www.netlock.com**)

Network Analyzers

▼ Cinco (**http://www.cinco.com**)

▲ Microsoft (**http://www.microsoft.com**)

Security Scanners Products

▼ Netcat (**http://www.l0pht.com/~weld/netcat**)

- ■ NetProbe (**http://www.qualix.com/sysman/product/netprobe.html**)
- ■ Portscan (**http://www.fbsolutions.com/clbrown/ntfnt.htm**)
- ▲ SATAN (**http://www.fish.com/satan**)

NT Security Web Sites

- ▼ Microsoft Security Page (**http://www.microsoft.com/security**)
- ■ NT Security.Net (**http://www.ntsecurity.net**)
- ▲ R. C. Consulting, Inc. (**http://www.ntbugtraq.com**)

THE NT 5.0 SECURITY MODEL

The main difference in terms of security that you find in NT 5.0 is the Active Directory. It is Microsoft's answer to critics that claim Banyan and Novell have a more robust directory. Active Directory is an extensible database containing information on all parts of the network. It is based on Lightweight Directory Access Protocol (LDAP) and the X.500 standard. You may have run across this naming convention already with other networking products. An X.500 name is read from right to left. Here is an example:

CN=Sean Corcoran,OU=Printing,O=NCS,C=US

The X.500 interpretation is that the user's country (C) is the United States, his organization (O) is NCS, he belongs to the printing organizational unit (OU), and his common name is Sean Corcoran.

Another important part of Active Directory is the way it addresses resources. Active Directory enhances the universal naming convention (UNC) names by building in more flexibility. For instance, in NT 4.0 if you want to move a shared resource from one server to another, you must move the data, create the share on the new machine, and then tell all users to now look for the share on the new machine.

For example, without Active Directory:

\\machine1\share →\\machine2\share

With Active Directory, the machines are part of a larger group (i.e., Servergroup). The path now becomes:

\\servergroup\share

Hence, you simply move the data and redefine the share as being on the new machine. The move is completely transparent to the user. Microsoft previewed an NT 4.0 version of this feature with the Distributed File System (Dfs). It has immense implications in terms of network resource availability. You can even move data off one server so you can do basic maintenance without having to interrupt your users!

SUMMARY

This chapter serves as a basic NT security overview and alerts you to some of the more common NT loopholes. For a more thorough examination of NT security, see the *Windows NT Security Handbook*, by Tom Sheldon.

The security of an organization's NT network can be an essential component in its success. Companies must analyze their security needs and risks and weigh them against costs to come up with a comprehensive protection plan. This plan must include protection of critical data from both internal and external intruders. Remember the importance of protecting your passwords, auditing, and locking down your servers. Do not forget that as NT grows in prominence, more and more developers are going to try to come up with new ways around its security scheme. You can stay on top of NT security changes at the Microsoft security page (**http://www.microsoft.com/security**).

WINDOWS
NT
Professional
Library

CHAPTER 8

Network Considerations

A network system is the entire collection of hardware, firmware, and software necessary to provide a desired functionality. A component is any part of a system that, taken by itself, provides all or a portion of the total functionality required of a system. A component is recursively defined to be an individual unit, not useful to further subdivide, or a collection of components up to and including the entire system.

—The Red Book

The above definition of a network by the United States Department of Defense is an excellent starting point for this chapter. Networks represent one of the most fundamental building blocks in the operations of most companies. In fact, networks are considered a necessity for modern companies. It is the network that allows workstations and people to communicate with each other and with servers. In fact, if the network is not available, many people cannot even perform their basic job functions. Therefore, network reliability needs to rank at the top of the list when it comes to planning for overall system redundancy.

From the above definition of a network, it is also important to notice that a network is comprised of many different components. Obviously, redundancy in a network must be applied to all component aspects, including computers, hubs, routers, wiring software, and even personnel. (Of course, the most important personnel on the system are the network administrators.)

On the software side, it is also imperative to build in redundancy. The software includes the different sets of network services such as Domain Name Service (DNS), Dynamic Host Configuration Protocol (DHCP), and Windows Internet Naming Service (WINS). These are the services that are basic requirements for the operation of the network. For instance, if the DNS server or some other name-resolving server is not available, no systems will be able to communicate with the server. This chapter will talk about these services and the other network components, and discuss methods to increase the reliability of them.

The bulk of the chapter is comprised of discussion of TCP/IP networks. Although much of the material is relevant to many networks, certain aspects (especially the network services mentioned) are applicable only to TCP/IP networks. With the massive move of companies to an Internet-based structure (TCP/IP), other protocols such as IPX or NetBEUI will not be fully considered.

POINTS OF FAILURE

As mentioned in Chapter 1, the first task to consider in making any system fault tolerant is to determine the system's points of failure. Today's networks and computers are much more robust than those in the past. Many people remember the early coaxial Ethernet and other implementations that required a computer to be rebooted if its network connection was dropped for any amount of time. Thankfully, network topologies have progressed much further. For instance, an 10BaseT Ethernet connection can be disconnected for almost any amount of time and data will start flowing almost the moment it is plugged back in.

So, where does most of the trouble exist in today's networks? The answer is simple: anywhere a person can touch something. Cables can be plugged into the wrong jacks, or some software or firmware parameters can be changed. Either of these simple events can be devastating to a network. For example, an errant router parameter can be extremely destructive to network operations. Routers commonly have dozens of parameters. There are some parameters that, when changed, will have dramatic effects on a network. There are also parameters and security entries on servers and other equipment. One wrong entry on an NT server can bring the whole NT network to a standstill. For instance, there are several documented cases of an unknowing NT administrator changing the "Access this computer from the Network" user right on a domain controller. This results in the majority of the users on the domain not being able to access any logon servers. It effectively locks them out of the domain.

NETWORK SOLUTIONS

So, how are these problems handled? Good company network policy goes a long way towards a solution. The network policy should include sections for wiring, network devices, network services, and security.

In terms of software, the same good management policy is also needed. Router configurations need to be determined before installation—do not simply guess at your configuration. If you do not have qualified network personnel, hire contractors or consultants to do the work. Many times, a working configuration can be immensely improved by having a knowledgeable person change a few parameters beforehand. Most importantly, document the configuration. Print it out, make notes about nonstandard or nondefault entries. Save the configuration documents in a safe place where you will be able to find them several months or even years down the road.

Finally, a realistic approach must be taken in establishing user hierarchy, access control lists, and permissions. One way to prevent any user from changing parameters on a router, switch, or managed hub is to simply not allow them access to these pieces of equipment. This lack of access should be at both the physical and machine password level. As certain types of redundancies on a network are increased, security can become compromised. In reality, network jurisprudence is one of the most critical aspects of any network. In the following sections, these issues are examined in detail.

Documentation

One important step in creating a fault-tolerant network is preparing adequate documentation. Faults will occur, and having procedures in place and practiced will allow for the quickest recovery from a disaster. The documentation needs to be readily available and continually updated as the network changes. In addition, the appropriate support people (users with appropriate permissions) must be aware of the changes and the documentation must be implemented. If you can manage the documentation, you are on the way to greatly increased network reliability.

Documentation should always be created based on the assumption that the entire operations staff will be gone the next day. This will assure that meaningful information will be documented. There are three types of documentation that are required for proper operation: network, design, and operation.

Network Documentation

Network documentation should include information on what things are, where things are, and where things go. It can range from the extremely detailed information to the basic information. For instance, some telephone companies require detailed knowledge of their internal wiring structures. They use computers and databases that keep track of every wire. Every time a wire is moved, its location has to be updated in the computer. This is wonderful because you can know from a remote location exactly what to expect before you get to a specific location. But for many companies, this is overkill. The things you should be documenting in the physical network are wiring plans and general locations of equipment. It is recommended that you label wires both as they come into a patch panel and at the jacks.

Design Documentation

The design documentation provides a high-level view of your system. It is important for both internal and external personnel to be able to quickly get a grasp of your network layout when there is an emergency. This type of documentation can point you and them towards the problem area. Where the network documentation focused on the physical aspects of the network, the design documentation should focus on the logical interconnectivity of the network and the methods used to interconnect devices.

Operation Documentation

The operation documentation primarily consists of the manufacturer's documentation. It can be supplemented with specific operational items to clarify and summarize the material from the manufacturer. It should include any customizations that you have made to both the hardware and software devices.

Impractical Redundancy

Let's take a moment to look at the issues of overkill and even invalid or impractical redundancy. There are some so-called redundant solutions that really do not add much to the overall network fault tolerance. For instance, suppose you have a system with multiple network adapters in every computer—will it truly increase network redundancy? First of all, it is a very expensive proposition. Secondly, it can be very hard, if not impossible, to do without specially designed software. Some devices only allow for one network connection, and others don't necessarily operate the way you might think they would. For example, spreading the load on and increasing the reliability of Web servers is a large concern today. At first look, it would be simple to add another network adapter and another TCP/IP address and share the load. But the problem is that DNS and TCP/IP stacks don't necessarily allow it. DNS and the TCP/IP stacks have no consistent method for assigning more than one address to a specific name for load balancing or providing redundancy. Most devices will only use the first IP address to communicate, even if the server is down or busy. The point here is that you must fully consider these types of propositions.

An example of the complexity of multiple adapters in a server is a secondary network for backing up servers to tape drives. Initially, it might seem easy to add an additional network adapter to all of the servers and then assume that you can perform backups over the new network without affecting the production user network. But how do the computers know to use it? Let's assume that two of the servers normally communicate with each other over the production user network. When the additional adapters are added, how do the servers know to run production traffic over one set of adapters and backup traffic over another? It can be done, but it requires sophisticated manipulation of routing tables in all of the servers and network devices. It also requires some interesting manipulations to the DNS and WINS servers. If the DNS returns an address of a server port that isn't connected to the production network, then you have broken your network. What you might construe as increased redundancy is actually a decrease in network operability by adding potential points of failure. In other words, you have decreased overall network security and integrity.

A much better solution for this scenario is products like the Intel EtherExpress PRO/100 Server Adapter with Adapter Fault Tolerance (**http://www.intel.com**). In the Intel product, two EtherExpress PRO/100 Server adapters are installed in the server and are joined together in an adapter "team." The team is controlled by an intelligent software agent. One of the adapters is designated as the primary, the other as secondary. Both of the adapters are connected in the network hub or switch. The software agent uses the secondary adapter to monitor the link and the connection status of the primary card with what are known as probe packets. When a failure occurs, such as a port failure, cable disconnect, or adapter failure, the probe packets fail to reach the primary adapter. The Adapter Fault Tolerance software agent detects the change in status of the primary adapter and the fail-over process takes place. It is actually transparent to the server's application software. All configuration information, including the MAC address and IP address, is given to the secondary adapter. In this way, no network changes are perceived by either the client's or the server's operating system.

Budgetary constraints are also important issues in deciding how to add redundancy to a network. Most companies cannot afford to be completely redundant. In fact, in a standard network, providing a redundant connection to all of the workstations is probably not important. What is important is providing high availability for the servers.

Other basic implementations can also increase availability. One of the simplest (and commonly overlooked) is the striping of resources across multiple devices. For example, a company might have a building with four floors. They purchase a router with four ports, one for each floor, and each router port is on its own board. If one of the ports fails, then an entire floor has failed. To avoid this, the network could have simply been designed differently. If the network connections are changed so that each router port serves a random quarter of each floor, a single port failure will only disable a quarter of the users (not entire departments). This will allow most departments to continue to operate, albeit in a partial fashion. This is just one example of a network change that is virtually free, and that can have a great impact on your system.

Network Wiring

The network cabling and wiring on your network should not be an unsettling sight. It is not uncommon to see ceilings that have collapsed from the cable load and wiring closets that have wires with no apparent destination. Likewise, you may have cables running directly over electrical wiring harnesses or fluorescent lights. You may also have rolls of wire in your ceiling, which can be another source of network problems. A great deal of noise is introduced into networks by faulty installation of cable. Wiring may seem like an expensive portion of installing a network, but by doing it right the first time, it can save many dollars and eliminate aggravations over the years. Additionally, installing high-quality cable in organized configurations can drastically reduce problems and expedite the resolution of many other troubles.

The standard network installation today calls for the Category 5 wiring for the networks and standard twisted pair (i.e., Category 3) for the telephone system. Where possible, try to stick with Category 5 wiring for both uses. This makes future system upgrades much easier and adds flexibility to your wiring infrastructure. Many designers like to configure either three or four cables for each drop, allowing multiple computers and/or phones to be installed at each desktop. The cost of adding a quality cable initially is cheap when compared to adding it at a later date.

In the wiring room, proper routing and location of wires is very important. All cables to workstations should be terminated into a patch panel and then patched with a short cord to the proper port on the hub or router. All of the workstation wiring should be labeled and carefully dressed to keep it from moving or getting tangled in any other wiring.

Patch cables should be short and run from one panel to another in cable trays, not in front of other equipment. Patch cables should never be tied down or labeled. If you have to trace a cable from one place to another, the proper method is by slightly tugging at the wire and following the movement. If you were to label a patch cable, the label would probably quickly be wrong as it will probably be moved from port to port and device to device.

When deploying Ethernet networks, there is one major limitation. That, of course, is the length of the cable from the workstation to the wiring hub. This should be no longer than 100m. For a 100m cable run, you can expect the physical distance between the workstation and the hub to be less than 60–70m, assuming that the wiring must snake up, down, and around walls. This means that in some buildings, two wiring closets must be used on each floor. All wiring closets should be interconnected with fiber to reduce electrical potential differences that exist between devices and electromagnetic noise.

Network Services

As mentioned above, there are several network services that need to be maintained in some sort of reliable and fault-tolerant manner on an NT network. The first step is to have the process on servers that are highly stable and seldom need to be touched. WINS, DHCP, routing, and remote access are services that should be set up once and then for the most part not tampered with. Of course, DNS, BOOTP, and security, are other services that have to constantly be updated.

With the advent of NT 5.0, Microsoft has combined WINS, DNS, DHCP, BOOTP, and security into one database. So, to make for an easier migration, it is generally recommended that these services be run on a single set of dedicated servers.

WINS—Windows Internet Name Service

WINS is used for NT NetBIOS name resolution. In fact, as you will soon see, it is like DNS for NT. It allows Windows and other NetBIOS-based machines to find each other on IP-based networks using the common name (instead of the IP address). WINS provides two features not commonly found in DNS. The first is a dynamic registration and the second is a service registration. A computer that is using WINS will contact the WINS server when it is starting, and actually register itself with the WINS server. The computer will also periodically refresh its registration to assure that the database is up to date. When a computer registers itself, not only does it register its name, but it also registers other information, such as the services that it is providing. If you were to examine a WINS server on an NT network, it would not be uncommon to see several entries for each computer.

The biggest drawback to WINS is the fact that it is completely NetBIOS-related. UNIX systems—or for that matter, most any non-Windows system—cannot access a WINS database. Before NT 4.0, DNS and WINS, which are actually closely related, were completely separate. In NT 4.0, the DNS service was modified to query the WINS database (the WINS directive) when processing a name lookup. In this case, if an NT system is acting as a DNS server and a non-Windows system queries for a name, DNS will check its databases and, if not found, query the WINS database. This then allows all computers on an NT IP-based network to find all other computers on the network.

WINS is a fairly easy to implement and reliable service. Clients will need to know the physical addresses of the WINS servers, so once the addresses are determined they should almost never be changed. WINS servers are fairly efficient and can serve a large number of clients from a medium-sized server. WINS understands how to provide backup services and allows two or more servers to replicate data among each other.

From the client side, a WINS client will always use its primary WINS server if the server is available. Only if the primary server is unavailable or inaccessible will the client attempt to query the secondary server. For this reason, many companies set up one half of their clients to use the first server as the primary and the other half of the clients to use the second server as the primary. It will depend on the specific network layout whether or not you should use this scheme.

The WINS service is relatively simple to install:

1. Open up the Network Control Panel Applet (NCPA) and from the Services tab select Add.

2. Highlight the Windows Internet Name Service from the list and click Okay.

3. When prompted, enter the path of the NT installation files and click Okay.

4. Close the NCPA and reboot the system.

5. Repeat the process on both of the machines that will run the WINS service.

NOTE: WINS must be installed on an NT server with a static IP address

After WINS is up and running on both machines, WINS replication needs to be started. Microsoft implements their replication through what they call "push" and "pull" partners. There are very few instances where you would need to install only one or the other. You will generally want both processes enabled. To enable replication, go into the WINS Manager Administrative Tool. You can bring up connections to both servers from either one of the consoles. Select Server | Add WINS Server and enter either the name or address of both servers. Replication is enabled on the Replication Partners screen. To access this screen, select each server individually and then click Server | Replication Partners. The Replication Partners screen is shown in Figure 8-1.

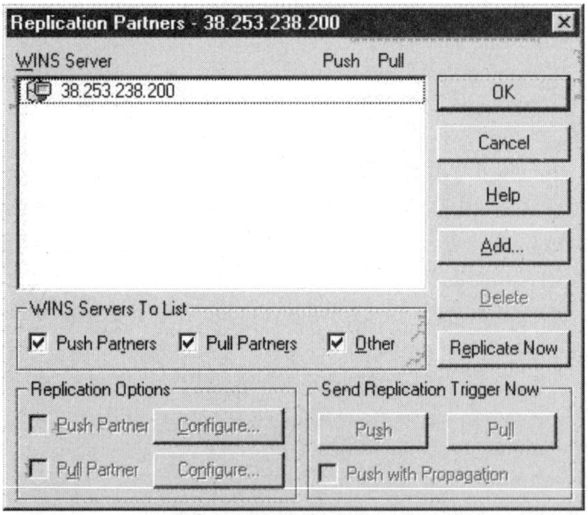

Figure 8-1. WINS replication configuration

To enable replication, select Add and enter the name or address of the servers that you want to replicate with. As they are added, the Replication Options in the lower left of the screen need to be enabled by checking off the Push and Pull Partner boxes. Check marks should then appear under the Push and Pull columns next to the server name (or IP address). After you perform these steps on both servers, replication should start. With the default configuration, it could be up to 15 minutes before replication commences.

If you are going to have more than two WINS servers, you should configure them in a star so that all servers replicate to one central site. This helps prevent entry ghosting problems as machines are removed from the network.

To verify that replication is occurring, select Mappings | Show Database, as shown in Figure 8-2. In the Owner window, select Show All Mappings, and in the window below select the remote WINS server. This should result in a listing of the mappings from the other server if replication has successfully occurred.

WINS also allows for the inclusion of static addresses. However, this is not necessary for most installations. If a static address needs to be added, it probably should be added to DNS instead of WINS.

All of the WINS information is kept in a database that can sometimes become corrupted. This information is stored in the %SYSTEMROOT%\SYSTEM32\WINS directory. Care should be taken to make sure that this database has been correctly backed up to tape. The database is usually open when the backup process is running, resulting in a bad copy on the tape. Periodically stopping and copying the directory is suggested to assure a good backup. If your database does fail, there are two options, depending on the

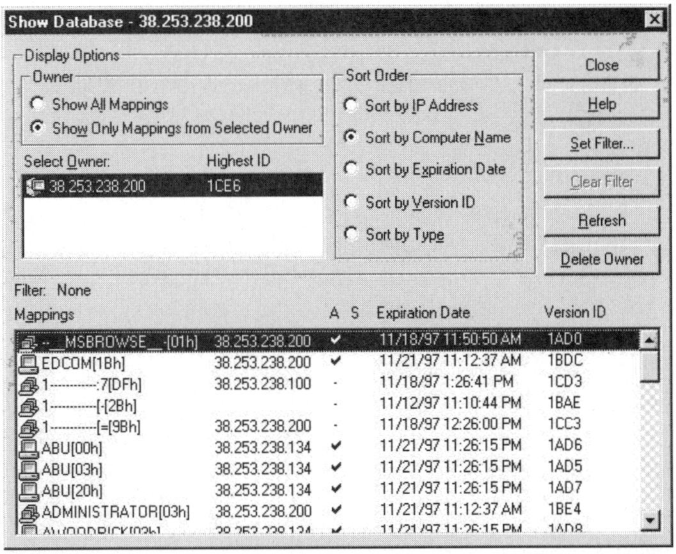

Figure 8-2.   WINS registrations

severity of the failure and the size of the organization. The first option is to restore the database from a backup and restart the process. The second option is to create a new database and allow all systems to reregister themselves. This will cause havoc on the network for a period, but it does attempt to assure that no old entries will exist in the database. Time to rebuild the WINS database is relatively short, and is dependent on the time to live configuration parameter in the WINS server. The default time to live is set at four days; however, rebooting all computers after initializing the database can accelerate the registration process.

DHCP—Dynamic Host Configuration Protocol

DHCP can make TCP/IP networks extremely easy to set up and manage. DHCP can automatically assign various bits of information to a DHCP client including IP address, subnet mask, default gateway, WINS server information, and DNS server addresses. When the client that is set up to use DHCP is started, it simply makes a network query for a valid DHCP server. If a range of open IP addresses exists on a DHCP server for the client's physical subnet, the server will answer with a valid IP address for the client (it can also give other information, as mentioned above).

Before DHCP, there were two alternatives to assigning IP addresses to hosts. Both required a great deal of administrative intervention. The standard method of assignment was a notepad or spreadsheet that was maintained by an administrator. The address was written down and then given to the installer, who had to manually enter it into the client's IP configuration screen. The second method was via BOOTP, which required the administrator to create a record on a central server for each client on the network. This is similar to setting up a reservation for a particular address on a DHCP server. Since Microsoft doesn't support the BOOTP Protocol directly, that left manual configuration of the network as the only option.

Manual configuration led to what was often an unreliable network. Duplicate addresses were fairly common. Either the administrator or installer used the wrong address or a user, unwilling to wait on the administrator, used a random address. DHCP increases the reliability of the network by reducing the number of parameters that require configuration on each workstation and by assuring that addresses are unique. The majority of NT networks now use some sort of automatic IP address distribution.

The utilization of DHCP requires configuration of the server, the workstations, and sometimes the routers. The workstations are quite easy; you simply tell them to use DHCP in the TCP/IP protocol properties pages (usually just a single check box!). The routers must be configured to send DHCP requests to the DHCP servers if you require IP addresses to be passed through the router (RFC 1542). Therefore, like many other network services, the addresses of the DHCP servers need to be dedicated and should not be changed. Changing the address will require configuration changes in all of the routers. That is, the new address will have to be entered in the routers manually.

Most new routers are capable of routing DHCP requests. DHCP requests are extensions to the BOOTP Protocol and have been supported by major router manufacturers since 1994. Each router segment needs to be set to send requests to the appropriate DHCP server and, on failure, to the backup DHCP server. One of the ramifications of a router being able to pass a DHCP request is that one DHCP server can handle dozens of different subnets.

DHCP, unlike many network services, does not handle having backup servers very well. But all is not lost. Fortunately, DHCP services are not constantly required on the network. A DHCP server is only required when a new machine is introduced to the network or when an IP lease time has expired.

The DHCP lease time is a specific time you set during DHCP configuration that the client will have control of the address. The default lease time is three days. If a client accepts an address from a DHCP server, it will continue to use the address for one and a half days (one-half of the lease). At that time, it will try to renew its lease with the same DHCP server for an additional three days. If a server is not available, it will continue using the lease until 85 percent of the lease time has expired. Then, it will attempt to renew its lease with any DHCP server that is available. If it is unsuccessful, it will give up its lease when the total time has run out. This process means that in a properly operating DHCP environment, no client should ever be below 50 percent of its DHCP lease time. If the servers are operating, the lease should always be refreshed at its halfway point. That is to say that unless you add a new machine, the DHCP server can be offline for up to the remaining 50 percent of the lease time (1.5 days) without presenting even one problem on the network. If there are no backup DHCP servers available at that point, clients would slowly begin to lose their IP addresses. When a server has been down the full lease time, all clients will have lost their address assignments.

So, what should you do? To provide fault tolerance, DHCP servers can be configured independent of each other by splitting the address pools between servers. If an abundance of addresses are available, then half can be assigned to the primary server and half to the backup server. Remember that the address pools cannot overlap. In this scenario, a client will start up and request an address from any DHCP server. The server that answers first with a valid IP address will be selected. The easiest way to ensure that a specific server answers first most of the time is to separate the DHCP servers (i.e., with a router). If you can separate the servers in this way, you can assign a much smaller number of addresses from a particular pool to the backup server.

If you are fortunate enough to have an abundance of IP addresses, you can set the lease time to a much higher number (i.e., two months). A lease of two months would theoretically give you an entire month to fix the broken server.

The low amount of traffic generated by the DHCP server makes it an ideal process to run with other network services such as DNS and WINS. A single DHCP server can handle thousands of clients easily.

Configuration of the DHCP is based upon the concept of "global" parameters and "scopes." A DHCP scope is an administrative grouping that identifies the configuration parameters for all DHCP clients grouped together on a physical subnet. Each subnet on the network will need a separate scope. All scopes for an organization do not need to be on the same set of servers, but doing so reduces the administrative overhead of configuring parameters.

Setting up DHCP is straightforward:

1. Open the Network Control Panel Applet (NCPA).
2. Under services, click Add.
3. Highlight Microsoft DHCP Server from the list and select Okay.
4. Enter the location of the install files when prompted and select Okay.
5. Close the NCPA and reboot when prompted.
6. Repeat the process on any other machines that will be running DHCP.

Now it is time to configure the scopes. Before configuring a scope, the following is needed:

▼ Scope name

■ Subnet mask

■ Subnet address

■ Reserved addresses

▲ Excluded addresses

For example, suppose you have a network in which each subnet is a Class C address space and has the standard subnet mask of 255.255.255.0. The router is assigned address 1 (by convention, the router is usually the first or last valid host address of a segment). The 255 address is reserved for broadcasts. For simplicity in this example, the primary and secondary scopes will be split into roughly 100 address chunks. The primary DHCP server will use the 51–150 range for all subnets and the backup server will use 151–254. The range from 2–50 will be reserved for devices that do not understand the DHCP Protocol or otherwise require a static address. The lease time will be set to 45 days.

For the scope name, a brief description can be used such as the building or floor name. After you have installed the DHCP service, open up the DHCP Manager Administrative Tool. The DHCP Manager main screen is shown in Figure 8-3. To start a new scope, select Scope | Create. If you already have DHCP installed on your other server, you can create its scope from this same console.

The scope information is straightforward. Simply fill in the blanks referring to start and stop addresses, subnet mask, and so on. If any addresses in the scope should not be passed out, add them to the excluded address list. Click Okay when finished.

Now you need to set the parameters for the server. Parameters can be added on a per-scope basis (apply only to a specific scope) or a global basis (apply to all scopes on the server).

Of the six supported parameters in Windows networks (see Table 8-1 next) the Domain Name, DNS servers, and WINS-specific items should be configured as global. The router value (same as default gateway) and sometimes the Scope ID are entered as scope specific.

NOTE: The DHCP parameters are all optional.

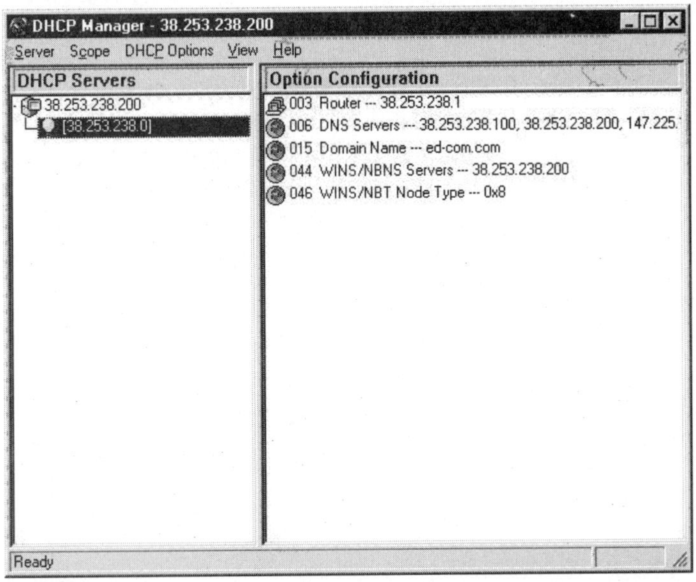

Figure 8-3. DHCP Manager

After all of the scopes have been defined and routers configured, you should be able to introduce a client to the network and allow it to request an address. You can confirm the acquisition by using the IPCONFIG /ALL command on NT clients (or WINIPCFG on

Option	Definition	Type
003	Router	Scope
006	DNS server	Global
015	Domain Name	Global
044	WINS/NBNS servers	Global
046	WINS/NBT node type	Global
047	NetBIOS scope ID	Either

Table 8-1. DHCP Options

Windows 95/98 clients). You can also check the server for active leases in the DHCP Manager.

A great deal has been made of the security problems with DHCP. The issues are twofold: 1) machines automatically connecting to the network and 2) fear of not having historical information concerning which IP addresses are assigned to which machines at any given time. The first issue is a problem with most network protocols anyway. If you are running NetBEUI or IPX\SPX, a person with physical access to a live jack can also join the network. The administrative benefits of using DHCP far outweigh this complaint. The better way to stop this sort of intrusion is to use intelligent hubs and switches on which unused ports and jacks can easily be disabled from a management console.

The second issue holds a little more water. Even if you have a relatively long lease period, there is actually no way to automatically determine which machine had a particular IP address at any given time. This can be an issue if corporate policy requires this information. The easiest way to handle the problem is to set up a script that does periodic dumps of the WINS database using the WINSDMP NT Resource Kit utility. By dating and saving these dumps (and possibly parsing them), you can gain historical information on who has which IP addresses and when someone has a specific address.

DNS—Domain Name Service

People in our culture like to be known by specific names. Therefore, it is not surprising that people like to give their computers names. Numbers are just not acceptable. So, for TCP/IP networks, a process called DNS was created. DNS provides the translation of names into numbers (IP addresses) so computers can find one another. This process is known as name resolution. DNS is very important for proper operation of TCP/IP networks. For most users, if DNS is not available, then the network will seem to be nonoperational even though the transport may be working perfectly.

DNS was designed for the Internet, a distributed network of large numbers of computers using various speeds for connections. Many of the features of fault-tolerant systems are already built into DNS. DNS provides a hierarchical architecture that allows multiple servers at all levels. These servers are known as primary and secondary DNS servers. A primary server is the server at which changes are normally made. Secondary servers periodically replicate the information from the primary server. As far as a client knows, a secondary server is identical, and just as reliable as a primary server. On the Internet, InterNic (the organization that more or less controls the Internet) requires at least two DNS servers to be configured for every valid domain. This policy should, of course, be followed for corporate networks.

It is possible to get carried away with the number of DNS servers on a particular network. This is not necessary. Most DNS platforms can handle thousands of clients. DNS has been optimized over many years to provide quick, reliable service. The hierarchical nature of DNS was created to reduce the load on any single server. For most networks, two DNS servers are more than satisfactory. DNS queries are short and do not put very much of a load on the network.

DNS addresses are configured into the TCP/IP protocol parameters of the network clients. Any changes in a network that require the changing of the IP address of a DNS server can affect the configuration of every other computer on the network. Clients have the addresses of the DNS servers configured in their TCP/IP protocol stack. Unless the client is running DHCP, which can dynamically pass out the new DNS information, a change in a DNS address can require a visit to every system on the network.

Basic DNS server configuration has been made easier under Windows NT. The location of DNS servers should normally be the same as the WINS servers—two servers located at geographically disperse locations.

> **NOTE:** If your company is connected to the Internet, use split DNS with one set of DNS servers inside the firewall and another set outside. This can prevent hackers from getting unnecessary information about your internal network structure.

DNS uses the concept of primary and secondary servers. The primary server is the one on which changes are made, while the secondary servers automatically replicate the information. From the client side, the client will always use the primary DNS if the server is available. Only if the primary server is unavailable or inaccessible will the client attempt to query the secondary server. For this reason, many companies set up one-half of their clients to use the first server as the primary and the other half of the clients to use the second server as the primary. Doing this can give a slight performance boost (DNS is actually a very fast service anyway).

The NT DNS Manager makes it easy to modify DNS entries and makes selection of the location of the primary server almost irrelevant. The generally accepted practice would be to locate the primary DNS at the primary data center.

Installing the NT DNS service is much like adding the WINS service:

1. DNS should be installed on an NT server with a static IP address.

2. Open up the Network Control Panel Applet (NCPA) and from the Services tab select Add.

3. Highlight the Microsoft DNS Service from the list and click Okay.

4. When prompted, enter the path of the NT installation files and click Okay.

5. Close the NCPA and reboot the system.

6. Repeat the process on both of the machines that will run the DNS service.

The NT DNS comes preconfigured with the Internet "root" servers' entries. This means they automatically know how to get domain information from the Internet. The only requirement is to enter your own domain. To accomplish this, open the DNS Administrator (an NT Administrative Tool). Select DNS | New Server and enter your server name or IP address. Now select your server and add a new zone by selecting DNS | New Zone. The screen that comes up should look like the one in Figure 8-4.

Select Primary as the zone type and click Next. This brings up the Zone Name screen, as shown in Figure 8-5. Enter the zone name (the domain name) and the name of the zone

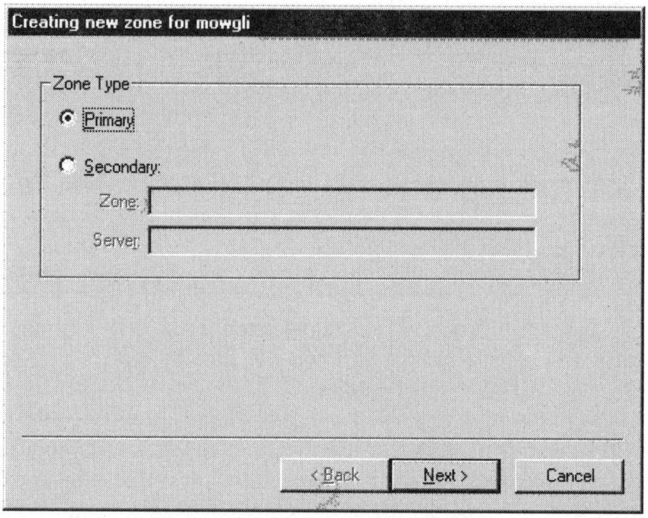

Figure 8-4. Zone Type screen

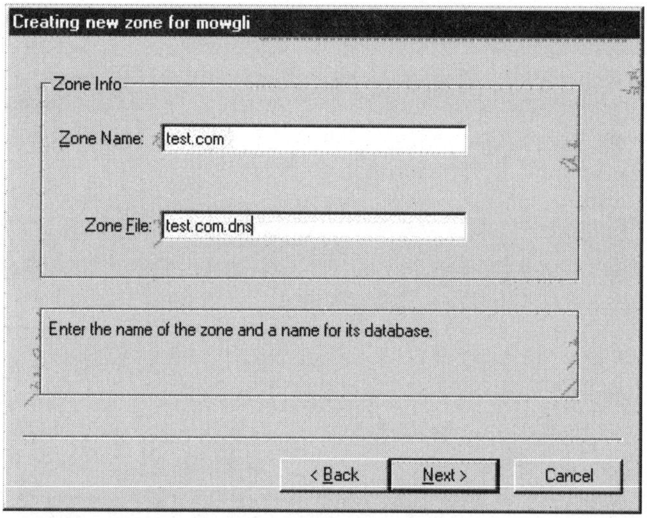

Figure 8-5. Zone Name screen

file. After entering the zone name, if you tab to or select the Zone File field, The DNS Administrator will select a filename for you (DOMAINNAME.DNS). Normally, this filename is sufficient. When you click next, the domain will be created.

On the General tab, the information is the same as that entered when you set up the domain, as shown in Figure 8-6. Select the SOA (Source of Authority) tab before moving on.

Go to the "Responsible Person Mailbox DNS Name." field. It should be the e-mail address of the person responsible for the domain. To create the field, add the responsible person's e-mail address. You can replace the default period with an at symbol (@) if you want to show a normal-looking SMTP e-mail address, as this area is simply a text entry field (i.e., change aaron.allsbrook.com to aaron@allsbrook.com). However, the period designation has been the standard method of denoting contact e-mail addresses for many years. The other fields on this page, as shown in Figure 8-7, are automatically generated and should normally be left at the default values.

NOTE: The period designation is used in the Responsible Person field because the @ symbol has a specific meaning in other parts of a DNS server: it means "at the domain name." This means that if the name were used in a true DNS process (and not just a text field), it would come up duplicated (i.e., Aaron@allsbrook.com. allsbrook.com).

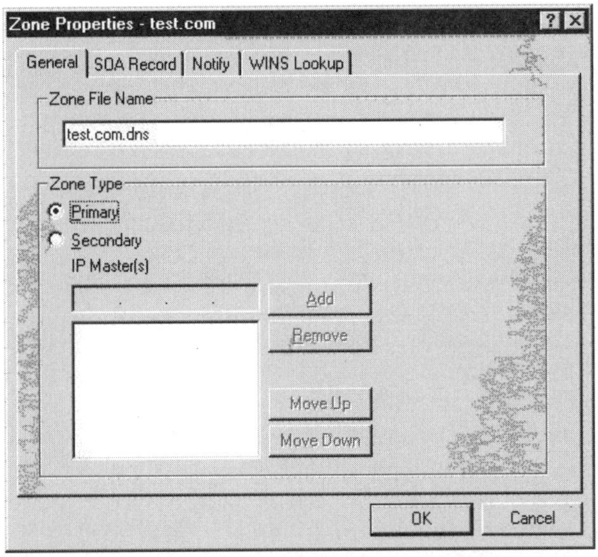

Figure 8-6.   Zone Properties screen

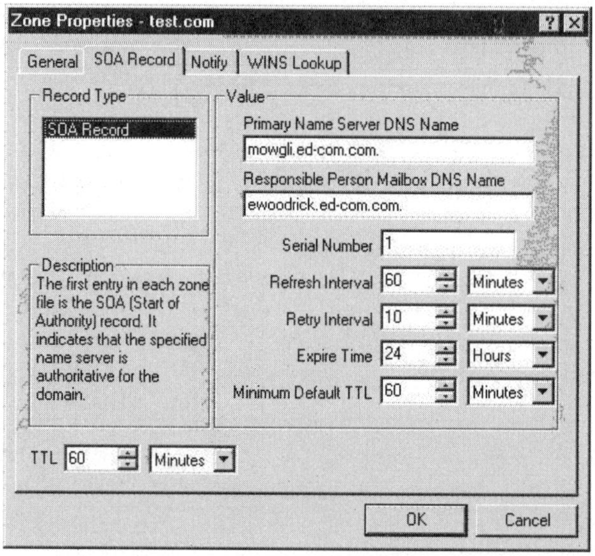

Figure 8-7. Source of Authority tab

The Notify tab is not utilized when only one DNS server is available. It will be configured after the second server is set up. Microsoft's DNS also provides the ability to use WINS to resolve names (the WINS directive). It is enabled on the WINS Lookup tab, as shown in Figure 8-8. If the DNS server does not find the requested name in the DNS table, it will send a request to the WINS server for address resolution. This allows systems that do not utilize WINS to communicate with all of the Windows workstations and servers. It actually provides a somewhat dynamic registration of DNS names.

At this point, the installation is moved to the secondary server. This assumes that the DNS service has already been installed. Like the other NT network services, both DNS servers can be configured from a single console. First select Server List and then the DNS | New Server menu item. Enter the name of the second server and select Okay. The utility will attempt to locate the second server. If it does not, be sure you can at least ping the second server at a command prompt.

To install the domain on the secondary server, select the new server and the Choose the DNS | New Zone menu item. This will bring up the Zone screen shown in Figure 8-9. When you select the secondary button, the Zone and Server text entry fields will be enabled. It will also enable the Secondary Zone Creation Wizard. Notice the new text and the little hand at the lower right-hand portion of the screen in Figure 8-9. To create the secondary zone, drag the hand and drop it on the primary zone, and just about everything will be automatically created. Simply click through the remainder of the

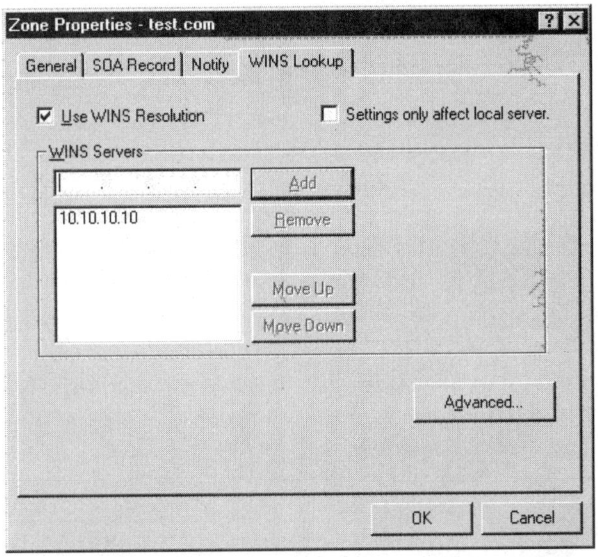

Figure 8-8. WINS Lookup tab

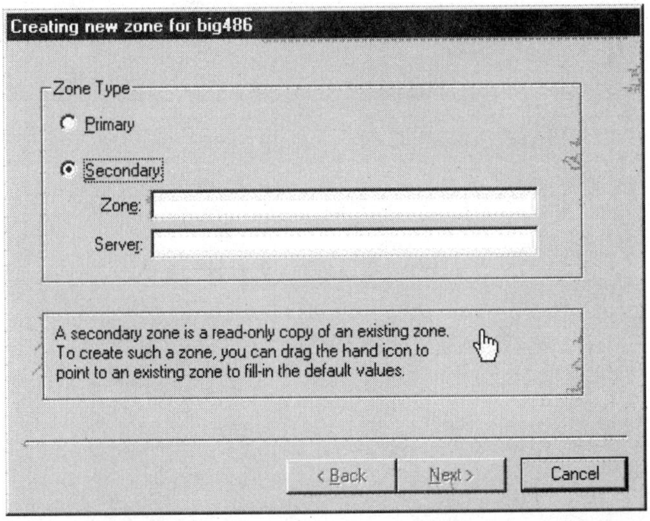

Figure 8-9. DNS secondary zone

screens until the zone is added. The information for the zone will not be available immediately; it will require the server doing an update or being restarted before the information becomes completely available.

To minimize the update time for future updates, the primary server can be configured to automatically notify the secondary server that an update has occurred. This feature is only available between NT 4.0 servers and does not work with other DNS servers such as BIND. Figure 8-10 shows the screen that is accessible through the primary server's Zone Properties | Notify tab. Change the properties so that the Notify tab includes the addresses of the secondary server. To enable additional security, the "Only Allow Access From Secondaries Included on Notify List" can be enabled.

BOOTP—Bootstrap Protocol

BOOTP is commonly used to provide IP address information for TCP/IP protocol stacks in network devices such as print servers, X terminals, routers, and switches. A BOOTP device will ask for its network address as well as the location of a TFTP (Trivial File Transfer Protocol) server from which the server's executable code can be loaded. A well-configured BOOTP server can be very reliable. The protocol has been around for many years and most of the bugs have been worked out. The usual problems with a BOOTP server concern the configuration of the individual entries by the administrator.

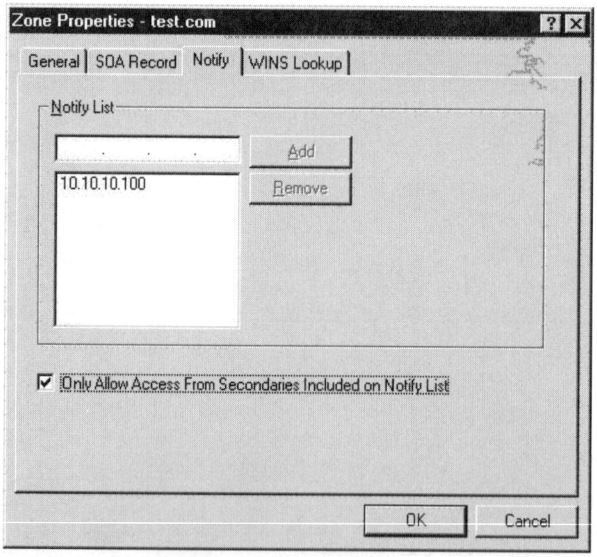

Figure 8-10. Notify tab

As with any manual intervention, mistakes can occur. BOOTP is not usually a viable protocol on NT networks because it is not supported natively by NT.

> **NOTE:**   DHCP is actually an extension of BOOTP protocol.

Luckily, most modern devices support BOOTP and DHCP for address allocation. This means that for most NT-based networks, BOOTP becomes unnecessary.

NT Domain Controllers

An NT domain controller is essentially a server that runs a logon service for NT networks. The best configuration of domain controllers for an organization can be a hotly contested issue. Suffice it to say that the model that Microsoft used for security doesn't necessarily fit any organization; therefore, compromises are usually made. Many organizations are moving toward a single master domain with resource domains. This might not fit your requirements, but it does make a lot of things easier. All is not lost, because NT 5.0 implements a new structure that will hopefully better fit the operations of most organizations.

From a fault-tolerance point of view, it should be remembered that all domains should have at least one BDC. This allows redundancy and can add to logon performance. The other main issue to understand about domain controllers is that any changes made in the User Manager for Domains will affect all domain controllers. Domain controllers are examined more closely in the security chapter of this book (see Chapter 7).

Routing

Routing is commonly viewed as one of the largest problem areas on IP-based networks. It is not that routing is unreliable. It is more that an administrator can simply incorrectly configure routing. Many of the recent problems with the Internet have been caused by incorrect routing configurations. Routing is a very complex item, not something for a novice to perform. Proper configuration of routing can also make a difference between high availability and failure. Complete routing configurations, when properly made, can change the flow of data around problem areas, actually circumventing disastrous situations.

The configuration of routing is highly network and equipment dependent. Some of the basic things that need to be addressed are multiple routes and fault-tolerant configurations.

In TCP/IP networks, routes can be manually configured or automatically updated. The Routing Information Protocol (RIP) is one of the most common methods of advertising routes. RIP has some advantages in the configuration of reliable networks, as routes can be automatically updated when links fail. But, as with anything, simplicity has its cost. It is fairly easy to configure a network so that if a link fails, a routing loop occurs and very little works. So, from the standpoint of reliability, it's hard to beat static routes.

Security

An often-overlooked aspect of reliability is security, from two vantage points—the first in keeping unwanted people from causing problems on the network, and the second in allowing the right people to access the network. You can design and implement a very reliable network, but without the proper security the network can be a considerable detriment to a corporation. From remote access intruders to visitors in your wiring closets, a network without security becomes an unsafe network. How much security is necessary? That's dependent on the level of reliability that you want, but basically you should attempt to provide basic security for all parts of the system, and if any portion of your network is available to "public access," those portions should implement significantly higher levels of security.

You should look at the network as needing different levels of security based upon accessibility by others. Even if a server is in a locked room that only certain individuals have the keys to, do not leave the room without logging off of or securing the workstation. This gives you an additional layer of security (intruders have to first get by your lock and then through your password security). If the computer is in a public area like a mall, then you should be completely paranoid. Make sure that all passwords are almost impossible to guess (see Chapter 7). Be sure that the machine is configured so that access is only into defined areas, and be sure to use locking screen savers. Lastly, it is recommended that you use NT Workstation with NTFS drives (with very tight profiles) in these types of areas.

For cable concentration areas (wiring closets), there is a tendency to place them in storage rooms. This is not typically recommended. Usually, too many people have access to the area, but most importantly, it becomes too easy for accidents to happen. Boxes can accidentally snag cable as they are carried, power plugs get pulled for other uses, all sorts of dangerous things can occur. So, it is obvious that part of network security is physical as well as electronic.

Speaking of electronic security, climate control and monitoring systems can greatly enhance your security and reliability. Temperature-monitoring devices can notify you if there are cooling problems and possibly save an entire data center before it overheats. Access monitors, badge readers, and surveillance cameras also become very handy in reducing unauthorized access. People don't tend to perform unscrupulous acts when they believe they are being watched.

Internet Security

Internet security should be an extension of the existing security built into your network. Internet security becomes a major issue in overall network security mainly because of the sheer number of possible intruders. Simply the realization that some people can, either maliciously or accidentally, perform actions detrimental to your operation should force you to implement strong Internet security.

An example of a malicious interference is when someone uses breaches in your security wall to access your network. These accesses can range from simple viewing of your network to the retrieval of information from your servers and the deletion or modification of information on your network. One major problem for NT systems has been utilities that run a "ping attack," in which unusual ping sequences are sent to servers on your network. This can result in a denial of service on your NT systems. Some servers will completely stop operating if this occurs, requiring a reboot of the server. To date, all of these types of problems have been quickly fixed by Microsoft through Service Packs and Hot Fixes. However, it is important to monitor these types of problematic utilities as they appear on the Internet. As mentioned in the security chapter of this book, two great sources of the most recent NT security information are the Microsoft Security page (**http://www.microsoft.com/security**) and The NTBugtraq home page (**http://www. ntbugtraq.com**). NTBugtraq has an excellent mailing list that always seems to report NT security problems before the rest of the world catches on. Be sure to assign a security administrator to your network who can follow these types of developments. No matter what the problem, though, Internet security requires a heightened awareness and restriction of your network when compared to an isolated network.

When you connect a network to the Internet, it is important to set up a firewall. The firewall acts as a one-way filter that is designed to keep things from transiting from one network to another. It allows internal users to access the Internet, but it does not allow Internet users to access your corporate network in undesirable ways.

There are many ways to implement a firewall, from filtering on routers to shareware to commercial products. Many commercial products allow for simplified setup as well as guarantees of security. A few major manufacturers are IBM, CheckPoint Software, and Raptor. All of these manufacturers have products that are suitable for protecting the enterprise network. In most enterprise installations, a firewall should be more than a basic address-translating proxy server. Look for a full-service firewall, such as those offered by the companies above, that inspects both packet content and source/destination.

Some firewalls integrate with your network better than others. Firewalls based on the NT platform can utilize your existing NT user account base, while UNIX-based products commonly require a new, separate authentication database. Many experts have argued the advantages of each method, and it comes down to what best fits your organization.

Firewall Manufacturers	URL
Border Network Technologies	**http://www.border.com**
CheckPoint Software	**http://www.checkpoint.com**
Cisco Systems	**http://www.cisco.com**
Gauntlet Firewalls	**http://www.tis.com**
Milkyway Products	**http://www.milkyway.com**
Raptor	**http://www.raptor.com**
IBM	**http://www.ibm.com**
NetGuard	**http://www.ntguard.com**

Other Methods for Security

Many other security methods do exist. Some provide minimal security, while others provide exceptional security. These newer methods include voice, face, and fingerprint recognition. Each method has its advantages and problems, and must be studied individually to determine what its reliability is. Understand that these can be expensive solutions, but may be necessary for extremely secure networks.

Windows NT Security

As mentioned, Microsoft Windows NT 4.0 and earlier versions used the Domain security model of the Primary Domain Controller and Backup Domain Controller for authenticating all resources under the control of the NT server and its clients. The NT security model provides centralized and encrypted transfer of security tokens on the network.

NT Domain documentation is available in many sources. The introduction of Windows NT 5.0 has significantly changed the method of implementation of domain security. NT 5.0 domain services are backward compatible with previous versions, but many of the limitations of the NT Domain Model are lifted, allowing for easier design of corporate networks. One concept that disappears with NT 5.0 is that of the Primary Domain Controller. All domain controllers in NT 5.0 are peers of one another and contain replicas of the database.

The NT security model centralizes much of the security authentication into a single database. Domain security is utilized for file and print services, Exchange Server access, SQL Server access, and web and RAS access. Microsoft attempts to implement a single logon capability with its current generation of products, and comes much closer to this goal with NT 5.0.

One of the more frustrating aspects of NT security is the lack of a true granularity of administration. This means that you cannot easily assign partial administrative support to individuals. People seem to have no rights or all rights when it comes to using tools like User Manager for Domains. Because of this issue, many NT networks have too many administrators. Here, careful design needs to be implemented. You can easily argue that any network with more than one administrator is a security breach. The practicalities of business require some administrator redundancy. Policies have to be established to allow the minimum acceptable number of administrators on the network. Likewise, care has to be taken to prevent the destruction of the network as stated above. There are no hard and fast rules for administrator numbers, but fewer are better.

The are actually products that can help solve the lack of security granularity in NT. These products—such as Trusted Enterprise Manager (TEM) from Master Design Development, Inc. (**http://www.mddinc.com**)—allow you to configure very specific administrative rights to specific users for specific resources. That is to say that you can allow a lower administrator to perhaps reset a user's password but not allow him or her to make changes in user rights.

Remote Access

A solid remote access system is important to the reliable operation of any modern network. Remote access can also be a point at which a high number of failures occur. Many installations consist of separate modems—with multiple cables tangled together—connecting to the access device. Anytime that you have a lot of unnecessary cables and devices, the reliability of the system goes down.

Other problems with RAS solutions are the reliability of the telephone lines and the ability to determine that there is a problem. RAS solutions must be devised so that if there is a problem with one line, it can temporarily and automatically be removed from service. It must be set up in such a way as to allow calls to roll over to other circuits.

Security on a remote access solution is also a problem. If the security is too light, then intruders may find an easy way onto the network. If security is too heavy, then it may be impossible to get through if there are basic network problems. It may become too troublesome for people to use.

The configuration of RAS is very similar to configuring workstations and networks except that physical security is no longer available. To connect to an Ethernet network, you physically have to perform the connection. For remote access, all you need is a phone line. This means that just about anybody from anywhere can attempt to connect to your network with very little, if any, evidence of the connection (or the attempt).

RAS Security

The first concern in a RAS design is the determination of which solutions meet your security requirements. There are three categories of security for remote access devices. The basic type is devices (i.e., modems) in which the administrator creates the account and the password on the device itself. Sometimes it is possible that the user can change the password, but many times it is not possible. Passwords are commonly passed across to the modems in clear text.

NT RAS SECURITY   In most instances, this standard NT RAS security will be sufficient. It utilizes the standard NT security database (SAM) and provides fairly secure access. It can also provide encryption of all data across the modems, making eavesdropping rather difficult. When compared to the basic authentication, NT Remote Access is significantly harder to break. In this sense, NT over RAS is actually more secure than NT over a network. A line monitor in the correct place on a basic security system will yield a username and password, whereas the same line monitor would require cryptography programs and expert knowledge of the protocol to break the security of the NT RAS system.

The middle-level security is the type of security the NT uses. The security database is not kept on the access device, but on the computer. Users can easily change passwords, password aging is enabled, and passwords are encrypted on the network.

HARDWARE TOKENS   The highest level of security uses constantly changing passwords. This is usually implemented with hardware password generators. In this way, the need to encrypt the password is reduced since a password can only be utilized once. The hardware token and server are related using a preset hardware key.

Products like SecurID, by Security Dynamics (**http://www.securid.com**), provide a higher level of RAS security than most products provide out of the box. The SecurID hardware token is commonly a credit card-sized device with a continually changing display. Each device is programmed with a key, which is known by the security server. Both the device and the server generate a pseudorandom sequence of numbers which, when combined with a user's secret PIN, provide a continually changing, virtually unbreakable method of access. SecurID is commonly used on remote access devices to assure authenticated access, but can also be used to secure access to many directly connected systems, including UNIX and NT servers.

RADIUS—REMOTE AUTHENTICATION DIAL-IN USER SERVICE   The RADIUS Protocol is commonly used to secure and monitor remote access devices. The RADIUS server nominally holds for each account the security information as well as any access information. This is a centralized and encrypted process that tremendously eases the administration of remote access devices. The manufacturers of the remote access servers—such as Ascend (**http://www.ascend.com**), Livingston (**http://www.livingston.com**), and CISCO (**http://www.cisco.com**)—provide RADIUS servers for utilization with their equipment. The RADIUS Protocol was initially defined by Livingston, but was subsequently offered to the IETF and is now published as a standard.

RADIUS is published in source code and has been ported to many different computing platforms. Some manufacturers, such as Ascend, have modified the code to provide some additional features. Microsoft has started to combine the use of RADIUS and security in a number of products; especially the Internet-related products such as Web servers and some remote access products.

RAS Configuration

After the security requirements have been determined, the physical configuration becomes an important issue. It is too easy to create a remote access solution that has hundreds of wires and modems, and power supplies lying around the server. This is not a reliable configuration. It is really only feasible for configurations of under a dozen ports. Above this number, cable, modem, and port management become overriding factors. One of the best-packaged systems for large numbers of ports is the Ascend Max 4004 Access Server. This chassis is in a rack mount configuration, four inches high. It supports up to 72 modems, digital or analog, and has only six connections—four T1/PRI, an Ethernet, and the power connection. With a configuration such as this, it becomes a lot harder to accidentally trip over a wire. By the way, if you will be using NT for large numbers of modems (over 32), be sure to check with Microsoft for the proper CPU and memory configuration. This kind of application can require a large amount of processing power.

When configuring remote access for Microsoft Networks, four parameters are important for each port: the DNS server addresses, the WINS server addresses, the port address, and the user authentication. The WINS address was introduced by Windows Networking and will eventually disappear as Windows NT 5.0 fully permeates the marketplace. Many remote access servers don't allow configuration of WINS addresses (this should be used as selection criteria for remote access devices if it will be required). If the device does not transmit the WINS addresses to clients, then significantly more configuration is needed on the client.

For address assignment for each port, one of two methods can be used. Some RAS servers, including the NT RAS server, can utilize DHCP for allocation of addresses. This has an advantage in that configuration can be simplified and management eased. If DHCP allocation is not available, the remote access server has to be assigned a pool of addresses for each port. These addresses have to be excluded from the DHCP scope for the subnet that the remote access server is on. If the addresses are available, there can be speed advantages to assigning pools of addresses directly on the RAS server.

When working with telephone circuits, as in remote access, care should also be taken to configure the telephone circuits so that they can assist with fault tolerance. A common configuration for multiple phone lines is to put them in a "hunt group" so that a new phone call always comes in on the lowest-numbered phone circuit in the group. One problem is that if the first phone line has problems, either in the circuit or the modem, it can just about completely disable the network remote access. One solution to this problem is to change the method of hunting for the group. Each telephone company and telephone switch is different, but many have a type of "least utilized" hunting. Others offer a revolving hunt group. This will route a new call to the circuit that has been idled the longest or to different circuits. If a circuit exhibits a problem, the user will see the problem, but upon dialing again, another modem will be accessed and should be functioning normally.

Monitoring of a remote access package is very important, and also somewhat difficult. Depending on the remote access solution chosen, there can be minimal or very good remote monitoring. The NT RAS solution does not provide a great deal of monitoring, and is one reason why many organizations pick other solutions. Other offerings—like those from Ascend (**http://www.ascend.com**), 3COM (**http://www.3com.com**), and MultiTech (**http://www.multitech.com**)—are designed for unattended operation and have significantly more complex monitoring and fault-tolerance tools built in. Some products can automatically detect failures and either compensate or disable the circuit to assure proper operation.

Network Topology

Many networks can be described as having two main sections. The first is the local office or building setup, and the second is the connections to other office and sites. The local office wiring is referred to as the local area network (LAN) and the wide area wiring is referred to as the wide area network (WAN). Although commonly connected together, the protocols, devices, and media are quite different between the networks. In a LAN environment, networks will probably operate at 10 or 100Mbps, or even greater speeds. In a corporate WAN setting, connections generally range from 56Kbps to 1.544Mbps. The cost is also significantly different. In the LAN, all wiring is installed by the customer and represents a one-time charge of about $200 per workstation. WAN connections are shared by many workstations and users, but the wiring and equipment are leased from telephone companies and can range from a few hundred to a few thousand dollars per month.

Wide Area Network

Although commonly supplied by the telephone companies, there are many different means of providing WAN connectivity. If you have right-of-way between buildings, it is actually possible to install your own fiber between buildings (such as on a campus). This is sometimes much cheaper than expected, especially when compared to the comparable costs of leased lines. For locations within a few miles of each other, there are LASER, microwave, and radio solutions that are available and should be looked at. Since WAN connectivity is so expensive, the correct determination of your needs can save large amounts of money. If you only have a few people at a remote site accessing centralized resources, a 56Kbps circuit might be all that is necessary. On the other hand, dependent on the tariffs, it might be just as cheap to provide a T1 connection. Knowing your options and having a good relationship with your telecommunications provider can be very important in setting up these connections.

In terms of redundancy, facilities can be connected by WANs over multipoint circuits like Frame Relay, ATM, or SONET. By connecting to network systems such as these, the network itself can provide redundancy. The tail circuit to each facility may still be a single point of failure, but it can be duplicated to add additional reliability.

One last note on WAN equipment. This type of equipment—like routers, CSU/DSUs, etc.—can be very complicated. There are also a large number of parameters in a router, and the proper configuration is crucial. As mentioned above, a small configuration error can seriously degrade WAN performance. If you do not have personnel that know how to configure this equipment, contract someone who does.

Local Area Network

Although there have been many alternatives in the past, 10Mbps Ethernet seems to be the most pervasive network topology in the current market. Ethernet adapters and cabling are less expensive than the alternatives, and have basically become a commodity in the marketplace. However, be sure to watch the available bandwidth on these systems. If traffic on the network reaches 40–60 percent of maximum bandwidth, Ethernet performance will seriously degrade. In this case, look at segmentation options, switches, or faster Ethernet speeds (100Mbps).

In terms of wiring, run fiber-optic cable between wiring closets and across any runs exceeding 100 meters. Fiber is also an excellent choice in industrial areas as it is unaffected by electromagnetic radiation and most environmental factors. Here, you should run Category 5 twisted pair from the hubs to the workstations.

As far as the actual network layout goes, try to make the network identical for each floor in the building. Each floor will consist of runs of cables from the workstations to the wire room and to the hubs, switches, or routers. As mentioned above, these devices should then be connected via fiber-optic cable to the master wiring room for the building.

HUBS   The proper selection of hubs is an important decision to make. Hubs can be grouped and managed, and come in different physical configurations. A hub is a loose term for a device that is a central place to connect workstations. It applies to many different types of networking, and even other disciplines. For this book, a hub will be referred to as an Ethernet wiring concentration device that commonly uses twisted pair for connection to workstations and other devices. There are currently three basic speeds of hubs: 10Mbps, 100Mbps, and 1Gbps.

A rather interesting turn of events for Ethernet is that most new network adapters are capable of 10 or 100Mbps speeds, depending on the hub that they are connected to. Connected to a 10Mbps hub, the adapter will operate at 10Mbps; connected to a 10/100Mbps hub, the adapter will operate at the maximum speed of all devices connected to the hub. For example, if you have eight devices connected to a 10/100Mbps hub and all have 10/100Mbps cards, then all will operate at 100Mbps. If one of the cards is 10Mbps only, then all devices will communicate at 10Mbps. To mix devices on a network, you will need a 10/100Mbps switch. Hubs come in a couple of electrical/operational configurations. Some hubs can actually be combined into a single virtual hub. Other hubs can be remotely managed to view activity or enable and disable ports. Many larger, dispersed companies use managed hubs. A managed hub allows for remote management of the hub, from monitoring individual ports to configuring ports into virtual LANs. Managed hubs can add drastically to the price and complexity of a hub; however, they offer capabilities far exceeding those of a basic hub.

ETHERNET SWITCHES   Ethernet and other switches have become extremely popular in the last few years, especially as their prices have come down. The configuration for switches is very similar to that of hubs. The primary difference is the method in which they operate, the configuration, and the manageability of the switch. A switch will actually try to separate (or segment) out packets so that the packets are only sent down the port that contains the destination host of the packet. This separation can greatly increase the overall capacity of the network. In terms of this segmentation ability, a switch can offer benefits that were traditionally found only in routers. If you plan on moving to 100Mbps Ethernet, a switch is certainly the way to go.

As far as adding redundancy to the network, a switch can be a double-edged sword. On one side, a switch adds reliability, bandwidth, and security by providing more isolation between segments than is provided by a hub; but on the other side, troubleshooting network problems through a switch is sometimes more complicated. Switches can actually increase the time it takes to diagnose problems. For instance, network monitoring of all but broadcast packets is not typically possible through a switch. This is actually by design, as the switches try to segregate packets so that the packets are only sent to the necessary ports. If you want to monitor all packets going through a switch, you must purchase a switch with this functionality built into it or place network monitor agents on each switch segment.

Software and Data Issues

The final issue that must be considered on a network is the manner in which software and data are placed on the network. Software and servers that have critical data that is used over the network must be established with redundancy. If the server is up and the network is functioning but the software or data is corrupt, the network is useless. Whether the data is mirrored offsite or multiple copies are kept on the network, care must be given to maintaining this final aspect of network design. Part of this issue is explored in detail in the clustering (Chapter 5) and real-world example chapters (Chapter 11) of this book.

A SAMPLE NETWORK

In this section, a typical network scenario will be briefly examined. To aid with the descriptions, a corporation will be defined whose headquarters building is located on Main Street and whose operations facility is on Park Street. The remote sites will be on Ash, Cedar, Elm, and Maple streets, as shown in Figure 8-11.

Wide Area Network (WAN) Design

WANs can be designed and connected in many different ways. If uptime is a critical factor, look for WAN solutions that offer built-in reliability.

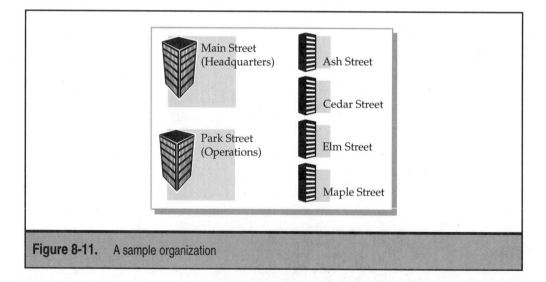

Figure 8-11. A sample organization

Point-to-Point Circuits

Suppose the park and main facilities each have three floors and a data center. Minimal connectivity between large facilities is normally T1 speed (1.544Mbps) and the connection to remote sites is at least 56Kbps.

The first point of configuring a redundant network is the interconnectivity between facilities. A basic configuration would be that all circuits originate in the operations facility. This does not provide any redundancy, but it is a very common configuration. It has one great advantage; it's most likely the cheapest of all configurations. This is shown in Figure 8-12.

The basic network provides all of the basic connectivity sites, but it does not provide any redundancy. To provide an extremely high level of redundancy, all of the circuits from the Headquarters building can be duplicated. This will effectively double the network cost. For a significantly lower cost, three circuits can be added, as shown in Figure 8-13. This will provide the ability to recover from any single circuit loss. The addition of these three connections between the two stores and a store and the headquarters provides the ability to continue operating in case of any single circuit failure. Note that the capacity may drop during failover, but the cost savings of the system would be significant.

Multipoint Circuits

Another method to connect the facilities would be through the use of multipoint circuits like Frame Relay, ATM, or SONET. By connecting to network systems such as these, the network itself can provide redundancy. Figure 8-14 shows a typical SONET network configuration.

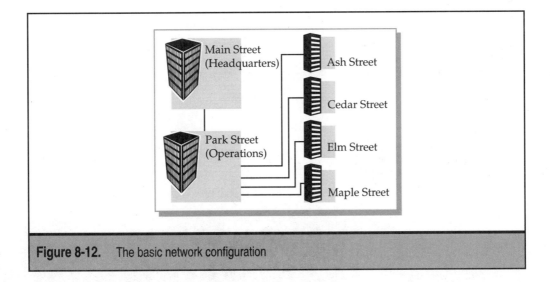

Figure 8-12. The basic network configuration

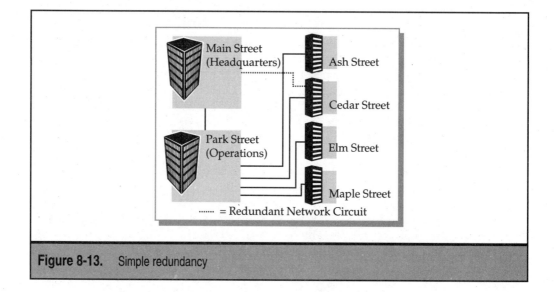

Figure 8-13. Simple redundancy

Local Area Network (LAN) Design

Once the WAN circuit is terminated into the local building and router, the network connections must be complete to all of the local devices within the building. These devices include the network cards in servers and workstations and also other devices (switches, hubs, etc.). In the local area network scenario, all connections are over relatively short distances. Therefore, you can use much higher-speed connections than

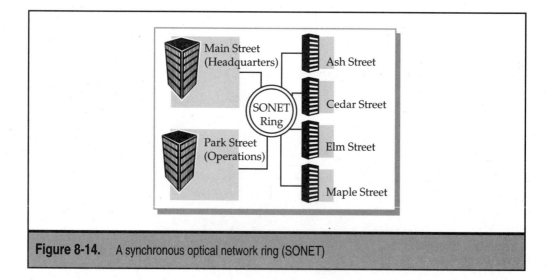

Figure 8-14. A synchronous optical network ring (SONET)

are available with WAN connections. For a LAN, speeds around 10Mbps are commonplace. In fact, with the cost reductions of higher-speed LANs, 100Mb and greater speeds are appearing more and more frequently.

Wiring Types and Designs

Although there are hundreds of different types of LAN and wiring configurations, we will limit our discussion to Ethernet and Category 5 wiring. This, although seemingly limiting, actually reflects the vast majority of LAN installations. Category 5 wiring supports Ethernet speeds of up to 100Mbps. As a de facto standard, it has made it possible for prices to decrease and for a large variety of equipment to become available.

With Category 5 Ethernet wiring, the workstations are configured into a star as shown in Figure 8-15. Each workstation only communicates with the hub. The hub is responsible for relaying the information to other devices. This introduces a single point of failure in the hub, but hub manufacturers have increased the reliability of their products to the point where hub failures are fairly uncommon.

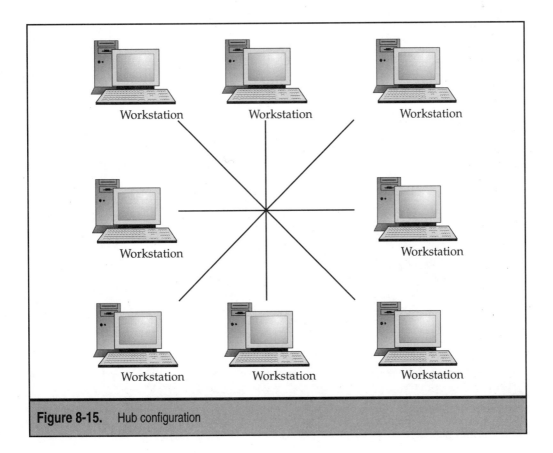

Figure 8-15.   Hub configuration

Wiring Closet

Wiring closets can be a source of network errors and security problems. To solve the security issue, they should be locked down in a manner similar to a server room.

Wiring from the offices should be terminated into a wiring panel (patch panel). This wiring should be tied down and should never need to be moved. To connect the workstation to a port on the hub, a short jumper cable (Category 5) is used. The location of the wiring panel and the location of the hubs and other network services should be well thought out before anything is installed. You need to make sure that patch cable lengths are minimized and that the cables are run in an orientation such that they can be readily viewed and moved. Figure 8-16 shows a basic wiring closet layout for both voice and data lines.

Workstation

On the workstation end, Ethernet cables and telephone wiring are commonly run together. To reduce the risk of people plugging the wrong device into the jack, many manufacturers allow for combinations of labels and color coding for the jacks. Be sure to make all phone jacks one color and Ethernet jacks another. Try to use a standardized placement scheme for all jacks. Always put the data jack in the same position on the plate (i.e., the right or left side). Also, be sure to have wiring installed by a reputable contractor and have all connections tested before being put into use.

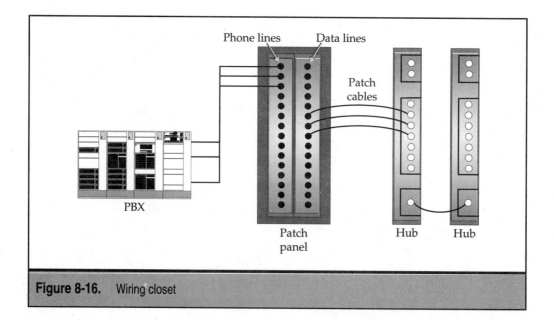

Figure 8-16.   Wiring closet

Since the network cable and the telephone cable are both connected to the same plate, it is highly probable that the telephone wires will terminate in the computer wiring room. Make sure that you leave enough room for all services. The methods for terminating the phone cable will be very similar to that of the network cables. Due to this, most companies hire a single contractor to pull both data and voice wiring.

NOTE: Voice and data wiring are commonly called "low-voltage wiring."

Configuration of Services

There are several network services that are important in an NT network. As mentioned above, these include domain controllers, DNS, WINS, and DHCP. These services should be located in a central area and in such a way as to provide high reliability to the network.

In our sample organization of Figure 8-11, it should be obvious that the operations facility and the headquarters facility are the most appropriate locations for network services. If either site fails, service servers in the other location will still be available, and if both sites fail, then most operations will probably be curtailed anyway. To this end, the servers will be set up so the primary services are in the operations facility and backup services are running in the headquarters facility. This keeps the primary services in the most reliable location, nearest the administrators.

CONFIGURING AND MAINTAINING RELIABLE NETWORKS

The following is a list of the basic steps you should take to ensure stable and reliable network operations.

▼ **Purchase solid, proven equipment from major manufacturers.** A network is not the place to skimp on equipment. Most major companies like 3Com (**http://www.3com.com**), Cisco(**http://www.cisco.com**), Bay Networks (**http://www.baynetworks.com**), and Cabletron (**http://www.ctrom.com**) build redundancy and reliability directly into their devices. In addition, they each offer plans to provide other forms of network reliability, such as backup networks and parallel devices.

■ **Test all configurations before putting them into production.** This point should seem obvious. However, it is not uncommon for a consultant to be called in to fix a solution that was "guaranteed" to work. People will go through and set parameters, not really knowing what they are doing, until the network works. They will then duplicate this "design" in all future devices. When the network is finally stressed, it fails and everyone is surprised. There are correct ways to design and configure networks, and they can all be done before the first piece of wire or the first router arrives. Many major corporations spend tens of thousands of dollars and more on testing so as to provide stable, reliable network operation.

■ **Monitor your network for problems.**   There are many ways to monitor a network. They range from inexpensive and simple through expensive and complex. They will be examined in the next section of this chapter.

■ **Keep the network layout as simple as possible.**   Sophisticated networks are quite often too complex for people to manage. You might be able to design it or have a third party design it, but can your support team support it?

■ **Be sure your disaster recovery plan includes the network.**   It has been mention several times in this book that you must provide power protection for your network devices. However, you must also have plans in place to recover your network in case of emergency. For instance, if a major router goes down, what is the procedure for replacement and the turnaround time? Try to understand the points of failure of your network and build plans and make purchasing decisions based on those areas.

■ **Document the network.**   Your network should be reasonably documented. The documentation should be readily available to anyone who needs it. At the minimum, include a broad overview along with device configurations. The device configurations are important so that you can verify what has been changed, and could possibly indicate what could have caused the problem. On the NT server side, be sure to document install directories and parameters.

▲ **Keep trained personnel.**   A major source of problems on networks can be someone who does not really know what he is doing. A network is not a place for guessing. Too many people can be affected by a simply error. In fact, trained personnel should also be the ones who design your network. If you do not have properly trained employees, hire outside consultants for the job. The extra money spent up front will be more than compensated for by a reliable network. If a network is built on trial and error, it may function—but it may not do so optimally or reliably.

You can plan all you want. You can put in some of the best equipment. But at some time in every network something adverse will occur. How do you know something has happened? A proper mixture of monitoring and benchmarking can help you solve situations before they become problems.

Monitoring

As mentioned above, the proper monitoring of your network can be extremely important in providing a high level of continuous service. The absolute best monitoring configuration is not one that simply displays all of the information. Too much information can actually be confusing and hard to follow. The best configuration is one in which only the necessary information is displayed. It should also notify network administrators when parameters go outside their normal range.

Monitoring solutions range from inexpensive and simple to expensive and complex. On the inexpensive side, there are utilities that can do "ping tests" across links to verify operability. They can be set up to page an engineer in the case of failure or a decrease in operation.

Also at the low-cost end is the Windows NT Performance Monitor. When run in the Alert mode, Performance Monitor will monitor counters and issue an alert if the counter exceeds a predetermined range. In Log mode, Performance Monitor will record events to a file for later playback. Performance Monitor can even be run as a service under NT so that it will run even when someone is not logged into the console.

It is not normally necessary to configure Performance Monitor to update the counter status every second. Depending on the counters that are being examined, the intervals between updates can be as long as minutes. If you set up logging with Performance Monitor and set too short an interval, the amount of information can quickly become unwieldy.

So, what should you be monitoring? As a general rule, try to only log or alert on a single counter for each critical application and some of the system resources. The typical resources to monitor are the CPU utilization and the memory usage. If any of these parameters go out of the normal operating range, it is an indication of trouble on a system. It is quite possible that some of the indicators do go to a maximum or minimum, but they need to be viewed in comparison to each other and previous operating values. In Chapter 2, running Performance Monitor as a service and its other aspects are examined more thoroughly.

To simplify the monitoring of NT networks, some companies have created products that utilize the existing NT monitoring mechanisms while others have developed their own mechanisms. These products are reasonably inexpensive considering the vital role they can play. NTManage by Lanware (**http://www.lanware.net**), SeNTry by Mission Critical Software (**http://www.missioncritical.com**), and NetIQ's AppManager Suite (**http://www.netiq.com**) are all products that can assist in network monitoring. NetIQ has implemented a two-pronged strategy for monitoring NT applications. The first is the standard NT event monitoring and the second is an impressive OLE implementation that actually drives applications remotely to determine their status. For instance, NetIQ can monitor an exchange server by the event counters that are exposed, and they can also monitor the operation by an OLE session of a set of mail clients, sending messages to each other and monitoring the activities.

On the more expensive side, management tools like HP OpenView (**http://www. hp.com**) can take monitoring to a higher level. Network General's Sniffer products (**http://www.ngc.com**) and similar products can also be used for diagnosis and monitoring. Be sure to monitor for both reduced capacity and complete failure. Monitor for the number of errors on each circuit. An unusually high number of errors can be indicative of impending failure.

Benchmarking

Benchmarking is good for catching problems in the network as well as monitoring for system capacity planning and sizing. As many parameters as possible should be captured and stored for each benchmark. It is worth purchasing benchmarking and capacity planning software for this purpose. In many of these products, the benchmarking collection process can be automated. With the collection of a few days or months worth of data, it becomes possible to compare parameters over time and locate any differences. Several computer industry magazine publishers like Ziff-Davis (**http://www.zdbop.com**) offer their benchmark products free of charge. They can be used for testing individual machines and components, and even stress testing networks.

Congestion

No matter how much work you do at providing fault tolerance and monitoring, if the network becomes congested, then reliability will deteriorate. If an Ethernet segment is constantly running over 40 percent capacity, then there are probably congestion issues that should be dealt with. Since Ethernet networks are collision-based systems, utilization parameters are important to monitor. Network bandwidth needs to be designed for the maximum utilization, not the average. If a circuit has an average utilization of 64Kbps and is sent across a 64Kbps circuit, then you are guaranteed that during 50 percent of the time, the circuit is overloaded. If you have careful control of the data passing through the circuit, then this situation may be tolerable. But if the circuit data is unpredictable, then a significant number of errors will be occurring.

Disaster Recovery Practice

At this point in this book, it should be clear that disaster recovery plans must be well thought out and, most of all, practiced. It is true for your network plan as well. This can be the most important part of ensuring network reliability—knowing what to do when something goes wrong. What are the steps when a router fails? What happens if a WINS server fails? What happens if the building floods?

When disasters occur, time becomes one of the biggest factors. All actions need to be well-planned reactions. During the disaster, the time to figure out what to do is at a premium. A disaster drill is can be an important step in keeping staff aware of the potential problems and solutions. If you are a manager, consider springing network problems on IS staff to see how well they know the drill. For example:

▼ A remote office router goes offline.

■ The central corporate router has power supply problems.

■ The DNS server is not responding.

■ The remote access server is randomly not answering.

■ A winter storm took out the main electrical feeder to your building.

▲ The disk drive on the primary DHCP server crashes.

So, how does your support organization handle the problems? Does it take them over a few minutes to decide on a solution? Do they get the right people involved? Do they notify the right people at the right time? These are just a few issues that will eventually come up in any operations center. Make sure you know the answers before situations arise.

SUMMARY

The aspects of your physical networks represent one of the most fundamental building blocks in the operations of most companies. The network must allow workstations and people to communicate with each other and with servers. If the network goes down, essentially all computers (server and otherwise) go down with it. This chapter examined the network and broke it down into the pieces that are most likely to fail. It is important to understand that each of these pieces (points of failure) must be examined, protected, and included in any corporate disaster recovery plan.

Power Considerations

Power problems account for nearly 50 percent of the events that cause computer data loss. A Windows NT computer, like any other form of electronic system, is susceptible to the various types of power disturbances. When you are considering fault tolerance and disaster recovery issues in your NT enterprise system, high-quality power protection devices should be an automatic decision. You have several options to protect an NT machine from these problems. This chapter will analyze these options and explain how to choose those that are compatible with your needs and budget.

PROBLEMS WITH POWER

A common misconception is that utility power is consistent and steady. However, depending on where you are, spikes, sags, surges, and other power problems pose potential hazards to your computer. If you are in an older building, you may also have inadequate wiring, which can become overloaded and cause power failures. Older buildings are also very susceptible to ground loops. (Ground loops are discussed in more detail in the "Data Center and Facility Power Considerations" section of this chapter.) Even in newer buildings, power problems caused by human error or miscalculation can plague a computer system.

Businesses are becoming more reliant on a utility supply that is often pushed beyond its capacity. Despite advances in the capabilities of modern personal computers, a momentary power outage is still all it takes to lose your data. More dangerous is the loss of recently written files, or even an entire hard disk, which can occur if a major power problem strikes while your computer is saving a file. Network file servers that are constantly writing to disk are particularly at risk.

Power protection should be provided to not just LAN servers and critical workstations but to your network equipment as well. When your business depends on your network, you cannot afford the downtime. To ensure continuous operation through any power problem, you must protect your entire data path, including hubs, bridges, switches, routers, and gateways. A continuous power source is crucial to the operation of these isolated pieces of your network. They must be shielded against power problems to protect the valuable data they carry, not to mention the configuration stored in their memory.

Undesirable power events can occur from several different sources: acts of nature (such as storms and earthquakes), human error and accidents, and large electrical equipment start-up (such as elevators and furnaces). The resulting power disruptions take many forms, including power surges, sags, high-voltage spikes, switching transients, brownouts, and complete power failure. With any power fluctuation, you have the potential for data loss, file corruption, and hardware damage. It can also result in premature hardware failure and intermittent hardware malfunctions. Adding to the problem is the fact that this damage is not always immediately noticeable. Damage caused may not be detected until months after the power disruption.

Lightning

Lightning and surges can cause huge potential differences between line and ground points. The natural tendency is for this energy to equalize. Unfortunately, your equipment is used as the transfer mechanism.

Lightning travels 90,000 miles per second, and its stroke extends up to 20 miles long. The stroke can have up to 125 million volts of electricity, with a discharge temperature reaching up to 50,000° Fahrenheit. Lightning strikes somewhere on the earth approximately 100 times every second. That is over eight million lightning strikes every day! In the United States, lightning is responsible for over two billion dollars of damage annually. The number of lightning storms you experience is based on geographic location. Some areas of the southern United States can experience up to 90 electrical storms each year.

What happens when lightning strikes? Consider what happens when lightning hits a nearby transformer. If the surge is powerful enough, it travels instantaneously through wiring, network cables, serial cables, phone lines, and more. It is an enormously destructive pulse traveling through the web of wires in your building. The surge then finds its way into your computer via the outlet or other lines. Once in your computer, the surge can effect chips and other vital components as well as internal power supplies.

Sags

Sags are also known as winks, depressions, or brownouts. They are sudden, usually short-term decreases in voltage levels. Sags are by far the most common type of power disturbance. Most people recognize them because sags cause lights to temporarily dim. In separate power studies by IBM, AT&T, and others, it has been found that sags account for over 50 to 80 percent of power problems. This is somewhat dependent on geographic location and the quality of the power company's protective coordination system (relays, fuses, etc.).

Sags are usually caused by the start-up power demands of many electrical devices. These can include motors, compressors, elevators, and shop tools. Electric companies also use planned utility line voltage reductions to keep up with extraordinary power demands. In a procedure known as rolling brownouts, electric companies systematically cause 5 to 10 percent sags on distribution feeders that range from a few minutes to hours at a time. In the summer this is a common occurrence. The companies are faced with elevated air-conditioning power requirements at the same time their transformer capacities are lowered due to higher operating temperatures.

Sags can starve a computer of the power it needs to function and can cause keyboards to freeze up or systems to unexpectedly crash. Sags also reduce the efficiency and life span of electrical equipment, particularly motors. They can wreak havoc with your stored data and can cause unpredictable software problems. Some uninterruptible power supply (UPS) and other power protection devices provide line regulation features that detect sags and ensure proper power levels that prevent damage to connected equipment.

Surges

A surge is a short-term increase in voltage, typically lasting approximately 1/120 of a second. Surges can result from the presence of high-powered electrical motors, such as air conditioners, elevators, and household appliances. When this equipment is switched off, the extra voltage is dissipated through the power line. Computers and similar sensitive electronic devices are designed to receive power within a certain voltage range. Surges cause voltages outside of expected peak and average levels and can stress delicate components and cause premature failure.

Blackouts

Like it sounds, a blackout is a total loss of utility power. Excessive demand, lightning storms, car and construction accidents, and earthquakes and other natural catastrophes can cause blackouts. During certain major disasters, utility companies are sometimes forced to resort to rolling blackouts due to the high demand for power from consumers.

On NT server machines, blackouts pose serious problems. Ungraceful NT shutdowns can result in file corruption and data loss. Blackouts might also cause any work in RAM or cache to be lost. If a hard disk is reading or writing data at the time, the hard drive's allocation table may be corrupted.

Spikes

A spike is an instantaneous, dramatic increase in voltage, sometimes referred to as an impulse. It is a burst of voltage running down your lines that can enter electronic equipment and damage or completely destroy components. Spikes are typically caused by a nearby lightning strike. However, they can also occur when utility power comes back online after a blackout. Even substation and distribution line switching can cause spikes. For this reason, you should always unplug unprotected devices during a blackout.

Noise

Electrical noise, more technically referred to as electromagnetic interference (EMI) and radio frequency interference (RFI), disrupts the smooth sine wave you expect from utility power. Electrical noise is caused by many factors, including lightning, load switching, generators, radio transmitters, and industrial equipment. The noise may be intermittent, making it often difficult to detect. Electrical noise, superimposed on electric source lines, can actually effect internal computer circuitry. It can raise the reference voltage of the system. This may disturb internal computer logic and can result in unpredictable software function. This kind of noise can be prevented with conditioning filters.

Why is there so much noise on the lines? The quick answer is because there are so many different customers. With the number of varied users and devices connected to a power grid, a utility customer cannot rely on the electricity provider to filter one customer from another. For this reason you must ultimately take responsibility for protecting your own equipment.

POWER DEVICES

A fault-tolerant power device is one that will maintain a clean, steady output to the protected equipment during power system component failure or during transient disturbances in the input power. Transients are defined as momentary variations in source power that can be the result of surges, spikes, sags, blackouts, or line noise.

Typically, transients enter a computer through the alternating current (AC) power line. This is the main source of power and is consequently the most important area to protect. Other ways through which transients can reach the computer are through telephone lines, peripheral cables, and network cables. Your decision to protect against these will be based on your budget and fault-tolerance requirements. If you want to completely safeguard your equipment, you should consider protecting against all of the sources of possible disturbances.

The power device you could select to protect electronic systems from transients ranges from a surge protector to an uninterruptible power supply (UPS) to a large diesel-powered backup generator. You will need to protect your computer systems as well as peripherals. Some peripherals, such as color laser printers, can cost well over $10,000. They can also provide a separate path for transients to enter your computers. As with most fault tolerance issues, you need to find a balance between cost and protection. In the case of the UPS devices, the cost will be determined by the size in volt-amperes (VA) and the amount of time the UPS is expected to operate on battery power. With the other devices, cost will vary based on the quality of the power regulation they provide. Power protection equipment must ensure reliable, continuous AC power for your critical load, regardless of what happens to the source.

The quality of the input power is a major factor in assuring clean, reliable power. Unfortunately, it is an area in which you have minimal control. A study by IBM has shown that a typical computer is subjected to more than 120 power-related problems per month. The effects of power problems range from keyboard lockups and hardware degradation to complete data loss or even burned-out electronic components.

Luckily, your PC is not as fragile as you might think. Systems from quality vendors like Digital and IBM offer exceptionally strong tolerance to the daily barrage of power transients. You will more than likely be oblivious of the frequency with which power problems hit these types of systems. Even with these transient-tolerant systems, though, you will need to protect against the wider power disturbances with surge suppression and reliable battery backup power. These wide transients, for example a high surge or a power outage, can cause damage to any electronic system.

Power protection devices constitute a big-money industry. The overall UPS market in North America alone will grow from approximately $1.5 billion in 1997 to about $2.3 billion in 2001, according to a recent Darnell Group (**http://www.darnell.com**) study.

UNINTERRUPTIBLE POWER SUPPLIES

One of the best investments to protect your systems is an uninterruptible power supply (UPS). They should be automatically considered when you are designing an NT network. For this reason, much of the rest of this chapter is devoted to a discussion on the types and uses of uninterruptible power supplies.

In simple terms, a UPS is typically a box that contains lead-acid batteries, somewhat like the ones used on a motorcycle. Lead-acid batteries are not as susceptible to "memory" problems as are other types of rechargeable batteries. All UPS systems incorporate an inverter that converts direct current (DC) from the batteries into alternating current (AC). A UPS can protect your equipment from brownouts and power fluctuations by providing supplementary battery power to compensate for diminished capacity. In a total blackout, UPS devices can keep your systems up and running long enough to administer orderly shutdown procedures or maintain normal operation for several hours. They are not designed to keep your PC running the entire time the power is out. You would have to switch to a backup generator solution to achieve continual operation.

Depending on the size of your UPS and the power demands of your equipment, the UPS will last from about ten minutes to one hour before the batteries lose power. Graceful shutdowns are particularly important with NT, as improper shutdowns can lead to data loss. It is imperative that all critical computer and network components are properly protected by an uninterruptible power supply.

In addition to providing backup power, today's UPS systems also monitor the amount and quality of the power passing through their transformers. Moreover, they filter and regulate incoming power and provide surge suppression. Almost by definition, the online type of UPS has some ability to absorb spikes and regulate surges. However, this should not be assumed. Check with the manufacturer's specifications of each model.

Modern power supplies also need to be fault-tolerant. Aside from the normal line transients, they need to be able to withstand the failure of a single component, such as a rectifier diode, a filter capacitor, or a cooling fan. Some redundant UPS systems are actually two UPS devices that have automatic switchover capabilities. If one UPS goes down, the system immediately switches to the other. This can be particularly important with the online variety, as changing a battery may mean shutting down the protected server.

UPS protection was initially intended for large data centers. The data, applications, and computing resources were considered too valuable to be subject to power failures and other electrical disturbances. It is anticipated that UPS devices will be protecting 85 percent of all LAN servers by 2000. This should not be surprising. The fastest growing segment of the UPS market is in the devices that supply five kilovolt-amperes (KVA) or less of power. As UPS systems move out of the data center, manufacturers are modifying their products to meet the demands of the client-server networking environment. The LAN server products are smaller and less expensive, and they support lower power ranges than their data center counterparts.

Types of Uninterruptible Power Supplies

Uninterruptible power supplies come in three basic types: offline, hybrid, and online. An online UPS provides the highest level of power protection and is the ideal choice for shielding mission-critical computer systems. As we will see in this section, they are also the most expensive. In some instances, they may be overkill, especially if your system can withstand the longer switching times of the other UPS styles. A modern PC power supply is rated to handle a minimum 8.3-millisecond switching time. Reports from various PC labs have shown that a quality PC can handle as much as a 50-millisecond power lapse without restarting. That is far beyond most UPS switchover delays.

Offline UPS Devices

Offline UPS devices connect input lines directly to output lines. They switch to battery power when the main voltage fails. They are also known as standby or switching UPS devices. Power protection is available only when line voltage dips to the point of creating an outage. This direct path from input to output means that an offline UPS provides no intrinsic protection against spikes and noise. To compensate for this deficiency, several manufacturers of offline UPS systems add surge suppression and line conditioning circuits. A diagram of a basic offline UPS is shown in Figure 9-1. The battery side of the circuit is only used when the switch is turned over during a power event.

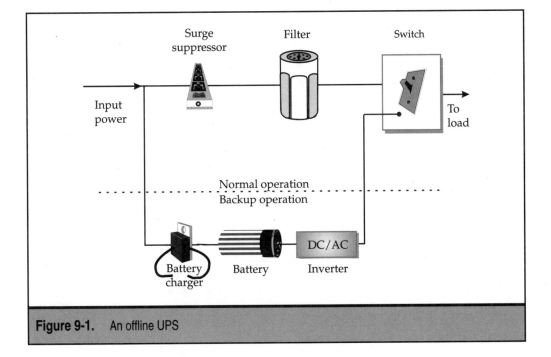

Figure 9-1.   An offline UPS

Offline UPS systems are generally the least expensive. They consist of a basic battery/ AC conversion circuit and a switch that senses irregularities in the electric utility. There is usually a lag time of around seven microseconds before the switch from AC to battery backup is complete. Some delicate electronic equipment cannot tolerate this disruption of power during the switching interval.

Complete power failure was the only event offline UPS systems were originally designed for. Luckily, today most manufacturers provide additional protection. If they include surge protection, the offline UPS passes any surge voltage to the protected system until it hits a predetermined voltage level. This level is usually less than a 15 percent over-voltage variance. At this surge limit value, the unit then switches to battery power. With high-voltage spikes and switching transients, they can provide reasonably good coverage but not the total isolation needed for complete protection. For power sags, electrical line noise, and brownouts, offline UPS devices protect only when switched completely over to battery power.

A similar limitation exists in the case of frequency variation. An offline UPS protects the system only if the inverter is operating and relying on battery power. This means that if the input frequency varies outside the device's range, the unit will be forced to use battery backup to regulate the output. In very unstable conditions, this may eventually cause the battery to drain, leaving the system without protection from a full blackout. Since an offline UPS offers only partial protection against many common power problems, they are most often used to shield single-user PCs and other less critical application servers.

Hybrid UPS Devices

Line-interactive UPS systems are hybrid devices that attempt to offer a higher level of performance by adding voltage regulation features to the more conventional offline designs. Like offline models, line-interactive UPS devices protect against power surges by passing the surge voltage to the computer until it hits a predetermined voltage, at which point the unit switches to battery backup. They also have traits of online systems in that they keep the battery and transformer constantly in the circuit. When power is at normal levels, the battery is only under trickle charge, thus extending its life. Switchover is faster and smoother than with offline systems, making this type of UPS appropriate for computers and other relatively sensitive components. However, this bridge from input to output can mean that surges can sneak through, so remember to provide surge and spike protection, if it is not already built in. An example of a line-interactive UPS is shown in Figure 9-2.

Line-interactive power supplies cost 25 to 40 percent less than a comparable online version. This can be a significant difference when you are buying dozens of UPS devices for a large network. While online UPS devices are considered the best solution, the added protection may not be cost-justified. The delayed switchover time of line-interactive units may not matter for most business applications. As stated previously, modern PCs are designed to accommodate a brief interruption in power (8.3 milliseconds). This means the inverter switches on before the server is ever aware of a power interruption.

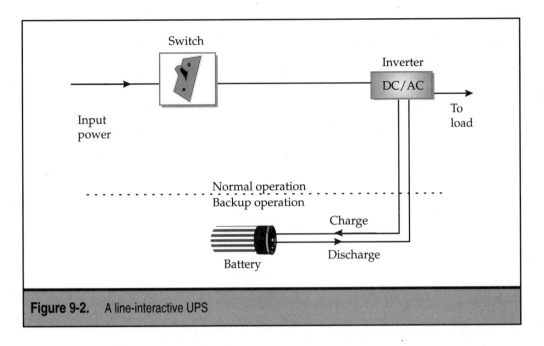

Figure 9-2. A line-interactive UPS

The UPS market leader is American Power Conversion (APC) of West Kingston, Rhode Island. The vast majority of its UPS systems are line-interactive units. The company also makes a handful of the online models up to 5KVA.

Line-interactive models provide moderate protection against high-voltage spikes and switching transients, although not with complete isolation. In the case of brownouts, they have tapped transformers that protect the system. This may reduce battery runtime if a power outage occurs before the recharge is complete. They will eventually go to battery full-time if the input voltage reaches a certain level. Line-interactive systems offer adequate protection as long as the power sags are not continuously occurring. This may reduce battery life and runtime. If sags are too frequent, the batteries may not be able to fully recharge and will not offer full blackout protection. For electrical line noise and frequency variation, these devices work only when the battery is the power source. Again, this has the potential to drain the battery during prolonged periods of unstable conditions.

Another variation of hybrid technology is the ferroresonant (FR) UPS. These devices keep the inverter in standby mode in a way similar to line-interactive and offline UPS systems. The protected system is powered through a ferroresonant transformer. This transformer is used to regulate voltage and filter incoming power during both normal and backup operation. The transformer also maintains a reserve of energy that is usually sufficient to power most computers for a brief period of time when a total outage occurs. This reserve maintains power to the computer until the inverter is completely switched over. This is a reliable design, and unlike a basic standby UPS it offers the advantages of conditioning input power. Moreover, it can maintain uniform output characteristics regardless of the operating mode.

In cases where the input power's frequency is unstable, the ferroresonant topology will subject the load to some voltage and frequency fluctuations. When the frequency variations exceed a certain limit, the unit will supply stable voltage and frequency to the load through the backup battery and inverter. Ferroresonant technology can also be sensitive to sudden input current surges. This can cause a significant change in the output voltage of the UPS. They can also have trouble with loads less than 100 percent, resulting in decreased efficiency, increased heat output, and loud operation. As a result, traditional ferroresonant devices work best with noncomputer technology or more linear loads, such as motors, heaters, and lights. This does not mean that the newer ferroresonant units should not be used with computer systems. However, it does mean that you should make sure you are purchasing a unit specifically designed for protecting computer equipment.

Online

At the other end of the UPS spectrum are online systems, which continuously monitor the input power as it passes through the transformer. They may even include some intelligence to determine whether power is lost or only fluctuating. Online systems use a double conversion power circuit (AC to DC, then DC to AC), which continuously powers the load, to provide both conditioned electrical power and full-outage protection. The battery is interposed between the input and output so it is always providing load power. The battery is kept in a constant state of charge from the utility power. This eliminates the need to physically switch to battery backup in the event of power failure, so the equipment is never without power. Full transfer to battery is accomplished in only two to four microseconds (note that it is microseconds, not milliseconds). Even the most delicate computer equipment can tolerate this switchover time. An example of a basic online UPS is shown in Figure 9-3. Note that not all online device manufacturers add the AC bypass circuit. This is a necessary feature, because it adds redundancy to the device. If the battery fails, power can still flow through the bypass circuit.

Online UPS devices also benefit from the battery's ability to absorb and smooth out transients. This means that online systems actually have intrinsic surge protection. Most manufacturers supplement this with additional protection against major spikes. The transformer further isolates the output and provides a steady sinusoidal current. These devices are ideal for protecting delicate equipment like high-speed network servers, which can be sensitive to even minor fluctuations of power.

If they are so effective, why doesn't everyone just purchase online UPS systems? Simply put, it is a cost issue. They can cost from 25 to 100 percent more than comparable line-interactive and standby systems. They have one other drawback: they keep their batteries under constant charge. This can be stressful to the battery and therefore increases the frequency of maintenance and replacement. Most online batteries have only a two- to four-year life span. In comparison, the batteries of line-interactive models last four to six years. Battery life can be an important factor, as it accounts for up to one-third of the cost of a UPS.

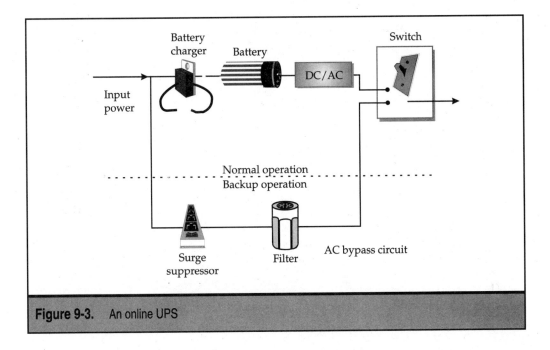

Figure 9-3. An online UPS

There is one other important point about online devices. Many so-called online UPS systems under 5KVA do not have their batteries connected constantly but actually have a standby DC to DC converter. This engages when power fails, and it backs up the UPS DC bus from a low-voltage battery. If you are looking for online protection, be sure that is what you are getting.

While online devices are expensive, there are times when they can be cost-effective. This is when truly comprehensive power protection is required. They offer complete protection and isolation from all of the common types of power problems, including surges, spikes, switching transients, sags, electrical noise, frequency variation, brownouts, and blackouts. Reaching this level of regulation in a standby UPS could require purchasing a separate line conditioner. The combined price might be higher than that of a single online unit. The point is to be certain that the UPS you are considering offers all of the protection you require.

UPS Software

By now, you should be convinced that you need a UPS for all of your NT server machines. Now you must consider monitoring your power supplies. Most of the high-end UPS models support serial or network connections for monitoring purposes. These connections pass information to UPS monitoring software that can give you a variety of information on your UPS status. They also allow you to set a variety of configuration parameters from shutdown times to testing frequency.

NT's Native UPS Management Software

NT offers native software support through a serial cable for several UPS models. There is a section in the NT Hardware Compatibility List (**http://www.microsoft.com/hwtest**) that specifies which UPS devices NT supports. To assure interoperability, select a UPS from this list or purchase software and cabling from the manufacturer that is designed specifically for Windows NT. Figure 9-4 shows NT's UPS applet, which is accessible from the NT Control Panel. Considering the fact that it is free, this program has a reasonable amount of functionality.

Once you're in the UPS applet dialog box, configure the UPS applet following these steps:

1. At the top of the dialog box, select the COM port to which the UPS is connected.

2. In the UPS Configuration section, check the Power failure signal check box if your UPS supports a power failure signal.

3. The low battery signal feature indicates whether your UPS can send a warning signal when power is low. Check this box if your device has this capability.

4. Some UPS models support a software UPS shutdown feature. If you would like it enabled, check the Remote UPS Shutdown box.

5. The Execute Command File box allows you to configure the applet to execute a command file immediately before system shutdown. Warning: This command file must completely execute within 30 seconds. If not, the computer may shut down before it is complete, causing unpredictable results.

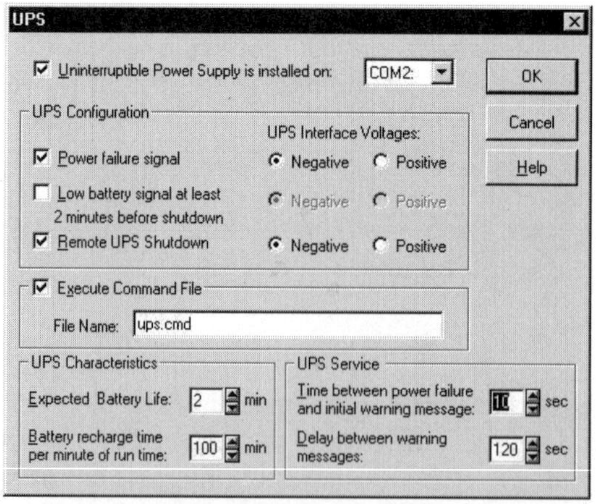

Figure 9-4. The Windows NT UPS applet

6. If your UPS does not support the low battery signal feature, you can estimate the values in the UPS Characteristics section. The expected battery life should be your best estimate of the *minimum* battery life you expect. The battery recharge time informs the applet how long to wait before assuming the battery is fully recharged.

7. In the UPS Service section, you can specify how long the applet will wait after a power failure before notifying users. You may want to increase this number from the default of five seconds if you experience a large number of short-term outages (there is no sense interrupting users' work if the outage is minor). The Delay between warning messages box indicates the frequency of UPS warning messages that will appear on the console.

8. After you click OK, the UPS service will attempt to start. It will not start if it does not find a UPS on the specified port or if there is a problem with the device or cabling.

In terms of cabling, a standard RS-232 serial cable will not work properly with the UPS service. You will need a special cable that has a specific pinout. This basic pinout is shown in Table 9-1. It is worth noting that the cable that works with the NT UPS applet will not necessarily work with third-party monitoring products. The best way to get a UPS cable is to purchase it directly from the UPS manufacturer.

There is a problem that sometimes occurs with serial-connected UPS devices at start-up. It occurs because NT attempts to determine what devices are connected to each of the serial ports when it boots. The problem is that when a UPS sees this signal, it may misinterpret it as a shutdown signal and power down the server. The easiest solution to this problem is to add the following line to your BOOT.INI file:

/NOSERIALMICE=COMx

This will prevent NT from checking the affected serial port.

NOTE: If your machine suffers from this problem, be sure to disable the UPS applet or remove the UPS cable when upgrading or reinstalling NT.

Pin Number	Signal from UPS
1	Low battery
4	Shut down UPS
8	Power failure

Table 9-1.   Serial Cable Configuration for Windows NT's Native UPS Applet

Third-Party Management Software

In addition to the built-in UPS applet, many of the third-party manufacturers offer their own UPS software. One well-known example of this software is American Power Conversion's PowerChute Plus. These programs generally run as services under NT and replace the native UPS service. The third-party products extend the functionality of the built-in applet with:

▼ UPS self-test scheduling

■ System shutdown and reboot scheduling

■ Battery replacement warnings

■ Battery runtime estimates

■ Enhanced reporting formats and graphical status information in real time

■ Enhanced alert functionality

■ Environmental monitoring capabilities, such as internal and external temperature and humidity

■ More advance and customized command files that can be run at different times throughout a power event

▲ Remote adjustments to the voltage within a predetermined range to accommodate fluctuations in power levels

Some manufacturers also offer hardware add-ons that can enhance the UPS software. These devices can be hardwired or the UPS can have special slots for upgrading feature sets. You can add a modem dial-in card to remotely control the UPS and automatically page you in case of emergency. You can also add a network card to support network management programs based on SNMP. The next section will look closely at the network card feature.

SNMP Monitoring Tools

Most UPS manufacturers now have Simple Network Management Protocol (SNMP) agents built into their power supplies for centralized control and monitoring capabilities on a network. This, of course, requires a network card internal to the UPS. SNMP is a very popular option, as most large enterprises already use SNMP to manage the rest of their networks. One of the main selling points of SNMP is that you can monitor devices from almost anywhere in the world.

SNMP is a protocol that allows remote management of networks. It has traditionally been used for managing TCP/IP networks. It is an open standard that is crucial for large network management. A device managed by SNMP must have a MIB and an agent. An *agent* is software or firmware that monitors and manages a particular network device, such as a UPS or a router. The UPS agent may be found in an SNMP adapter or in the host computer to which the UPS is directly connected. The MIB, or management information base, is the database of variables and traps (events) related to a particular device. It serves as a collection of guidelines that tell network management consoles what kind of information can be provided by individual or groups of devices. The agent maintains a device's MIB and responds to requests from the network management console.

The *network management console* is a central repository for SNMP traps. Some well-known network management consoles include Computer Associates' UniCenter, Hewlett-Packard's OpenView, and Sun's SunNet Manager. Compaq's Insight Manager is also based on SNMP technology. Deltec, Exide, APC, and other manufacturers allow their power management software to "snap in" to common network management platforms. This makes the agents very easy to configure. Unfortunately, some of the vendors have been slow to catch on to this snap-in feature. In those cases, the configuration is a bit more complicated. Check with your vendor to see if its SNMP implementation directly supports your network management platform.

The support that UPS manufacturers have added for SNMP greatly simplifies the administration of even a moderately sized network. A network manager must often oversee a complex network supporting many different types of hardware platforms that may be spread over multiple buildings or sites. UPS SNMP support allows you to keep a pulse on the power status of your entire enterprise.

Sizing and Buying a UPS

You will need to understand the capabilities and limitations of a UPS before you make a purchase. Select a UPS that can tolerate wide under-voltage and over-voltage variances without going to battery. Most low-voltage, 120-volt UPS systems will operate between 90 and 144 Volts Alternating Current (VAC), depending on the size of the load.

You will want to examine the manufacturer's service capabilities and compare them with your needs. If your computers are critical to your hour-to-hour business, then a 24-hour turnaround may not be enough. If you are using a data center–sized UPS that weighs thousands of pounds, then express shipping is clearly not an option. You will want to use a manufacturer that has seven-day-a-week, around-the-clock dispatch capabilities that can offer on-site support by factory-trained service specialists. The following list highlights some of the important features to look for.

▼ Less than 250-volts let-through on the 6,000-volts surge tests

■ Automatic testing for site-wiring faults (i.e., ground loops)

■ Replaceable batteries

■ Voltage regulation between 90 and 144 VAC

■ At least five minutes of runtime at full load

■ Avoid square wave outputs

■ Underwriters Laboratory (UL) recognized

■ Lifetime equipment protection against surge damage

■ For critical workstations: consider data interfaces

■ For servers: look for data interfaces for automatic saves and shutdowns

▲ For enterprise systems: look for standard SNMP support

The size of UPS you require will depend on the volt-ampere (VA) value of the load and the runtime requirements. A simple formula that is discussed next can be used to identify an appropriate VA level. If necessary, help is available from most UPS manufacturers via e-mail, telephone, or World Wide Web access. They even have charts that give VA requirements for specific computer systems. Some UPS manufacturers and systems integrators offer power consulting services and audits that can help identify weaknesses in power distribution systems and protective devices throughout an entire facility. This service is sometimes included free with some of the high-end data center devices. At the other end of the spectrum, you can expect to spend $150 per hour for the service.

The technical terms in the UPS equations deserve a closer look. UPS systems are not rated in watts as you might expect. They are rated in volt-amperes, which reflect the inefficiency of the AC power with a power factor term. The power factor inefficiency results from the fact that a PC's power supply actually draws more power than it puts out. The VA rating can be used to indicate the output capacity of a UPS or it can be used to indicate the input power requirement of a computer. The VA rating is also known as the apparent power. It is the product of the RMS current and RMS voltage. The RMS (root-mean-square) values are literally the square root of the average of the squares of all the instantaneous values of current or voltage during one half-cycle of an alternating current. With a sine wave (AC power should be a sine wave), the RMS value is approximately equal to 0.707 times the peak value of the waveform.

So what exactly is the power factor? The power factor is a number between 0 and 1 that represents the portion of the VA product delivered to the load that actually supplies energy. This means that some of the current supplied to the equipment is not converted to energy. This occurs if the current is distorted or if the current is not in phase with the voltage applied to the equipment. Computers always draw harmonic currents that cause their power factor to be less than 1. A typical personal computer has a power factor between .6 and .7.

One issue with the power factor is that power factor corrected internal power supplies are now appearing in the marketplace. A corrected supply draws low distortion current from the AC source and has a power factor very close to 1. The benefit of power factor corrected supplies is that they do not overheat wiring or distort the AC waveform. For this reason they are actually required on equipment in some foreign countries.

For AC power systems, the wattage rating is the product of the voltage rating and the amperage rating multiplied by the power factor. The VA rating of a load must be greater than or equal to the wattage rating, as the power factor is always less than 1. Watts denote the energy actually delivered.

Watts = Volts × Amperes × Power Factor

To find the VA requirements for your system, locate the AC voltage and amperage ratings for each piece of equipment to be protected. They are usually located on a sticker on the bottom or back of the equipment. An example of the information sticker is shown in Figure 9-5. Multiply these numbers together for each item. Add up all of the VA values to find your total volt-ampere requirements.

$$VA = Volts \times Amperes$$

If your components are measured in watts, then multiply the number of watts by 1.4 (this is an approximation):

$$VA = WATTS \times 1.4$$

There is an important issue regarding the values listed on the power label. The ampere values typically are the maximum amount the power supply can handle. This means that the rated amperes can sometimes be inflated by up to 50 percent. This is okay, because the result of over-specifying a UPS is that you end up with more available runtime. This can obviously be a big plus in some applications.

If you cannot determine the VA for your equipment, you can use Table 9-2 as a rough estimate. Remember, these are just estimates. Some PCs, especially the high-end and server models, have high output power supplies that can double VA requirements. For example, a Compaq Proliant 5000 server, a Pentium Pro workhorse, draws around 800 VA without the monitor.

Another good estimation technique is to purchase a UPS with a volt-ampere rating twice that of the computer's power supply wattage. Be sure to err on the side of over-protection. You will always want to get a UPS that is rated to handle more load than

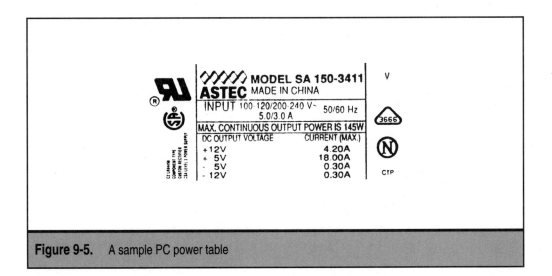

Figure 9-5. A sample PC power table

System Processor	Volt-Amperes
386	200
486	300
Pentium 90	400
Pentium 166	500
Pentium Pro 200	500
Digital AlphaServer 2000 (1 processor)	700

Table 9-2. Approximate PC Power Needs

you are planning to put on it. Luckily, UPS devices are designed to provide better-than-rated performance, so there is some grace built in.

Now that you have your volt-ampere requirements, you must determine the size and model of UPS required to support that load for the length of time you desire. Runtimes can range from a few minutes to several hours. The amount of amperes the load is drawing will be the major factor in available runtime. If you want more runtime, you can simply increase the UPS volt-ampere rating. Most manufacturers can give you close estimates of runtimes for a specific piece of equipment. You can find this information on product charts, Web sites, or by calling the manufacturer. Keep in mind that runtimes will decrease as the battery ages. Runtime is an important issue, even if you are only trying to give your systems time to do a graceful shutdown. An NT server machine can take several minutes to shut down with certain applications. You will have to customize your battery runtimes and VA requirements to fit your specific computers and applications.

How much runtime is enough? Studies have shown that complete power failures are usually very short in length. In fact, 90 percent of blackouts are resolved in less than one minute. Less than 3 percent of blackouts last more than 30 minutes. Like the other choices you have for providing system fault tolerance, your budget, application, and uptime requirements will dictate the correct runtimes. The higher the runtime, the more the system will cost. Some UPS systems offer add-on battery packs so you can increase runtime as need dictates.

You may be surprised at the relative affordability of UPS devices. A low-end desktop system can be as low as $100. A quality server UPS can be as little as $500, including data interfaces. The large (100KVA-plus) systems can go into the tens of thousands of dollars, but they can support a hundred or more computers.

UPS Maintenance

Once you have purchased a UPS, there are a few things you will need to keep in mind as far as maintenance is concerned. The batteries are the most common points of UPS failures.

Regularly check backup batteries to ensure they are fully charged. This step may not be necessary on high-end UPS systems, which usually have self-testing diagnostic capabilities. Some also have battery-monitoring devices capable of predicting battery failure.

Check to see if battery maintenance is part of your UPS service contract. This will depend on the manufacturer and the size of the equipment. If you do not already know, ask your UPS supplier what type of battery maintenance services it can provide.

When computers or other electronic devices connected to your UPS are not in use, consider shutting them off. Turning off electronic devices will prevent unnecessary battery drain on your UPS that may leave your computers defenseless against normal power fluctuations.

SURGE SUPPRESSORS

Some of the more frequent power line disturbances are transient voltage spikes and surges. Many devices, including air conditioners and elevators, cause them. They can also be created by power line crosses and lightning. These instantaneous increases in voltage through supply lines, data cables (especially RS-232), network cables, and phone lines can cause a great deal of equipment problems.

You can prevent these transients from damaging your equipment by purchasing the simplest and cheapest form of power protection device: the surge suppressor. They are often used to shield important, but not mission-critical office equipment, such as fax machines, printers, and copiers. They can also be used in conjunction with a UPS to provide a more comprehensive power protection scheme.

A surge suppressor may operate by absorbing the surge (shunt type), by stopping the surge from flowing (series type), or by some combination of the two. The shunt type suppressor has a characteristic clamping voltage that is normally chosen to be around the maximum safe operating voltage of the system. Most modern UPS devices have surge suppression circuits built into them.

To be completely protected, you will want to create an area of protection around your equipment. That means protecting against surges on every cable that enters your computer (AC power lines, peripheral cables, phone lines, and network cables). As mentioned previously, the most common source of surges is through the AC power lines. Do not forget to protect an AC powered peripheral if it is connected via cable directly to your computer. A surge can travel into that device along the data cable and into your main system. While surges along phone lines are not as common, you still need to protect mission-critical servers and workstations from their effects. Figure 9-6 shows the many

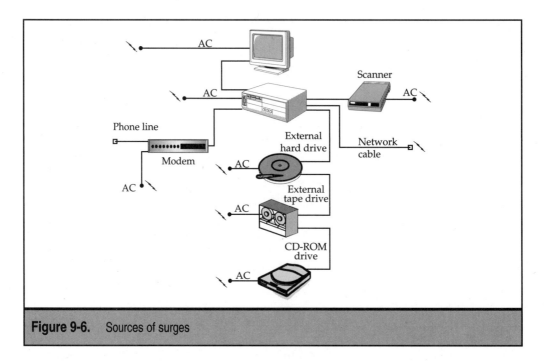

Figure 9-6. Sources of surges

ways AC power surges can work their way through to a PC. Some manufacturers offer modular systems that give you the flexibility of building custom surge protection solutions.

Probably the least common way a surge can affect your computer is through network cabling. Network protocols were specifically designed to resist the effects of noise, surges, and other transients. The IEEE 802.3 specification clearly explains the need to provide isolation between cables and computers. A series of small isolation transformers, capacitors (filters), and surge suppressors accomplish this quite effectively. Studies have shown that this barrier can sometimes be compromised. The worst cable problem offenders are the AUI connectors. They provide no isolation and should not be used on mission-critical systems. If you must use them, keep the cable length as short as possible. The isolation works quite well with UTP and coaxial cabling and their associated connectors.

To avoid cable transient problems completely on mission-critical applications, use fiber-optic cabling. It is the best form of cable available today in terms of surge protection. It does not conduct electricity and as such is completely immune to power transients like surges and noise. Even if a fiber-optic cable contacted a high-voltage distribution wire, it would have no effect on the system!

A quality surge suppressor should be protecting every piece of computer equipment in an organization from AC line surges. There are dozens of stories that illustrate this point. One recent incident involved a client that moved its main Internet gateway machine out of the computer room for easier access to it. The machine was a UNIX box that supported the company's DNS and IP address translating firewall, and it was simply plugged into an outlet, as it was assumed the location would be temporary. Shortly thereafter, the power company suffered a surge followed by a brief blackout. As you can probably guess, when the power came back up, this machine did not. The result was three days without an Internet connection and e-mail. A large portion of this company's contact with its customers is through e-mail. This was a costly public relations disaster that could have been averted with a $50 surge suppressor.

When a transient spike comes through your AC line, the surge suppressor diverts the excess power before it affects the connected equipment. Some voltage will always get through after the spike is diverted. The clamping or let-through level is the amount of voltage the protector will let through before cutting off any higher amounts. The suppression level numbers can be found on the back or side of the unit. Obviously, the best surge suppressors have the lowest clamping level voltage. You should look for suppressors in the 250 volt or less range.

Many surge suppressor companies actually provide a guarantee for the equipment they protect from surges. They will pay for the equipment if it is lost to a surge while their devices are installed. While these offers seem great, be aware that there are specific wiring connections that, unless followed correctly, will invalidate this warranty. For instance, the manufacturer will not warranty the system unless all AC power on the computer and all of the connected peripherals are connected through a surge protector to the same distribution ground. Check with individual manufacturers for specific details.

So what do common surge protectors do with the excess voltage? The energy is diverted from the hot line to neutral and ground wires. The hot line is the true source of dangerous external surges, as the neutral and ground wires are actually tied together and joined to a ground rod buried in the earth at the service entrance or to water pipes. For this reason, you should also look into your building's grounding system, especially if you are in an older building. Make sure all the grounds are connected and properly passed through to a grounding rod. Your building's main AC line should come from a single source. Multiple AC power entry points can lead to ground level differentials that can adversely effect computer equipment.

The Underwriters Laboratory UL 1449 rating is a main standard for surge suppressors. In this rating procedure, the suppressor is subjected to a 6,000-volt transient spike to see the maximum voltage that is let through to the device being protected. The suppression level numbers are the transient let-through levels, or the amount of voltage that gets past the suppression device after it diverts the spike. The suppressor manufacturer is not required to supply this information. However, a lack of disclosure probably means lack of protection. Obviously, a lower let-through value is better.

Be sure to select a surge protector that indicates when it has been damaged. Once damaged, a suppressor may not be able to adequately protect your equipment. The damage indicators are usually lights or audible alarms. Some protectors also use circuit breakers or fuses that stop all current flow in the presence of a component failure.

INTERNAL REDUNDANT POWER SUPPLIES

Another point of failure to address when considering power is the internal PC power supply. All of the surge and blackout protection in the world will not help you if your computer's internal supply burns out. For this reason, many of the major computer manufacturers, including Compaq, Dell, Digital Equipment, Hewlett-Packard and IBM, have high-end servers that offer two or more redundant internal power supplies.

These servers are quite effective because if one supply fails, the other one immediately takes over. If you specify redundant power supplies for your servers be sure to take the extra supply into consideration when sizing your UPS. Your choice to use this technology will be based on the required overall system fault tolerance and your budget.

POWER LINE CONDITIONERS

Power line conditioners were one of the first power protection devices to come on the market. They were originally designed to shield small computer installations before the introduction of low-cost surge suppressors and small-capacity UPS devices. These devices deliver clean AC power to your systems by offering regulation over a certain bandwidth of voltage fluctuations. They divert high-frequency, low-voltage disturbances to ground. Power line conditioners provide a level of protection similar to that offered by surge suppressors against power surges, spikes, and switching transients. They can also alleviate some electrical noise problems. Line conditioners actually provide some protection against power sags and brownouts for a couple of AC cycles, although this depends on the model. They can also filter out any voltage differential between neutral and ground (there should be none).

Most modern surge protectors and interruptible power supplies have decent line conditioning characteristics. For this reason, stand-alone line conditioners are becoming much less common in computer environments. In fact, even the meaning of the term "line conditioner" is becoming blurred. The term is now generally used to describe any equipment that provides some type of power filtering or regulation and may be applied to any of the devices described in this chapter.

DATA CENTER AND FACILITY POWER CONSIDERATIONS

To keep your enterprise's computers running smoothly, your first line of defense is properly designed and installed building electrical equipment. This is normally assumed but should be questioned in older buildings. All power equipment should be installed by qualified electricians, tested for conformance to specifications and codes, and then retested periodically at your critical locations.

One especially important problem in building wiring is improper grounding. As shown previously, most surge protection systems use the ground wire to shunt lightning strikes and other surges. This process will not happen unless there is a free path to ground.

Another condition that occurs on ground wires is known as a ground loop. It occurs when a ground current can take more than one path to return to the grounding point at the panel. The grounding system is a web of wiring that traverses your entire facility. Every ground wire throughout your building should be directly connected. A common source of ground loop is separate AC power sources in a single building. If possible, there should be only one entry point for AC power in a building, and it should be earth-grounded at that point. Another ground problem can occur as a result of computers being connected via data cables. This can give these systems two ways to get to ground and can result in a damaging potential voltage difference in the ground web.

The best way to ensure that the power quality is suitable for computers is to have it tested by competent professionals. Some UPS vendors will do this for you if you are purchasing a high-KVA device. Otherwise, these audits can be costly and should be considered where budgets permit. They should at least be considered if you are in an older building. If you think you have major problems, it is worth spending the money on an audit rather than spending it on damaged equipment.

Once you are sure of your electrical system's integrity, it is time to look at UPS devices. Do not assume that a large data center requires a 250KVA UPS system. It can sometimes be cheaper to have individual UPS devices customized to the particular power needs and runtime requirements of each server or set of servers. With today's remote monitoring and remote control capabilities, it can be similar to having one large UPS device.

If you are going to use a backup generator to supplement utility power during long blackouts, make sure the UPS has a reliable generator interface. Your UPS should seamlessly provide a bridge to the emergency generators when utility power is lost. It should also be able to accept a separate power load in the event of a generator failure.

The best data center solutions include management tools to decrease your support costs, increase reliability, and ensure server uptime. They will also offer line conditioning and surge suppression in a single unit. Look for a system with less than 250-volts let-through on the 6,000-volts surge tests. Almost all data center equipment can handle this amount of surge. For most servers, plan on a 15-minute runtime. For more critical applications, go to 30 to 45 minutes. This will protect you from 97 percent of power outages. Use UPS software to shut down machines at the 20 percent battery life level. For truly mission-critical applications, consider longer runtimes or even backup generators.

If you are purchasing a single, high-KVA unit for your data center, add at least 30 percent capacity for future growth. For 120-volt systems, purchase a UPS with voltage regulation between 90 and 144 VAC. The output wave peak to RMS voltage waveform ratio should be between 1.2 and 1.4. Avoid square wave outputs. Look for common mode and normal mode noise filtering greater than 20db. The UPS must be able to take abnormal interference and reduce it to harmless ranges. The data center UPS should automatically test for wiring faults and poor ground conditions.

For mission-critical applications, try to find hot-swappable battery packs. These battery pack modules can be removed and replaced without interrupting power to the protected devices. If hot-swappable battery packs are not available, consider redundant systems with manufacturer provided switchover capabilities. This is worth the extra costs if you truly need 100 percent uptime. You would not want a fault in the UPS to cause the data center to be brought down. Remember that batteries have a finite life span, even if they are rechargeable. Do not forget that a high-KVA UPS can weigh several tons. Be sure to plan accordingly. Finally, remember that large UPS systems or clusters of small ones will throw off heat due to inefficiency. Consider placing them outside the main computer room where wiring allows, to save on cooling costs.

POWER PRODUCT MANUFACTURERS

There are a large number of power product manufacturers. Several are listed here for your reference. Many of these Web sites contain online sizing utilities for UPS systems as well as a wealth of power-related information.

- ▼ American Power Conversion (**http://www.apcc.com**)
- ■ Best Power Technology (**http://www.bestpower-emea.com**)
- ■ Deltec Electronics (**http://www.deltecpower.com**)
- ■ Exide Electronics Group, Inc.(**http://www.exide.com**)
- ■ Hewlett-Packard (**http://www.hp.com**)
- ■ Liebert Corporation (**http://www.liebert.com**)
- ■ Merlin Gerin (**http://www-merlin-gerin.eunet.fr**)
- ■ Oneac Corporation (**http://www.oneac.com**)
- ■ Tripp Lite (**http://www.tripplite.com**)
- ■ Atlantic Scientific (**http://www.iu.net/atlsci**)
- ■ Panamax (**http://www.panamax.com**)
- ▲ Antec Inc. (**http://www.antec-inc.com**)

SUMMARY

This chapter covered the various problems an NT system is susceptible to due to power transients. It should be clear that, at the minimum, all computers should be protected by a quality surge suppressor. Any important NT server should be protected by an uninterruptible power supply that has a data link for automatic server shutdowns. The type of UPS you buy depends on the size of your server, your budget, and on the importance of your data. You should consider a line-interactive UPS for most applications and online solutions for your most critical systems.

Recovering Data

One of the worst situations that administrators face is an NT server that has completely stopped operating. At that point, the administrator must play the role of firefighter and try to recover the data at all costs—a situation that should be avoided by all means.

Chapter 1, which discusses fault tolerance and disaster-prevention techniques, is probably the most important chapter in this book because fault tolerance and disaster recovery are actually studies in prevention. You must study and analyze a system or an enterprise to uncover its weaknesses. The goal of all administrators and managers of NT enterprises is never to be surprised and always to be prepared. In fact, repair capabilities should be built into the initial design of the server.

Whereas Chapter 1 discusses prevention, this chapter is about recovering systems when you are *not* adequately prepared. It discusses techniques, emergency and otherwise, for recovering data in the worst situations. It also discusses tools that belong in your recovery kit for every NT server. These tools include

▼　An NT boot diskette

■　A DOS boot diskette

■　A recent tape backup of each server, including the Registry

■　A Full Registry Backup using REGBACK or a similar utility if you do not have tape backup

■　An updated Emergency Repair Disk for each server

■　A DiskSave image of each server

▲　Complete documentation concerning the installation of the server and its application programs (i.e., Exchange or SQL Server setup parameters)

What are the typical recovery scenarios? As a general rule, they fall into two categories. Either you have to repair a machine that stopped working for some inexplicable reason (possibly because it couldn't boot into Windows NT) or some mechanical problem has caused a drive to fail. In either event, nothing is more frustrating to an administrator than staring at a Blue Screen of Death (BSOD) or being called at 2:00 a.m. because the server is down. Sometimes the system simply needs to be rebooted and everything works out fine. Other times, the fix can be much more invasive.

No matter what problem you face, you must address these truly critical questions:

▼　Why did the system fail?

■　Will this happen again?

■　Did specific events precede the failure?

▲　What if the system cannot be rebooted?

Unfortunately, most engineers and administrators have had to answer these questions on many different occasions. Sometimes the system is recovered quickly and efficiently, but sometimes the operating system must be completely reinstalled. In fact, you may have to replace the entire server machine or some of its components. Having to reinstall can frighten a novice administrator, but sometimes reinstalling is the most effective solution. The main task is to reinstall and/or recover the server and all necessary programs in a timely manner. With the proper planning, you can even make a reasonable guess at how long the reinstallation will take.

This chapter discusses the basic nature of system crashes in Windows NT. Crashes can be caused by software or hardware problems and can range from the simple to the painfully complex. Remember that the key to these types of recoveries is proper planning beforehand.

THE NT BOOT PROCESS

The NT boot process follows a predefined set of events that occur each time the machine is started. For recovery purposes, understanding the NT boot process and exactly what can go wrong with it is imperative. You also need to consider what can cause a runtime error and crash.

For the purposes of this discussion, it is assumed that the system is running Windows NT 4.0 with the NTFS file format. As discussed in Chapter 1, NTFS should be the file format of choice. The benefits that it offers in terms of security, fault tolerance, and performance far outweigh the perceived recoverability benefits of the FAT format. In fact, NTFS combined with an NT boot floppy and a parallel NT install is arguably the safest method of running NT.

For a complete boot of Windows NT to be successful, the following events must occur. The boot process is relevant to data recovery because different types of system crashes can be related to many aspects of the loading sequences described here.

1. POWER ON SELF-TEST (POST)   The *power on self-test* (POST) is the system self-analysis that occurs in all personal computers at boot-time. The POST is a BIOS-engendered test of system hardware. Cards in the system that also run hardware examination, if there are any (i.e., SCSI bus mastering cards with BIOS), conduct their own POSTs. Typically, the system POST and card POSTs have routines that allow you to examine/format hard drives.

2. FIRST PHASE OF SYSTEM STARTUP   The first phase of system startup typically involves the system BIOS finding the Master Boot Record (MBR) and transferring it to memory. Usually the Master Boot Record is either on the floppy drive or, on X86-based systems, on the first BIOS-resident hard drive. After the transfer to memory occurs, the BIOS turns over further execution of startup to the Master Boot Record. Generally speaking, the MBR is operating system-independent. The MBR scans the partition table (located on the same sector as the MBR, beginning at 0x1BE) and finds the system partition. It then loads sector 0 of the system (or active) partition into memory. Typically, sector 0 contains a boot sector that begins the operating system boot or boot loader process.

3. SECOND PHASE OF SYSTEM STARTUP (NT BOOT LOADER) The boot loader portion of boot-up is operating system-dependent. This is where NT deviates dramatically from DOS. In DOS, all files must be on the first BIOS-resident hard drive, but in NT the system files can be on any drive in BIOS. However, NTLDR, NTDETECT.COM, and BOOT.INI must be on the root drive, whether the root drive is a floppy or hard drive. On an NT system, the partition table simply needs to be able to find NTLDR. (The search for NTLDR is evident when an NT-formatted floppy that lacks NT system files is left in the drive at system startup. In this case, the "Boot couldn't find NTLDR" system error pops up.) If NTLDR is found, it is placed into memory and the boot load begins. The boot itself involves many steps. First of all, NTLDR switches memory to a 32-bit flat memory model. NTLDR is able to read both FAT and BTFS mini-file systems. At this point, the appropriate file system is started. BOOT.INI is then loaded, read, and displayed on the screen. Assuming there is a user choice, one of two events occurs:

▼ If you dual-boot to DOS and have chosen DOS, NTLDR loads BOOTSEC .DOS and passes control to it. BOOTSEC.DOS contains the partition table information that existed prior to the installation of NT. As such, BOOTSEC.DOS is machine-specific and may or may not work between machines.

▲ If the user choice or default is NT, NTLDR executes NTDETECT.COM, which then gathers information about the attached hardware. The user is now presented with the choice of booting into NT, choosing a hardware profile, or, more importantly, choosing the Last Known Good configuration (discussed shortly). NTLDR now loads again and starts NTOSKRNL.EXE.

NOTE: The following files are needed to start an X86 system: The root of the startup disk must have BOOT.INI, NTLDR, and NTDETECT.COM. The remaining required files are all in the %SYSTEMROOT%\SYSTEM32 directory or a subdirectory. This directory is pointed to in BOOT.INI. Primary files needed are NTOSKRNL.EXE and HAL.DLL. The final files needed are the system key of the Registry (SYSTEM32\CONFIG) and the necessary device drivers (SYSTEM32\DRIVERS). Obviously, damage to any of these files can lead to a system crash.

4. THE KERNEL LOADS AND INITIALIZES The kernel load and initialization phase begins when NT switches the screen background to blue. The blue screen indicates that NT is loaded. A service pack number as well as the number of processors and the amount of RAM installed are listed. The device drivers are now loaded and the system fully initializes.

5. THE FINAL STAGE About the time the monitor switches in graphics mode, the system loads WINLOGON.EXE and a logon screen appears (the CTRL-ALT-DEL screen). The system continues and starts all necessary services.

▼ *NOTE:* NT actually considers a startup completed when any single user logs on successfully one time. At this point, the clone registry set is copied to the Last Known Good control set.

How is the boot process relevant to data recovery? Different types of system crashes can be related to many aspects of the loading sequences described here. In the next sections, a few of the more common types of crashes will be examined.

BIOS-RELATED CRASHES

Most BIOS-related crashes occur at system boot. They are caused by a variety of hardware-related problems. Typically, the system BIOS has a beep-related diagnostic code that indicates what the problem might be (that is to say, the machine beeps in a certain known sequence to aid in self-diagnosing the problem). These beep sequences or codes are listed in the manual for the specific BIOS type. For instance, three long beeps might indicate a memory mismatch.

The more common BIOS-related crashes are video card failure (infrequent), motherboard failure (infrequent), and, most often, a memory-related failure. The causes of memory-related failure range from mismatched SIMMs to NMI failures. Of course, the usual fix is to reseat or possibly replace the problem component. Another common fix is to replace or remove a bank of SIMMs.

Following is a list of suggestions to help you avoid BIOS related problems:

▼ Buy components from a single dealer. This is certainly true of SIMMs but also pertains to entire systems. Do not fall into the trap of buying each allotment of PCs and components from different vendors. Remember that different sets of tolerances are associated with different components.

■ Cheaper is not necessarily better. If yours is a large company, be sure to include the cost of ownership in your purchases.

■ When buying machines, try to specify at the time of purchase how much memory will ultimately be needed. By doing so, you avoid memory mismatches and other memory-related problems down the road.

▲ No matter how much a system costs, it is no better than its weakest component. (Ironic, isn't it, that a large server with a 250-watt power supply can ultimately cause the system to fail?)

The majority of these problem can be avoided with proper planning and commonsense purchasing. These issues are more thoroughly discussed in Chapter 1.

THE EASY BACKUP SOLUTIONS

Many different problems can strike a system and be a continual source of aggravation to an administrator. For instance, consider the so-called driver fix that has just been downloaded from the system vendor. After the update is run, the system is rebooted and it crashes. How can you fix this problem?

Reverting to the Last Known Good Configuration

Depending on how a new program or driver is handled by NT, the Last Known Good option can save considerable effort. When NT boots, copies of the system Registry entries are cloned. When the NT system successfully boots into a workable state, the clone entries are copied to the LastKnownGood entry in the Registry, as shown in Figure 10-1. Notice that the LastKnownGood entry shows current control set 3 as this value.

The benefits of using the Last Known Good configuration can be enormous if the process works correctly. After you add software or device drivers that crash the system, often you can hit the SPACEBAR when NT boots and invoke the Last Known Good choice. By doing so, you revert to the last successful logon and thereby load the appropriate system drivers, which causes the system to boot into the last successful logon profile (normally) and effectively ignore the new driver or software package. Unfortunately, 30

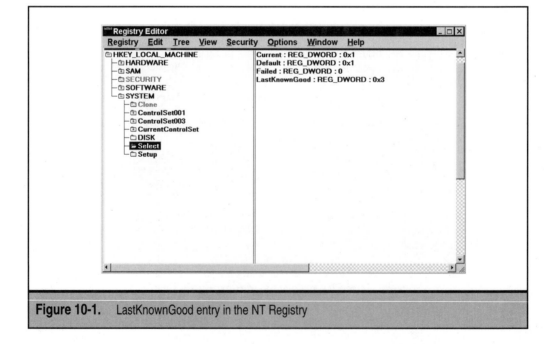

Figure 10-1.   LastKnownGood entry in the NT Registry

to 50 percent of the time the Last Known Good configuration is not as current as might be expected (Microsoft acknowledges this). In other words, the Last Known Good configuration might result in the loss of more than was expected. However, this is not much of a problem if you plan ahead and maintain a decent backup of the Registry.

Creating an Emergency Repair Disk

One easy way to make a backup of the NT Registry is by creating an Emergency Repair Disk (ERD). Every time you make a major change to or upgrade an NT system, you need to completely update the Emergency Repair Disk. This process is straightforward:

1.   Open an NT command prompt.

2.   Type **RDISK /S**.

This command makes an updated ERD without additional user input. It is important to note, however, that some systems have a Registry that exceeds the size of a floppy drive. In this case, the REGBACK and REGREST utilities from the NT Resource Kit can be used, as is explained in the next section.

Emergency Repair Disks should be created before and after a change is made to the hardware or software components of an NT server. Obviously, the "before" copy is for disaster recovery if the install fails. The "after" copy is for a later recovery of the system, if necessary. Third-party companies have come up with inventive ideas for keeping up-to-date copies of Emergency Repair Disks. One in particular is ERDisk from Midwestern Commerce, Inc. (**http://www.ntsecurity.com**). This product allows administrators to create Emergency Repair Disks for one or a group of servers over the network. Emergency Repair Disks are thoroughly covered in Chapter 2.

Using REGBACK/REGREST to Restore the NT Registry

The REGBACK and REGREST utilities allow you to back up and restore the NT Registry in a variety of ways. Using a tape backup program to do backups and restores is usually easier. NTBackup and most third-party NT tape backup software allows backups to be made to tape. However, if a tape backup option is not available, by all means use REGBACK.

In order to back up the full Registry to a folder or directory on a hard drive, the backup folder (C:\CONFIG) must be created. Following is the complete command-line argument for backing up the Registry to a directory on the C drive called C:\CONFIG:

REGBACK C:\CONFIG

Figure10-2 shows the results of this command.

As shown in Figure 10-2, a manual save is required for the two active users, the current *probob* account and the *repl* account user (The *probob* account is the logged in user and the *repl* account is a service account on this particular machine). You must back up

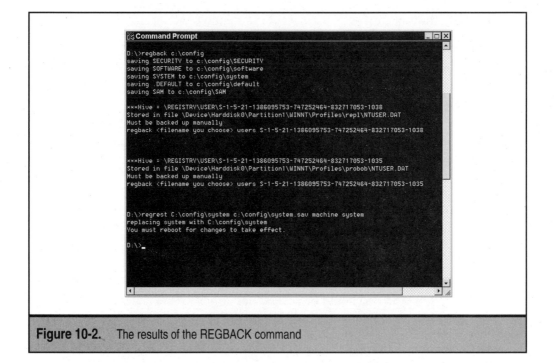

Figure 10-2. The results of the REGBACK command

this information separately if you want to be able to fully recover the information for those specific users. The easiest way is to run REGBACK as above and watch the output. REGBACK will give you the syntax required for the manual backup. You can then use the console cut and paste feature to create the manual backup commands or just manually enter them. As you can see from Figure 10-2, the cut and paste feature is much easier as the user account hive names (actually the user security IDs) are rather long. In the case of the *repl* user the command would be:

REGBACK C:\CONFIG\REPL.SAV USERS S-1-5-21-1386095753-747252464-832717053-1035

Backing up to a standard CONFIG directory on all machines is a good idea for consistency's sake. The backup directory must be on the same volume as the Registry because REGBACK uses the Rename function and not the Copy function. The files can then be copied to another volume or server with a script. Remember that you cannot use REGBACK to back up the Registry to a directory that already has files in it (the directory must be empty). To overcome this problem, simply delete files in the directory before a backup is performed. The following simple batch file works in our example of C:\CONFIG:

```
C:
CD \CONFIG
DEL *.* /Q
REGBACK C:\CONFIG
REM PLACE NECESSARY MANUAL REGBACK COMMANDS HERE
```

(The /Q on the DEL *.* line tells the command processor to delete the files in quiet mode; that is, without asking if it is okay.)

So how do you restore the Registry? There are two ways; automatic and manual. If you use the automatic method remember that it may not restore hives that had to be created with the manual REGBACK method (as the *repl* account above). The basic syntax is:

REGREST <*copiesdirectory*> <*savefiledirectory*>

where *copiesdirectory* is the directory that contains the hives that were backed up using REGBACK(C:\CONFIG in our example). The *savefiledirectory* is an empty directory you create for making copies of the active NT hives that you are replacing. It must be created and empty before running the restore command. For our example, to automatically recover all files from the C:\CONFIG directory to the actual NT Registry and make a backup copy of the replaced hives type:

REGREST C:\CONFIG C:\BACKUP.SAV

In a manner similar to the REGBACK command, REGREST will tell you which hives must be restored manually. You can again cut and paste the command into the console window. Remember that you can actually restore all of the hives by the manual method. This procedure simply restores the hives one at a time. Here is the command syntax:

REGREST <*copyfilename*> <*savefilename*> <*hivetype*> <*hivename*>

where:

<*copyfilename*> is the hive file that was created with REGBACK.

<*savefilename*> is the REGBACK backup file. (Any unused file name will actually do. This is simply a backup of the replaced hive in case something goes wrong.)

<*hivetype*> is either "machine" or "users" based on whether the hive resides in HKEY_LOCAL_MACHINE or HKEY_USERS.

<*hivename*> is an immediate subtree of the same HKEY_LOCAL_MACHINE or HKEY_USERS hives. If you are not sure which hive or subtree name to use, open the Registry Editor (REGEDT32) and check the hives. For instance, go to the HKEY_LOCAL_MACHINE window. You will notice that the SAM, Software, Security, and System subtrees all reside there. Therefore you always use machine for the hivetype when restoring these hives. The account (SID) hives are always found under

HKEY_USERS. The hivetype for accounts is therefore users. For instance, the following command restores the system hive of the NT Registry from the C:\CONFIG\SYSTEM file that was create with REGBACK:

REGREST C:\CONFIG\SYSTEM C:\BACKUP.SAV MACHINE SYSTEM

or to restore the *repl* account information mentioned above:

REGREST C:\CONFIG\REPL.SAV C:\BACKUP.SAV USERS S-1-5-21-1386095753-747252464-832717053-1035

Once either (or both) of the above lines are executed, the machine must be rebooted. It is absolutely imperative to understand that doing such backup and restore procedures is potentially lethal to an NT system. Be sure that you thoroughly understand these commands before executing them. It is generally recommended to test them on a nonproduction machine. After a few tests you should be quite proficient at using these commands. Wherever possible, use tape backup to back up and restore the Registry instead of REGBACK\REGREST.

▼

NOTE: The Registry Editor (REGEDT32) also allows hives to be saved and replaced from its interface.

MBR/BOOT SECTOR ISSUES

Tools like RESTREST and REGBACK are nice features of Windows NT, but what if you cannot even get the machine to boot up? In this case, recovering from a crash might mean recovering from damage to the boot sector. The hard drive might become inaccessible and simply not boot, which can be a disastrous problem in Windows NT. The most common causes of these types of problems are related to computer viruses (see Chapter 6). However, the problem can also be caused by failed installations of NT.

Virus-related boot sector problems are usually caused by a virus utilizing the beginning disk sectors of which NT is supposed to have full control (particularly with NTFS). The virus uses these additional sectors as working swap space. Depending on the virus, it moves the original sector 1 data onto the contiguous sectors. After the move, the virus copies itself to sector 1 and dumps its payload or operates in some way. Now the process becomes interesting. In order to effectively hide itself from detection, the virus next copies the original sector 1 data back to the original location (sector 1). On FAT systems, the Partition boot sector is typically one sector long, so using the contiguous sectors may not necessarily pose a problem. On NFTS, however, the same Partition boot can be up to sixteen sectors long. Overwriting these contiguous sectors on an NTFS drive is almost always disastrous. In cases such as these, it becomes important to understand how to recover the boot sector.

One of the easiest tools for examining these records is *DiskProbe*, the sector editor from the NT Resource Kit. DiskProbe allows a user with Administrator rights to directly alter and read data on a hard drive. The Master Boot Record, partition tables, and Partition boot sectors can be also be read and modified. As will be shown in the following sections of this book, you should only turn to Disk Probe to modify hard drives when tools like CHKDSK, EMERGNCY REPAIR, and NT SETUP do not work.

Remember that DiskProbe can also be used as a preventative maintenance tool. Data structures such as Master Boot Records and Partition boot sectors can be saved as disk files and kept with the Emergency Repair Disk. In the event of corruption caused by viruses or faulty hardware, these critical data structures can be easily replaced.

> **CAUTION:** Before you make changes with low-level tools such as DiskProbe, make sure that a reliable, complete backup of the drive is available. Misusing such tools can make all data on the drive permanently inaccessible.

DiskProbe and other sector editors function a level "below" the file system, so the normal checks for maintaining disk consistency are not in force. DiskProbe gives the user direct access to every byte on the physical disk without regard to access privilege, which makes it possible to damage or permanently overwrite critical data structures.

Actually, two different aspects of boot-related problems must be considered. The first area is the Master Boot Record and the second is the boot sector itself. Figure 10-3 shows the appearance of the MBR sector on a Micropolis 4221 hard drive using Disk Probe. Notice on line 0080 the reference to an invalid partition table. This is a normal looking Master Boot Record. The operating system references are also quite clear.

In contrast to the Master Boot Record, the boot sector shows references to kernel or even NTLDR files. The actual boot sector of the same Micropolis drive from Figure 10-3 is shown in Figure 10-4. Notice at 0130 that the ASCII string "a disk read error" is started. This is a normal view of a standard boot sector.

In the following sections, common instances where either the boot sector or the MBR is corrupted are examined.

Fixing the Problem

If an NT system suddenly does not boot (after no obvious system changes), the first things to search for are viruses. As noted in Chapter 6, viruses can play a major role in NT boot problems. There are also several other factors that can lead to these problems. These include software faults, operator error, and hardware problems. Let's examine the easy ways to repair a damaged boot sector of a drive (we are, of course, presuming that setup and repair do not work). The scenario here is that your system does not boot and you suspect an MBR\boot sector problem.

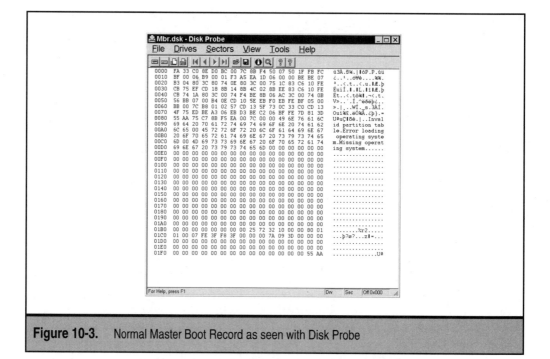

Figure 10-3. Normal Master Boot Record as seen with Disk Probe

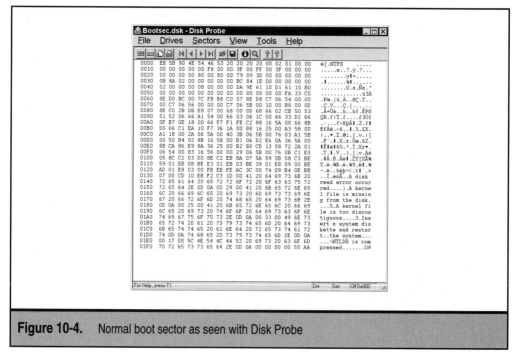

Figure 10-4. Normal boot sector as seen with Disk Probe

Create an NT Boot Disk

You need an NT boot disk to help determine where the problem lies. As noted earlier in this chapter, only a few files must be on the disk. In general, an NT boot disk can be used from machine to machine. If your service is dead in the water, simply make the disk on another NT machine. The BOOT.INI file must sometimes be edited (see the BOOT.INI section later in this chapter), but editing can be done with any text editor.

Copy NTLDR, NTDETECT.COM, and BOOT.INI to the floppy. Removing the hidden, system, and read attributes on these files before making the copy is a good idea. To copy the files, use File Manager (highlight the files, choose File | Properties, and change the attributes), NT's Explorer, My Computer, or a command prompt. After the files have been copied to the floppy, reset the attributes on both the floppy and the hard drive.

NOTE: Be sure to make the boot floppy read-only.

Boot to the NT Boot Floppy

Place the NT boot floppy in A: drive and start the system. Make certain that the system has *boot from floppy* enabled in its BIOS (if it does not, simply go into the BIOS and make this change). Choose the default BOOT.INI setting and press ENTER when prompted. If the system boots, the problem indeed resides in the boot sector. If it does not boot, the problem could be caused by a bad partition table or, more than likely, by corrupt or missing system files. MBR\boot record issues are discussed in the next few sections. The issue of a bad system file is addressed later in this chapter.

NOTE: Do not use these techniques if you have a third-party partitioning manager such as Partition Magic or OnTrack.

Fix the Master Boot Record

First assume that the Master Boot Record is corrupted. At this point, the second essential boot floppy, the DOS boot floppy (DOS 6.22 is recommended), is required. To create it, follow these steps:

1. Go to a DOS machine and place a floppy in the A: drive.

2. Type **FORMAT A: /S** from the C: prompt and press ENTER. This command formats the floppy and copies the system files to that floppy.

3. Copy FORMAT.COM, FDISK.EXE, and SYS.COM from the DOS directory to the floppy.

4. Remove the NT boot floppy from the machine and insert the DOS boot disk (be sure to set it to the read-only tab).

5. Restart the system and press ENTER when prompted for the time and date. The A:\> prompt should appear.

6. Type **FDISK /MBR** and press ENTER. This step replaces the MBR without replacing the partition tables at the end of the sector. As you recall, the MBR is operating system-independent. It is the same for DOS as it is for NT. This process can be very effective in repairing corrupted boot sectors, but it does not always work.

CAUTION: Before running FDISK/MBR be sure to scan the system for viruses using a reputable anti-virus software.

Recover the System Using Tape Backup

If the above steps do not work, the options become quite limited. If the files are accessible, back them up to tape or other media (a network boot disk works great for this purpose). Of course, you should be able to fall back on a tape backup. If no other backup is available, move on to the next step.

Hand-Edit the Boot Records

If all else fails, you must hand-edit the boot records of the system. The easiest way to accomplish this task is to use the utility from the NT Resource Kit called DiskProbe. This usually requires you to use the NT startup boot floppy. If the startup boot floppy fails to bring up NT you can use the floppy to boot to your backup NT installation (if you have one). If you have no parallel installation, you can use a DOS utility like Norton DiskEdit (**http://www.symantec.com**) to accomplish the disk modification tasks listed in this section or you can install a second copy of NT.

CAUTION: Do not install NT onto the bad drive or on *any* drive if the problem disk is your primary drive!

NT will run a CHKDSK and try to "fix" the errors. You may end up corrupting the entire primary drive. The trick is to make some other disk the primary drive while you are doing the repair. If it is a typical SCSI configuration, simply change the drive IDs of the second drive to zero and the drive ID of the disk in question to one or higher.

To use DiskProbe, you have to get a good Master Boot Record from another disk. This is copied to the failed startup disk (usually disk 0 on x86-based computers). The smallest disk write during the procedure will be one entire sector. Therefore, when you copy the Master Boot Record from another disk, you will also copy the other disk's Partition Table. Of course, this will not be valid for the current disk, so you must first write down the partition information in the Master Boot Record that you are going to replace. You must then manually enter the Partition Table information in hex format into the newly copied sector. Figure 10-5 illustrates the differences between the DiskProbe view of a Quantum 1080s drive and a Micropolis 4221 drive.

```
                            1080S
01B0    00 00 00 00 00 00 00 00 28 82 09 CF 00 00 80 01    ........(.......
01C0    01 00 07 FE 3F 82 3F 00 00 00 84 1C 20 00 00 00    ....?.?..... ...
01D0    00 00 00 00 00 00 00 00 00 00 00 00 00 00 00 00    ................
01E0    00 00 00 00 00 00 00 00 00 00 00 00 00 00 00 00    ................
01F0    00 00 00 00 00 00 00 00 00 00 00 00 00 00 55 AA    ..............U.

                            4221
01B0    00 00 00 00 00 00 00 00 25 72 32 10 00 00 80 01    ........%r2.....
01C0    01 00 07 FE 3F F8 3F 00 00 00 7A 09 3D 00 00 00    ....?.?...z.=...
01D0    00 00 00 00 00 00 00 00 00 00 00 00 00 00 00 00    ................
01E0    00 00 00 00 00 00 00 00 00 00 00 00 00 00 00 00    ................
01F0    00 00 00 00 00 00 00 00 00 00 00 00 00 00 55 AA    ..............U.
```

Figure 10-5.   The partition tables for a Quantum 1080s and a Micropolis 4221

The following steps walk you through the actual process of modifying or repairing damaged boot sectors with DiskProbe. Please note that this process is not recommended unless nothing else has worked to recover the disk.

1. Boot into NT with the NT boot floppy.

2. Click the Start button, choose Programs, select Resource Kit, select Disk Utilities, and click DiskProbe to open that application.

3. Choose Drives on the menu bar and select Physical Drive. A window opens showing you the drives available on your system.

4. Double-click the drive you want to examine.

5. Clear the check in the read-only box and click on the Set Active button, as shown in Figure 10-6.

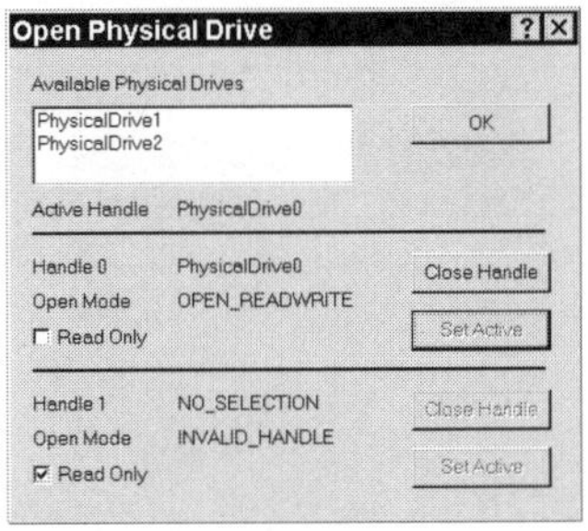

Figure 10-6.   The selection of the hard drive and the Set Active button

6. On the menu bar, choose Sectors | Read and set the starting sector to 0 and the number of sectors to 1, as in Figure 10-7.

7. Click on Read. You see the MBR, as shown in Figure 10-8. Note that this figure is the same as Figure 10-3, which was made by Disk Save.

8. Choose View | Partition table on the menu bar. Make certain that the boot indicator is set to system and the System ID is NTFS. If there is more than one partition, be sure to set it to partition 1, as shown in Figure 10-9.

9. On the bottom left window of the screen, note and write down the relative sector number. This is the actual area that will be repaired.

10. Click the Go button next to the relative sector value.

11. Choose View | Bytes on the menu bar. You see values in sector 63, as shown in Figure 10-10. The normal value is shown in Figure 10-8. If the boot sector is corrupt, many of the values are incorrect.

12. On the menu bar, choose View | NTFS partition.

13. In NT 4.0 and newer versions, the backup boot sector is located at the end of the drive. Click on the Volume End button as shown in Figure 10-11.

NOTE: The FAT file system does not have a backup boot sector.

14. On the menu bar, click on View | Bytes to identify the contents of this sector, as shown in Figure 10-12. Notice that Figure 10-10 (the actual boot sector) and Figure 10-12 (the backup boot sector) are identical.

15. Since this a good copy of the boot sector, you now need to copy (write) it to the actual boot sector area (in this case, sector 63). On the menu bar, choose Sectors | Write.

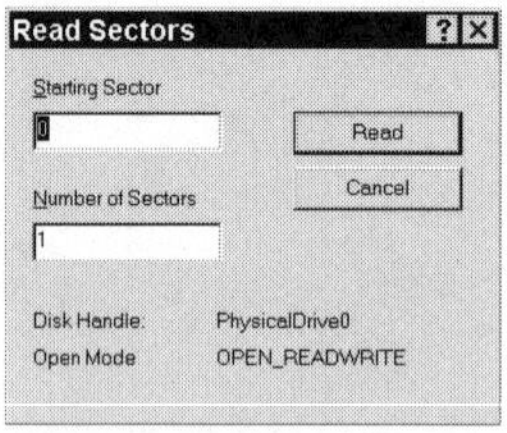

Figure 10-7.   The basic information necessary for the first read of the hard drive

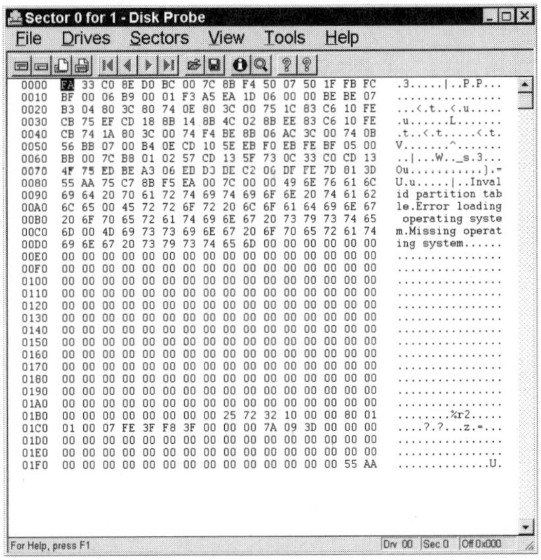

Figure 10-8. The MBR for the drive

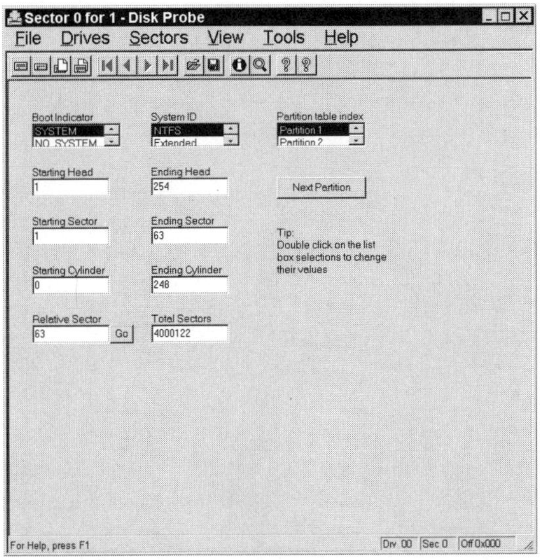

Figure 10-9. The partition table for the drive

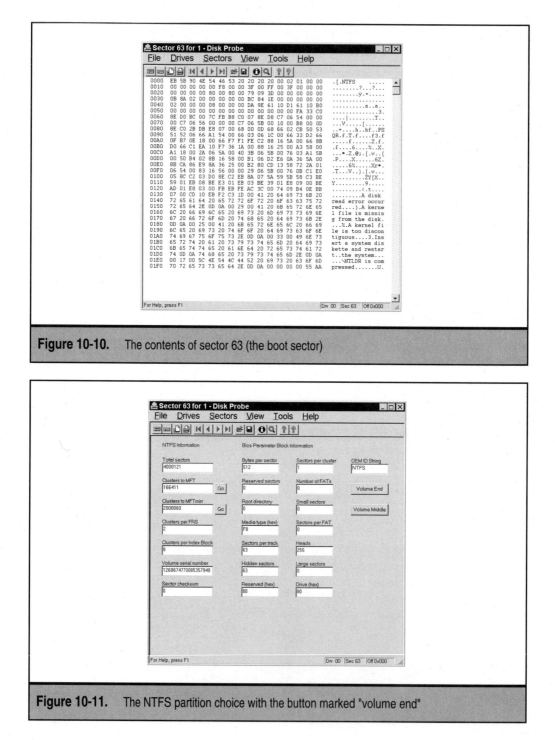

Figure 10-10. The contents of sector 63 (the boot sector)

Figure 10-11. The NTFS partition choice with the button marked "volume end"

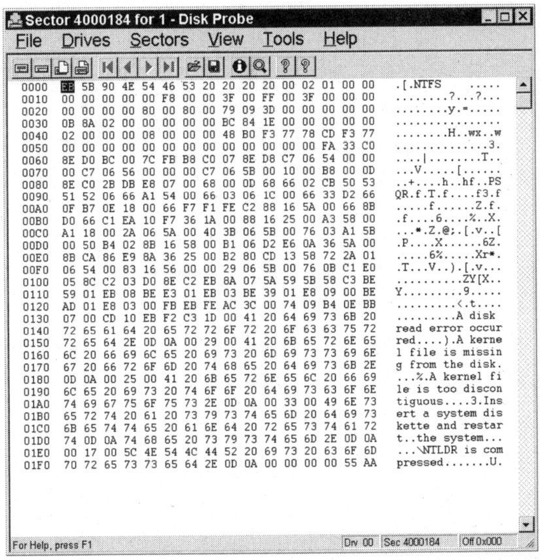

Figure 10-12. The backup boot sector at sector 4000184

16. In the box at the bottom of the screen, enter the relative sector that you wrote down in step 9. In this case, enter **63** and click on the Write it button, as shown in Figure 10-13. You are prompted to overwrite the data in sector 63.

17. Click Yes to complete the write process.

18. On the menu bar, choose Sectors | Read and enter the sector that you wrote to; in this case, enter **63**.

19. Choose View | Bytes and you should be able to read the normal boot sector.

20. Reboot the computer.

After reading these steps, it should be obvious that you do not ever want to go through them in a production environment. Using a disk editor for disk changes is always very risky. Prevention is the best medicine for these kinds of problems. Fortunately, Microsoft has provided several tools that make it easier to plan ahead and protect NT systems. These tools from the NT Resource Kit are straightforward, easy to use, and easily justify the cost of the entire Resource Kit.

Planning Ahead with DiskSave and DiskMap

The Microsoft NT Resource Kit provides several significant disaster recovery and repairing utilities. Two that every administrator should know about are DiskSave and

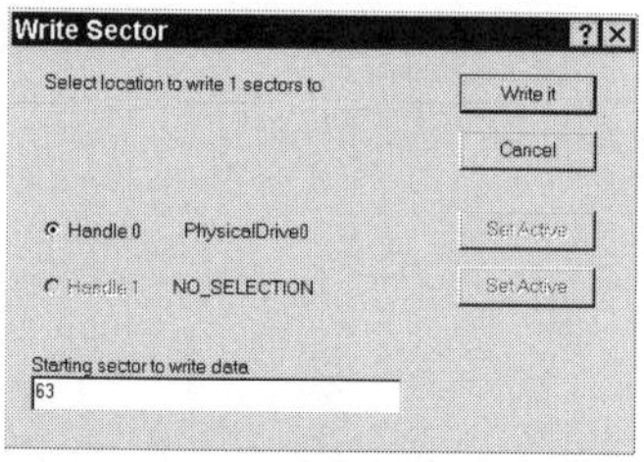

Figure 10-13. The final step of writing to the hard drive

DiskMap. DiskMap, an interesting utility, shows the physical setup of a formatted hard drive. It is useful for documenting a drive and is worth running. DiskSave, a critical utility, *must* be run to save significant trouble later on. It should be on your list of important utilities to run on every NT server.

As mentioned previously, the full list of items you should have is

▼ An NT boot diskette

■ A DOS boot diskette

■ A recent backup of each server, including the Registry

■ A Full Registry Backup using REGBACK or a similar utility if you do not have tape backup

■ An updated Emergency Repair Disk for each server

■ A DiskSave image of each server

▲ Complete documentation on the installation of the server and its application programs (i.e., Exchange or SQL Server setup parameters)

DiskSave

DiskSave runs under DOS and can save and restore the boot sector and partition boot sector of a hard drive. The utility should be run on all critical servers. Here are the steps for running DiskSave:

1. Start with a fresh diskette that has been formatted in DOS without the system files.

2. Boot into NT.

3. Copy DISKSAVE.EXE and DISKSAVE.TXT to the nonbootable DOS floppy.

4. Go to the machine in question and boot to the DOS read-only boot diskette (you will have created it earlier).

5. In DOS, remove the boot diskette and place the nonbootable Disk Save diskette in the A: drive.

6. At the A: prompt, type **DiskSave** and press ENTER.

DiskSave provides important safety features with regard to the Master Boot Record (MBR) and the boot sector. If this sector becomes damaged, the machine will not boot. Most administrators have encountered a system that hangs at a black screen or messages such as "Invalid partition table" or "Missing operating system." Corrupt boot sectors can also result in STOP: 0x0000007B failures during boot up into NT. The machine may also hang prior to loading NTLDR. DiskSave allows the Master Boot Record and boot sector to be saved as binary image files. Once these critical disk structures have been saved, it is easy to restore them if the copies on the hard drive become corrupted.

When you boot to the DOS diskette and run DISKSAVE, you are presented with several options. These options can be very powerful. They are explained in the following pages.

NOTE: DiskSave only works on Intel-based machines.

F2—BACKUP THE MASTER BOOT RECORD   This function prompts for both a path and filename for the saved MBR image. Limit the name and path to a simple yet descriptive name. Making the names compatible with the DOS 8+3 convention (i.e., A:\ MBRDISK0.DSK) is recommended. The saved file is a binary image of the MBR sector and is 512 bytes in size. The MBR is always located at Cylinder 0, Side 0, Sector 1 of the boot disk. DiskSave only works on the first partition, partition 0.

F3—RESTORE MASTER BOOT RECORD   This function prompts for the path and filename of the previously saved Master Boot Record file. Enter the filename and path (i.e., A:\MBRDISK0.DSK). The only error checking is for the file size (must be 512 bytes).

CAUTION: Copying an incorrect file to the MBR permanently destroys the partition table information and renders the machine incapable of booting.

F4—BACKUP THE BOOT SECTOR   This function prompts for a path and filename for the saved boot sector image. Again, limit the name and path to a simple yet descriptive 8+3 name (i.e., A:\BOOTSECT.DSK). This step searches for the active partition and jumps to the starting location of that partition. The sector at that location is then saved under the filename that the user entered. The resulting file is a binary image of the boot sector and is 512 bytes in size.

F5—RESTORE BOOT SECTOR   This function prompts for a path and filename for the previously saved boot sector file. The only error checking is for the file size (it must be 512 bytes).

> *CAUTION:* Copying an incorrect file to the boot sector permanently destroys boot sector information and renders the machine incapable of booting.

F6—DISABLE FT ON THE BOOT DRIVE   This function is useful when Windows NT will not boot from a mirrored system drive. This step searches for the bootable or active partition and then checks to see if the SystemType byte has the high bit set (i.e., the partition is part of a fault tolerant set). Disabling this bit has the same effect as breaking the mirror. Note that this function offers no reset option.

It is easy to see that DiskSave is a powerful utility. Every administrator should always use DiskSave on critical NT servers to make a backup of the boot-up data structures. The next important utility is DiskMap.

DiskMap

Disk map is an interesting utility in that it gives the user basic information about a hard drive. One use for it is to obtain an image of a drive and attach the image to the documentation of the system. Following is the syntax used in the application:

DiskMap /D# /H

The /D# switch denotes the *drive number*. The /h switch creates the dump as hex (decimal is default). Dumping the file as decimal is recommended for readability. On any system, the following sends information about a disk to the C drive as the file DRIVE0.TXT:

DiskMap /D0 >C:\DRIVE0.TXT

The output of DiskMap can be seen in the following three examples (the asterisk in the output denotes a system partition).

Quantum 1080s with a single primary partition:

```
Cylinders  HeadsPerCylinder SectorsPerHead BytesPerSector MediaType
     131               255             63            512        12
TrackSize = 32256, CylinderSize = 8225280, DiskSize = 1077511680 (1027MB)

Signature = 0xcf098228
     StartingOffset    PartitionLength StartingSector PartitionNumber
*            32256         1077479424             63               1
```

```
MBR:
          Starting               Ending          System   Relative    Total
   Cylinder Head Sector  Cylinder Head Sector     ID      Sector     Sectors
*      0    1    1        130   254   63        0x07        63       2104452
       0    0    0          0     0    0        0x00         0             0
       0    0    0          0     0    0        0x00         0             0
       0    0    0          0     0    0        0x00         0             0
```

Micropolis 4221 with 1 primary partition and an extended partition with 2 logical drives:

```
Cylinders  HeadsPerCylinder SectorsPerHead BytesPerSector MediaType
   249            255             63             512          12
TrackSize = 32256, CylinderSize = 8225280, DiskSize = 2048094720 (1953MB)


Signature = 0x4dcef888
    StartingOffset     PartitionLength StartingSector PartitionNumber
*          32256           526385664         63              1
       526450176           814270464         63              2
      1340752896           707341824         63              3

MBR:
          Starting               Ending          System   Relative    Total
   Cylinder Head Sector  Cylinder Head Sector     ID      Sector     Sectors
*      0    1    1         63   254   63        0x06        63       1028097
      64    0    1        248   254   63        0x05      1028160    2972025
       0    0    0          0     0    0        0x00         0             0
       0    0    0          0     0    0        0x00         0             0


EBR: (sector 1028160)
          Starting               Ending          System   Relative    Total
   Cylinder Head Sector  Cylinder Head Sector     ID      Sector     Sectors
      64    1    1        162   254   63        0x07        63       1590372
     163    0    1        248   254   63        0x05      1590435    1381590

       0    0    0          0     0    0        0x00         0             0
       0    0    0          0     0    0        0x00         0             0
```

```
EBR: (sector 2618595)
```

Starting Cylinder	Head	Sector	Ending Cylinder	Head	Sector	System ID	Relative Sector	Total Sectors
163	1	1	248	254	63	0x07	63	1381527
0	0	0	0	0	0	0x00	0	0
0	0	0	0	0	0	0x00	0	0
0	0	0	0	0	0	0x00	0	0

Micropolis 4221 with one primary partition configured as NTFS (note system IDs):

Cylinders	HeadsPerCylinder	SectorsPerHead	BytesPerSector	MediaType
249	255	63	512	12

TrackSize = 32256, CylinderSize = 8225280, DiskSize = 2048094720 (1953MB)

Signature = 0x10327225

	StartingOffset	PartitionLength	StartingSector	PartitionNumber
*	32256	2048062464	63	1

```
MBR:
```

	Starting Cylinder	Head	Sector	Ending Cylinder	Head	Sector	System ID	Relative Sector	Total Sectors
*	0	1	1	248	254	63	0x07	63	4000122
	0	0	0	0	0	0	0x00	0	0
	0	0	0	0	0	0	0x00	0	0
	0	0	0	0	0	0	0x00	0	0

DiskMap outputs an image of the disk configuration. In all cases, there is an MBR. On the drives with extended partitions, there is also an Extended Boot Record. If at all possible, make the boot drive a primary partition. Finding boot records on an extended partition can be more difficult than it is worth (Microsoft refers to this process as "walking through the drive"). As mentioned, the asterisk in the DiskMap output above denotes a system partition.

One interesting value in all three of the examples is the system ID. These values describe the nature of the partition:

System ID Value	Interpretation
0x05	Extended partition
0x06	BIGDOS FAT partition or logical drive
0x07	NTFS partition or logical drive

Understanding the BOOT.INI File

As mentioned previously, an NT boot floppy is an important part of any disaster recovery kit. While most of what is on the boot floppy is generic, the BOOT.INI can change from machine to machine, depending on the hardware and the location of the NT install directory. As such, understanding the ARC-based syntax of BOOT.INI is important. Figure 10-14 shows an example of a BOOT.INI taken from a basic Intel-based NT system.

In Figure 10-15, the same BOOT.INI file has been modified to include an entry for the parallel installation of NT on a second drive. This could also point to an NT installation on a mirrored drive.

In Figure 10-16, the multi( ) is replaced by SCSI( ), denoting a SCSI controller that is not supported by the motherboard BIOS. The SCSI( ) notation indicates that Windows NT will load a boot device driver (NTBOOTDD.SYS). This file is actually the driver for the SCSI controller renamed to NTBOOTDD.SYS and located in the primary root directory. For example, if the controller were an Adaptec 2940, NTBOOTDD.SYS would be a copy of the AIC78XX.SYS available from Adaptec. Note in Figure 10-16 that there are actually two SCSI adapters, SCSI(0) and SCSI(1). This could be a duplexed drive set or simply a machine with parallel NT installations on separate drives that reside on separate controllers.

Multi( ) is only found on Intel-based systems. Multi( ) can indicate a non-SCSI disk drive supported by either the ATDISK.SYS or ABIOSDSK.SYS driver, or a SCSI disk drive supported by a SCSI BIOS that loads when the SCSI adapter detects a bootable device on the lowest SCSI ID (on most SCSI adapters). Originally in the days of NT 3.1, the Multi() syntax could only be used on IDE and ESDI drives. It is now the more common designation.

Multi( ) syntax tells NT to use the system's BIOS to load NT system files. This means that NT will use interrupt 13 BIOS calls to find and load NTOSKRNL.EXE. The syntax of the BOOT.INI with the multi( ) designation is based upon the following:

multi(X)*disk*(Y)*rdisk*(Z)*partition*(W)\<WINNT_DIR>

where

▼   X is the ordinal number of the adapter and should always be 0 for multi( ).

■   Y is always 0 (zero) for multi( ), as the parameter is not required.

■   Z is the ordinal for the disk on the adapter. It starts at 0. This number is also indicative of how the disks will show up in Disk Administrator.

```
[Boot Loader]
Timeout=5
Default=multi(0)disk(0)rdisk(0)partition(1)\WINNT
[Operating Systems]
multi(0)disk(0)rdisk(0)partition(1)\WINNT="NT Server"
multi(0)disk(0)rdisk(0)partition(1)\WINNT="NT Server [VGA mode]" /basevideo /sos
```

Figure 10-14.   A basic BOOT.INI file

```
[Boot Loader]
Default=multi(0)disk(0)rdisk(0)partition(1)\WINNT
[Operating Systems]
multi(0)disk(0)rdisk(0)partition(1)\WINNT="NT Server"
multi(0)disk(0)rdisk(0)partition(1)\WINNT="NT Server [VGA mode]" /basevideo /sos
multi(0)disk(0)rdisk(1)partition(1)\WINNT="NT Server Parallel"
multi(0)disk(0)rdisk(1)partition(1)\WINNT="NT Server Parallel [VGA mode]" /basevideo /sos
```

Figure 10-15.　A BOOT.INI showing an entry for a parallel NT installation

▲ W is the partition number. All partitions receive a number except for type 5 (DOS Extended) and type 0 (not used) partitions. Primary partitions are numbered first and are followed by logical drives.

With the SCSI( ) controller designation it is based on the following syntax:

scsi(X)*disk*(Y)*rdisk*(Z)*partition*(W)\<WINNT_DIR>

where

▼ X is the ordinal number of the adapter as identified by the NTBOOTDD.SYS driver and starts at 0.

■ Y is the SCSI ID of the target disk.

■ Z is the SCSI logical unit number (LUN) of the target disk. This number is almost always 0 (zero).

▲ W is the partition number, which always starts with 1. All partitions receive a number except for type 5 (DOS Extended) and type 0 (not used) partitions. Primary partitions are numbered first and are followed by logical drives.

```
[Boot Loader]
Timeout=5
Default=SCSI(0)disk(0)rdisk(0)partition(1)\WINNT="primary drive"
[Operating Systems]
SCSI(0)disk(0)rdisk(0)partition(1)\WINNT="Primary NT Installation"
SCSI(1)disk(0)rdisk(0)partition(1)\WINNT="Parallel NT Installation"
```

Figure 10-16.　A BOOT.INI with SCSI drives that do not use the system BIOS

The SCSI syntax can also be used when mirroring SCSI drives. If the system is using a SCSI adapter and the primary boot drive of a mirror set fails or becomes inaccessible and the SCSI adapter BIOS does not load, the multi( ) identifier option may fail to locate the healthy mirrored drive. As a result, the BOOT.INI file on the fault-tolerant floppy disk may require the use of the SCSI designation to boot the remaining mirror drive. The other option is to remove the bad primary drive and change the SCSI ID of the second drive to the boot ID (typically 0).

Generally speaking, the easiest way to create a BOOT.INI for an NT boot floppy is to copy the existing BOOT.INI from the C drive and modify it as necessary. You can even create several copies of the BOOT.INI on a single floppy by naming them BOOT. MACHINE1, BOOT.MACHINE2, and so on. Simply go to an operational machine and rename the appropriate BOOT.INI file when needed.

All of the above tools are superb when it is necessary to recover from a boot sector or MBR failure. In fact, if you have the above diskettes, have run DiskSave, have an up-to-date ERD, and recent tape backup, you have fulfilled many of the basic requirements for NT data recovery. Unfortunately, sometimes NT does not boot at all. An errant driver or incorrectly loaded service pack may have damaged the NT installation, in which case an improper system file simply produces a BSOD every time the system boots. These issues are examined in the next section of this book.

SOLVING DRIVER, SERVICE PACK, AND SYSTEM FILE CORRUPTION PROBLEMS

Many administrators have at one time or another fallen prey to the "apply the latest driver or patch" syndrome, a syndrome that smart administrators quickly learn to avoid. For example, several unfortunate people installed Microsoft's Service Pack 2 for NT 4.0 with disastrous results. Administrators should follow the basic rule of service packs: Let 30 days pass after release before installing them, unless absolutely necessary!

The same rule holds true for software drivers. Sometimes drivers simply do not load and their associated services fail; other times they cause a Blue Screen of Death.

If a service does not start, make sure that all of the drivers necessary for the service have been loaded. An easy way to do this is to use the DRIVERS.EXE utility from the NT Resource Kit. Figure 10-17 shows this utility in action. The DRIVERS Resource Kit utility verifies that drivers were successfully loaded. To display the list of Kernel mode drivers that were loaded, type the following at a command prompt:

DRIVERS.EXE

Table 10-1 describes the DRIVERS.EXE output.

Drivers are loaded in many different phases of the NT system startup process. Their load sequence is based on their startup priority number. If a driver is not starting,

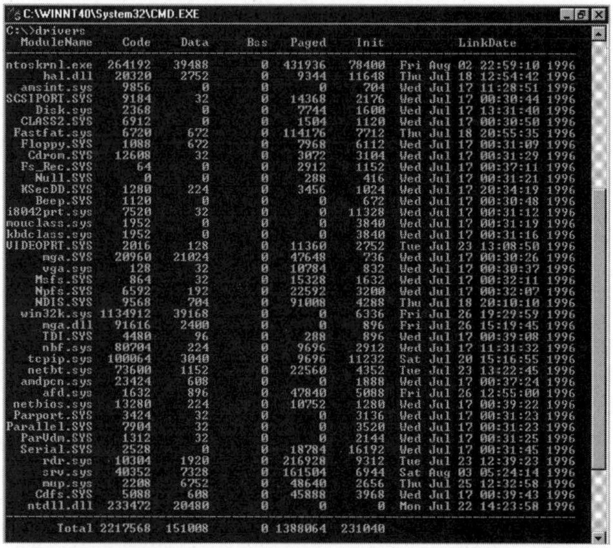

Figure 10-17. The DRIVERS.EXE utility

Module Name	Driver Name
Bss	
Code	Nonpaged code
Data	Static data (initialized)
Init	Data not used after initialization
LinkDate	Date that the driver was linked
Paged	

Table 10-1. DRIVERS.EXE Output Description

knowing when it is supposed to start can be helpful. The driver startup parameters can be examined and changed in the Registry or, more easily, in the Devices Control Panel applet. The startup priority numbers are as follows:

▼   **0 Boot**   Loaded by the NTLDR during the boot sequence.

■   **1 System**   Loaded at Kernel initialization (NTOSKRNL.EXE) during the load sequence.

■   **2 Automatic**   Loaded or started automatically at system startup.

■   **3 Manual**   Either the user or another process, including other drivers or dependent services, manually start the driver.

▲   **4 Disabled**   Driver will not start under any circumstances.

The first drivers (with a priority of 0) are loaded by NTLDR during the boot sequence. Then, during the load sequence, the Kernel attempts to initialize all drivers loaded by NTLDR, after which all drivers with a priority of 1 are loaded. The Session Manager then loads all drivers with a start value of 2. Device drivers with a start value of 3 are loaded as required by dependent services and applications as they are initializing. For more information on services and drivers and their dependencies, you can run the Windows NT Diagnostic Administrative Tool. The WINS Client Service Properties dialog box is shown in Figure 10-18.

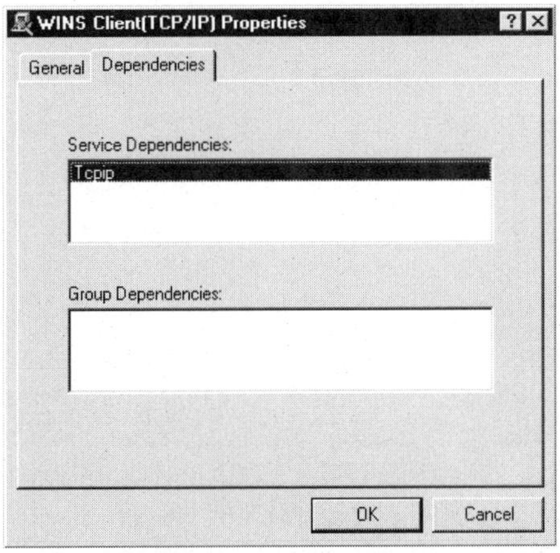

Figure 10-18.   Windows NT Diagnostics tool (WINMSD)

Recovering from a Blue Screen of Death

True story: An administrator is searching the Web and comes across a new driver for the trusty old Adaptec 2940. The administrator adds the driver and reboots only to see a blue screen of hex dumps, all of which seem to point to the new driver. The system is down and must be brought back. How can this be done?

Of course, the screen of hex dumps mentioned here is the industry standard Blue Screen of Death, or BSOD. A BSOD is very frustrating, but it supplies you with critical NT data. These basic debug screens can offer you information on the driver that caused the crash. The following example comes from Microsoft:

```
*** STOP: 0x0000001E (0x80000003,0x80106fc0,0x8025ea21,0xfd6829e8)
Unhandled Kernel exception c0000047 from fa8418b4 (8025ea21,fd6829e8)
Dll Base  Date Stamp -  Name                Dll Base  Date Stamp - Name
80100000  2be154c9  -   ntoskrnl.exe        80400000  2bc153b0  - hal.dll
80258000  2bd49628  -   ncrc710.sys         8025c000  2bd49688  - SCSIPORT.SYS
80267000  2bd49683  -   scsidisk.sys        802a6000  2bd496b9  - Fastfat.sys
fa800000  2bd49666  -   Floppy.SYS          fa810000  2bd496db  - Hpfs_Rec.SYS
fa820000  2bd49676  -   Null.SYS            fa830000  2bd4965a  - Beep.SYS
fa840000  2bdaab00  -   I8042prt.SYS        fa850000  2bd5a020  - SERMOUSE.SYS
fa860000  2bd4966f  -   kbdclass.SYS        fa870000  2bd49671  - MOUCLASS.SYS
fa880000  2bd9c0be  -   Videoprt.SYS        fa890000  2bd49638  - NCR77C22.SYS
fa8a0000  2bd4a4ce  -   Vga.SYS             fa8b0000  2bd496d0  - Msfs.SYS
fa8c0000  2bd496c3  -   Npfs.SYS            fa8e0000  2bd496c9  - Ntfs.SYS
fa940000  2bd496df  -   NDIS.SYS            fa930000  2bd49707  - wdlan.sys
fa970000  2bd49712  -   TDI.SYS             fa950000  2bd5a7fb  - nbf.sys
fa980000  2bd72406  -   streams.sys         fa9b0000  2bd4975f  - ubnb.sys
fa9c0000  2bd5bfd7  -   mcsxns.sys          fa9d0000  2bd4971d  - netbios.sys
fa9e0000  2bd49678  -   Parallel.sys        fa9f0000  2bd4969f  - serial.SYS
faa00000  2bd49739  -   mup.sys             faa40000  2bd4971f  - SMBTRSUP.SYS
faa10000  2bd6f2a2  -   srv.sys             faa50000  2bd4971a  - afd.sys
faa60000  2bd6fd80  - rdr.sys               faaa0000  2bd49735  - bowser.sys

Address  dword dump                 Dll Base - Name
801afc20 80106fc0 80106fc0 00000000 00000000 80149905 : fa840000 - i8042prt.SYS
801afc24 80149905 80149905 ff8e6b8c 80129c2c ff8e6b94 : 8025c000 - SCSIPORT.SYS
801afc2c 80129c2c 80129c2c ff8e6b94 00000000 ff8e6b94 : 80100000 - ntoskrnl.exe
801afc34 801240f2 80124f02 ff8e6df4 ff8e6f60 ff8e6c58 : 80100000 - ntoskrnl.exe
801afc54 80124f16 80124f16 ff8e6f60 ff8e6c3c 8015ac7e : 80100000 - ntoskrnl.exe
801afc64 8015ac7e 8015ac7e ff8e6df4 ff8e6f60 ff8e6c58 : 80100000 - ntoskrnl.exe
801afc70 80129bda 80129bda 00000000 80088000 80106fc0 : 80100000 - ntoskrnl.exe
```

How do you interpret the above message? Basically, this message offers a snapshot of all drivers that were loaded at the time of the crash. In the second line, you can see that the memory call that was invalid was located at fa8418b4. Examining the list of drivers, you can see that the closest memory space for a driver is the I8042PRT.SYS driver. Hence, I8042PRT.SYS is probably the driver that caused the crash. Other parts of the message are meaningful to engineers, but for the purpose of most NT administrators, identifying the errant driver is the key to the puzzle.

If NTOSKRNL.EXE (the NT operating system kernel) is identified as the errant "driver," little useful information can be obtained from the BSOD. In this case, a different set of problems and circumstances are at work and they affect a broader piece of the NT operating system. No operating system is truly 100 percent robust and crash-free. Quite simply, an NTOSKRNL.EXE Blue Screen of Death means that a system error has occurred and that the error has proven fatal to the integrity of the system. Writes to the hard drive may get corrupted and render the system unusable. These issues are related to "error trapping." A BSOD is an "untrappable error." This becomes important in understanding the stability of NT, which is discussed in the next section.

Maintaining NT Stability

When the computer industry touts the stability of NT, it's actually referring to NT's ability to handle errant applications. This is something NT is remarkable good at. An application running in NT that goes haywire usually does not affect the kernel or the system. NT is designed to isolate applications from the system level. As such, one application can go down without affecting all the other applications or the system itself.

When an application running in NT begins to experience trouble, one of two things can happen: the problem can be dealt with by the application using error trapping or the application itself can terminate. The specific event that occurs is related to the severity of the error. In other words, if the error is serious enough, the programmers of the application might decide not to trap the error because it could cause damage to a data file or a database. Due to the isolation of applications in NT (which is automatic for 32-bit applications and can be set for 16-bit ones), closing down an application usually has no deleterious effect on Windows NT or other applications running at the time.

However, if a problem affects the kernel itself (as happens if an attempt is made to write to privileged memory space), the entire NT system usually crashes and you see the classic Blue Screen of Death. The reasoning behind this crash is quite simple: kernel-level crashes are considered a cause of great instability, so the system is shut down to prevent damage to the system and all of its components. Serious system crashes can corrupt drivers and even cause cross-linked files. Shutdowns help avoid these types of problems.

FAT vs. NTFS for Repairing Corrupt Drivers and Cross-Linked Files

What if a problem occurs with corrupt drivers or cross-linked files? There are two schools of thought on this problem. One school says to make the system partition FAT so you can go into the Windows NT directory and replace the faulty files. The other school says to have an NTFS system partition with a second parallel install of NT in which to boot.

The FAT system partition idea seems okay on paper. In fact, the people at the Microsoft Support Center might even recommend it. However, you should put some thought into the FAT system partition idea before setting up your systems in this manner, because this type of setup is not optimal for several reasons. To start with, NTFS is far more secure than FAT. In fact, having FAT on a server is a violation of C2 level security. Likewise, FAT does not have the built-in fault tolerance that NTFS has. When was the last time you saw a FAT-based system run CHKDSK and fix files automatically on reboot or hot-fix the files on the fly? NTFS automatically makes a copy of the boot sector at the end of the partition (on NT 4.0 and later). NTFS also offers the ability to hot-fix sectors and maintain a recovery transaction log. In effect, NTFS can actually double-check itself on every pass. FAT does not provide hot fixing. If a sector corruption occurs in the FAT table, large sections of data could be lost. Throughout this book, the recommendation is to run NTFS on all volumes, including those used by databases for temporary files and transaction logs.

Solving Common Problems

By this time, it is obvious that the system is down with a fatal reboot situation. The Last Known Good configuration does not work because the driver or file has been replaced. First of all, if the system was a production server, the driver or service pack should not have been installed without serious testing. In fact, as mentioned above, the best first way to test a service pack is just to delay implementation for 30 days or so. However, if the driver or service pack was applied and the system crashed, all is not lost.

As part of any fault-tolerant NT setup, two copies of NT should be on the system. For simplicity, the first copy is called the "primary install" and the second the "parallel install." If finances afford, one of the best configurations is to have the primary copy of NT on the C drive, a parallel copy on the D drive, and all data on a third drive or RAID set. Of course, used here the term *drive* means just that—a physical drive (not a partition). In this way, if you apply fixes and patches to the primary set and the system does not boot, simply boot the parallel NT installation and replace the files that were changed.

Following are a few common problems and how to solve them.

A Service Pack Problem

When Service Pack 3 for NT 4.0 was released, some attempts to run it across networks resulted in corrupt system files (this corruption was caused by checksum mismatches). Administrators had no idea that this was happening until they did a system reboot and saw the dreaded "corrupted system file" message. Needless to say, the data on such a system is no longer accessible. If this happens, simply boot to the parallel installation and replace the corrupt files one by one. You may have to reboot several times until all of the corrupt files are replaced. However, with this technique the entire installation can be repaired in a few minutes.

A Hardware Driver Problem

You decide that you need a new network card, you purchase the latest card, and you discover that it is not on the Microsoft Hardware Compatibility List (HCL). However, because you own the business, you decide that you are beyond IS control, so away goes the old card and in goes the new. You reboot and the system crashes with a KMODE_ Exception_Not_Handled message and a hex dump. You now have two choices: fix the problem yourself or suffer the indignity of calling in a consultant or the IS department. The Last Known Good configuration is unlikely to work on a network card driver, but it is certainly worthwhile trying.

> **NOTE:** If the driver actually loads *before* you are presented with the option of Last Known Good, this will not work.

How should this problem be approached? Fixing any system requires a very logical set of deductions and attempted fixes. In this case, it seems logical that the network driver is the culprit. Hopefully, this is information that you can obtain from the BSOD, as described earlier in this chapter.

To verify this, load NT but use the [VGA Mode] choice in the boot loader (/basevideo /SOS). The /SOS switch runs the startup in verbose mode and shows each driver as it loads. You should see the driver that caused the crash (hopefully, the new network card driver). If this is the case, power off the system and remove the new card. In most cases, a driver does not load if the card is not present. You should now be able to boot and replace the new card with the old. This usually works, but if it does not work, you need to go to a second installation of NT and manually remove the driver or do a tape restore of the older NT directory (make sure you have the correct registry!).

Corrupt Sectors

Suppose someone calls and says that a message has appeared on the server screen. The message states that there was a problem flushing the cache to the hard drive and that files may be corrupt or the drive may have corrupted sectors. A message like this is truly very dangerous because it is important to figure out why the message occurred. In general, these types of messages occur when some type of hardware failure has occurred. Assume that the hard drive is starting to fail. If the drive is part of a RAID 5 set, the system should be able to recover from the failure. With luck, your hardware RAID set simply places the drive offline and regenerates the set with a hot spare.

In a worst-case scenario, what are your options? You can go to a command prompt and schedule that drive to have CHKDSK /F /R run on it. Most likely, you are told that it is impossible for the drive to be locked for exclusive use and that the drive will be fixed on the next reboot. Before you reboot, make a backup of the drive. If the backup fails because of excessive errors, the hard drive is indeed damaged. Hopefully, you will be able to do the backup or you have a recent backup to restore from. Your options are CHKDSK /F /R, as stated above, or to use a SCSI controller BIOS application such as verify to rebuild the drive. Many times, salvaging a drive is doomed to fail (see the final section of this chapter).

Intermittent BSODs

In this scenario, everything seems to work fine, except once every few days or so the machine crashes for no apparent reason. You check out the BSOD and can gather little information from it. The only thing left to do is examine the memory dump from the crash. However, crash dumps can be unwieldy and typically yield very little useful information to administrators. The DUMPEXAM utility can be used for this purpose because it might tell you the component or application that caused the error. However, your best bet for making sense of this information is to send it to Microsoft for analysis.

To set up your system so that it dumps its memory contents in the event of a crash, the following conditions must be met:

1. Debugging must be enabled in the Control Panel System applet. To enable debugging, select the Startup/Shutdown tab and check the Write Debugging Information To box. Specify the name of a file in which to save the dump information. The default is %SYSTEMROOT%\MEMORY.DMP, as shown in Figure 10-19.

2. The paging file on the system drive must be at least 12MB larger than the physical RAM.

For DUMPEXAM to work properly, you need to copy the following from the SUPPRT\DEBUG\PLATFORM directory on the NT CD: DUMPEXAM.EXE, IMAGEHLP.DLL, and either KDEXTX86.DLL (if you are running an Intel-based machine) or KDEXTALP.DLL (if you are running an Alpha). You also must install the symbol files associated with the build and service pack of NT that you are running. The symbol files replace the debug code that runs on the checked versions of NT that are used to debug the system. Checked files cause NT to run very slowly and are not applicable to active servers or workstations. The symbol files are used in the following DUMPEXAM syntax (which is run at the command line):

DUMPEXAM –Y D:\SYMBOLS D:\WINNT\MEMORY.DMP –F
D:\SYMBOLS\MEMORY.TXT

The above is translated as "run DUMPEXAM." The location of the symbol files (-y switch) is D:\SYMBOLS and the location of the MEMORY.DMP file is in D:\WINNT. Write the debugged file to D:\SYMBOLS\MEMORY.TXT (-f switch).

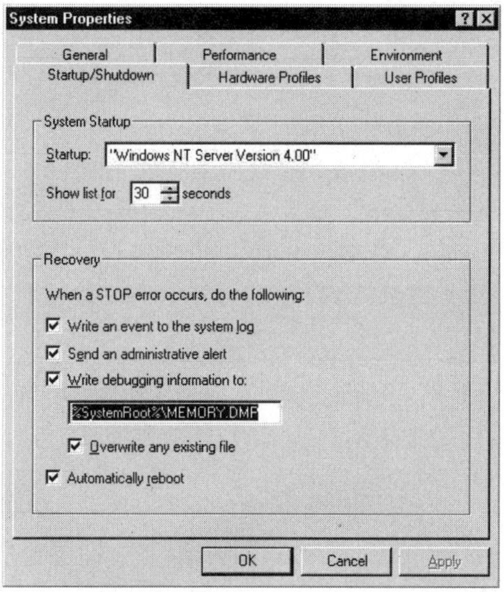

Figure 10-19. The Debug file location

The output of DUMPEXAM is very straightforward. Following is an example header:

```
****************************************************************
**
** Windows NT Crash Dump Analysis
**
****************************************************************
*
Filename . . . . . . .D:\winnt\memory.dmp
Signature. . . . . . .PAGE
ValidDump. . . . . . .DUMP
MajorVersion . . . . .free system
MinorVersion . . . . .1381
DirectoryTableBase . .0x00030000
PfnDataBase. . . . . .0x83f9f000
PsLoadedModuleList . .0x8014ce10
PsActiveProcessHead. .0x8014cd08
MachineImageType . . .i386
NumberProcessors . . .1
BugCheckCode . . . . .0x00000077
BugCheckParameter1 . .0x00000103
```

BugCheckParameter2 . .0xc000009d
BugCheckParameter3 . .0x00000001
BugCheckParameter4 . .0x0005b000
ExceptionCode. 0x80000003
ExceptionFlags 0x00000001
ExceptionAddress . . .0x801237f9

If you examine the stack trace, you will be shown a screen that is probably not meaningful to you but does show you the line in which the system trap occurred:

```
****************************************************************
** Stack Trace
****************************************************************
*

ChildEBP RetAddr  Args to Child
f904befc 80122f5f c03e323c c03e323c 00000001
MiMakeOutswappedPageResident+0x27b (FPO: [0,0,0])
f904bf2c 8013a1d4 80697dc0 00000000 00000000 MmInPageKernelStack+0xf5
(FPO: [0,0,0])
f904bf3c 8013a19d 00000000 00000000 00000000 KiInSwapKernelStacks+0x2c
(FPO: [0,0,0])
f904bf4c 8013471a 00000000 00000000 00000000 KeSwapProcessOrStack+0x97
(FPO: [0,0,0])
f904bf7c 8013f9ca 8013a106 00000000 00000000 PspSystemThreadStartup+
0x54 (FPO: [0,0,0])
f904befc 80122f5f c03e323c c03e323c 00000001 KiThreadStartup+0x16
f904bf2c 8013a1d4 80697dc0 00000000 00000000 MmInPageKernelStack+0xf5
(FPO: [0,0,0])
f904bf3c 8013a19d 00000000 00000000 00000000 KiInSwapKernelStacks+0x2c
(FPO: [0,0,0])
f904bf4c 8013471a 00000000 00000000 00000000 KeSwapProcessOrStack+0x97
(FPO: [0,0,0])
f904bf7c 8013f9ca 8013a106 00000000 00000000 PspSystemThreadStartup+
0x54 (FPO: [0,0,0])
000003e0 00000000 00000000 00000000 00000000 KiThreadStartup+0x16
   801237A9: AE              scas    byte ptr es:[edi]
   801237AA: 01 74 0C 8D     add     dword ptr [esp+ecx-73h],esi
   801237AE: 45              inc     ebp
   801237AF: A8 50           test    al,50h
   801237B1: FF 75 B4        push    dword ptr [ebp-4Ch]
   801237B4: E8 61 A1 FF FF  call    MiMakeOutswappedPageResident+237h
   801237B9: 39 5D F8        cmp     dword ptr [ebp-8],ebx
   801237BC: 7C 05           jl      MiMakeOutswappedPageResident+245h
   801237BE: 39 5D D         cmp     dword ptr [ebp-2Ch],ebx
```

```
801237C1: 7D 36                     jge   MiMakeOutswappedPageResident+27Bh
801237C3: 81 7D D4 9A 00 00  cmp dword ptr [ebp-2Ch],offset
MiMakeOutswappedPageResident+248h       C0
801237CA: 75 1A                     jne MiMakeOutswappedPageResident+268h
801237CC: 83 7D EC 14               cmp   word ptr [ebp-14h],14h
801237D0: 73 14                     jae   MiMakeOutswappedPageResident+268h
801237D2: 68 38 7F 14 80            push offset
MiMakeOutswappedPageResident+255h
801237D7: 53                        push   ebx
801237D8: 53                        push   ebx
801237D9: E8 CA 1F FF FF            call     MiMakeOutswappedPageResident+
                                            25Ch
801237DE: 89 5D E0                  mov    dword ptr [ebp-20h],ebx
801237E1: FF 45 EC                  inc    dword ptr [ebp-14h]
801237E4: EB 87                     jmp    MiMakeOutswappedPageResident+
                                            1EFh
801237E6: FF 75 CC                  push   dword ptr [ebp-34h]
801237E9: FF 75 F0                  push   dword ptr [ebp-10h]
801237EC: FF 75 D4                  push   dword ptr [ebp-2Ch]
801237EF: FF 75 F8                  push   dword ptr [ebp-8]
801237F2: 6A 77                     push   77h
801237F4: E8 B9 14 FF FF            call
MiMakeOutswappedPageResident+277h
--->801237F9: FF 15 84 0B 14 80  call      dword ptr
[MiMakeOutswappedPageResident+27Dh]
801237FF: FF 75 FC                  push   dword ptr [ebp-4]
80123802: E8 C5 83 00 00            call     MiMakeOutswappedPageResident+
                                            285h
80123807: 8B 45 F4                  mov    eax,dword ptr [ebp-0Ch]
8012380A: 8B 4D 08                  mov    ecx,dword ptr [ebp+8]
8012380D: C7 40 10 80 00 00         mov    dword ptr [eax+10h],offset
MiMakeOutswappedPageResident+292h
      00
80123814: E8 53 75 00 00            call     MiMakeOutswappedPageResident+
                                            297h
80123819: 8B CE                     mov    ecx,esi
8012381B: C1 E1 0C                  shl    ecx,0Ch
8012381E: 0B C1                     or     eax,ecx
80123820: 8B 4D F4                  mov    ecx,dword ptr [ebp-0Ch]
80123823: 0B 05 F0 7F 14 80         or     eax,dword ptr
[MiMakeOutswappedPageResident+2A7h]
80123829: 80 49 0C 01               or       byte ptr [ecx+0Ch],1
8012382D: 89 45 FC                  mov    dword ptr [ebp-4],eax
```

```
80123830: 80 4D FC 40          or     byte ptr [ebp-4],40h
80123834: A1 C0 81 14 80       mov
eax,[MiMakeOutswappedPageResident+2B7h]
80123839: 23 45 10             and    eax,dword ptr [ebp+10h]
8012383C: C1 E0 08             shl    eax,8
8012383F: 33 45 FC             xor    eax,dword ptr [ebp-4]
80123842: 25 00 01 00 00       and    eax,offset
MiMakeOutswappedPageResident+2C5h
80123847: 31h
80123848: 45                   inc    ebp
```

So how do you make sense of this data? Move through the data until you find the arrow. The line that is marked with the arrow "--->" is the line that was running when the trap occurred. In this case the error was at the following line:

```
--->801237F9: FF 15 84 0B 14 80     call     dword ptr
[MiMakeOutswappedPageResident+27Dh]
```

In the proper circumstances, this information is invaluable for determining the cause of the crash.

RAID FAILURES

Assumptions are made all the time concerning RAID and its robust and stable nature. However, as was shown in Chapter 3, RAID statistically increases the chance of a server hard drive failure. The more drives a system has, the greater the likelihood of a hard drive failure. The power behind RAID comes from the fact that a drive failure is expected and compensated for. Most system professionals suggest and highly recommend using hardware RAID. Unfortunately, both software and hardware RAID can fail.

Recovering from Software RAID Failures

RAID can be a powerful complement to the fault tolerance of an NT system. Unfortunately, RAID also comes with significant overhead. In software RAID, the operating system maintains this overhead. To understand this overhead better, consider the fact that when a process intends to write to a disk with software RAID, a software driver (shunt) intercepts the write. The shunt, which takes processing time from the CPU, then writes the information to the necessary drives, usually more than one.

Is this bad? The answer is obvious. Any processing that can be removed from the CPU speeds up overall system performance, results in less overhead to the OS, and causes far fewer problems. Software RAID problems can be severe or minor, but all require a serious work-through. The major problems are discussed here.

Software RAID Problems

To repair most software RAID problems, the RAID set must be regenerated. Doing so requires gaining exclusive control of the hardware, which is not always an easy task to accomplish if the server is a production machine. The most common problem you encounter when trying to repair a software RAID 5 set is the inability to lock the drive for exclusive use by Disk Administrator. If this happens, check to see if some applications are currently accessing the drive (Explorer, File Manger, or Command Prompt, for example). If so, close them and try again. Sometimes parts of applications or even DLLs can be open. Check for the following:

▼ A DLL file was loaded and is still open.

■ A data file is open in an application.

▲ A paging file is on the volume.

NOTE: Never place an NT page file on a software-generated RAID 5 set. The parity writes slow down the page file significantly.

RAID 5—STRIPE SET WITH PARITY   It should by now seem obvious that using a software RAID 5 array in Windows NT is far from ideal. You must plan carefully how to use it and what files are placed on the volume set.

If a software stripe set with parity fails on your NT server, replace the drive in question and regenerate the set using Disk Administrator. If the drive appears fine, be sure to delete its partition information before you run regenerate to prevent corruption problems.

MIRRORED AND DUPLEXED SETS   Repairing mirrored drives is far easier. In an ideal world, when drive 1 fails, drive 2 immediately takes over. This is the case with hardware RAID 1 but not necessarily with software RAID 1 because the MBR and Boot Record might not have been copied to the mirrored or shadow drive. A failure to switch drives immediately is not really a problem if you have planned ahead and have prepared a proper NT boot floppy with the correct BOOT.INI on it. Basically, the BOOT.INI on the boot floppy needs to point to the operational drive. See the BOOT.INI section of this chapter for more information.

To replace the mirror, you must first break it by using the Disk Administrator tool. Then replace the defective drive. When the machine reboots, simply reestablish the mirror and you will be back to the fault-tolerant state.

NOTE: When using fault-tolerant software configurations, try to use the same components. For example, never use different types of drives on a mirrored set. Likewise, use SCSI rather than EIDE drives. The money you might save with EIDE is often offset quickly by NT's compatibility with SCSI systems. If duplexing rather than mirroring is to be implemented on the system, be sure to use the same controllers.

Recovering from Hardware Raid Failures

Hardware RAID is the best choice for a RAID configuration, assuming it falls within the IS budget. Hardware RAID unloads RAID overhead onto the RAID controller and is far more stable than software RAID arrays.

It is generally assumed that hardware RAID does not present many problems. Indeed, this is normally the case. Like software RAID, hardware RAID assumes that the drives fail one at a time and that sufficient regeneration times will be available between failures. (It boils down to this: if two drives fail, it is back to restoring from tape.)

Hardware RAID on the newer controllers does allow you to have hot spares set in standby mode. If one drive goes down, the hot spare automatically goes online, which can make the regeneration almost automatic and of short duration. Remember, however, that there is a serious impact on system performance during a regeneration.

Another nice feature of the newer controllers is that cache can be placed on the controller to overcome the parity overhead on a RAID 5 set. These benefits are significant, but it must be understood that hardware RAID does have liabilities as well. Most limitations of hardware RAID can be overcome by reading the RAID hardware manuals. In particular, double-check the manual before you replace a RAID drive and regenerate the set. The order of events is different for most manufacturers and can cause disastrous results if not followed properly. In some sets, including the high-end RAID configurations available from Compaq, the process is automatic. All you do is replace the drive and the firmware does the rest. Obviously, cutting costs on RAID sets is not always cost-beneficial in the long run.

In some types of hardware RAID controllers, if a drive goes offline you should not set it online without regenerating the set. If the other drives had storage activity while the offline drive sat there unused, then the RAID set can become corrupted when the drive is returned. You have to synchronize the drive set. Again, be sure to read the drive replacement procedure for the specific manufacturer.

Of great importance is the question of why the drive went offline. Several factors can contribute to this state. First of all, drives can get too hot and shut down. If five drives are placed in a small enclosure without adequate ventilation and cooling (we have seen it), it is not uncommon for one of them to go offline from time to time. In the case of powerful servers like the Digital AlphaServers, the entire machine is a well-engineered cooling box. If the sides are removed, the drives can actually overheat!

Timing issues can also contribute to the problem. You can encounter SCSI bus time-out issues on the bus due to improper termination or internal cabling problems such as cable touching a case (see the following section of this chapter, which concerns incidental hardware failures). For RAID to work properly, the hardware has to be ideal.

It also is essential for fault-tolerant RAID to use the same hard drives. Purchasing spares up front when you purchase RAID hardware can save valuable replacement time as well as avoid hardware incompatibilities down the road. Planning ahead is essential. If you cannot find identical hard drives for replacement, you may need to buy new hard drives and rebuild the set completely. Not being able to purchase identical hard drives is a strong argument for purchasing NT server equipment from a first-tier computer company such as HP, Compaq, Digital, and IBM. These companies typically have identical drives in inventory and so can guarantee compatibility.

Finally, be sure to monitor all RAID arrays, including drive status and up times. All of the tier-one systems mentioned above offer monitoring through agents within NT. Monitoring is one of the most important and overlooked aspects of RAID on NT. It is important to know if a drive has failed and that a hot spare was activated. Remember that if two drives go offline in RAID 5, all data is lost. Finally, always regenerate RAID member drives as soon as possible to maintain the fault tolerance of the system.

AVOIDING INCIDENTAL HARDWARE FAILURES

An incidental hardware failure is simply one that is not normally thought of as significant. These are the circumstances that occur which make no sense whatsoever. These failures range from vibrations to heat problems to cable issues. They cause a variety of symptoms: NT may spontaneously reboot, a drive may simply go offline, or a drive may suddenly become inaccessible. Here are some pointers to avoid these types of failures.

Vibration Issues

Computers are generally considered passive systems that operate as intended. Such might be the case with the high-end servers that you buy from tier-one vendors, but even these normally robust systems can crash for no apparent reason. One of the major causes of this type of problem is vibration, which causes components to move within the case.

Vibrations can be caused by spinning hardware within the case. Power supply fans, cooling fans, and disks drives top the list of culprits. Drives can be particularly bad. Many new drives run at 7200 or 10000rpm and can cause serious vibration inside a case. In such instances, option cards and cables can come loose and make the system act as if the hard drive or some other component were failing.

In many clone systems, cable runs in nightmare configurations and can be dislodged easily by vibrations. If your budget demands building or purchasing clone systems, always allow plenty of space for drives and cables and make certain that the drives are in fact mounted properly. Each drive should be secured in a mounting bracket with all four screws intact.

Other Cable Issues

It is interesting to see where IS people try to pinch pennies. SCSI cables have got to be at the top of the list. Most vendors tell users that all SCSI cables are the same, but that is absolutely untrue. For example, Adaptec discovered that the 1542cf cables had to be made to exacting specifications. Time and time again, systems succumb to bad writes that corrupt data over inferior cabling. This problem is easy to fix but can be very frustrating until proper cables are used. Be sure to buy only quality internal cables.

Another problem with cables is that they can short out against a case or onto an option card. This problem can be particularly bad if the system experiences a great deal of vibration. These types of problems are easy to resolve. Simply use the proper cabling and the proper cable lengths.

Power Surge Issues

When most networks are put together, there is a discussion about protecting the system from a lightning strike or other power problem, but, typically, no serious attempt is made to deal with all of the culprits in such events. One of the most exposed aspects of any network is a phone line. A destroyed modem is not too bad a problem, but, as is discussed in Chapter 9, a lightning spike to a phone line can destroy hard drives and even complete systems as easily as a spike through a power connection. Short of a tape backup, recovering from a power surge is impossible. Be sure to protect phone lines and hubs, switches, and routers. A power surge at any of these points can lead to serious system problems and data loss.

Bus Issues

The typical bus issue is a poorly seated card. It is interesting to note that very few written standards on the height of an option card are available. When a card that is slightly off is screwed into a slot, it can tilt and short out the bus, with the result being a myriad of system problems, from intermittent crashes to complete failure. Be sure that the cards are inserted and screwed in at a 90-degree angle to the bus slots.

Several other problems are related to buses. For instance, consider what happens when an option card is added to a system. When the system goes to boot, nothing happens. After a card being inserted improperly, the next most common cause of a boot failure is dirt. Simply moving a PC or opening a case can cause dirt to short out bus connections.

Cleanliness around servers is an extremely important issue. Normally, servers are left in one place for long periods of time. The longer they sit, the more dust particles build up inside. Always try to maintain a clean environment in and around critical servers. At some data centers, server down time can cost thousands of dollars. A clean server room is well worth the cost. Managers of high-end data centers often mount pressurizing fans inside the data center so that there is always a negative airflow (that is to say, when a person opens the data center door, the air flows out and not in).

SIMMs Issues

The usual problem with SIMMs can be summed up this way: Do not attempt to mix unmatched SIMMs in NT systems. Microsoft has documented many instances of mismatched SIMMs that cause Blue Screens of Death. SIMMs as the cause of BSODs can be particularly difficult to detect if the BSODs occur intermittently. Sometimes mismatched SIMMs actually cause NT to operate more slowly. In addition, make certain that the system cache and motherboard can handle new memory. SIMMs are a common cause of BSODs. If you have tried everything else to stop a BSOD, replace the SIMMs and see if the problem goes away.

Heat Issues

One way to cause problems to a computer system is to expose it to excessive heat. Generally speaking, the first-tier system manufacturers take heat into consideration when they specify drives for specific computer enclosures. The Digital AlphaServer mentioned earlier this chapter is a study in heat control. These machines use extremely high-speed, high-end (and hot) drives. As mentioned, simply running the systems with one side off can cause the drives to overheat and go offline.

In the clone world, however, there is a decided lack of heat consideration. It is not unusual to see RAID systems built out of standard computer cases. Four or five high-speed drives can quickly overcome a standard cooling fan. Eventually, these drives fall offline. The culprit is most likely heat. Adequate cooling must be provided for large systems. The ultimate price is the loss of hard drives or other components.

WHAT TO DO ABOUT IRRECOVERABLE CRASHES

Sometimes a failed drive or failed NT system absolutely cannot be repaired by "normal" means, even after calling Microsoft. What is the next step? Can you still recover the data? The answer is that all is not lost if the data is worth the expense of recovering it.

Destroyed drives can be sent to a data reclamation and recovery center. These centers, which do their work in a clean room environment, can do amazing operations on disk drives to recover impressive amounts of data. The technicians are professionals at recovering data drives damaged by water, file corruption, mechanical and electrical failure, virus attacks, system malfunctions, accidental erasure and/or formatting, smoke damage, and even burned or dropped drives. Most of the centers can work on a variety of media from hard drives to optical disks to floppies.

However, the process can be somewhat expensive and prices generally start in the $600 to $1200 range. Some large RAID-arrayed drives may be prohibitively expensive, costing up to tens of thousands of dollars, but if the data is important the expense is often worth paying.

NOTE: If you are interested in a reclamation cost estimate, most companies offer an evaluation in the $100 to $200 range, plus shipping. In addition, many companies charge only the evaluation fee if no data can be recovered.

CAUTION: Several low-end shops claim to be able to recover high percentages of data. Sent to one of these places, a drive could end up worse than before. Always check a company's references. Two of the better-known companies are DriveSavers (*http://www.drivesavers.com*) and OnTrack Data (*http://www.ontrack.com*). Chapter 11 has some interesting real-world examples that were obtained from the folks at DriveSavers.

In the case of catastrophic damage to an entire building, it is sometimes necessary to bring in electronic salvage experts to recover equipment and even data. For instance, if a fire occurs in your facility, you have to contend with heat damage, water damage, and soot damage among other things. People who have seen the inside of a piece of computer equipment after a fire understand that the soot damage can be as bad as heat damage, in terms of equipment loss. There are companies like RestorTek (**http://www.restortek.com**) that will come to a site and dismantle and clean every piece of your equipment. They use special brushes, dryers, and solvents to restore electronic equipment. Of course, cost consideration will determine if this is the right process for you.

SUMMARY

This chapter examined some of the major retrieval methodologies for recovering data from a downed NT system. Sometimes you can recover the entire system and other times you can simply recover the data from the disks. Fixes range from the simple (Last Known Good) to the complex (DiskProbe) to the expensive (data reclamation centers). We hope that the techniques discussed in this chapter and in this book will enable you to avoid such unnecessary expenses and system downtime. Always think prevention and err on the side of caution. That way, you make these techniques unnecessary on your NT network systems.

CHAPTER 11

Real-World Examples

It is instructive to look at some examples of how fault tolerance and disaster recovery techniques are being implemented in companies in the real world. This chapter is a conglomeration of such examples. It includes some desktop examples, some server examples, and some examples of entire enterprise plans. It starts out with examples of what not to do and offers explanations. The next section concentrates on using the clustering solutions examined in Chapter 5 to implement fault tolerance on a network. Finally, a variety of enterprise-size examples are considered. These include examples of entire data centers being replicated for complete redundancy.

WHAT NOT TO DO

The following anecdotes illustrate how things can go bad in the worst way. You can make plans and document what needs to be done, but users don't have to pay attention to what you suggest. Sometimes you can solve problems and sometimes you can't. These first few situations may seem like mundane issues, but each one provides an understanding of how small problems can escalate. The problems reflect what not to do rather than what to do and can really be applied to larger server systems. Understanding the seriousness of a small problem helps understand the issues with very large and dramatic problems.

Not Having Adequate Documentation and Having No Protection at All

An associate dean needed her home machine fixed. There was a power surge in her house and the machine would not boot because it presumably had lost all BIOS settings. After setting up the machine, we noticed that it was an older 486/33 with 8MB of RAM and, indeed, no hard drive listed in BIOS. The machine had no autodetect utility in BIOS, so we had to open the machine and find out what drive was in it and how it was configured. While this was not a hassle, it did take about 15 minutes to identify the drive and determine its parameters. We booted the machine and realized there was no operating system present. We booted to a DOS floppy and had no problem reading the C: drive. At this time, we knew that there was a problem with the boot files. We tried to run FDISK and were informed that the file was bad. When we asked what operating system was on the system, we were informed it was Windows. We booted to a DOS floppy and ran SYS.COM from the floppy. The system would now boot fine. Then the fun began. The system was not running Windows at all, but was actually running Windows 95.

We asked for the 95 installation CD and it was an upgrade. We created a Windows 95 boot floppy and made certain that the AUTOEXEC.BAT and CONFIG.SYS files had the real-time CD-ROM drivers listed. We then booted the system and ran the upgrade and all was well. The time-consuming solution to the problem was in determining the issue and making boot disks on other machines. In reality, the total time to get the system to what we considered an ideal state (which included running SCANDISK and DEFRAG) took about three hours. What are the lessons from this experience?

1. No documentation came with the system. We had no idea what was running on either the system or the hardware parameters available for the hard drive.

2. The person who asked us to fix the system was a user who was not concerned with the intricacies of the system. She used her computer for writing grant proposals and the only screen she ever looked at was WordPerfect for Windows.

3. The power surge had not only caused BIOS settings to be lost, but also blew away the boot sector.

4. We did not have the necessary tools to easily diagnose and fix the problem.

If the system had the necessary information and had been on a decent UPS, probably no problems would ever have developed. You can argue that this example is an isolated event but, in fact, we have seen the same types of problems occur on network workstations. Every time the crisis would happen, we were working on something else and, depending upon the issue's severity, might not be able to fix the problem immediately. In any event, such problems are inexcusable in any enterprise environment. Documentation and recent backups are essential. The dean could easily have lost all her grant proposals and correspondence. A system call can never be called unimportant.

Thinking You Are Protected, but Surprise!

After our success with the dean's machine, we were called to look at a machine in a professor's office. Surprisingly, the problem seemed to be exactly the same as the dean's. We booted to a Windows 95 floppy and tried to read the C: drive. The drive was not available, although another partition on the drive could easily be read. We ran FDISK /MBR to see if the problem was a bootstrap issue. This did not help. Finally, we simply booted the system and, amazingly, the drive was available. The professor was happy and we left after spending less than five minutes in the office. We agreed to examine the drive in more detail in the morning.

We arrived at the office early in the morning only to find that the C: drive possessed an unknown operating system (according to BIOS) and would not boot or be read. The message on the screen was ominous—"media failure on drive C." By turning the system off and on a few times, we could boot to a floppy and partially read the hard drive, but sooner or later the problem reading the drive would appear. It was apparent that the drive was failing. Immediately, we asked if there was a backup of all critical files. We were handed ten ZIP disks—all unlabeled. When asked what was on the disks, the professor told us that he had no idea but they represented copied files that were considered important. Then came the significant issue; he had last copied files three weeks earlier and had no idea if a copy of critical grants and papers had been made. To make matters even worse, some of his graduate students also used the computer.

As we left his office wishing him great luck, we told him of his options: Try to do a cold boot of the system and copy files before the drive got hot. Take the ZIP disks to another computer to see if all necessary files were hidden somewhere on the disks. Finally, we told him that he could send the drive to one of the reclamation centers, have the files removed, and have the files copied off the drive (probably a $500 minimum charge).

What problems are evident here?

1. No realistic backup of files or operating system was available. Imagine the time required to install an operating system and all programs, then find and restore all files (if they were present). The project would probably have taken all day.

2. Critical files, including some essential for career development, were placed upon an entirely nonsecure, non-fault-tolerant system.

A Near-Total Disaster

A small business in Mobile, Alabama (Southern Chemical Formulators) maintains all its data, including accounting and sales/inventory, on a Novell 3.12 server. Because of money constraints, the system was built of old parts—but, hey, it worked fine so don't mess with it. Two and a half years ago, we got a panic call from them. The server was down. After listening to the message, we realized that a serious problem had indeed occurred. The drive was mirrored and should have recovered on reboot. Either a power surge had occurred or something had killed both drives. We rebuilt the system and were able to easily restore everything because backups were done routinely. Everybody involved was pleased at the outcome.

About six months later, we were called in to look at their database. The company file seemed to have vanished. It turned out that an employee had run a utility to check the integrity of the database and had accidentally deleted the company ID file. Sometime that same day, the network supervisor had run PURGE /ALL, so salvage would not work. We decided to simply use the tapes and restore the file (it took us awhile to determine which file it was). The tapes were no good. Apparently, the heads of the tape were corroded and this was destroying tapes. Finally, we found a valid tape and were able to restore all the information.

In order to prevent such problems from happening again, we added another measure of redundancy to the system. The owner had just gotten a Pentium notebook. We installed a stand-alone copy of the application on the notebook to be used in an emergency situation. At the end of the day, a simple batch file was run and all files copied to the notebook. We told the owner to take the notebook home in the evening. In addition, another tape drive was placed on the network and the entire server backed up every night. The owner was also told to take the tape home with him. Assuming all was done as requested, the network was safe and actually reasonably protected, given the fact that all would have to be reconstructed.

A year ago in December, we got a message that one hopes to never hear: "The plant had burned down." We immediately rushed to the facility and the firefighters were still working on the blaze. Thank God for the remote storage. Actually though, it turned out that the tapes and notebook were left in the building. There was no backup. Fortunately, someone had the foresight to save the server and one workstation along with the old Proteon hub and cables. Over the weekend, we were able to rebuild their network (and throw away the Proteon hubs and cables). Their data were intact, and today the company is thriving and obeying the rules of system backup. They were indeed very lucky because without their database, the company would have gone out of business.

What can be learned here?

1. If a company is small enough, you can establish a fault tolerance strategy that is reasonable and inexpensive.

2. Test your tapes. They might not work when you need to do a restore.

3. Always have off-site storage that is accessible and up-to-date.

4. Expect and prepare for the worst.

SPECIFIC EXAMPLES OF FAULT TOLERANCE USING CLUSTERING SYSTEMS

Although clustering on the PC is new, there is considerable evidence that clustering is indeed being used successfully. The solutions listed here range from inexpensive to massively parallel.

Octopus

Octopus can be easily used as a primary replication. Two different uses of the product are listed here.

Countrywide Home Loans

Countywide Home Loans, based in Pasadena, CA, is one of the primary users of Octopus. This company has been around since the late 1960s and has been instrumental in providing the assets necessary for home buying by providing nationwide home loans. Countrywide relies on a WAN that connects local offices to 50 servers running Microsoft's SQL Server on Compaq ProLiant servers.

The company decided that it could withstand a maximum of two hours downtime on any server before the time became intolerable. This is an interesting criterion because Countrywide estimated that downtime costs would be, at a minimum, $100,000 per hour. The important issue, though, is that a policy had been established. Through an investigation of the network (based on affected users and supported applications), 11 machines were identified as critical. These 11 machines were prepared with RAID 5 drive volumes and Octopus data mirroring. It turned out that Octopus met the company's design criteria. The software was easy to install and, in the event of a primary failure, could be up and running again within 15 minutes. This was considered ideal for the company.

With Octopus installed on the critical servers, high availability was easily achieved. When a mirrored server went down, users could log into the backup servers within 15 minutes. This boot was well within the company policy of two hours acceptable downtime. Since this design was finalized, Countrywide has not had any major detrimental downtimes.

U.S. Web

Ian Chronister, Manager of Network Operations for U.S. Web, has instituted Octopus differently than the example provided with Countrywide Home Loans. He decided to do a manual reboot rather than use any type of automatic switchover routine. All machines are HP NetServers that are ideally suited for remote control and management. The SQL database and associated databases are replicated to a local second machine. If the primary server goes down, a message is sent to Ian and he responds accordingly. If he is off-site and has access to his notebook, Ian uses PCAnywhere to connect to the servers and rename the secondary machine to the same name as the primary. He also resets the IP address to the same as the primary. The secondary recovery machine is then rebooted. If Ian does not have access to a computer, a message is sent to his beeper and he simply calls the company. He lists specific instructions that allow anyone to easily implement the necessary changes. In any event, the total switchover time is minimal. The current setup is being switched over to Microsoft's Cluster Server with Octopus replicating the server. The basic approach being chosen is to use Cluster Server for failover capability and Octopus to mirror the important databases. Clearly, this is an example of genetic determinants of sound and well developed fault-tolerant designs.

Vinca

The Vinca Corporation has a number of large and serious clients worldwide for their cluster/server mirroring products. We will only deal with a few of these clients. This information was edited based on information supplied by Vinca and is used here with permission.

Sumitomo Bank Capital Markets

For the second largest bank in the world, data accessibility is critical. Sumitomo Bank Capital Markets, Inc., is the U.S. subsidiary of The Sumitomo Bank, Limited of Tokyo, Japan. It is the first commercial bank to begin trading rate swaps on a portfolio basis. With the high volume of customers served every day, Sumitomo Bank relies on its network to keep operations running smoothly and efficiently. If the network goes down, millions of dollars could be lost.

"Our customer database is accessed through the network as well as e-mail," said Lucie Onderwyzer, networking engineer for Sumitomo Bank in New York City. "We also keep the information for the Risk Management Department that does all the analysis of the market and investment positions. These are all vital services of our company."

If Sumitomo Bank's network goes down, employees do not have access to customer information. Additionally, the risk management team cannot move money and potential investment opportunities could be missed.

"We want to maximize our investment opportunities," said Onderwyzer. "To do that, we've got to have our servers running at all times. That's why we implemented StandbyServer. Even though we have multiple ways to ensure that our risk management team can keep running without StandbyServer, the time and inconvenience of the alternatives would be immense. With StandbyServer, I avoid all the problems of downtime with the assurance that we have not missed a billion-dollar investment opportunity."

Onderwyzer uses two Compaq ProLiant 1500s, each with 20GB storage space, for the primary server and standby machine running Vinca's StandbyServer for Windows NT. With this solution, data is automatically mirrored to the standby machine. If the primary server fails, the standby machine takes over with complete copies of the data, keeping Sumitomo Bank's risk management team current on investment opportunities.

Another obstacle Onderwyzer wanted to tackle was providing disaster recovery for their NetWare servers. With the announcement of StandbyServer's new data vaulting feature for it's NetWare products, Onderwyzer found the solution she was looking for. StandbyServer for NetWare now allows a primary machine to be connected to local standby machines and remote vault machines for disaster recovery. With this configuration, data is simultaneously written from the primary server to the local standby machine and to the remote vault machine. In the event of a disaster that destroys both the primary and standby machines, the vault machine will be able to take over and function with complete copies of data. This type of functionality is especially attractive to financial institutions like Sumitomo Bank that could lose billions with the loss of their data.

"Vinca's solutions are perfect for a company like ours running on two platforms. We can provide solutions for both our NT and NetWare servers that help us protect our data and provide disaster recovery where needed," said Onderwyzer. "StandbyServer is one of the best investments this company has made."

UniSource Business Networks

Vinca's StandbyServer software and Compaq's servers are a strategic part of our network configuration. They are key in meeting our government mandate of 99.4 percent uptime and in helping us reduce or eliminate the monetary penalty we pay for each hour of downtime. Vinca and Compaq also help enhance UniSource's worldwide reputation for dependability and reliability as a data communications provider.

—Theo Ekelmans, product specialist

UniSource Business Networks, headquartered in Zurich, Switzerland, is comprised of privately owned segments of Europe's Postal Telecommunications and Telegraphy (PTT). UniSource quickly grew into a global telecommunications company, and currently has more than 3,000 people employed at 140 sites in Europe, Asia, and the United States. The company specializes in building computer networks, providing everything for its clients from file and print services to long-distance lines. In 1994, UniSource earned more than $2 billion in revenues.

UniSource implemented, and currently maintains, a NetWare network for the Dutch PTT Telecom Division, one of Europe's largest telecommunications providers. The Dutch PTT network, which handles all of the provider's business and billing data, consists of more than 350 servers and 30,000 workstations. Because of the large volume of mission-critical work done on the network, UniSource is required by contract to keep the network running 99.4 percent of the time during normal working hours or pay a sizable downtime penalty.

With such a strict uptime requirement, UniSource needed to design a foolproof network. Selecting the hardware came first. "We needed hardware that performed well and would be compatible with the other components needed to make our network perform to our standards," said Theo Ekelmans, a product specialist at UniSource. "We also wanted hardware from a manufacturer whom we could depend on for support. After looking at multiple options, we found Compaq to offer all the solutions we were looking for."

UniSource currently has 600 Compaq servers installed throughout their customer sites. "Support from Compaq has been incredible and our Compaq servers are very reliable and scalable. They have provided the solid base we need for our network," said Ekelmans, "but even the most reliable machine needs to be protected and that is why our next step was looking for a compatible high-availability solution."

UniSource researched several options and finally installed a leading high-availability solution on their servers. They soon realized it was not what they were looking for. "A few years ago," said Ekelmans, "the fault-tolerant system we were using deleted the bindery information on a primary and secondary server, causing both to crash. That incident alone cost us 400,000 Guilders/$242,520 U.S. in downtime and kept thousands of Dutch PTT users idle for four hours."

The system backed up data by searching the primary server for new files and copying them to the secondary server. But as the Dutch PTT NetWare network grew, so did the system's search cycle, until it was taking three to four hours to cycle through the primary server to look for new files to copy.

In addition, because the high-availability system could not copy open files, if the system went down before a search cycle was completed, up to four hours of work would be lost. "That happened several times," said Ekelmans. "Obviously, we had a lot of upset users. And our 8mm tape backup didn't help out in those cases. We only backed up to tape once a day."

The system was also expensive to operate. It not only sat on a third machine between the primary and secondary servers, but both servers had to be identical. "That's a lot of hardware and a big budget item," explained Ekelmans. "In addition, because the system ran on a separate workstation and had to copy data twice over the network, it could only use half the available bandwidth, which slowed down the backup process. The system just wasn't working out. Finding a replacement became a top priority."

After carefully considering ten fault-tolerant solutions, UniSource decided to replace its existing fault-tolerant system with Vinca's Standby*Server* mirroring system. "It's powerful, easy to use, and works seamlessly with our Compaq servers," said Ekelmans. "I especially like Standby*Server*'s simplicity, and the fact that it makes use of NetWare's built-in mirroring. Simple solutions are always the best."

With 300 copies of Standby*Server*, UniSource connects warm online Compaq servers directly to their clients' primary servers. All data is automatically mirrored to the standby machine over a high-speed dedicated link. If the main server's hardware or software fails, Standby*Server* automatically switches to the standby machine, giving users continuous access to network services with little or no interruption.

"With Standby*Server*, we no longer have a three- or four-hour window where users can lose data," noted Ekelmans. "All files are simultaneously written to the primary and secondary server in real time." The Standby*Server* mirroring system also proved to be a cost-effective solution. "Unlike the previous fault-tolerant system, Standby*Server* doesn't require identical servers or a third workstation. With the money we saved, I've been able to provide more service to end users. Considering all the solutions we looked at, Standby*Server* had the least impact on our customers—we didn't have to change anything on their workstations and we could continue using the Compaq servers we've come to rely on.

"I also save money by being able to simply switch to the secondary server in order to perform maintenance or repairs on the primary server during regular working hours. Best of all, our clients don't even know when we take down the server for maintenance. It's all transparent. All they know is that the network is virtually never down. And if there is a crash, we can recover faster with little or no loss of data."

UniSource was able to use all of Dutch PTT's Compaq servers to implement Vinca's Standby*Server* mirroring system. Ekelmans explains "Vinca's Standby*Server* software and Compaq's servers are a strategic part of our network configuration."

JR Simplot

JR Simplot is a multibillion dollar highly diversified agribusiness with headquarters in the Western region of the United States. This company is involved in food processing and the production and manufacturing of chemicals and minerals, such as fertilizer. The agriculture group raises potatoes, cattle, and food for cattle. JR Simplot also has a transportation division and a real estate division that contribute to the company's $2.8 billion in revenues. An interesting sidelight is that the company supplies the french fries to all the McDonald's restaurants worldwide.

JR Simplot's network is as diverse as the company. The following describes what network systems they use:

▼ Mainly IPX over Ethernet

■ Some Frame Relay

■ T1 to the Internet

▲ DECNet, LAT and TCP/IP, and FDDI

The network is used company-wide, except by the corporate farmers while they are in the field. They run a useful intranet. Simplot is running NetWare and Windows NT as network operating systems. The main applications are Microsoft Exchange and Lotus Notes, along with large custom databases with vendor and customer information. Each division is quite different in the applications they run. This configuration makes them an obvious candidate for Vinca products.

When All Else Fails—The Word from DriveSavers

DriveSavers is a data recovery company located in Novato, California. Their specialty is retrieving damaged or lost data from a variety of storage media for individuals, corporations, educational institutions, and government agencies. They have been doing this for more than a decade, successfully recovering data from storage media damaged by viruses, accidental deletions, fire, concussion, and other causes. They are known worldwide as the one of the most trusted and respected data recovery companies in the industry. The following is a short list of some of their more memorable recoveries. DriveSavers can be reached by calling (800) 440-1904 or by going to their Web page at **http://www.drivesavers.com**.

Example 1

DriveSavers works very closely with all of the major drive manufacturers and many vendors. They received a call one afternoon from a very nervous CFO at a well-known drive reseller. He had lost all of the company's financial records for the previous quarter and it was tax time. The CFO had been backing up the files religiously to numerous tapes but unfortunately never checked the contents. When his drive failed he discovered his backup tapes were empty.

The CFO was so desperate he decided to fly to the DriveSavers facility in the San Francisco Bay Area and hand carry the drive rather than risk losing it in shipping. When he arrived the next day, he said he'd be stopping off to take a dive off the Golden Gate Bridge if they couldn't get his data back.

Two technicians worked around the clock on the drive, which had suffered electromechanical failure and directory corruption. After several days working with the drive in their specially designed clean room, they were able to get the drive to a ready state and extract the needed files. The CFO was, of course, very relieved and left that day for the earliest flight home.

Example 2

The people at DriveSavers frequently hear about drive failures and crashes that occur when users are under tight deadlines to finish projects and don't have time to properly back up their data. Such was the case with a designer working on the latest catalog for a New York–based fashion designer. The data (which was 10Gb of CAD files), was spanned across two drives in a set, one of which had failed. The catalog was nearly finished and set to go to press in four days.

This was an extremely complex recovery because the data spanned two drives. This required DriveSavers to re-create the volume set so the spanned data would line up properly. Most of the work was accomplished by tediously assembling the data at the sector level. The job was completed in under 24 hours and the data was returned overnight to the customer.

Veritas Software

The examples listed here present several interesting uses of Veritas software. In both instances, the advanced file system components are used. While these will not be completely available until NT 5.0 ships, they give some idea how clustering and advanced file management systems can aid in protecting data from any failure.

Knight-Ridder Industries

Knight-Ridder maintains a large amount of news information that is used 24 hours a day by industry, science, and the news media. In fact, all the information is maintained on nine 30GB volume sets that support a library system, a database search engine, and extensive amounts of news information. Obviously, this amount of hardware and software requires extensive planning and careful implementation.

Originally, all the information was maintained on mainframes, but it has now been ported to a UNIX environment and uses the Veritas Volume Manager (VxVM) and the Veritas File System (VxFS) to manage the large data sets. These applications allow the use of very large data volumes, but in an open system environment readily amenable to standard C++ and C development.

The use of VxVM and VxFS allows Knight-Ridder to run an Oracle7 database engine to query across the volumes. Furthermore, the use of the Veritas products allows a very flexible RAID array, allowing optimal tuning of performance with the preservation of fault-tolerant data storage.

Because the operation cannot afford any downtime at all and must be available 24 hours a day, seven days a week, serious design and planning has gone into the 270GB of data. The file management systems provide storage availability, and FirstWatch is being evaluated to provide failover support. While this effort may seem large, Knight-Ridder has more than 200,000 customers that constantly query a real-time, fault-tolerant enterprise environment.

Bay Networks

Bay Networks is attempting to store and manage data in all possible means of storage: local, LAN, and WAN environments. In reality, Bay Networks has more than 30 million nodes installed worldwide. These nodes are connected by all possible means, ranging from 10Base-T to ATM and use everything from hubs to multiprotocol routers and switches. In order to maintain a database of sufficient size and expandability to allow scalable applications for this large environment, Bay Networks has decided to run the Veritas solution for SAP R/3 against an Oracle database.

Obviously, the environment to provide such a system is very complex and cumbersome to maintain. Veritas has developed several tools that allow easy management and great fault-tolerant abilities:

1. Monitoring has been developed that allows easy examination of the database's state of health through constantly updated charts and graphs. Staying in tune with the environment is easy.

2. Veritas has developed a clustering system for SAP R/3 that allows multiple servers to fall over to single servers. This failover can be implemented automatically and thus requires minimal user intervention.

3. A Web interface also allows the management of the entire range of components from application servers, database servers, and the network itself.

This environment is complex and includes mirroring as well as cluster solutions. While these implementations are currently being accomplished on a UNIX environment, there are ports of these applications in progress to Windows NT. They will be readily available when NT 5.0 is released.

ServerNet

Tandem and its partners are aggressively targeting ServerNet clustering for the Windows NT market. They have released specific products for NT that will add a great deal of power to the clustering environment of enterprise NT. Because most of ServerNet is hardware related, some of these early products will use Microsoft's Cluster Server software. Examining some of the current implementations of ServerNet or ServerNet-like approaches from Tandem can provide an appreciation of parallel processing capabilities.

New York Stock Exchange and NASDAQ

These two exchanges account for more than 90 percent of world securities transactions, and the number of shares sold on a single day has approached the 1.5-billion share level.

Clearly, any computer solution to this environment must have the highest availability and a fault-tolerant design. On both of the exchanges, the transactions are maintained on Tandem Himalaya servers. These servers have functioned flawlessly and maintain not only adequate bandwidth but also failover support in real time. The NYSE uses a large configuration of NonStop Himalaya K20000s for its equity trading systems while NASDAQ uses Himalaya K20000 servers for its core equity trading operations. These Tandem servers handle everything, including the order execution and trade reporting systems as well as the trade confirmation system.

While the above example might be an extreme one, Tandem is providing parallel cluster support for the maintenance of much of the world's investment community. Such an adoption demonstrates the robustness and proven technology developed in ServerNet.

Cellnet—A Multimillion Dollar Wireless Intelligent Network System

Formed in 1983, Cellnet was given a license to act as a mobile communications network operator. The company currently has almost 3 million customers and has built up a $1.7 billion network in the United Kingdom that handles about 10 million calls per day. To make matters somewhat more complex, Cellnet forecasts a dramatic increase in subscription rates over the next several years. Obviously, key to the growth of Cellnet is the ability to deliver high-quality service at a realistic price to its customer base. This ability includes reliability, fault tolerance, bandwidth, and availability.

Because Tandem's RISC-based NonStop Himalaya servers are known to offer continuous availability and scalability, and have an excellent price-performance ratio, Cellnet is scheduling the implementation of the NonStop servers over several years. Cellnet chose the Himalaya product for several major reasons:

▼ NonStop Himalaya servers provide linear scalability; that is, each additional NonStop Himalaya server delivers a full processor's worth of performance.

■ The systems maintain an open architecture and are easily integrated into any existing intelligent network infrastructure.

▲ Tandem has a proven reputation for delivering the technology and software for large-scale enterprise environments.

Once more we are dealing with very large and complex environments that have never been considered possible on Windows NT networks. This is changing rapidly. The ability to have multiple-server cluster environments that scale well on the PC is on hand, or at least close at hand. Tandem and its colleagues are committed to providing strong support for ServerNet in Windows NT. Tandem is porting its NonStop Platform to Windows NT and is a Microsoft clustering partner. In fact, ServerNet drivers are provided with the Microsoft Cluster Server.

For now, much of this NT fabric may be considered pie-in-the-sky by many IS managers, but such is a foolhardy consideration. Low-cost servers providing high-cost function will dramatically change the face of enterprise computing.

ENTERPRISE EXAMPLES

The following examples are of large-scale NT installations at major corporations. The first, CIPCO, is an example of a solid NT design. The second two contain major contingency plans for the loss of an entire data center.

CIPCO

CIPCO is a large U.S. company with approximately 12,000 employees. The name was required to be anonymous, as the Internet firewall information has been included. The company has 14 buildings in the headquarters city as well as 75 service outlets that are all connected through a private network. They have a single (redundant) high-speed connection to the Internet. Remote offices connect first to the headquarters data center and then to the Internet. The basic layout follows.

Network

3COM was chosen as their network hardware vendor of choice. This includes hubs, switches, routers, and network interface cards. They run fiber from all servers back to separate switch ports. All building wiring closets are connected to the central closet via fiber to a separate switch port. All switch ports support a 16-node, 10Mbps collision domain for the workstation connectivity. The 14 buildings in the headquarters city are connected via high-speed fault-tolerant SONET rings. Remote offices are connected via T1 with a minimum of dial backup.

This network is 100 percent TCP/IP. Network General Sniffer products periodically scan the networks for bottlenecks and unsupported protocols. They use static IP addressing on all servers, printers, and network devices (hubs, routers, switches, and print servers). DHCP is running on NT Servers and is used for the dynamic addressing of all workstation machines. The IP lease time is set to 30 days, which keeps most addresses fairly static. Incoming remote access IP pools are assigned from a static list of addresses and not through standard DHCP. To keep historical data on who has what address at any time, they download hourly dumps of the Windows Internet Name Service (WINS) database. The WINSDMP Resource Kit utility is used for this purpose.

The company is protected from the Internet with CheckPoint Firewall 1 running on a HP NetServer LH. Address translation has been implemented with the valid IP addresses translated to a private Class A network (10.x.x.x) They use a mask of 255.255.255.0 for subnetting into thousands of possible Class C sized IP subnetworks. Virtually all clients are allowed basic access to the Internet. From the outside looking in, CIPCO allows typical access to mail, FTP, and Web servers on a separate DMZ, as shown in Figure 11-1. They have several salespeople that make encrypted connections to the internal network with Checkpoint's SecuRemote product. This essentially allows a virtual private network connection from the client to the network from any site on the Internet.

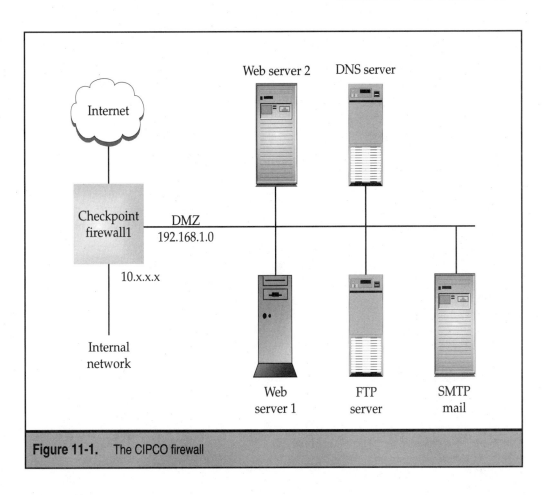

Figure 11-1.   The CIPCO firewall

In addition, CIPCO uses the firewall's built-in Web address rollover functionality to automatically bounce Web requests between the two Web servers. This gives some scalability while also adding a backup if one server is down. In fact, if one server needs to be worked on, they simply disable the rollover until it is back online. The Internet connection is T3 with a T1 backup.

Network management is a combination of HP OpenView, Tivoli, and Compaq Insight Manager. OpenView was selected as the primary system, as it had built-in support for both the UNIX and NT systems.

Power

In the headquarters city, all servers are located in a centrally located data center. This data center has a high-end Liebert UPS system that feeds power to distribution transformers. Feeds from these transformers supply power to the specific server banks. The UPS system is backed up by redundant diesel-powered generators. These generators are operated and tested on a monthly basis. The UPSs can sustain the data center for a maximum of 20 minutes. The backup generators are typically operating within eight minutes of a severe failure.

This brings up an interesting issue—that is, the fuel contracts. Most companies with diesel generators work out contracts with local suppliers to bring additional fuel in case of emergency. Any person who has been in a major disaster lasting several days will tell you that the first thing that happens is the supply companies cannot keep up with the demand. Be sure to take this into consideration when setting up these types of contracts. Set up contracts with a local supplier as well as another supplier at least 50 miles away, or design a system that can store many days' worth of fuel.

Server Hardware

The NT Servers at CIPCO are all Compaq ProLiant series systems with hardware RAID controllers. These range from ProLiant 800s for low-use utility servers up to ProLiant 7000s for high-end applications, including their Microsoft Exchange and SQL Server applications. As mentioned, Compaq Insight Manager is used to monitor all servers.

On some server systems, CIPCO includes at least one hot spare system. On critical systems, they employ Compaq's Standby Recovery Server configuration. In this system, two Compaq ProLiant servers are attached to a common set of storage systems that contain a single copy of the operating system, applications, and data. If the primary server fails, each ProLiant storage system automatically switches from the primary to the recovery server. The recovery server then boots, and the system is back online in minutes without intervention.

Server Software

CIPCO has a myriad of possible software configurations on its servers. Almost all of the NT Servers are now at version 4.0. All databases are either Oracle or Microsoft SQL Server. The internal e-mail is 100 percent Microsoft Exchange running on 14 servers. All Internet mail passes through the Exchange bridgehead server to the external mail server (in the DMZ) and then out to the Internet.

Tape Backup

HP Omniback is CIPCO's backup platform of choice. These network-level backup servers and associated software have banks of high-capacity 70GB DLT cartridges with multiple readers. A robot arm loads and changes the tapes. This company is typically working with extremely short backup windows so they have several of these machines. Omniback has agents that run on both their NT- and UNIX-based servers and allow complete system backups in this heterogeneous environment. They run differential backups during the week and full backups on Friday nights. Omniback also seamlessly integrates with their HP OpenView infrastructure.

RAID

In terms of RAID, all of the CIPCO's servers use Compaq SMART-2 Array Controllers. These controllers are based on an intelligent I/O architecture, which has some very useful features. They offer the standard levels of RAID plus online capacity expansion and an easy-to-use array configuration utility. The graphical user interface greatly simplifies array configuration and facilitates the online capacity expansion. Compaq Insight Manager is used to monitor both the array performance and status. This company also utilizes an online spare drive so that in case of a drive problem, the failed drive is immediately replaced with a spare and data is reconstructed automatically. This particular controller supports up to four spare drives.

Antivirus

CIPCO has set up strict antivirus policies. IBM Antivirus has been chosen as their product of choice for desktops, with Norton Antivirus protecting all NT servers. Virus definitions are updated periodically through a central distribution server. CIPCO has chosen not to scan incoming Internet e-mail at the firewall, but is considering taking such action as the need presents itself.

Security

In terms of general security, CIPCO has made great strides to limit the number of personnel with full NT administrative equivalence. To this end, they have implemented the Trusted Enterprise Manager (TEM) product from Master Design Development, Inc. (**http://www.mddinc.com**). This product allows a great deal of added granularity to the administrative rights, by assigning sub-rights to specific users. For example, it can be set up to allow a person to create user accounts and passwords without giving them the rights to add workstations to the domain.

Koalinex

This example is anonymous mainly due to time constraints. Most of the design and implementation work was done by a group of engineers and application developers from an international consulting company. This example is of a large U.S. manufacturing company that offers a consumer processing service. Koalinex is currently made up of a corporate headquarters, a main and backup data center, seven customer service/manufacturing locations, and 55 purely manufacturing locations. The backup data center is actually run by a separate division of IBM. This backup data center is set up as a virtual replica of the main center. It is actually backed up to a division of IBM that makes its money doing just that—acting as a backup for a variety of companies. It is interesting to note that the complete backup data center plan is tested every November by operating the company from the backup site for an entire week.

The company's main product is a processing service that guarantees customers a 24-hour turnaround. Any product not returned within 24 hours is returned free. This puts an enormous strain on the system, as even relatively minor problems can quickly escalate into expensive propositions. On the other hand, each of the manufacturing centers is nearly a duplicate of the others, so that work can be routed to other plants if capacities allow. Any plant can handle any other plant's packages. Figure 11-2 shows the basic layout.

This original NT project is particularly interesting because it was not necessarily cheaper to go with NT over an AS/400-only solution as there are over 60 separate locations. When $30,000 IBM NT servers are being used, this adds up very quickly. However, it does turn out to be more fault tolerant using NT. One of the design goals included the capability to run any manufacturing plant for at least two weeks, even if the plant network is completely separated from the rest of the system. There is a maximum of two weeks because the local databases would simply run out of space in that time.

The individual NT Servers allow this two-week uptime window to occur. They are basically database servers whose data is frequently moved back to the New York data center. It should be noted that there is very little or no NT server expertise at the remote

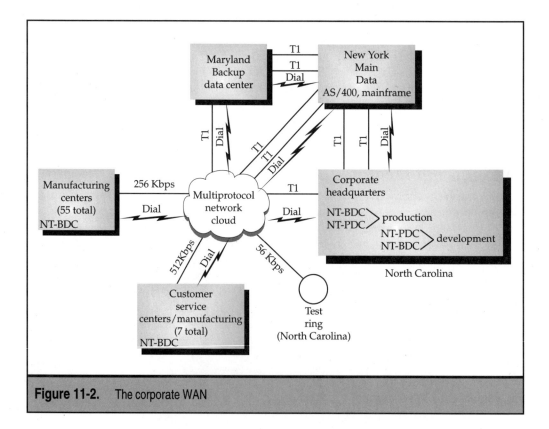

Figure 11-2.   The corporate WAN

manufacturing sites. This has a tremendous design implication in that all systems had to be configured to allow remote administration and control.

Network

The local networks indicated in Figure 11-2 are all token ring. Token ring was chosen originally because of the ease of integration with the AS/400 and IBM mainframe systems, so there was no overriding reason to change it. The major protocols are SNA and TCP/IP. All locations are connected by a minimum of a single 256Kbps line and a backup dialup connection. The multiprotocol network cloud is a series of redundant network spaces that offer built-in fault tolerance. The headquarters building is also connected to the main data center via separate redundant T1 lines. They are configured at the router (with costs) to both be handling traffic at all times.

The designers also indicated that a major problem they ran into was ensuring the T1 connections were actually separate. In several instances, they found that the separate T1 lines they had ordered actually went through the same wire bundle somewhere down the road. This led to a disturbing single point of failure. An accidental cable cut in the single bundle would result in both connections going down. To be sure of line separation, the two lines were ordered through different telecommunications companies. However, the end result was often the same. The telecommunications companies were leasing the same fiber bundle just down the road! The point is that you should always be sure your redundant schemes are truly redundant.

Power

The data center has its own separate power scheme. However, Koalinex had to purchase UPSs for each of the 60+ manufacturing plant servers. They chose American Power Conversion's BackUPS 1400, which can supply power for 25 to 30 minutes (estimated) for a server that is running at peak operational levels. APC PowerChute software is used to monitor the UPSs. In case of power failure, a general alert is sent to all users telling them to log out or risk losing their work.

NOTE: It was determined that all servers in this system would be rebooted weekly at a predetermined time. APC PowerChute was used to schedule and initiate this weekly shutdown.

Server Hardware

The servers are all high-end IBM PC Server 704 machines with 512M of RAM and dual Pentium Pro processors. They can be expanded to four processors and come with a 512KB L2 cache. They support a maximum of 2G of memory and have dual I_2O-ready PCI bus architecture. These machines have 12 internal drive bays that can accommodate up to a maximum of 109GB of hard drive storage.

In terms of warranty, these machines come standard with three years of IBM's international on-site warranty service. Like any other top-tier network server provider, IBM also offers NT-specific telephone support 24 hours a day, seven days a week.

For emergency server connections and repair, all servers have dedicated analog lines and two modems. They use a Call Director box to select which modem to use at dialup time. This box essentially allows two modems to share the same phone line. The first modem is a standard RAS connection. The second modem is used to dial into the IBM Advanced System Management Adapter (ASMA) server manager product. The ASMA is a separate hardware controlling/monitoring package that allows the remote operator to initiate shutdowns and monitor internal temperatures, drive usage and conditions, and several other hardware-related parameters. This dual-modem configuration allows the administrators back at headquarters to dial in to either the server console or directly to the server hardware in case of problems.

They currently keep three hot spare servers online at the company headquarters. If a complete server crash occurs at any of the remote sites, the server is boxed up and flown air cargo to the location. Koalinex has a preestablished agreement with the airlines.

These servers also have three hot swappable power supplies. In the current configuration, any one of these power supplies can run the entire machine. No spares are kept in stock as they can use the power supplies from the hot spares mentioned previously, if required.

Server Software

The servers currently run NT 4.0 with Service Pack 3. They are used for some minor file and print services. Koalinex also uses the Tivoli system management product line for software distribution, remote control, inventory, and alert monitoring.

The primary function of the NT Servers at the remote manufacturing sites is to run IBM DB2 Database Server for NT and a separate product called IBM DB2 Apply. The DB2 Apply software enables hourly database propagation from the mainframe-based data center databases to the local NT-based databases (the mainframe stores all account master and master tables). Microsoft's FTP Server is used to transfer data (invoices, orders, and manifests) back to the mainframe every 15 minutes. It is also used to transfer the data to the AS/400 midrange machines that are at the data center. Since these transfers occur every few minutes, there is a high level of fault tolerance against a single server crash. If a server completely fails, the only data lost is the amount that has changed since the last upload (a few minutes before). As mentioned previously, a complete replacement server can be sent from the headquarters office via air shipment in a few hours. If the problem is simply a single drive, the RAID systems (discussed next) provide backup until a new drive arrives.

NOTE: Koalinex has implemented custom three-way software controls to make sure that the data is the same on the NT Servers, the mainframe, and the AS/400s.

Tape Backup

Because the operation is 24 hours a day, seven days a week, Koalinex works with very limited backup windows during the week. On Sundays, they are allotted a four-hour window for maintenance and backups.

All of the NT systems at the manufacturing plants run two 4mm tape drives. The first tape drive is used as a database dump device. This backs up the database-specific files and devices. The second tape drive currently uses NT's built-in back up program to run a complete backup of the server, including the database transaction log files. In this way, the database is actually backed up twice. They are considering using IBM ADSM to replace the built-in backup product in the future.

In terms of backup schemes, Koalinex runs full offline backups on Sundays during their four-hour maintenance window. They run daily differential backups during the week. In addition to the local tape backups, the database's information is also continually being transferred back to the main data center databases during the work day (as mentioned previously).

RAID

They run the IBM ServerRAID hardware RAID controllers with 4GB to 4.5GB hot swappable drives in an enhanced RAID 1 configuration. In this configuration, drives can be mirrored across several physical drives, as shown in Figure 11-3. Koalinex uses two SCSI channels to pair up the drives in sets of two. The third channel is used to run only the tape devices. They also run the IBM RAIDMon monitoring software to keep tabs on the arrays. This software issues audible alarms in case of RAID failure. They use the SRVANY utility from the NT Resource Kit to run this product as a service.

Antivirus

Koalinex has set up a tight antivirus policy on all workstations. They chose IBM Antivirus for this purpose. They do not currently run any real-time virus scanners on their servers. Monitoring is left up to individual users.

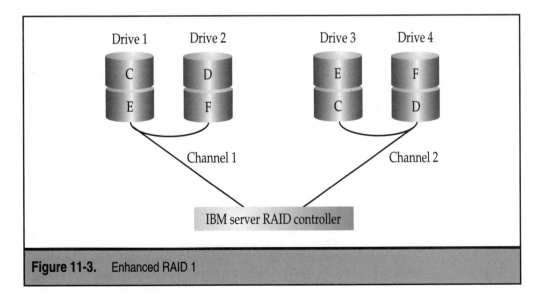

Figure 11-3. Enhanced RAID 1

Unusual Hardware

The BDC servers at the remote site also use 16-port Digi AccelePort EPC/X PCI adapters for multiple serial interfaces. These are currently used to connect to a legacy IBM Series 1 computer that in turn monitors custom production equipment. This equipment will eventually be directly connected to the NT servers once the software interfaces are complete.

Workstations

The workstations are all running Microsoft NT Workstation. They are locked down extremely tightly via profiles, so the local users cannot make any local changes. This stringent lack of machine customization helps keep support costs down. They also run the DB2 client, DDCS, Tivoli, and IBM Personal Communications package for 5250 and 3270 emulation. In terms of hardware, the workstations are IBM PC 35GCs with 200Mhz Pentium Pro processors, 64MB of RAM, 2.5GB EIDE hard drives, and IBM PCI token ring cards.

Miscellaneous

One last decision that had to be made here was which domain(s) model to employ. They decided to go with a single-domain model with backup domain controllers (BDCs) at each remote site. The single domain was chosen for the NT 4.0 network because the remote sites have no local NT administrators. They considered network traffic and found this to be acceptable. As mentioned earlier, each of the separate manufacturing facilities is required (for reasons of fault tolerance) to be completely self sufficient for a period of at least two weeks. This meant that an authentication server (BDC) had to be local to the sites. This configuration also prevented them from having to deal with the trust relationship problems of connecting over 60 separate domains! Koalinex also has several users that require access to data at multiple sites (and many mobile users). In the future, they have plans for passing more data between the separate site servers and certainly do not want to manage a messy multidomain trust environment. This had to be a robust, stable system. Only one hour of downtime at peak manufacturing times can result in huge losses for the company.

Kobe

This example is of a large U.S. food products company whose main Japan office is located in Kobe, Japan. When the now-famous Kobe Earthquake hit in 1995, their entire Japanese operations center was destroyed. This included all office space, computers, and phone systems. This also included their major data center that contained computerized records of orders to be filled, inventories, and other critical day-to-day operational information for the entire country. This crippled their entire distribution system throughout Japan. The problem, of course, was that the earthquake affected only the region around Kobe. Their customers in other parts of the country still required the normal service they had always expected. This lack of service forced the customers to go elsewhere for their food supplies. The loss of both short- and long-term orders and customers was estimated to be in the hundreds of millions of dollars. In this example, we will briefly outline the systems before the earthquake and the new system implemented after the earthquake.

Before the Disaster

The system that existed before the earthquake consisted of NT servers located at both the data center and other sites. Also in the data center was an IBM AS/400, which was used for their main database. Their mail system ran on the NT side and was Microsoft Mail. All sites were connected to the single data center with multiple redundant, high-speed WAN links. High-quality tier-one NT servers were used and standard practices were employed for backing up all information to tape. This was a solid, stable system that was sound enough to withstand a variety of disasters, including a partial loss of the data center. However, it was not set up to handle the loss of the entire data center, offices, and the surrounding infrastructure.

The New System

After the disaster, a few main points became clear:

▼   The system had to have complete redundancy to a second site.

■   Kobe had to make contingency plans that included the computer systems, alternate office space, and some sort of phone switch.

■   They needed to test and train any implemented plan.

▲   They could afford a plan that might cost millions of dollars. They could not afford to be unprepared for another disaster.

With these points in mind, Kobe set out to build as fail-safe a network as possible. The first thing they did was to rebuild their AS/400 infrastructure. Then, they re-created their mail systems using Exchange instead of Microsoft Mail. They built in the standard mechanisms to compensate for virus problems, security, etc. The next step was to work on reconnecting the physical network. The new network was essentially the same except that it included redundant connections to a backup data center. This backup center was the key to their new plan.

THE BACKUP DATA CENTER   The backup data center was actually a hotel located several hours away from the city of Kobe. The company worked out a lease plan with the hotel with the following conditions. Kobe would:

▼   Install network wiring to all rooms

■   House their backup center in the bottom level of the hotel

■   Lease enough storage space to house additional preconfigured client desktop PCs

■ Claim responsibility for all fees and maintenance associated with these systems

■ Pay a set fee per year for the lease plus a separate fee if the disaster plan was actually put to use

▲ Test the plan for one specified week each year

This agreement, essentially stated that in case of emergencies, all guests are moved out and the company takes over the hotel. A backup redundant phone switch was also preconfigured at the hotel. In disaster mode, anyone calling the main corporate number would almost immediately be redirected to the backup site, where the phone would be answered as if it was the company's main system. The voice mail and e-mail systems would be almost immediately turned over as well, allowing almost continual customer contact. The major lag is the time it takes to remove the hotel guests and transfer company personnel to the new site.

The required turnaround times were 1 hour for the phone switch and e-mail, 12 hours for relocation of all guests, 24 hours for 50 percent operational capacity, and 36 hours for 90 percent operational capacity. The remaining 10 percent operational capacity was considered nonessential and could wait out the rebuilding/relocation of the primary center. The estimate used for the rebuilding of this primary center to a functional state is 90 days.

THE TEST PLAN   One of the most important and interesting parts of the Kobe plan is the testing. There are two sets of tests that go on: continual and annual.

The backup data center personnel carry out the continual tests. The servers are checked and monitored for faults and so forth, and the network connections are closely observed. The idea is that in case of an emergency, these systems are always ready. There is a remarkable amount of work that goes on at the backup center. As new programs and services are being developed at the primary site, the backup team works out the redundancy issues.

The annual tests are much more involved. At some time during a predetermined and preannounced day, an announcement is made that the main data center and main headquarters building are to be evacuated. Employees leave the building carrying nothing but their personal belongings. The employees then board buses and are brought to the backup center.

About the time the employees arrive at the backup center, the power to the main servers in the primary data center is turned off. The employees then go to the assigned rooms to find their backup computers waiting. They typically operate in this state for up to three days. During the first year, several bugs were worked out of the system as a direct result of these test scenarios.

Kobe Follow-Up

The Kobe example is indicative of disaster-related problems that occur frequently in large corporations. This even becomes more of an issue with the recent increase in sales of thin client servers like Citrix Winframe, Tectronics Windd, and now the Microsoft Terminal Server (formerly Hydra). Thin clients are an excellent way to connect outlying sales offices back to a corporate center. One of the nice features is that they do not require an IS person (or a dedicated server) to be located on-site. The are simply remotely connected into the main data center. This can result in huge corporate-wide cost savings. However, the problem occurs when the main data center is the object of a disaster. In that case, instead of taking down one site, a disaster can cripple the entire network. Be sure to keep this in mind when you are designing networks in a single hub configuration as shown in Figure 11-4. In this figure, it easy to see the effect of losing the main corporate data center in New York. The result is a countrywide disaster. Be sure to include this consideration in your disaster plan.

During Hurricane Fran in North Carolina in August 1996, several companies had this same hub configuration. The result was a country-wide shutdown of the systems

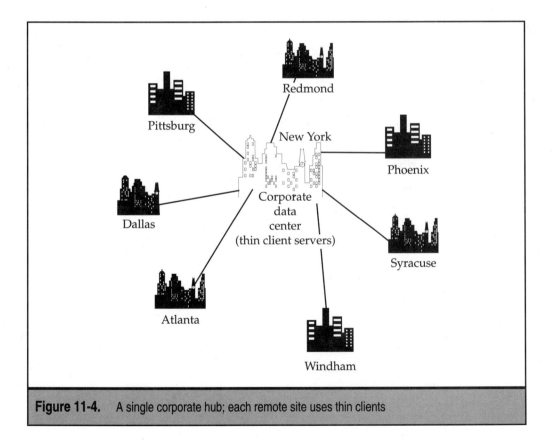

Figure 11-4.   A single corporate hub; each remote site uses thin clients

dependent on the data centers (i.e., a disaster in one city led to a country-wide disaster for the companies). It is interesting to note that a relatively low-cost diesel generator would have solved the majority of the problems. Of course, this will not help you if the entire data center is burned down. In that case, a scenario like the Kobe company above is about the only solution.

WORKING WITH CLONES

In many instances in the book we have counseled people to steer clear of server systems that are not from major server manufacturers. Generally speaking, you should be purchasing server systems from vendors like IBM, Digital, Hewlett-Packard, Compaq, and Dell. The reasons for sticking to these manufacturers are varied, however the overriding issue is support. The tier-one companies have thousands of NT engineers that can help you through your NT issues. In addition, the more variation you have in your systems, the more difficult they are to support.

Even with these warnings, many people have expressed interest in an examination of which components and configurations actually work in terms of clone systems. To find some of these systems, we spoke with Scott Blanchard, a network engineer with Cadre Systems, Inc. in Cary, North Carolina. Cadre is an AutoCAD reseller and an installer of small network systems and high-end CAD workstations. The typical network they deal with is between 10 and 25 workstations and between 1 and 3 servers. The main requirements for these CAD environments are stability, large amounts of storage and a high rate of data retrieval.

Selecting Components

When Cadre first started installing NT servers and workstations several years ago, one thing became clear. To make NT work on clone systems, you need to experiment with solid components and make decisions on what combinations actually work together. Once compatible combinations are determined, Cadre sticks with these systems and stresses the necessity of this consistent selection to their clients. The following sections describe the components with which Cadre has had particular success.

Network

The physical network is a key feature for the CAD environment. To this end, Cadre has found a great deal of stability in 3COM and Intel network adapters. For hubs and switches they also stick with the 3COM and Intel product lines. In terms of routers they use the 3COM and Ascend lines. The key, according to Mr. Blanchard, is to find a network solution that works and stay with it. He doesn't have time to reinvent the wheel at every job site. Because of the relatively large size of the files being pulled off the servers, they try to use 100MB Ethernet wherever possible.

Power

Cadre uses APC uninterruptible power supplies on all servers and network components. When budgets permit they purchase units that support the automatic server shutdowns through a serial port connection. High-end surge protectors protect all other devices. In terms of internal power supplies, they look for cases with certified 275 to 350 watt power supplies like the Acer Open or the Intel Columbus units. On the most critical servers, they go for cases with a minimum of one redundant swappable power supply like the units in the Hewlett-Packard server series.

Hardware

The actual hardware that Cadre uses on the servers and workstations is key to the success of these systems.

SERVER HARDWARE   Cadre has worked hard to determine which motherboards and other components are the most compatible with NT. The servers are assembled by hand and generally take a few hours to complete. All systems are bench-tested in the lab environment for one week to ensure proper operation. The following is a list of the components that are used:

- ▼ **Motherboards (Intel only)**
  - ■ Pentium Series
    - ■ Endeavor
    - ■ Zappa
    - ■ Explorer
  - ■ Pentium Pro Series
    - ■ VS440LX Venus Pro
    - ■ Pentium II Series
    - ■ R440LX Dual P2 Server Board

- ▼ **Memory (Kingston RAM Only)**
  - ■ DIMMS with ECC support (where available and supported)

- ▼ **Hard drives (they try to use IDE for workstations and SCSI for servers)**
  - ■ Quantum
    - ■ Fire Ball 1 GIG IDE
    - ■ Fire Ball 2.1 GIG IDE
    - ■ Fire Ball 3.2 GIG IDE

- Fire Ball 4.3 GIG IDE
- Fire Ball 9 GIG SCSI
- Western Digital Series
  - 1.6 GIG 1600 Series
  - GIG 2300 Series
  - GIG 3200 Series

▼ **Video**

- S3 Trio/64
- Trident 9000 Series

WORKSTATION HARDWARE   For workstations they stress a fast drive and a high-end graphics adapter.

▼ **Motherboards (Intel Only)**

- Pentium Series
  - Endeavor
  - Zappa
  - Explorer
- Pentium II Series
  - AL440LX AGP Workstation Board
  - DK440LX Dual P2 Workstation Board

▼ **Hard Drives**

- Quantum
  - Fire Ball 1G IDE
  - Fire Ball 2.1G IDE
  - Fire Ball 3.2G IDE
  - Fire Ball 4.3G IDE
  - Fire Ball 9G SCSI
- Western Digital Series
  - 1.6G 1600 Series
  - 2.3G 2300 Series
  - 3.2G 3200 Series

Mr. Blanchard's workstation of choice is currently a Pentium II 330 MHz 128M RAM box on a Intel AL440LX chipset motherboard (by Intel only). This board has integrated sound and an independent integrated AGP slot. For high-end video he uses the Diamond Stealth Fire GL 1000 (4/8 MB) AGP video accelerator card.

Server Software

In terms of server software, they have been using the Microsoft Small Business Server since its release in 1997. Cadre particularly likes the ease of installation and feature set of this entry-level product. The most common components they use are the mail server, proxy server, and fax server. The total feature set includes:

▼ Microsoft NT Server

■ Microsoft Exchange Server with Microsoft Outlook

■ Microsoft FAX Server

■ Microsoft Internet Connection Wizard

■ Microsoft FrontPage

■ Microsoft Proxy Server

▲ Microsoft Modem Sharing Server

Tape Backup

Cadre considers their backup plans to be a crucial component of these networks. They generally use several methods for backup.

On the servers, they use Hewlett-Packard SureStore and WangDAT 9600AT tape drives (normally 4mm). They usually use NT's built-in backup software. When deemed appropriate, they use Seagate BackupExec for a full-featured, third-party backup solution.

In addition, CD burners and Zip storage are used to backup or archive CAD drawings. In this area they use Iomega Zip or Jazz drives, JVC 6X RXCDRs and Hewlett-Packard SureStore CD writers.

RAID and SCSI Support

The following list is completely comprised of SCSI controllers from Adaptec (**http://www.adaptec.com**).

▼ Low end (Mainly for separate tape drive controllers)

■ AHA-1510

■ AHA-1515

■ AHA-1520

■ AHA-1535

▼ Higher end

■ AHA-2940 (U2W for highest performance)

■ AHA-3940 (2 channel)

▼ RAID

- AHA-3985 PCI RAID adapter
- AHA-3985W PCI RAID adapter

Where budgets permit Cadre always tries to go with hardware RAID solutions. In particular, they use the Adaptec 3985 series, which brings high-performance PCI hardware RAID to entry-level servers. The 3985 delivers high performance through three independent SCSI I/O channels. It supports multiple RAID levels (0, 1, 0/1, 5). User-friendly menus make configuring, installing, and managing these adapters easy. The arrays can also be monitored in real time from the server console. In addition, the Adaptec CI/O software allows monitoring from any Windows based client on the network.

Antivirus

On servers, Cadre uses Intel LANDesk Virus Protect. They run the auto scan feature in real time on these systems. They have found the product to be both stable and reliable in terms of eliminating viruses without interfering with normal server operations. They use the same product on all workstations.

Miscellaneous Advice

The last important issue Cadre contended with is component vendors. They try to use as few major vendors as possible for their components. They stick to major suppliers like Merisell, Gates/Arrow, Ingram Micro, and Tech Data. Keeping vendors to a minimum makes it much easier to determine where equipment has come from. This becomes extremely important when things go wrong. In addition, Cadre recommends staying away from the so-called gray market suppliers. They have had a great deal of problems in the past with incompatible components from these types of vendors.

SUMMARY

This chapter looked at some examples of how fault tolerance and disaster recovery techniques are being implemented in companies in the real world. It provided examples of how to use some of the products and technologies discussed in the rest of this book. The most important thing to remember when developing your own plan for disaster recovery and fault tolerance is that you need to analyze and test every possible problem area. Then, make the financial decisions on what to protect and what not to protect.

NT Resource Kit

This appendix is an alphabetical listing of several of the NT Resource Kit utilities useful in managing NT from a fault-tolerance or disaster recovery perspective. A short description of each tool is included. The NT Resource Kit can be purchased as a set of books and CD-ROMs at most large bookstores. The utilities are also included in a subscription to Microsoft TechNet. For more information on TechNet see Appendix B.

▼ **AUDITPOL.EXE** This command line utility allows the modification of the audit policy of a local or remote computer. Administrative equivalence is required to run this program.

■ **AUTOEXNT** This service allows a batch file (called AUTOEXNT.BAT) to run at system startup without requiring a user to log into the console. It even allows programs to be started interactively with its interactive switch.

■ **BROWSTAT** This is the command line browser diagnostics tool. It can be used to determine a great deal of browser information on a network and on a domain. It can also be used to cause a new browser election (this is called tickling). To use BROWSTAT, you must run it against a specific transport bound to a specific NIC. To find the transport name, run NET CONFIG SERVER.

■ **C2CONFIG.EXE** This is the NT C2 Configuration Manager. It is a tool that can be used to compare the current system security settings with the C2 requirements of the NCSC. This utility is shown in Figure A-1.

■ **COMPREG.EXE** This is a command line program that allows you to compare any two local or remote Registry keys for differences.

■ **COUNTERS.HLP** This is a help file that includes a description of all of the standard NT Performance Monitor Counters. It also includes information on the optional counters that can be installed from the NT Resource Kit and Internet Information Server.

■ **DH.EXE** This is a character-based tool for displaying information about heap usage in kernel-mode memory.

■ **DHCPCMD.EXE** This is a command line tool for administering a Dynamic Host Configuration Protocol (DHCP) server.

■ **DHCPLOC.EXE** This command line utility can be used to detect DHCP servers on a particular subnet. It can be used for both troubleshooting purposes and for detecting unauthorized DHCP servers on a network. It can be set to show packets from all DHCP servers or only from unauthorized DHCP servers.

■ **DIRUSE.EXE** This utility shows disk space usage on a per-folder basis. If you run the utility with administrative equivalence, it can be used to show information on all NTFS directories regardless of permissions. It also allows you to set up alert thresholds so it will mark any folders that exceed a specified value.

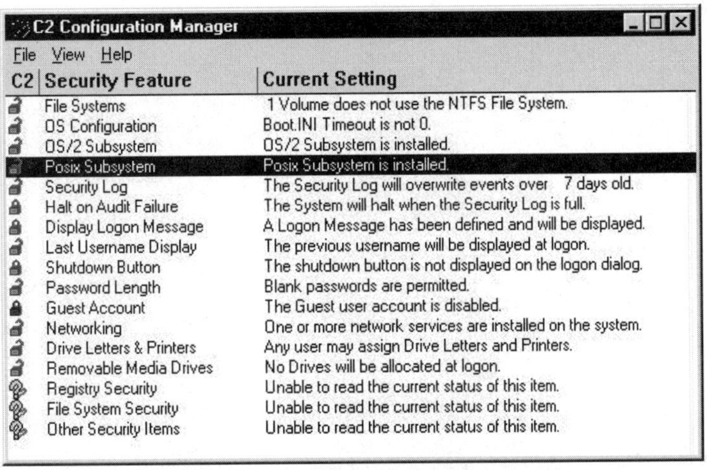

Figure A-1. NT C2 Configuration Manager

- **DISKMAP.EXE** This command line utility produces a report on the configuration of a hard drive. It is discussed in detail in Chapter 10. You should run this utility on all critical servers as a disaster recovery tool.

- **DISKPROBE.EXE** This utility allows a disk to be edited at the sector level. It allows an administrator to directly edit, save, and copy data on the physical hard drive. It can be used to replace the master boot record, repair damaged partition tables, and repair other file system data. This utility is discussed thoroughly in Chapter 10.

- **DISKSAVE.EXE** This utility allows you to save the master boot record and partition boot sector as image files. These disk structures can then be restored in case of a later corruption. DISKSAVE is discussed in detail in Chapter 10.

- **DNSCMD.EXE** This character-based tool allows DNS administration on local and remote DNS servers.

- **DOMMON.EXE** This tool enables you to monitor the status of servers in a local domain and in trusted domains.

- **DRIVERS.EXE** This command line utility lists all loaded device drivers. A partial list of the DRIVERS.EXE output is shown in Figure A-2.

- **DUMPEL.EXE** This utility allows you to dump an event log on a local or remote system to a tab-separated text file.

- **EXPNDW32.EXE** This is a GUI version of the Expand utility. You can use this utility to expand any file from the NT Install CD or any other Microsoft source.

```
Command Prompt                                                        _ □ ×
ModuleName     Code    Data    Bss    Paged    Init        LinkDate
─────────────────────────────────────────────────────────────────────────
ntoskrnl.exe  270272  40064     0    434816   82880   Sun May 11 00:10:39 1997
    hal.dll    20384   2720      0      9344   11936   Mon Mar 10 16:39:20 1997
  amsint.sys    9856      0      0         0     704   Wed Jul 17 11:28:51 1996
SCSIPORT.SYS    9824     32      0     15552    2208   Mon Mar 10 16:42:27 1997
    Disk.sys    3328      0      0      7072    1600   Thu Apr 24 22:27:46 1997
  CLASS2.SYS    7040      0      0      1632    1152   Thu Apr 24 22:23:43 1997
 Fastfat.sys    6720    672      0    114368    7712   Mon Apr 21 16:50:22 1997
  Floppy.SYS    1088    672      0      7968    6112   Wed Jul 17 00:31:09 1996
   Cdrom.SYS   12608     32      0      3072    3104   Wed Jul 17 00:31:29 1996
    Null.SYS       0      0      0       288     416   Wed Jul 17 00:31:21 1996
  KSecDD.SYS    1280    224      0      3456    1024   Wed Jul 17 20:34:19 1996
    Beep.SYS    1184      0      0         0     704   Wed Apr 23 15:19:43 1997
i8042prt.sys   10784     32      0         0   10976   Mon Apr 21 16:03:54 1997
mouclass.sys    1984      0      0         0    3968   Mon Mar 10 16:43:11 1997
kbdclass.sys    1952      0      0         0    3840   Wed Jul 17 00:31:16 1996
VIDEOPRT.SYS    2080    128      0     11296    2752   Mon Mar 10 16:41:37 1997
    mga.SYS    20960  21024      0     47648     736   Wed Jul 17 00:30:26 1996
    vga.sys      128     32      0     10784     832   Wed Jul 17 00:30:37 1996
    Msfs.SYS     864     32      0     15328    1664   Mon Mar 10 16:45:01 1997
    Npfs.SYS    6560    192      0     22624    3200   Mon Mar 10 16:44:48 1997
    NDIS.SYS   11744    704      0     96768    4640   Thu Apr 17 22:19:45 1997
    Ntfs.SYS   68160   5408      0    269632    8704   Thu Apr 17 22:02:31 1997
── More ──
```

Figure A-2.   The output of the DRIVERS.EXE utility

- **FINDGRP.EXE**   This utility locates all indirect or direct group memberships for a specific user in a domain. Administrative access is not required.

- **FIXACLS.EXE**   The FIXACLS tool resets the NTFS permissions of system files and folders for NT machines to their default values. It is typically used after a conversion is run on a file system to change it to NTFS from FAT.

- **FLOPLOCK.EXE**   This is an NT service that controls access to floppy drives on an NT machine. When this service is running on an NT server, only administrators can access the floppy drives.

- **FTEDIT.EXE**   This is a GUI utility that allows you to modify and view software fault-tolerant disk sets on local and remote NT computers.

- **GETMAC.EXE**   This great tool quickly determines the MAC address and binding order of a NIC in an NT machine. This is very useful when running the NT Network Monitor.

- **GETSID**   This utility compares the security IDs between two accounts.

- **HARDWARE COMPATIBILITY LIST (HCLNTX.HLP)**   This is the NT Hardware Compatibility List (HCL) for the version of NT you are running. The latest HCL can be obtained at **http://www.microsoft.com/hwtest**.

- **HEAPMON.EXE**   This is a character-based utility that shows the system heap information.

- **INSTSRV.EXE**   This is the command line utility that is used by the SRVANY.EXE tool to run any program as a service. This process works best with 32-bit applications.

- **KERNPROF.EXE**   This utility shows counters and profiles of various functions of the NT kernel.

- **KILL.EXE**   This command line utility ends one or more NT processes. To use KILL, you must first determine the process ID (PID). You can determine PIDs by running the PULIST or TLIST Resource Kit utilities.

- **LEAKYAPP.EXE**   This is a GUI tool that can be used to determine how applications run in memory-stressed conditions. To use it, first start your applications and then run LEAKYAPP. LEAKYAPP essentially grabs as much memory as possible for itself, and allows you to watch the effects of this "grab" on the other applications and on the system as a whole. When LEAKYAPP is stopped, it releases the memory.

- **LOGEVENT.EXE**   This event-logging utility creates entries in the application event log. It enables you to follow the progress of batch files and tailor the event description. Adding LOGEVENT entries to a batch file enables you to monitor and troubleshoot batch program execution. LOGEVENT is also resourceful when used with login scripts and the AT command. For example, putting LOGEVENT "Login script started" at the beginning and LOGEVENT "Login script finished" at the end of a login script allows you to time how long the script takes to execute.

- **MONITOR.EXE**   This is the configuration tool controlling the DataLog Service. The two utilities (DATALOG.EXE and MONITOR.EXE) combine to allow the Performance Monitor alerting function and monitoring function to be run as a service. This process is described thoroughly in Chapter 2.

- **NETSVC.EXE**   This is a very useful utility for remotely starting, querying, and stopping NT services. It is particularly useful for controlling services over a slow link. If you are not sure of a service's name, simply run NETSVC with the /list switch. You do not need special access to query or list services. However, you do need specific privileges on the target machine if you wish to start and stop any services with this tool. The results of the /list switch are shown in Figure A-3.

- **NETWATCH.EXE**   This utility shows which users are connected to shared resources on a server machine. It allows an administrator to remove users from resources and can simultaneously monitor multiple computers.

- **NLTEST.EXE**   This command line tool allows you to force a user account database into synchronization, get a list of domain controllers, force shutdowns, and check trust relationships.

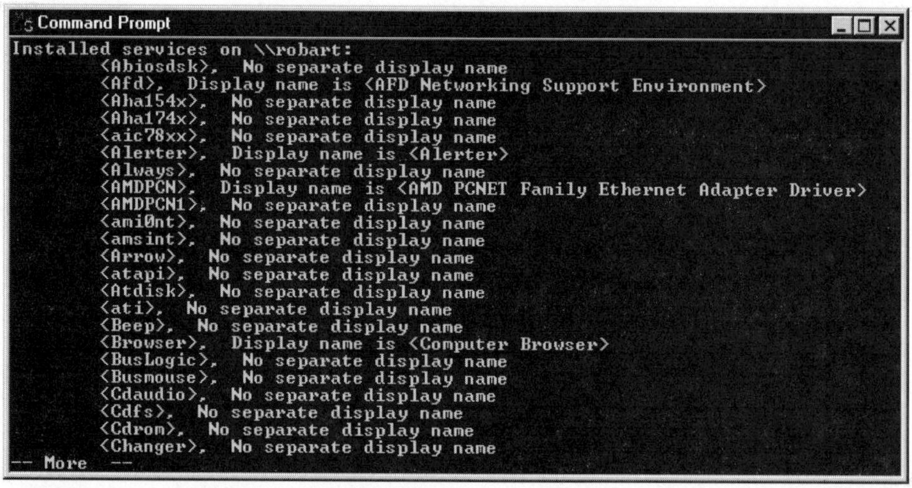

Figure A-3. The NETSVC command

- **NTDETECT.COM** The INSTALLD.CMD script installs the debug version of the NT hardware detector, NTDETECT.COM. It is used to troubleshoot startup problems. Be careful to always be sure at least one copy of NTDETECT.COM is residing in the startup directory of the system or NT will not boot.

- **NTEVNTLG.MDB** This is a database in Microsoft Access format that lists messages and other information related to the NT event log. The database contains possible messages from the system, security, and application logs along with their corresponding event IDs, sources, and types.

- **NTMSGS.HLP** This is a Windows help file that lists many of the possible errors and informational messages generated by Windows NT. It provides explanations and suggestions on how to correct the problems.

- **OH.EXE** This is a command line utility that shows the handles of all open processes. This is a nice utility to use to figure out which process has a file open after a sharing violation occurs.

- **PASSPROP.EXE** This is a command line utility that sets two security policy flags: 1) it sets the complex passwords flag and 2) it allows the administrator account to be locked out. These options are discussed further in Chapter 7.

- **PERFMTR.EXE** This command line utility displays information on the performance of an NT system in text format.

■ **PFMON.EXE**   Page Fault Monitor allows the monitoring of the page faults that occur as you run an application. It lists both hard and soft faults. This information can also be shown using the memory counter in the NT Performance Monitor. Page faults are discussed in Chapter 2.

■ **PMON.EXE**   This is a command line utility that allows you to monitor process, resource, CPU, and memory usage.

■ **PULIST.EXE**   This is a command line utility that tracks what processes are running on local or remote NT systems. It is especially useful to determine process IDs for the KILL.EXE utility mentioned above.

■ **PVIEWER**   Process Viewer is a GUI-based tool that shows information about running processes. It also allows you to KILL errant processes.

■ **QSLICE**   This utility shows the percentage CPU usage for each process in an NT system.

■ **RCMD.EXE**   The Remote Command Service is a secure way to run command line programs on an NT server. It requires the Remote Command Service (RCMDSVC.EXE) to be running on the remote machine.

■ **REG.EXE**   This utility allows you to view and modify Registry entries from the command prompt.

■ **REGBACK.EXE**   This is a command line utility that backs up the Registry hives to files while the system is running and has the hive files open. The files it creates can be used to restore the hives with the REGREST.EXE tool. These tools are fully discussed in Chapter 10.

■ **REGDUMP.EXE**   This command line utility dumps all or part of the NT Registry to standard output. A typical use for this output is for REGINI.EXE scripts.

■ **REGENTRY.HLP**   This Windows format help file is a list of Registry entries. It includes modification instructions and a list of possible keys and values. The basic format is shown in Figure A-4.

■ **REGFIND.EXE**   This is a command line utility used to search the NT Registry for data, keys, or values. It also supports a replace function.

■ **REGINI.EXE**   This utility can be used in batch files to add keys to the NT Registry by specifying a Registry script. Using the REGDUMP.EXE utility mentioned above can easily create this script.

■ **REGREST.EXE**   This command line utility uses the files created with the REGBACK.EXE utility above to replace NT Registry hives while the system is operational.

■ **REMOTE.EXE**   This tool allows you to run command line programs on remote computers. It requires the remote server to be running. This service does no authentication of the sender and should not be used on security-critical

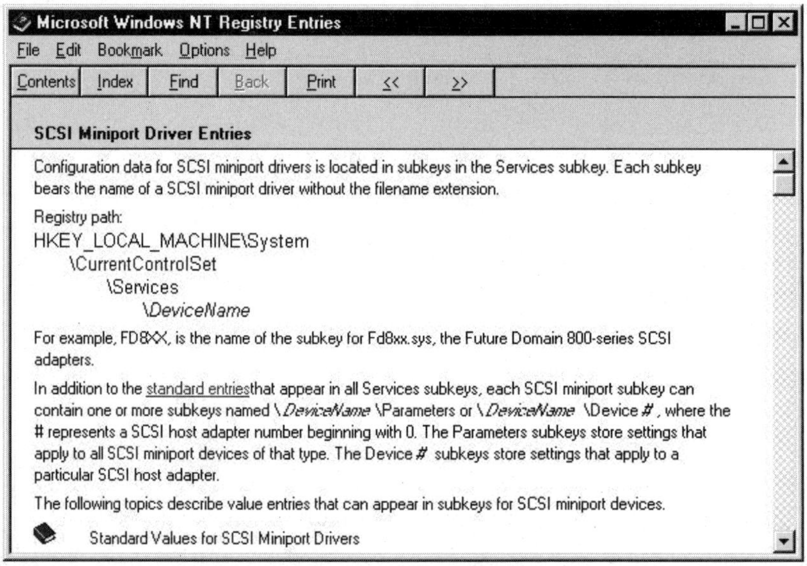

Figure A-4.   The REGENTRY help file

servers. For most servers, you will want to use the RCMD.EXE utility
mentioned above.

- **ROBOCOPY.EXE**   This is an easy-to-use 32-bit command line tool that can be
  used to make replicas of directories in multiple locations and on multiple
  computers. It is essentially an intelligent copy program in that it can be set up
  to copy only changed files and it also has many other useful parameters. It is
  great for copying files over slow or unreliable network links, as it can restart a
  copy in the case of network errors. ROBOCOPY works best when copying from
  an NTFS partition to another NTFS partition. You can also use ROBOCOPY in
  batch files to schedule periodic replication.

- **SC.EXE**   This command line utility allows you to connect to and communicate
  with NT services via the service controller.

- **SCANREG.EXE**   This is a 32-bit command line Registry search tool. It
  allows you to search for any string in keys, values, or data in local or
  remote Registries.

- **SCLIST.EXE**   This command line utility shows information on NT services on
  a local or remote server.

- **SCOPY.EXE**   This is a very useful utility for copying files on NTFS volumes to other NTFS volumes while retaining all security information.

- **SECADD.EXE**   This command line tool allows you to add specific permissions to Registry keys.

- **SECEDIT.EXE**   This is a GUI security context editor that enables you to change privileges of the current user and any running processes. It also lists the security contexts that are in use.

- **SHAREUI**   This is an add-on to the NT Explorer interface. When it is installed, it gives you a quick method of managing server shares through a folder (named Shared Directories) that shows up in My Computer. One special feature is that it allows you to modify permissions on remote shares directly if you have the necessary permissions.

- **SHOWACLS.EXE**   This is a command line program that shows access rights for files, folders, and directory trees. It allows wildcards and masking, and works only on NTFS partitions.

- **SLEEP**   This is a small utility that is useful for adding delays to batch files. It causes the process to wait for the specified amount of time.

- **SNMPMON.EXE**   This is an SNMP MIB monitor. It can pick up MIB variables across multiple SNMP nodes. It can also log the results to an ODBC data source. The basic screen is shown in Figure A-5.

- **SNMPUTIL.EXE**   This is an SNMP browser utility that allows you collect SNMP information from other SNMP hosts.

- **SOON.EXE**   This is an interesting scheduling utility. It actually creates the appropriate NT AT scheduler jobs based on the user-provided information. It requires the Schedule Service to be running.

- **SRVANY.EXE**   This utility allows you to run any NT application as a service. It works best with 32-bit applications.

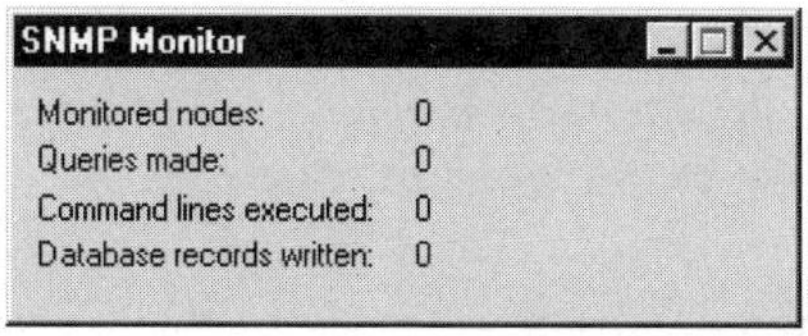

Figure A-5.   The SNMPMON screen

- ■ **SRVCHECK.EXE** This is a command line utility that lists all shares on a server and shows the ACLs for the shares.

- ■ **SRVINFO.EXE** This is a command line tool that shows information about the local server or a remote server. The information displayed includes uptime, protocols, services, drives, OS versions, and service pack levels as well as other information.

- ■ **SRVMON.EXE** This useful utility monitors the services on local and remote machines for changes in operational state. If a change is detected, SRVMON can be configured to issue an alert or send an e-mail. This can be very useful to monitor problematic services.

- ■ **SU.EXE** This utility allows you to start a process running as any specified user. It is based on the standard UNIX su utility.

- ■ **TDISHOW.EXE** This utility collects and displays packets that are crossing the Transport Driver Interface (TDI) layer.

- ■ **TIMESERV.EXE** This command prompt utility (and service) allows you to maintain global clock synchronization.

- ■ **TIMETHIS.EXE** This utility shows the time elapsed during a specified command.

- ■ **TLIST.EXE** This command line utility shows a list of running processes. It shows the PID, which can then be used with the KILL.EXE command to halt the process.

- ■ **TRANSLATE.EXE** This utility converts Win32 error codes into more informative text strings.

- ■ **TWEAKUI** This utility allows full customization your NT user interface.

- ■ **USRSTAT.EXE** This is a command line tool that displays the user statistics, including last logon times for users in a specified domain. The output of the USRSTAT command is shown in Figure A-6.

- ■ **WAITFOR.EXE** This is a command line utility that "waits" for a specific signal. One nice feature is that multiple machines can wait for the same signal. It can be very useful for testing and diagnosing capacity planning issues.

- ■ **WINAT.EXE** This is the GUI version of the NT Command Scheduler interface. It is explained in detail in Appendix C of this book.

- ■ **WINMSDP.EXE** This is the command line version of the Windows NT Diagnostics Administrative Tool.

- ■ **WINSCL.EXE** This is a command line Windows Internet Name Service (WINS) administrative tool.

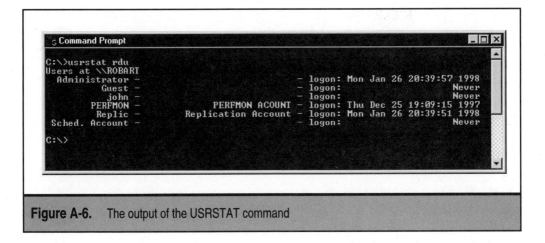

Figure A-6. The output of the USRSTAT command

- ■ **WINSDMP.EXE** This is a command line utility that dumps all records in a WINS Database and prints them to STDOUT. This can be used as a quick way to gain historical data on who has what particular IP address on a network running DHCP.

- ■ **WNTIPCFG.EXE** This is a GUI version of the IPCONFIG.EXE command line utility native to NT. It displays a great deal of information relating to the IP configuration parameters for an NT server.

- ▲ **XCACLS.EXE** This command line tool allows you to set and modify access control list information for an NTFS file structure. It is particularly useful in changing ACLs in a script (i.e., for backup) and then changing them back to the original values. It can also be used to create the proper ACLs during an unattended NT installation.

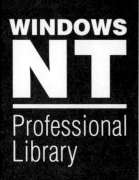

WINDOWS
NT
Professional
Library

APPENDIX B

Sources of NT Information

As mentioned many times in this book, any disaster recovery plan must also include a plan for the escalation of problems. Sometimes the problems may indeed be pressing. At those times, you are probably going to want to speak to someone on the phone. Of course, as we are now in an era of paid support for just about everything, you can expect that the call is going to cost you. If you are simply trying to figure out some issue within NT, or if time is not of the essence, there are many alternative, low-cost, or even free sources of information. This appendix is a list of the many sources of NT-based information. Under some of the headings, a brief description is included. Some are quite obvious, so they are left to the reader to interpret.

▼ **Microsoft NT Resource Kit** The NT Resource Kit is a series of books and a CD that contain volumes of NT-specific information. Most people are familiar with the many useful utilities that come with the NT Resource Kit. These utilities are generally unsupported by Microsoft, but have become absolute "must haves" in any administrator's arsenal of tools. The full Resource Kit costs around $200 and includes four books and a CD-ROM. It is available from Microsoft or most large bookstores. If you are only interested in the utilities CD, it is probably more cost effective to purchase a copy of TechNet. TechNet includes the utilities CD plus all of the Resource Kit books in online format.

■ **Microsoft TechNet** Like the Resource Kit, no NT systems engineer or administrator should be without copy of TechNet. TechNet is a set of informative CDs that include white papers, the Microsoft Knowledge Base, resource kits, patches, and utilities. It covers all of the common Microsoft products, from DOS to NT to Exchange. The most often-used portion of TechNet is clearly the Knowledge Base information database. It has an easy-to-use front end that accepts a wide variety of queries. Prices for TechNet start at around $300 for a single license and $700 for a server-based copy. For more information call the Microsoft TechNet line at (800) 344-2121 or check out their Web page at **http://www.microsoft.com/technet**.

■ **MSDN** Have you ever wondered where those guys at the user group get access to the latest and greatest Microsoft software. The most likely place is from a subscription to the Microsoft Developer Network (MSDN). MSDN membership comes in three flavors: Library, Professional, and Enterprise. The costs range from $200 to $1,500. The Enterprise version MSDN gets you access to the latest release versions and beta versions of operating systems and BackOffice products. It includes development products like Visual Studio, the Software Development Kits (SDKs), and the Driver Development Kits (DDKs). It also includes the online documentation for all of the products. While not a necessity for administrators, a subscription to MSDN is crucial for NT developers. For more information call the Microsoft Developer Network Service Center at (800) 759-5474 or check out their Web page at **http://www.microsoft.com/msdn**.

- **Microsoft technical support** Microsoft offers technical support for all of its products at the Microsoft technical support hotline—(888) 677-9444. Be prepared to pay. A five-pack of BackOffice support calls will run in the $1,000 range. However, a correctly placed call can save you much more money. If time is not critical, try one of the newsgroups or forums mentioned below.

- **Microsoft Authorized Support Centers (ASCs)** Microsoft has certified several other companies to support a wide variety of their products. Depending on the problem, support calls will range between $30 and $200. At complete list of ASCs is available at **http://www.microsoft.com/Enterprise/asc.htm**.

- **Major vendor support centers** Many of the major NT server vendors, including HP, Dell, IBM, Digital, and Compaq offer paid support for NT-related problems. Most have both software and hardware support options. In fact, many of these companies are actually Microsoft authorized support centers. The Compaq support center does a particularly good job at NT support.

- **Microsoft Consulting Service** Microsoft has its own set of big guns for installing and designing Microsoft BackOffice solutions. This is the Microsoft Consulting Service (MCS). They are available at **http://www.microsoft.com/ MSConsult**.

- **Independent consultants and integrators** Most cities of any size are likely to have a wide variety of professionals that support Microsoft products. However, be sure to check the references of these companies. In general, you will want to find a company that is a member of the Microsoft Solution Provider Program that has experience in the particular area of your need.

- **The Microsoft Solution Provider Program** A Microsoft Certified Solutions Provider (MCSP) is a company that has been qualified to support Microsoft products. They are required to have a certain number of Microsoft certified professionals on staff. Solution Providers have access to TechNet, MSDN, and several direct lines of communication to Microsoft. Just as with any consultant or integration company, be sure to check references. A complete list of MCSPs is available by calling the MCSP line at (800) SOLPROV. There is also an online version at **http://www.microsoft.com/mcsp**.

- ▲ **Microsoft Authorized Training Centers** If you are looking for solid professional training for Windows NT and Microsoft BackOffice products, then you will be interested in the list of Microsoft ATECs at **http://www. microsoft.com/atec**. ATECs offer Microsoft-designed classes at locations worldwide. All trainers at ATECs are actually Microsoft Certified Trainers (MCTs). This simply means that they have passed the certification test, taken the course, and passed a speaking competency audit. As you would expect, many MCTs are extremely knowledgeable about their subject matter. However, this is not always the case. The quality of ATEC classes is completely dependent on the quality of the *speakers*. Be sure to ask for the instructor qualifications for each class before signing up.

The following table is a list of Web sites for your reference:

Web Site	Description
http://www.microsoft.com	
/support	The full Microsoft support site. Includes the Web version of the Microsoft Knowledge Base, support alerts, FAQs, support phone numbers, and more. This site is also accessible at **http://www.support.microsoft.com**.
/security	The Microsoft security page. All companies should have a least one administrator checking this page periodically.
/train_cert	Microsoft training and certification page (includes lists of ATECs).
/technet	Microsoft TechNet page.
/ntserver/tool	Microsoft Internet resource page.
/windows/dailynews!	Microsoft daily news.
/backoffice/promo/lsdowntrial	Microsoft BackOffice download and trial center.
/hwtest	Windows Hardware Quality Labs (WHQL); this is the home of the NT Hardware Compatability List (HCL).
http://www.backoffice.microsoft.com	BackOffice live; the BackOffice-focused site at Microsoft.
http://www.winntmag.com	The Windows NT Magazine Web site includes moderated forums and a great deal of NT-related information.
http://www.bhs.com	The Beverly Hills software Web site. Another good NT-related site.
http://www.ntinternals.com	NT Internals Web site. Great location for the latest NT utilities.

Web Site	Description
http://www.ntxtras.com	An excellent online catalog of NT-related software.
http://www.ntadmintools.com	NT administrative tools Web site.
http://www.ntsystems.com	*NT Systems Magazine.*

The following is a list of Internet newsgroups for your reference.

NOTE: Most of the NT-related groups start with **comp.os.ms-windows.nt**.

▼ comp.os.ms-windows.nt.admin.misc

■ comp.os.ms-windows.nt.admin.networking

■ comp.os.ms-windows.nt.misc

■ comp.os.ms-windows.nt.setup.misc

■ comp.os.ms-windows.nt.setup.hardware

■ comp.os.ms-windows.nt.pre-release

■ comp.os.ms-windows.nt.software.backoffice

▲ comp.os.ms-windows.nt.compatibility

A list of Internet newsletters and discussion groups follows.

Newsletter/Discussion Group	Description
NTBUGTRAQ	The first list to mention has to be the NTBUGTRAQ mailing list that is available at **http://www.ntbugtraq.com**. This is a tightly moderated list (moderated means all messages are screened before being sent out) that always seems to be one of the first places that NT and the latest NT security issues are discussed.
ISS	Internet Security Systems (ISS) hosts a security list as well **(http://www.iss.net)**. It has good information but is not as tightly monitored as the NTBUGTRAQ list.
Update	Update is the *Windows NT Magazine* mailing list **(http://www.winntmag.com)**. It is sent out periodically and contains the latest of the goings-on in Redmond. For solid general NT information, this list is tops.

Newsletter/Discussion Group	Description
Microsoft-related user groups	There are NT-related user groups in many major cities across the United States and throughout the world. A list of user groups can be found at the Worldwide Association of NT User Groups' Web site (**http://www.wantug.org**). This organization helps promote and build NT user groups. If there is not an NT user group near you and you would like to start one, the WANTUG Web site puts a great deal of information at your disposal.
CompuServe	CompuServe has been an excellent source of computer information for many years. While arguably not as popular as they once were, CompuServe forums still offer one of the most organized and accessible information interchange formats. The following are some of the NT-related sections.
GO MICROSOFT	Windows support forum.
GO NTSERV	The Windows user group's network (WUGNET's) Windows NT Server forum (For network-related questions).
GO NTWORK	WUGNET's Windows NT Workstation forum (for install questions).
GO WINNT	WUGNET's Windows NT forum (for hardware and OS questions).

NT Scheduling with AT

Any high-end operating system must be capable of scheduling jobs. The AT command, NT's built-in scheduling utility, schedules commands and applications to run on an NT computer at specific times and dates. You can also use the AT command to automate processes and enhance logon script functionality.

In order to take advantage of NT's built-in scheduling utility, a user must have administrative rights on the machine on which he or she will run AT.EXE. In addition, the Schedule service must be running. If you are not sure it is running check out the Control Panel Services applet for the Schedule status. The command interpreter (CMD.EXE) must also be running before any commands are run unless the commands are executable (.BAT, .EXE, or .COM).

The following pages explain how to activate the scheduling service and the AT command syntax. They also include some common examples of how to use the AT command.

ACTIVATING THE SCHEDULE SERVICE

By default, the Schedule service is not activated automatically. However, activating the service is easy by completing the following steps:

1. From the Control Panel, double-click the Services icon.
2. Select the Schedule service and click the Start button.
3. Click OK.

To configure the Schedule service to automatically run at startup, follow these steps:

1. From the Control Panel, double-click the Services icon.
2. Select the Schedule service and press the Startup button.
3. In the Startup Type section, select Automatic.
4. You can now set the logon account in the Log On As: Box.
5. Click OK.

NOTE: It is advisable to only use the Default System Account for the Schedule service or to create a nonadministrator account for this purpose.

AT COMMAND SYNTAX

The AT command can only be executed at the command prompt. The syntax for scheduling commands (programs) and deleting scheduled events, respectively, is as follows:

AT [*computername*] *time* [/*interactive*] [/*every:date*[,...] | /next:date[,..]] "*command*"
AT [*computername*] [[*id*] [/*delete* [/*yes*]]

The parameters for the command are the following:

▼ *computername* specifies a remote NT workstation or NT server computer. Commands and programs are scheduled on the local machine if this optional parameter is excluded. This is a very nice feature.

■ *id* is the identification number for each scheduled event.

■ /*delete* deletes all scheduled commands unless an ID is specified.

■ /*yes* answers "yes" to all queries from the system when deleting scheduled events.

■ *time* specifies the time in 24-hour format when the event is scheduled to run.

■ /*interactive* permits the user who is logged on at the time of the scheduled event to interact with the job as it executes.

■ /*every:date*[,...]indicates that you want the event to run on the specified day(s) of the week or month. If this optional parameter is omitted, the event is scheduled to run on the current date.

The date parameter follows these rules:

■ To select specific days of the week use M,T,W,Th,F,S,Su. Be sure to place a comma between each entry.

■ To allow a job to run on one or more days of the month, use the numbers 1 through 31. Note that multiple date entries must be separated by commas.

■ /*next:date*[,...]executes the job on the next specified date. The current date is assumed if this field is omitted. The date and day rules previously mentioned also apply.

▲ "*command*" is the command to be executed.

AT Command Examples

Using the parameters listed above, the scheduling process is quite straightforward. Here some basic examples of using the AT command:

    AT \\GRANT1 8:00AM /INTERACTIVE /EVERY:M,T,W,TH,F,SA,SU
    "PERFMON1.CMD"

This job will run at 8:00 a.m. on the computer \\GRANT1. It will be interactive and will run on every day of the week. The command to be run is PERFMON1.CMD.

    AT \\ANDREW1 8:30PM /NEXT:T "EVENTDUMP.CMD"

This job will run at 8:30 p.m. on the computer \\ANDREW1. It will be noninteractive and will run on the next Tuesday. The command to be run is EVENTDUMP.CMD.

AT \\ROBART 9:00AM /NEXT:2,3,4,5,6 "23456.EXE"

This job will run at 9:00 a.m. on the computer \\ROBART. It will be noninteractive and will run on the next second, third, fourth, fifth, and sixth day of the month. The command to be run is 23456.EXE.

AT \\ROBART 9:00AM /EVERY:2,3,4,5,6 "23456.EXE"

This job will run at 9:00 a.m. on the computer \\ROBART. It will be noninteractive and will run on every second, third, fourth, fifth, and sixth day of the month. The command to be run is 23456.EXE.

AT 9:00 "DIR>DIR.TXT"

This job will run at 9:00 a.m. on the local computer. It will be noninteractive and will run one time. The command to be run is 23456.EXE.

VIEWING SCHEDULED COMMANDS

Information about scheduled events can also be viewed with the AT command. Viewing AT command information is a good way to verify that events are properly scheduled. Two types of displays can be produced, information on all scheduled events and information on a particular event. Used without parameters, the AT command displays information on all events. Figure C-1 shows sample listings produced from the AT command when it is used without any parameters.

If no jobs are scheduled and you run the AT command without parameters, the output looks something like Figure C-2.

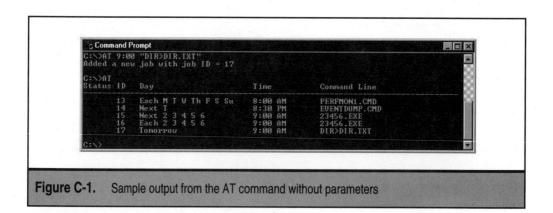

Figure C-1. Sample output from the AT command without parameters

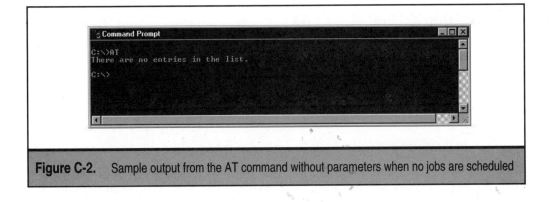

Figure C-2.   Sample output from the AT command without parameters when no jobs are scheduled

In order to display information on a particular event, you must include the event ID. Figure C-3 shows the results of using the Event ID 15 with the AT command.

INCORPORATING AT WITH DISASTER RECOVERY

Backing up system resources reliably and routinely is a key component to an enterprise's disaster recovery plan. A notable disaster recovery solution that can be achieved with the AT command is providing automation for the Windows NT Backup utility. NT Backup does not directly include scheduling, but you can use the AT command to schedule routine system backups. For more information, see Chapter 4. Meanwhile, the following pages explain how to schedule unattended backups and some useful Resource Kit utilities.

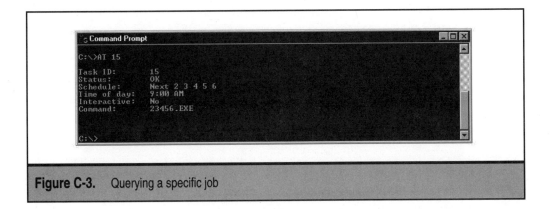

Figure C-3.   Querying a specific job

Scheduling Unattended Backups

To schedule an unattended backup, the basic procedure is to create a command file that runs NTBACKUP.EXE with the proper switches and schedule the job, like so:

1. Using a text editor such as Notepad, create a command file (.CMD) to carry out the commands to back up files. For example, the contents of BACKUP.CMD might be the following:

   net stop server

   This command prevents access to the machine being backed up and is optional:

   NTBACKUP BACKUP C: /V /D "FULLBACKUP.TXT" /B /L "C:\BACKUP.LOG"

   where

   - ■ /V verifies the operation.
   - ■ /D provides a description of tape contents.
   - ■ /B backs up the registry.
   - ■ /L specifies the filename for the backup log.

2. Schedule the command file to run by using the AT command, like so:

   AT 1:00 /INTERACTIVE /EVERY:M,T,W,TH,F "C:\BACKUP.CMD"

CAUTION: Be sure to use the /INTERACTIVE parameter when initiating NT Backup by way of the AT command. If you do not and an error occurs, NT Backup may stop responding to the system and will not be able to execute again without restarting the system or killing the process. The ability to interact with NT Backup allows for the correction of any errors. The backup can then be continued after the error condition is resolved.

Related Resource Kit Utilities

The NT Resource Kit contains several utilities that are useful in writing your scripts and automating NT jobs. These include SLEEP.EXE, TIMEOUT.EXE and WINAT.EXE. They are briefly described in this section.

SLEEP.EXE   SLEEP.EXE is a utility that pauses execution for a specific period of time before performing the next operation in a batch or command file. Here is an example:

SLEEP *time*

where *time* is in seconds to wait.

TIMEOUT.EXE   TIMEOUT.EXE is similar to the sleep command in that it makes the system wait a specific period of time. The difference, however, is that a user keystroke causes the program to continue even if the timeout period has not expired. Here is an example:

TIMEOUT #

where # is in seconds (-1 to 100000) to wait before continuing the operation (-1 signifies an indefinite waiting period that can only expire with user intervention).

WINAT.EXE   WINAT.EXE, another Resource Kit offering, is the graphical version of the AT command schedule. It is an easier-to-use front-end to the Windows NT Schedule service. Of course, WINAT.EXE requires the Schedule service to be running. In addition, it relies on the Workstation service to function properly. Figure C-4 shows the WINAT.EXE program.

To schedule with the WINAT.EXE utility, follow these steps:

1. Open WINAT.EXE. The main screen automatically shows all scheduled jobs on the selected computer. In Figure C-4, notice that the commands are the same as those listed when AT was run from the command line in Figure C-1.

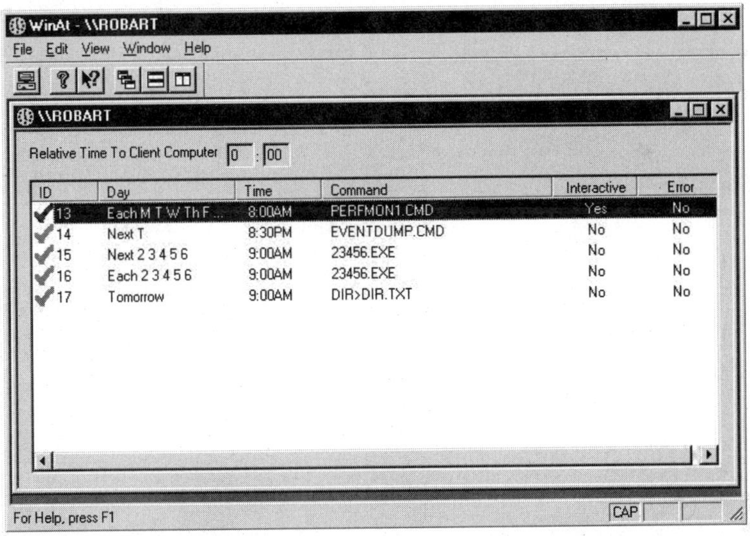

Figure C-4.   The WINAT.EXE main screen

2. Select the Edit | Add command.

3. Enter the required information and click OK, as shown in Figure C-5. The new job should appear in the WINAT.EXE main screen.

WINAT.EXE also allows modifications to existing jobs. These more common modifications include Change and Remove. To modify an existing job, highlight the job and select the Edit menu.

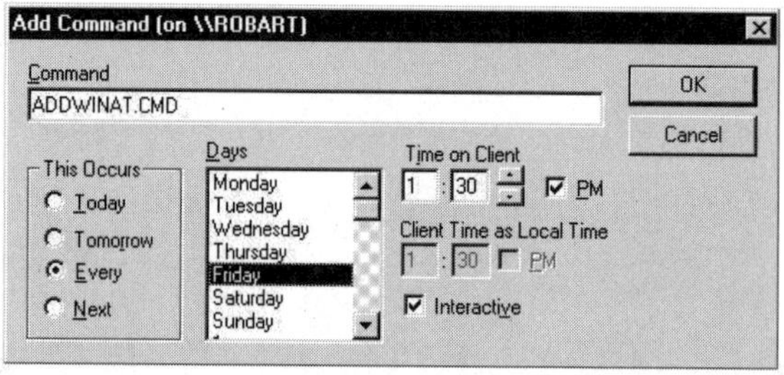

Figure C-5. Entering job parameters

WINDOWS NT
Professional Library

Index

▼ D

▼ T

▼ U